PROJECTIONS 11

in the same series

PROJECTIONS 1
John Boorman fires the starting-gun for the series; includes interviews with Michael Mann, Gus Van Sant by River Phoenix and Demme on Demme

PROJECTIONS 2
Interviews with George Miller, Willem Dafoe, Jaco Van Dormael, as well as Altman on Altman

PROJECTIONS 3
The diaries of Francis Coppola, interviews with Quentin Tarantino, Chen Kaige, Sally Potter, as well as Kasdan on Kasdan

PROJECTIONS 4
James Toback's diary, an interview with Gene Kelly, Lindsay Anderson's tribute to John Ford, Walter Murch on sound design and Arthur Penn on Arthur Penn

PROJECTIONS 4½
What is your favourite film? Answered by Clint Eastwood, the Coens, Elia Kazan, Mike Leigh, Stephen Frears, Steven Soderbergh, among others

PROJECTIONS 5
Animation issue. Also includes Jamie Lee Curtis and Tony Curtis, Quentin Tarantino and Brian De Palma, and Jimmy Stewart's last interview

PROJECTIONS 6
Pieces by Mike Figgis, Eleanor Coppola, Tom DiCillo, Robert Towne and interviews with Vittorio Storaro and Stanley Donen

PROJECTIONS 7
Scorsese issue; also includes Jamie Lee Curtis talking to her mother, Janet Leigh, Willem Dafoe with Frances McDormand and an interview with Robert Mitchum

PROJECTIONS 8
International critics answer the question: Does film criticism have any value today? Also, Christopher Doyle's diary of his work with Wong Kar-Wai and interviews with Abbas Kiarostami and Abraham Polonsky

PROJECTIONS 9
The legacy of French cinema from Robert Bresson to Matthieu Kassovitz's *La Haine*

PROJECTIONS 10
The Hollywood issue. Mike Figgis explores the System in conversation with Mel Gibson, Salma Hayek, Paul Thomas Anderson and others

PROJECTIONS 11
New York Film-makers on Film-making

edited by Tod Lippy

executive editors
John Boorman and Walter Donohue

faber and faber

First published in 2000
by Faber and Faber Limited
3 Queen Square London WC1N 3AU
Published in the United States by Faber and Faber Inc.
an affiliate of Farrar, Straus and Giroux LLC, New York

Typeset by Faber and Faber
Printed in England by Clays Ltd, St Ives plc

© Tod Lippy, 2000
Tod Lippy is hereby identified as author of this work in accordance
with Section 77 of the Copyright, Designs and Patents Act 1988

A CIP record for this book is available from the British Library

ISBN 0–571–20591–7

10 9 8 7 6 5 4 3 2 1

Contents

Foreword *by John Boorman*, vii

Introduction *by Tod Lippy*, ix

Ted Hope and James Schamus, 1

Frances McDormand, 19

Carter Burwell, 36

Thérèse DePrez, 53

Spike Lee, 67

Tim Robbins, 79

Stacy Cochran, 93

Wes Anderson, 108

Jonas Mekas, 122

Christine Vachon, 139

John Pierson, 153

Sidney Lumet, 168

Ulu Grosbard, 183

David Picker, 198

Nora Ephron, 213

Sam Cohn, 219

Juliet Taylor, 233

Jim Jarmusch, 251

Harmony Korine, 268

Buck Henry, 276

Walter Bernstein, 291

Karyn Kusama, 308

David O. Russell, 322

Acknowledgements, 333

Foreword

John Boorman

In the last edition of *Projections*, Mike Figgis negotiated the labyrinths of Hollywood, lighting its murky nooks and crannies, probing its concentric anxieties. It was about status and hierarchies and paranoia and money.

Tod Lippy read it and proposed to Walter and me the volume that is before you. If the LA film-makers are cocooned by their town, the New Yorkers, like it or not, are buffeted by the turbulence of their urgent city. This is another world – gritty, wildly diverse, irreverent, harrowing.

From Jonas Mekas's account of the origins of the Independent movement through to the young producers and directors in the front line, Tod ferrets out the state of the art and the state of the business.

David O. Russell, talking about working in LA, says the cultural ghosts are very strong there. 'They get into your cerebellum and you don't even realize it.' These ghosts insist on narrative resolution.

Many of these New York characters are haunted by spectres too: above them, God-like, hover the figures of Scorsese and Woody Allen; and below, with the promise of fame and fortune, lurk the Brothers Weinstein.

Tod has the knowledge and the scoop, his penetration is deep. I learned a lot and laughed a lot.

Introduction

Tod Lippy

Samuel Fuller's *Pickup on South Street* (1953) – for my money, the quintessential New York movie – opens on a crowded subway car during rush hour. In the middle of the scene, the train pulls into a station. The doors open and passengers spill out, pushing their way past the throng of commuters on the platform waiting to enter. As the commuters sweep into the car, hats are knocked askew, ribs jabbed by elbows; skin brushes against skin, eyes meet, wander, meet again. Every inch of available space is taken, every human contour broken.

In the *Pickup* screenplay, Fuller describes the subway car as a 'human sea'. The term is apt for New York City, suggesting density, movement and shifting energies. This sea washes into every public space: bus shelters, building lobbies, street corners, the cramped confines of Korean delis. And it forces the individual into constant proximity to others – an exceptional collection of others – thereby creating many of the paradoxes that New York embodies. It familiarizes all difference. It subverts intimacy with anonymity. It forces the private into a public arena. It creates unwitting voyeurs and reluctant exhibitionists.

Virtually everyone interviewed in this book alludes to this sea. Tim Robbins, speaking for many of the interviewees, is convinced that the constant exposure to such a wide variety of humanity helps him to write and act more complex characters. Jim Jarmusch, citing the city's inevitable and continual melding of cultures, claims that all of his work has sprung from the resultant 'blurred edges' between them: that fertile area 'where synthesis occurs and gardens grow'. Spike Lee can't imagine anyone with an open mind not being affected by exposure to 'so many different types' of people. Buck Henry perhaps puts it best: 'One trip on the subway is worth a hundred limousine rides.' (Take that, John Rocker.)

That heterogeneity not only stimulates film-makers' imaginations; it also presents an antidote to the 'company town' aspect of LA (as Stacy Cochran puts it, film-making in LA is like 'politics in Washington'). In effect, the sea 'dilutes'. Despite the success of their production/distribution company Good Machine, James Schamus and Ted Hope have resisted opening an office in what they refer to as the 'black hole' of Hollywood. As Hope says, 'I don't know how I'd get my mind off the movies I'm working on if I didn't wander the streets of Manhattan, which instantly give me something else to think about.' Ulu Grosbard echoes that thought: 'The minute you step onto the street you're part of a larger sense of life, a life that has nothing to do with making movies.' Frances McDormand asserts that the proximity to people with different interests and occupations prevents complacency: 'You just simply have to articulate your thought differently from other people because you can't fall back on clichés.' Nora Ephron finds that in LA, people 'are obsessed with the details of . . . who just got cast in what, which script just got auctioned for a trillion dollars, who's about to be fired, etc. These things are not important, and it's nice to live in a place where that's understood.'

Interestingly, agent Sam Cohn views being here as a tactical advantage that creates a 'back-door kind of insider-ness'. He adds, 'I've deluded myself into thinking there's a certain mystery connected with the fact that you're not there, and they don't see you every night.' Both Walter Bernstein and Sidney Lumet suggest that the distance from LA and its industry saturation might have even made the fifties more livable for blacklisted film-makers located in New York.

All of those comments suggest an urge to escape the confines of the clearly circumscribed Hollywood community and to disappear instead into something whose all-encompassing physical form necessitates a more elusive, personal 'marking of territory': creative self-definition. The history of New York film-making is, by and large, a history of individual expression, whether embodied in the work of experimental film-makers like Stan Brakhage, Shirley Clarke and Jack Smith or the distinctive narrative films of directors such as Woody Allen, Martin Scorsese, John Sayles, Jim Jarmusch and Spike Lee. That tradition is immensely appealing to the younger directors who still locate here – directors like Karyn Kusama, who aspires to make the same kind of films, in which 'you never feel anything but the stamp of personal cinema'. That same term can be used to characterize the work of 'auteurist' indie producers like Christine Vachon or Schamus and Hope, as well as the entrepreneurial efforts of definition-resistant 'one-man bands' like Jonas Mekas or John Pierson. Even David Picker, who was head of production of United Artists during its heyday in the sixties and early seventies, describes the UA environment as being less about studio hierarchy and more about 'four men' – the company's principals – 'talking to each other every day.'

Considering the fact that the film-makers gathered together here run the gamut from Ephron, famous for her homages to classic romantic comedies, to Harmony Korine, already, at twenty-five, well-known for his experimental film-poems, it might seem somewhat ridiculous to suggest a link between the majority of them. But, keeping that 'human sea' in mind, I'll offer one observation: New York films, more often than not, share a similar approach to narrative. Here, a typical walk in the streets will lead you into, and past, any number of unresolved stories: did that couple break up after their screaming match at 31st and Park? Did anybody ever find the bulldog whose face graced the 'Missing' posters in the West Village? Why is that bike messenger crying? Was that who I thought it was? New York film-makers often resist easy resolution or over-simplification in their films (or, as Spike Lee puts it, 'tying everything up in a neat little bow') and it's worth considering that such resistance comes from recognizing the beauty of the lack of closure, not to mention the enormous complexity, in the environment around them. Composer Carter Burwell, while allowing for the fact that film is necessarily an 'escapist' medium, still says, 'I don't think most people go to films to have their understanding of the world contradicted – "No, it's all fine! Everybody's happy, and everyone will find love" . . . I don't think that's the escape people look for.' Loose ends, equivocal messages and unpredictable characters abound in the work of virtually all of the film-makers gathered here, from Wes Anderson to Walter Bernstein, from Stacy Cochran to Sidney Lumet. David O. Russell, a somewhat reluctant (and temporary) resident of LA after moving there from New York to make *Three Kings*, has an even more metaphysical explanation: he is convinced that the density of New York somehow crowds out the 'particularly American ghosts' of narrative resolution that glide freely through the open, unpeopled spaces of LA, insinuating themselves into the work of even the most independent-minded film-maker.

In the following pages, this neat thematic bow I've attempted to tie will, of course, be fiddled with and tugged on until it's pulled apart. The observations made here stand to be refuted, or ignored, perhaps even dismissed out of hand. Other, more tangible influences – New York's theatrical and literary traditions, for instance – will be justifiably cited, and in one interview the city and all it represents will be not only dismissed, but cursed. Careful readers will notice contradictory assertions and conflicting opinions about everything from 'Indiewood' politics to New York real estate; recollections of particular events will vary enough among individuals to turn the remembered moment into something like a Cubist collage.

Confusion, complexity, shifting perspectives – all generated by a rather arbitrary grouping together of people. Resulting, in its best moments, in art. I'd like to think that sounds a little like New York.

Ted Hope and James Schamus

James Schamus and Ted Hope co-founded Good Machine, a New York-based independent production company, in 1991. They have been involved in the production of over forty films, including *Happiness*, *Walking and Talking*, *The Myth of Fingerprints*, *The Brothers McMullen*, *Safe* and Hal Hartley's *Trust*, *Simple Men*, *Amateur* and *Flirt*. Their long-standing relationship with director Ang Lee, both as producers and, in Schamus's case, screenwriter, began with Lee's first feature, *Pushing Hands*; Schamus's script for *The Ice Storm* won the Best Screenplay Award at the 1997 Cannes Film Festival. In 1994, Hope and Schamus received the Brian Greenbaum Award for outstanding achievement in producing from the Independent Feature Project-West.

Tod Lippy: Is either one of you from New York?
James Schamus: [*Laughs.*] Who's *from* New York? Are you?

Ted Hope: I read the obituary in the *Times* of the guy who wrote the obituaries in the *Times* over the weekend, and one of the lines was, 'He was the quintessential New Yorker, in that he had spent three months in New York, then moved to Los Angeles, where he spent eighteen years hating it and wanting to get back to New York before he finally returned.' [*Both laugh.*] My mom grew up here, but I didn't move here until I was nineteen.

What about you, James?
JS: I came after graduate school in Berkeley.

TH: I would say that, in an odd way, I never felt relaxed until I moved to New York. There was so much going on I didn't have to worry about finding something interesting to do. I knew that there would *always* be something interesting to do.

James, why did you come here after graduate school?
JS: I was actually still in graduate school, having finished everything but my dissertation, and I thought it would be interesting to check out for a semester what the film business was like, so I took out a student loan and proclaimed myself on 'independent study', flew to New York and got stuck here, basically.

I got here on January 1st, 1987. The night after I arrived there was a cocktail party in the neighbourhood in Brooklyn I was staying in, and I met a guy named Jack Lechner who was leaving a job he had had as story editor at a small company called Program Development Company. At the time there were making a lot of theatre-for-television stuff for American Playhouse. They would tape, for example, a Sam Shepard play with John Malkovich —

TH: *True West* —

JS: *True West*, and then put it on American Playhouse with Lindsay Law. I contacted them, and they said, 'Hey, if you want an internship, come on by.' But already that afternoon I had landed a job as director of theatrical distribution for

Troma, and so I declined because, you know, I had this big job. When I think about it, it was ninety-nine dollars a week. I'd come directly from Berkeley, where the weather was great, the people were incredibly groovy, the coffee was good – remember, this was before New York had good coffee – and I'd go to work in the morning, slogging through this slush to get to the Troma building on Ninth Avenue, for these guys who I know are heralded often as, you know —

TH: 'The kings of independent film' —

JS: The kings of independent film. But you know, when I was there, maybe they were just having a bad week. Anyway, I lasted a week and a half – basically, I just couldn't take people screaming at each other all day. But I did manage to walk out with a lot of great one-sheets – *Surf Nazis Must Die, Toxic Avenger,* all that kind of stuff. So I ended up doing an internship for Program Development. Now, here in New York, by 'internship' you mean 'slave labour', and the first day there, I said, 'Maybe I should look at the screenplays you guys have here in development, just to see what you're doing.' I took home, I don't know, 14 or 15 scripts, including four different drafts of a script based on the life of Clara Bow, which the company was developing at the time. I stayed up all night and read everything, and came in the next day with a two-page proposal to rewrite the Clara Bow script for next to nothing – something, just so I could survive – and after a couple of little glitches, I landed that job.

TH: It took James a little time to return to his screenwriting roots . . .

How about you, Ted?
TH: I had dropped out of college, and had been working for various arms of Ralph Nader's organization out in Oregon. I started the Oregon Public-Interest Research Groups canvas, and it was incredibly successful —

JS: That's going to sound really nice, Ted. 'It was incredibly successful, and Ted was the sole reason for its success. In fact it was a stunning, astonishing success.'

TH: Whatever. There were many reasons why it was successful, Oregon being such a prime place to do door-to-door canvassing, but it was like the first time something had actually gone right for me – somehow that really depressed the hell out of me, so I decided I really had to get out of there. I started applying to schools, and I'd always wanted to go to film school but felt that it was really self-indulgent, and I shouldn't do it. But because I was so depressed that day, I filled out my NYU application and NYU ended up giving me more money than the other places I applied to, so I decided to go. At that time I thought I would make radical documentaries.

So it brought me to New York, and while I was at NYU I answered an ad in the *Village Voice* and got a job for a small film company inspecting their 16-mm. prints. They had a big non-theatrical business. While I was there, they released their first big hit film, which was *Nightmare on Elm Street*, and I was soon able to become their first paid scriptreader.

This was New Line, right? Didn't you both end up there as readers?
TH: Well, right around that time James had come in and pitched New Line a silent, black-and-white Wooster Group version of *The Hunchback of Notre Dame* starring Willem Dafoe. And the week before, I had delivered my coverage of Whitley Strieber's alien abduction book, *Communion*. I found it really fascinating, and recommended that they hire Godard to direct it, because I loved that in its efforts to show that the material was true, the book created a *bad* narrative. I'm sure they thought, 'This guy's coverage is not exactly what we were looking for . . .'

So I was kind of aligned with this nutbag who had just come in to pitch us this Wooster Group thing.

JS: But I was already doing coverage for them.

TH: Maybe.

JS: Yeah. I was doing really, really great – in fact, astonishingly successful – coverage for them.

TH: Well, Janet Grillo suggested the two of us meet, and given that James was somebody who was addicted to good coffee, he suggested that we meet at De-Roberti's coffee shop in the East Village. He's always been driven by the quality of the caffeine.

JS: I really tried to get Ted to work on this feature-length video that we were doing at the Wooster Group which ended up being called *White Homeland Commando*, but Ted was busy doing *Frankenhooker* . . .

TH: No, they didn't hire me on *White Homeland*. But one thing we discussed was our mutual affection for Raul Ruiz's films —

James, you ended up producing his feature, *The Golden Boat*, right?
TH: Well, I ended up getting a job at the same place James had just left – Program Development Company. It had become Vanguard Films, John Williams's company. I started there just after coming off of AD'ing *Basket Case II*, and I had been there about four or five months, and nothing much was happening. James got money together for *The Golden Boat* and offered me the AD gig, but we were getting close to getting the money for *Trust*, Hal Hartley's film. And I had to make a big career decision – do I go off and work with this guy that I had a good time getting drunk with – Raul Ruiz – and this guy that I like, James Schamus, or do I stick it out maybe two or three more weeks and see if we get money for *Trust*. I opted for the latter. I think it was about the same time as *Thank You and Goodnight*, wasn't it?

JS: Yeah, I was working with Jan Oxenburg, helping her complete this really interesting film that she had gotten funding for from a lot of different sources, including American Playhouse. It was a film that eventually took her almost ten years to finish. But I think it was really a signature piece for that era.

TH: One of my mom's favourites.

JS: On the one hand, a documentary about the death of the film-maker's grandmother, and on the other hand, a real inventive mix of genres and approaches to film-making, inspired by this documentary situation.

Speaking of 'signature pieces', can you characterize for me what was happening in New York at that particular moment – the late eighties – as far as films, particularly indie films, were concerned?
JS: When we were starting out, there was this very interesting hybrid – three or four strands of production which New York still retains the archaeological traces of. One was B-movie production, and really, B-movie production that was supported by an ongoing stream of pornography production. So that crews that were working on the porn productions and were trying to break into more professional movies as a rule had résumés that listed their B-movie credits. For example, when I was on the set of *The Golden Boat*, we had Annie Sprinkle do a cameo walk-on – fully clothed, by the way. And the second she came on the set, the entire crew was like, 'Hey, Annie! Haven't seen you in a couple of months!' So people were really getting their training on these films, because there was still a fair amount of 35mm pornography production at that point, although it was beginning to wane.

The second strand was that the NEA, state or private foundations were funding a lot of 16mm work that was documentary and experimental. So there was a whole group of film-makers that were coming out of short-form experimental or long-form doc/experimental work. This is where Christine Vachon and Todd Haynes and the whole Apparatus Productions thing comes in, in that little room on Lafayette Street. There was a whole ethos of grabbing a little money here and a little money there. So that was another river flowing in.

Then there were the independent distribution companies that had sprung up in New York, many of which had been based on the college circuit – particularly New Line, Miramax – who were picking up European art films and finding a way to base their assumptions about the film business in the arthouse cinema that New York really had so much of at that time. In the early nineties, these theatres kind of disappeared, but now they're slowly coming back in a more institutional form – Walter Reade, Film Forum, all this other stuff.

Finally, you had the centre of all media – electronic media. The television studios were here, so you had a lot of higher-end, studio-based video stuff.

TH: You could even break it into a fifth or sixth strand at that time, too, frankly. In addition to porno stuff there were all the horror films going on —

JS: That's why I said B-movie.

TH: And then there was also the beginning of the home-video business. I remember there was a film that got made that a lot of people I knew worked on; it starred Philip Bosco as a cab driver who wants to be a Shakespearean actor.

JS: Oh, yeah . . .

TH: All these kind of 'quality', Playhouse-type films that were getting funded by these New York distributors. For instance, as soon as New Line had a hit with *Nightmare on Elm Street*, they got their first video deal . . .

JS: One of the first big infusions of capital. Like with Vestron, which was based in Connecticut, there was a real flush of money that came in. So you had this kind of coagulation of different kinds of film-making that the home video money fuelled into feature-length narrative. It was coming from all different pockets of film-making activity in New York, but different, obviously, than what was out in LA.

TH: It was how I really learned how to make movies. I came out of film school – I didn't stay there very long – and I didn't even know what a production assistant was. I was lucky that I had this scriptreading gig. And then I ended up getting hired by a producer who made these kind of sleazy horror films. He thought I could write coverage for him to get his movies made and he started hiring me to do business plans, which I knew nothing about, but it taught me a lot. Same with my friends – Bob Gosse, who PA'd with me and is now a director and was one of the founders of The Shooting Gallery – and Hal Hartley's cousin, though not really; they thought they were cousins, but they weren't –

JS: Just kissing cousins.

TH: Bob worked for a company called Cinema Sciences. They had one of these video deals. They would basically shoot three movies simultaneously, with the same cast. They'd hire some name actor to come in for a day or two of work, and they travelled with sets of paramilitary costumes, civil-war uniforms, revolutionary-war uniforms, gangster costumes, and they'd just go in and just run the same actors. Then they'd give the footage to a screenwriter to try and make it fit, to piece it together. And they would be shooting this stuff, you know, using car headlights for lighting.

Anyway, Bob would talk to Hal Hartley about how they got these movies made, and meanwhile I was working on these horror films. I got hired by another company, called Films Around the World, to find locations where they could shoot an entire movie. Basically, you'd have a three-week prep, and that would be it. They'd be casting young men and women who were willing to run around in their bathing suits, and one guy who'd wear, like, a heavy monster costume. The one I'm thinking of was called *Doom Asylum*. We found this place where they performed the first lobotomy in New Jersey. It ended up being a tuberculosis clinic for a while, but it was abandoned by the time we got there.

With that one, we had started production and were casting and there was still no script whatsoever. So the screenwriter sort of cobbled together a script, and the movie came out to seventy-one minutes. We had a contract to deliver eighty, so we used all this public domain footage. You know, we built a 'lair' – it may have been in the old Good Machine offices – and the monster sat and watched these old movies on TV so we hit the eighty minutes.

There was also this guy, Chuck somebody out in Queens, who would shoot the softcore and hardcore porn at the same time . . .

JS: Oh yeah, Chuck Vincent. Didn't he die of AIDS?

TH: Yeah, he did. So all of the same crews would go from the Apparatus Productions to the Cinema Science productions to Chuck Vincent's movies. So anyway, that was kind of how we figured out how to do a movie like *The Unbelievable Truth* for $65,000. It was like, the basic rules came down to: you had to shoot in nine days; all the locations had to be within walking distance of one another; you'd shoot on a two-to-one ratio, boom.

And you had a crew that was not only experienced, but willing to work for peanuts.
TH: Yeah, exactly. I mean, I thought everybody in film put orange gel over headlights. I thought that was how you made movies.

James, what was your experience in LA when you were out there in 1988?
JS: Well, I ended up writing another screenplay, after the Clara Bow one, that got a lot of good reads, and was being cruised by a major agency. An agent there promised me he'd set up twenty-five meetings for me and all this stuff, and lend me all this money – tens of thousands of dollars. The screenplay was based on Richard Price's first novel, *The Breaks*. In any case, the option was running out a week later. I'd come on to do the rewrite really quickly, because they'd had it in development for several years, and it was a really expensive option. Anyway, we literally had a week to set it up.

I landed in LA at noon on the first day of the 1988 Writers' Guild strike. The entire town just shut down. I mean, no one would take a call, except for a couple of very sleazy people who will remain unmentioned. So it was my introduction to the Hollywood side of the screenwriting business. I met a lot of people out there, and learned a few lessons.

Such as?
JS: Such as, I thought I better get back to New York and learn how movies are really made – understand the process – before I put myself in a business where writers in particular were being very well paid but turned into gigantic, overweight, macho, whiny, snivelling, ego-driven maniacs. I mean, people were insane. [*Laughs.*] Not that I'm not an overweight, snivelling egomaniac, but at least I'm in New York.

TH: Prior to moving to New York I had gone to LA *once* to see The Clash when I was nineteen or something. I didn't go again until *Wedding Banquet* got nominated for an Academy Award. That was my first real trip there, and I was completely petrified. Dependent on James – I didn't want him to leave my sight. 'You have to drive in the city? Oh my God!'

James, you've said before that 'you can create your own version of the film business in New York'. Could you both elaborate?
TH: I don't know about James, but I was pretty ignorant about the whole thing, and I think that was probably the greatest advantage I had. That whole line, 'If I knew then what I knew now, I probably wouldn't do any of it.' I just really wanted to make movies that I wanted to see, and had a willingness to just go forward and get it done. And there were enough people in New York who had a similar energy and commitment that a lot of it ended up happening. So I guess in a sense it's true. But it wasn't so preconceived.

JS: Yeah. I had dinner with Ang [Lee] last week, and after a while we lapsed into the 'So whatever happened to so-and-so . . .' thing. And I turned to him and said, 'My God, we're old enough to be having these conversations. This is frightening.' But anyway, looking back, you can find patterns to things you've done which in the end are as much determined by environmental factors as anything else. But the fact is, a number of confluences, many of them structural and economic, as we've discussed, but also quite frankly political, helped create the scene in New York, and the so-called independent film movement.

What do you mean by 'political'?
JS: Well, I think there are two things. One is that there's a kind of residual but long-forgotten politics to independent feature film-making in New York that really started in the fifties with people like Abe Polonsky —

TH: Shirley Clarke —

JS: Well, yeah, Shirley Clarke. A lot of people engaged from a social/political point of view who were creating a kind of destiny for their film-making that was outside of the system. And a lot of that was being influenced by some of the hype around companies that were here, like United Artists, who really had the publicity ethos of being 'creator-driven' in terms of their economics. So the residual feel of that still informs a lot of what we're about.

But really, fundamentally, the decision to make feature-length narrative films puts you in an economic sphere of activity that by necessity is going to be dominated by Hollywood. Dominated not only economically, but also ideologically. I look at what we do and no matter how aesthetically daring, and bold, and provocative and new and original, we're really committed to doing work within a very narrow bandwidth of aesthetic and political activity. We don't step out that much because if you do, the hatchet comes down.

At the same time, within that very narrow range of activity is a very wide range of potential audiences. So you're trading off constantly in terms of those two sides of the business.

TH: When I came to film school here there was a very vibrant, Super-8, no-wave, downtown New York film scene. Nick Zed, Beth B., Lydia Lunch – all those people. I had a romantic notion about the times of Warhol's Factory, all that stuff. So there were these little film showings, and I went and wasn't connected to the movies at all, but it seemed like these people were successful. Their movies were getting shown, and it was exciting. It seemed to me that if you made your movies and you really believed in them and pushed them, there was some way people would see them. Plus, I didn't have any clues as to the economics of the business. I was working at New Line, and they had this great library of Pasolini films, you know, mixed in with *Evil Dead* and so on, and I just felt that, because these existed, somehow everybody was making money.

But your definition of success at that point wasn't directly linked with financial concerns?
TH: I didn't see a difference. If it showed on the Lower East Side, then it meant it worked somehow.

JS: Just to interject one factoid. *The Golden Boat* was made with this mixture of grant money, tiny little overseas investments, tiny little this, tiny little that, and we made it in two long weekends. Didn't cost much at all, but the fact is, it never made any money. But I remember when the film was selected for the New York Film Festival. At that moment, everybody who invested in and worked on the film truly believed that I as a producer was hoarding the incredible amount of money that must have been made because the film was showing at the New York Film Festival.

TH: I remember the New York Film Festival where *Blood Simple* and *Stranger Than Paradise* premièred. I had, like, the cheap seats up front to see *Blood Simple*, and all of a sudden the Coen Brothers get up on the stage, and I recognize them from my local supermarket. They were always there buying cold cereal after midnight when I was there buying cold cereal after midnight. I was like, 'Oh my God, it's those stoners from the neighbourhood!' And like two days later, after seeing *Stranger Than Paradise*, there was Jim Jarmusch on the subway. Somehow it just felt really *possible*.

That certainly hasn't changed here.
TH: That's true. Todd Solondz told me that a month or so ago he went to see some movie at the Angelika on Saturday afternoon, and as he was waiting to get in he noticed that he was standing next to Wes Anderson and Vincent Gallo. He was like, 'God, we're all such big losers, going to see a movie by ourselves on a Saturday afternoon.'

And I've experienced that in reverse now, too. When I was a PA, all of the people that were above me I just looked up to like real gods, and since then I've been able to collaborate with them – Michael Nozik, Bob Colesbury, the whole production world – and having that awareness, knowing that these people I'd PA'd with were now directing their own films. It was all right there, and the reason that people are here is not because they want to drive that cool sports car —

JS: Well, some of them do, and that's their right.

TH: But there's that hunger to really make the movie.

A very broad question: how have things changed since you've founded Good Machine, both for you and for the city as a film-making centre?
JS: We just don't look as good as we used to.

TH: At that time, I wasn't aware of producer collaborations that extended beyond, you know, Rollins/Joffe. None of it seemed accessible. There wasn't a way I could go in as the young film-maker and meet some of these people. Now, there's a huge proliferation of producer-driven, director-driven companies. I think that there are more points of access. To me, at least, it felt like if you wanted to make an independent film of any sort you could never even get to a producer who had made movies before, let alone one of the film companies that financed them. Now there is such an apparatus of things sucking things in.

JS: Well, basically, when I started out, anybody who would introduce themselves as a 'producer' was by definition somebody who'd never made a movie before, and never would. You know what I mean? All those people with the business cards printed up? Now, for better or worse, although the American independent movement sells itself on the *auteur*, writer/director concept – and I think that's legitimate – in fact, structurally, it is very much a producer's cinema. The *auteurs* themselves function as producers in many ways. We ourselves emerged as characters or 'figures' at a time when structurally we were able to adapt the concept of producer to a situation that was crying out for it.

You see now, quite frankly, that that construct is more and more marginalized in the studio system. I used to think that writers got treated badly out there, but the producers are really taking a beating now that the studios themselves 'know how to produce'. Obviously it's a pathetic mistake, and part and parcel of mismanagement. But there's a reason for that mistake. It's not that people are stupid, it's just that there's this structural change taking place and people haven't adapted to it yet.

TH: There are a couple other things that have changed that I'm aware of. First of all, back then it was tougher to gain the proprietary knowledge associated with producing. I got hired for jobs because I'd done script coverage and no one else had, because I knew how to do a budget on a computer. You know, because I had the Teamsters' phone number and I knew where to buy recanned film stock. All that stuff is so available right now – budget templates, information on crews – so that a person who's PA'd on one film who's relatively intelligent can get access to that information. It took me two or three years to accumulate that originally. So I think that's changed and allowed people to get movies made.

Also, the awareness of how to go out and then bring your film to market was something that very few people knew how to do. If it wasn't for Jim Stark, in some ways, talking about how to go about all of this, we wouldn't have had the courage or the knowledge to do it. Now, everyone knows when you go to Sundance, how to handle Berlin . . .

JS: There were two kinds of discourse about independent film ten years ago that were replaced by a very different public discourse. I remember when I was editing the precursor of what is now *Filmmaker* magazine, called *The Off-Hollywood Report*. We filled it up with stuff like, 'How to Shoot Car Scenes' – you know, how to rig cars if you don't have anything to rig them with. Really kind of artisanal approaches, which had a kind of kick-shit ethos attached to them. And the other discourse was a real high-art, aestheticized approach to discerning what was valuable in any kind of independent film. So you had these two tracks: on the one hand, this very get-your-hands-dirty thing, and on the other hand, this extremely rarefied, analytical approach to understanding film.

TH: And you also had the people who did both. I remember grips arguing on film sets I was on about how long a close-up should be held, or talking about Michael Snow's films, things like that.

JS: I remember taking a one-day 16mm film-making workshop at Collective for Living Cinema, which seems so ephemeral now, but it was one of those institutions in that period that were so important.

And there was Millennium Film Workshop, founded by Ken Jacobs.
JS: Now this has all been displaced into what I call a kind of personality model, in terms of discourse about film. Very much about people like me and Ted, or people like Todd Solondz, how these people do what they do, what their tastes are, how they mix business and aesthetics, blah blah blah. And again, I'm not saying there's anything wrong with that, anything incorrect or invalid, but it's a discourse that hovers around a very particular economic model of what independent film is.

TH: Also, when we started out, we were able to bring our film, *The Wedding Banquet*, to market as producers. You'd meet the foreign buyers, have access to the two or three people in a given territory who would actually buy these films. You'd do that deal, and have a level of trust that was sometimes warranted and sometimes wasn't. These companies that became the investors in movies grew to be big conglomerates. Now you're dependent on a Good Machine International, or

Miramax or New Line to place your films in the right hands. That part of the knowledge/information circuit is no longer accessible.

So that has adversely affected your ability to get product into the market?
JS: Well, that is simply an index of a fundamental problem, which is the relationship between the cost of making a film and the cost of bringing it into the marketplace. The maturation and saturation of the so-called independent marketplace and the arrival of really deep-pocketed, sophisticated, structured capital into the system has meant that, on the one hand, you can make a movie for three dollars, but on the other hand, it's going to cost a million dollars to get that film into the marketplace – even one little tiny toehold into the marketplace. You can open an arthouse film, or a foreign-language film, for less than $100,000, and see if it can grow, but frankly, you'll fail.

I don't know of a successful release that has spent less than $100,000 – by 'success' I mean a release in which the economics were in a real relationship to the negative cost of the film and the recoupment of that cost.

TH: Around the time we started Good Machine, Bingham Ray and Jeff Lipsky had founded October Films here, and one of their first releases was *Life is Sweet*. And I remember their eighth-week gross had surpassed any prior week gross on a per-screen average. Those days of being able to get a film out there for a while, get some good reviews, get Roger Ebert or somebody to champion it – they don't exist any more. And it starts to affect the kinds of movies that get made – at least the ones that get financed. So that's changed tremendously.

The other thing that I always find really interesting – and it kind of goes from the independent world into the studio world – is that change in definition of producer. Originally it was the guy with the business card and the Rolodex; the guy with the good idea. Then it was the guy who did that but also sort of oversaw the production. Then it was the one who did that and brought money to the table. For a long time, that's what distinguished independent film – financing a movie like *Walking and Talking*, or *Safe*, took year upon year and five or six companies. Now, also on the studio level, the definition of producer is the person who brings in a big chunk of the money. In another year, the only people with studio overhead deals will be those companies that also bring money to the table.

By the way, now I think it's gone another step, if you look at the *Blair Witch* model. Now you not only have to come up with the good ideas and the connections and the know-how and the money, but you also have to bring your audience to the film before the film is ever shown in public. How else do you open a movie with word of mouth on day one?

It's a tired question, but are you planning on getting involved in this whole digital-video phenomenon? There are a number of other New York production houses – Open City, GreeneStreet – which have started specialized DV divisions.
JS: Actually, we are making a gigantic announcement next week: we're buying AOL.

TH: We did the first digital movie, by some people's accounts: *Love God*. It's not something that we have as an agenda item, though. We've certainly explored it for different films, but you know, we make movies, and some will be shot digitally, some shot 35, some 16.

Ted, you mentioned several years ago how the most successful marketing of a recent film was the Pamela Anderson–Tommy Lee sex video over the Internet, asserting that traditional distribution venues for independent film-makers were for the most part a dead end.
JS: Pure bluster.

TH: No, I actually think, frankly, that *Blair Witch* is an offshoot of that kind of phenomenon.

JS: Actually, I think there is something essentially true about what Ted was saying in that article, which ties in with what we were saying about the role of the producer. At this point, you're going to have to figure out new ways to cost-effectively find and deliver an audience to your movie that is not simply the expenditure of P&A for national TV, etc. You're gonna have to get your photograph on the back of the milk carton and make sure that people are staring at it when they're eating their cereal after midnight.

TH: And I think that audiences want something that feels authentic – not to say it *will* be authentic – and that sort of thing really informs both the Pamela–Tommy video and the *South Park* guys' *Spirit of Christmas* short, as well as *Blair Witch*. The audience could feel like 'this is our own', not something that one of the seven major media companies had preconceived and developed. People always hate to compare the music business and the film business, but it's the way that records are still broken – starting a single in the dance clubs before it gets radio play, and before the album comes out. A perfect example is when Guns 'N' Roses were signed to a major label. The first thing they did was release an independent album on an 'indie' label, so they could get their authenticity in place.

James, you were recently quoted as saying that Good Machine is now doing 'the pseudo-independent Hollywood thing'. What does that mean?
JS: It means that the economics of the so-called 'independent' film business have become simply a simulacrum of Hollywood, just on a more miniaturized scale, which requires you to bifurcate your potential audiences, and means you address more specialized and specific audiences. So therefore you can look either smarter or dumber, depending on which direction you want to go. And you make films that are specific to a target audience, the size of which relates to the overall cost of your budget and the marketing. It's no different from what Hollywood does, except for the fact that at the end of the day, the thresholds now in terms of casting and budget are economically higher than they've been in the past.

Something that's been absolutely successful about Ted and myself, I should say, is that we've never been snobs. We haven't worn our eclecticism on our sleeves as some great value, but at the same time we've always recognized that great movies can cost a dollar or $200 million. The economics of them impact on what they are, but they don't necessarily impact on the valuation of them as aesthetic/cultural objects, so we're having a great time making movies the studio way, the independent way, the digital way, the whatever way.

Not that long ago Good Machine signed a first-look deal with Universal, and before that you had another similar two-year deal with Fox. Have you ever considered opening an office in LA?
TH: I think we felt if we opened a Los Angeles office, the vacuum, the magnet, the black hole – whatever it is you want to call it – would draw all of our attention in that direction. We like our lives here. It also helps to think about other things. I'm slightly obsessive, and I don't know how I'd get my mind off the movies I'm working on if I didn't wander the streets of Manhattan, which instantly give me something else to think about.

JS: It's not like we're placing a distance between ourselves and all those 'evil Hollywood types', but rather that we're able to use our ignorance about who had lunch with who, or which spec script is going out on Friday, or whatever, to clear out time to do stuff that we think is really interesting and cool and important. So it's a real luxury, quite frankly, to have that distance. And Ted's right, I think that if we opened an LA office – which some day we may, by the way – it would serve as a kind of vacuum for everything else to get sucked into, because all the agents, all the managers, all the studio execs would be having lunch with whoever was in that office . . .

TH: I used to say we had to be in New York because we were more dependent on Europe for our independent films, but frankly, these days we have to be in New York because we're more dependent on Europe for our Hollywood films! Because of that whole co-financing thing, we need the response of the international community for the big-budget films. With the small films, it's different: You make a film and you want everyone to be unaware of it until it goes to Sundance or whatever, and then they can respond naturally to it. But when you're trying to make *Ride with the Devil*, or even *Happiness*, you have to make sure that Europe knows about it even before LA does.

You mentioned the 'who-had-lunch-with-who' paradigm of LA – isn't there some version of that here in New York as well?
JS: You'd have to ask Ted, because I never go out. Here's it's more about who's having sex with who, which is much more interesting.

TH: I think it's that way out there, too . . .

JS: I'm always so surprised at how collegial the film world is here. It's amazing. I mean, we work with just about every person who could be conceived of as our competition in New York. Actually, the only person I have a long-running feud with in New York is Ted. But from Christine Vachon, or Jim Stark, or Larry Meistrich, to a lot of the newcomers, like GreeneStreet – I hate to use that word 'community', but it just feels right. You don't have a feeling of a specific pie that has to be carved up. You feel that people are generating situations and energies that are helpful to each other.

I assume you don't get into bidding wars with, say, Shooting Gallery over a spec script, then.
TH: It's never happened. I think some of it is that it's *never* been an easy time to make films in New York. I talk to people in LA and they tell me how hard last year was: 'Nobody got any movies made.' Well, it's always kind of been that way in New York. And you know that you're not going to get a movie made unless somebody gives you that little piece of information here, and another person gives you something else over there. We're across the street from The Screening Room, which is now a really well-programmed theatre. Often you'll go in there for a drink and they'll be three or four other downtown film people there, and you'll get to talking and somebody will say, 'Oh, you should show that to so-and-so', or, 'Call this person'. It's always been that way here because the feeling is that it's so impossible to get a movie made, each time it happens should be a cause for celebration whether you're involved with it or not.

Good Machine is known for cultivating long-term relationships with directors, Hal Hartley and Ang Lee being perhaps the two most obvious examples —
TH: One of the first things James and I did when we decided to work together was to draw up a list of directors we wanted to work with. Among them was Ang Lee. I'd wanted to work with him since I'd seen his film at NYU, and I thought he was too beyond my reach – which he was, for a while.

What this whole relationship with directors comes down to, I think, is a real love of film, rather than a love of the business side. I really want these people to make movies. Hal and I stopped working together for a while because there really wasn't a need for either of us to work with each other, but during that whole time I never stopped asking myself what I could do to help him get his movies made.

Could you talk a bit about your development process with the directors you work with?
TH: Well, James and I early on adopted this credo of 'production as development'. First of all, you have to hear the stories that people want to tell, figure out what the current climate allows for in terms of budget and then work out how you'll hit that number. For example, do you want to make the sacrifices you'll need to make to get a star in the lead? We usually have a very conservative approach as opposed to saying, 'Yes! We'll get Cameron Diaz and Brad Pitt and then this little indie film will become a big hit!' So you work through that and figure out what the right

number is going to be for this piece. Then you determine who the folks are who want to work in that venue, in terms of the buyers, the financers.

Then you have to figure out how to get it into the marketplace. I'm always really nervous about knowing when to introduce a script into the marketplace – how do you get it to the point where it's really going to allow people to focus on it the way it should be focused on? And that's really tough, because people need feedback. You may bring things out too early, but then that input level helps the director to go back and do another series of rewrites.

Basically, our development process is about allowing someone's skills to reach the level where they will get somebody to give them the money they need to make the movie they want to make.

It sounds like a relatively intensive process.

TH: It's funny, I had an experience with a director we're doing a first feature with that's technically independent, but which in a lot of ways is kind of 'Indiewood'. I was meeting with him and the writer and the other producer, and it was a six-hour story meeting where we only dealt with three or four scenes. He'd already had several films in studio development prior to this, and he said, 'I don't see why anyone wants to make these indie films. It's so hard! The studio didn't care about what I was doing with the final scene. I never had a story session like that. I want to go back to Hollywood!'

I'm assuming the process would be somewhat less laborious – at least regarding the script – with more seasoned directors ...

TH: Oh, yeah. After three or four films, what I can personally give a director starts to get rather limited – other than my experience and passion and a couple of good ideas. But with those first, second and third films you really kind of work them through the process of exactly how they want to make movies and what matters most, let them know what compromises are necessary for the choices they're making. And that remains incredibly rewarding for me on a personal level, although it means frequently that someone's going to go off and do movies without me. But, hopefully, there's always that desire to still work together.

Are you guys sick of talking about *Happiness*? I read recently, James, how you pitched Todd Solondz's script – not an easy sell – to potential financers with a sort of post-Marxist soliloquy about late capitalism's overproduction of desire and the inability of the social structure to absorb that excess properly, resulting in paedophilia and the like in suburbia. I couldn't quite imagine what those pitch meetings must have been like.

JS: It was weird because it worked. I really did end up doing that, it was my shtick. We did that pitch in Cannes.

TH: That's been your shtick ever since our first meeting at the coffee shop. 'Capitalism is the manufacture of desire.'

Did Universal read the script before you went into production?
TH: I have no idea.

JS: Don't know.

TH: I think October had a level of autonomy that allowed that movie to get made, and people that were committed to making that film. There probably wasn't much of a desire to see it at Universal until after it won the Critics' Prize at Cannes.

JS: Well, it was interesting, because what on the one hand was the downside of working within this 'Indiewood' system, this faux-independent Hollywood system – being under the heavy hand of corporate censorship, that is to say – was at the same time their Achilles heel, because Universal, and their parent company, Seagram, really didn't want to be seen that way. So we could sort of use the system to negotiate a distribution deal that allowed the film to find its way into the marketplace. But again, those are very specific negotiations, and it's sobering to think that there is an enormous amount of censorship we practise unconsciously that keeps out some of the other things. This experience made it clear how certain things can get in and stay in, once they work, but it doesn't necessarily mean that it's a wonderful world and late capitalism is groovy for everybody.

TH: At the end of that whole cycle, we were trying to figure out if there was a way to release an R-rated version on video – which we ended up not doing. We thought about putting a black bar across certain scenes that said 'Censored'. We were told we could put in the black bar but we couldn't use the word 'Censored'. So, in essence, 'censored' was censored.

Do you ever find that you turn down a project because its prospects for commercial success are limited, despite great promise?
JS: Oh yeah, absolutely. Look, there are two things to say about that. One of the things that we have to do in terms of exercising our judgment as producers is to have an instinct for the relationship between the budget and the market. One of the luxuries of being self-identified as 'New York independent film-makers' is that we're not scared of the lower budgets, so long as we think there's a marketplace for them. They don't have to be crossover indie hits – although, these days the system is set up so that if you don't think that way, you almost don't have a chance of making a film. But for us, still, we try to work within producable margins, even if the system is really working against that.

That's the biggest change from years past. You used to be able to nurture a film and let it grow, but now, however much the movie is made for, in order for it to receive distribution, someone along the way must believe that it can eventually get to 1,000 screens. I mean, I'm overstating the case, but the system is set up in such a way that if you don't believe that could be a possibility, there's an enormous disincentive to getting involved. And so what we're trying to do is figure out a way to say, 'Hey, if it costs a million, you can make 1.3 million, you're good.' Whereas in fact the system says, 'No, you can't do that any more.' I remember when *Poison* broke a million at the box office and there was a sense of almost unreality to the magnitude and significance of that achievement. Now, no matter how tiny your film is, getting a million dollars is like, 'OK, so they paid for the party.'

Are you going to distribute any more films?
TH: Hopefully not. I mean, if we were in the same situation I'd do it again, but I can't say I'd like to repeat the *Happiness* experience. Unfortunately, there are films we're drawn to that will cause trouble, so maybe if it's cost-efficient . . .

What are you working on right now?
TH: I think we have a handful of really difficult movies to get made right now, and some of them might have distributors come on because it's a 'cool' project, hip and daring or whatever, and it shows their indie cred, but on the other hand, what will happen at the end of the day? I now know enough to go through the 'what if' thing every time.

Well, in the end, *Happiness* did quite well. What about movies like *Safe*, which appeared on virtually every critic's best-of-the-decade list, but barely registered at the box office?
TH: I know, it made like $200,000 or something.

How many movies – movies that are not only critically lauded, but actually have the potential to change perceptions – like that can you make a year?
TH: Well, that's the reason you make the movie, because you feel you have the potential to do that. Up until a certain point, I really thought that *Ride With the Devil* would have that kind of impact. It was an even bigger entertainment, and it seemed like people would really grab hold of it. And yet it's really kind of a similar experience, but one that cost thirty times the budget of *Safe*. There's nothing more demoralizing than walking through that.

JS: It was basically dumped by the studio. Did you notice that the ads for it were basically the size of postage stamps? We thought it was kind of a nice little movie . . .

TH: We wanted to go see it at the Kendall Square Theater in Boston at Christmas, and you had to go to the 4.30 screening – it was the only time it was playing.

JS: But you know, I have to say that I was surprised at my own lack of professional jealousy when I saw the whole slew of really interesting studio films this year that were doing well. So many people at the top of their form.

TH: It was invigorating. I had a period where I was a little down, and frankly what brought me up was that I saw a bunch of fantastic Hollywood films.

Frances McDormand

Actress **Frances McDormand** has appeared in *Blood Simple*, *Raising Arizona*, *Chattahoochee*, *Hidden Agenda*, *Darkman*, *Short Cuts*, *Beyond Rangoon*, *Primal Fear*, *Madeline* and *Wonder Boys*, among others. She was nominated for a Best Supporting Actress Oscar for *Mississippi Burning*, and won the Best Actress Oscar in 1996 for her portrayal of Marge Gunderson in the Coen Brothers' *Fargo*.

Tod Lippy: Did you come directly to New York after you got your MFA at Yale?
Frances McDormand: Yep.

What brought you here, the theatre?
Yeah. I expected to be a classical theatre actor; that's the way I'd been trained. Of course, it's impossible to do that in this country. 'Wake up, young child.' I mean, Cherry Jones has proven that you can; there are certain actors who've proven it. But you have to ply your trade in small cities around the country and not make any money, and that's the way it goes. And I quickly learned that I had to pay back my school loans.

Was Yale's curriculum more theatre-intensive?
Twenty years ago, yeah. I'm not really sure what it is now. I think that they've started to be a little more responsive to training actors in the business of being actors. I mean, when I left there I had no idea what an agent was for. I was really naïve. Craft only, basically. We had only had one class at school that involved cameras. I don't know if it was Super-8 or 16mm or video, but that was the only experience we had doing scenes on tape. We never talked about film, we never talked about television, we never talked about auditions.

Once you'd arrived here, how did the city strike you?
It was really exciting. Actually, my first job after school was in Trinidad, acting in a play that the poet Derek Walcott had written, so I came back to New York at the end of summer, in August, with, you know, a piece of batik fabric wrapped around me, wearing sandals. I remember I took the D train down to my agent's in midtown in this outfit. I walked in, and the first thing he said was, 'You cannot ride the subway like that!' It was like, 'I'm back from the islands!' [*Laughs.*] I moved in with the man I was seeing, who was living in the Bronx. We lived up near Bainbridge Avenue, near Montefiore Hospital. And then I got a job as cashier at Richoux of London, which was a restaurant in the basement of the Citicorp building – they had shepherd's pie, afternoon tea, that kind of stuff – I had to wear a little doily on my head and a brown polyester skirt. I worked there until I went to Austin for *Blood Simple*.

That wasn't very long, then.
No, that was September.

From what I understand, Holly Hunter was up for the role of Abby originally. Weren't you two roommates around that time?

She lived right down the street from us, two blocks away. She and my roommate Vito both auditioned for *Blood Simple*. I hadn't read the script, but I'd helped them learn their lines. Joel and Ethan were very interested in Holly – they offered it to her – but she'd just gotten her first really big theatre job, in Beth Henley's *Crimes of the Heart*, so she said, 'Wait. I have a six-month contract and then I'll be free.' But they couldn't wait. They needed to do it in September. So they kept looking, lucky for me. I finally got in for an audition. Four or five months after that, Holly and I both changed our living situations at the same time, and I moved in with her.

You've claimed that you had absolutely 'no clue' about film acting when you were shooting *Blood Simple*.
No. None. I didn't even know how to read a script.

What was your audition like?
Well, the casting agent had told my agent that they were interested in a 'Debra Winger type'. They always do that. It's the same thing as 'This is a cross between *Porky's* and *Apocalypse Now*.' Because of limited imagination, and expedience.

So the night before the audition I watched *An Officer and a Gentleman* on tape, which I loved, in fact. [*Laughs.*] But I'm not Debra Winger. And there were the love scenes, and the nudity in the movie – 'Oh my God, I'm *nothing* like her!' So I went into the audition with a 'Fuck you, you're not gonna cast me' attitude. But then I walked in to discover these two chain-smoking geeks my own age. Huge ashtray on the table. I thought, 'This is great', because I chain-smoked myself. I also remember asking Joel some question about motivation, and he proceeded to give me a twenty-minute dramaturgical essay about how they'd written the scene. He didn't know how to talk to actors.

Anyway, they asked me to come back in the afternoon to read with John Getz, who they cast as Ray. I said, 'What time?' '3.30.' I said, 'I'm sorry, I can't.' Because at 4.00 my boyfriend had his first soap opera – he had five lines – and I told them I had to watch him. And it was great, because it was true. Anyway, finally they asked me if I could come back after the soap opera, and I said, 'Well, yeah, OK.'

Up to that point, they'd only given me sides, so I took the script to a friend's house and read it. First of all, there's hardly any dialogue in it, and everything's 'POV' this, 'POV' that. I didn't know what 'POV' was. And they describe all the camera moves, which I read as a stage direction, which of course you skip in a play – you're not supposed to cry when the playwright tells you to cry, you're supposed to *feel* it – so I didn't know what it was about. Of course, every once in a while I'd read, you know, 'Stabs him in the hand on the windowsill', that kind of thing.

How was your experience on the set?
The set was great. A lot of really long-lasting relationships were formed, not just Joel and I. There are so many people who worked on *Blood Simple* who Joel and Ethan still work with, or who will come in and out. It also informed the way so many of us now work, or how we choose our work. I am interested in working

with film *directors*, people who know technically how to make a movie. I mean, it would be nice if they know how to work with actors, but that's not essential. I'd much rather they know how to use a lens. And on that film, everybody was there because of the script. And then the added plus of getting to know Joel and Ethan and thinking, 'Hey, they might actually know what they're doing.' They were putting across an air of confidence.

Even though it was shot in Texas, would it be stretching it to call that shoot a very 'New York independent' kind of production experience?
I think it's too general. But I do have to say one specific thing about Joel and Ethan's films – they cast a lot of theatre actors, because their work is dramatic, not just visual – it's consistent the way a playscript is. And they depend on character actor/theatre people that you only find on the East Coast, or in places like Minneapolis, where there's a company. Theatre in Los Angeles is different. You can get it a little bit in San Francisco or Seattle, but LA is not the same thing. It's a transient hobby, not a profession. I mean, Holly is involved in a theatre company in LA that she established with some other actors. They've done good professional work because they're committed to it, but she can, financially. That's the problem with theatre there. People leave, and you worry whether you're going to have the same cast all the way through a production.

It's a different set of ethics. That's what I think is different about the two places. You have to live differently in New York.

You once said about acting that 'if you work constantly you're living in a fantasy world and you have nothing else to offer but fantasy'. Do you think New York offers a more resonant kind of reality check?
Definitely. I find it stifling to only talk to people who do exactly the same thing I do. Now, I'm an actor, and I love to get together with other actors and talk jargon. If you're rehearsing something in the theatre, for instance, and a bunch of actors go out to dinner, you can actually keep on rehearsing – you can intellectually keep working through a scene. But generally, you don't have to hang out with people who do the same thing here. In fact, you're forced to hang out and meet other people who don't, every day. So you're jarred out of the complacency of whatever field you're in, and you just simply have to articulate your thought differently from other people because you can't fall back on clichés. I think that's really important. In New York, you can't escape reality.

Also, in the acting profession, just working in film is way too seductive a lifestyle. You know, somebody gives you a call sheet, tells you when to wake up, where to go, when to eat. Every single time I do it, I have to adjust. When I start working, I'm like, 'Get away from me! I'm gonna get my own coffee. Leave me *alone*, for God's sake!' And then a couple weeks into it, I'm like, 'Excuse me, could I just ask you one more little favour . . .' And then after the job's over it takes me a couple more weeks to adjust back. 'Where'd I put my coffee? What time is it?!'

I wanted to back up for one second and ask you about your auditioning experience. You must have been doing a lot of it during your first few years in New York. Could you talk about that a little bit?

I conducted the first ten years of my auditioning life in total defiance, with my jaw locked every time I went in for something.

Was that a protective measure?

Definitely. When I first moved to New York, my agent would get me meetings with casting people. I met this one woman, I don't remember her name. She'd been around for a long time, and met with me as a favour to the head of the agency. I came in, sat down, probably looking exactly like I look now – no make-up (less wrinkles), chipped tooth, etc. She looked me over and said: 'Here's the thing: you would be perfect as a pioneer woman. Unfortunately, they're no longer doing Westerns. You're gonna have trouble.' I left her office mumbling to myself, 'I'm a pioneer woman . . . they aren't doing pioneer movies any more . . . gonna have trouble . . .'

This was the early eighties, and I'd just been told I would be perfect for *Little House on the Prairie*. So anyway, I spent the majority of my time trying to figure it all out. I was always walking into auditions either falling off high-heeled shoes or carrying along prosthetic breasts —

You've talked before about your 'breast roles' and 'non-breast roles' —

Yeah, they've become a tool for me. I mean, I would get scripts where the description of the woman character was, you know, 'big, beautiful breasts'. 'The breasts emerge through the door before she does.' [*Laughs.*] I'd see that in a script and go, 'Well, hah! So they think I have breasts, do they? I'll show 'em.' But I never wore them to an audition – that would really be lying – I would just take them along with me. I remember I went into one audition for one of those 'big, beautiful breast' roles, and the star of the movie, who'd I'd only seen in the movies, was going to be there. So I wore these big tall trashy shoes and I was at least a foot taller than him. Miscalculation.

Did you ever go out to LA for auditions, pilot season, that kind of thing?

No. Right after *Blood Simple,* Joel and Ethan went out there to try to sell it, and I drove out from Minneapolis, where I was doing a play, to basically hang out. We all got a house together with Sam Raimi in Silver Lake. And then I got a job on *Hill Street Blues*, a recurring character, for six episodes. So I stayed out there and finished that and then came back.

I know you lived in Santa Monica during the filming of *The Big Lebowski*; did you do any work out there then?

Actually, I was busy being a stylist for myself because of all the award things. I had planned to hang out with our son in LA while they were filming. But then we started going to all of these events. It was the only time I'd see Joel. He'd put on a tuxedo, and I would put on a gown, and we'd go to awards ceremonies. It was amazing. So I spent a lot of my time finding the right shoes for the dress, that kind of thing. It was extraordinary.

A huge percentage of the press I found on you dates from around this period.
Well, that's for two reasons. One was the phenomenon of what happened with *Fargo*. It found a broad audience that nobody expected, so it kind of became something that nobody could ignore. But also, that year I had done four different movies, and I made the decision to work with a publicist. I wanted people to see these movies. Only one of them was going to get any kind of publicity – *Primal Fear*, a studio movie. But I felt that if people were going to see me in that, then I wanted them to see me in *Fargo*, *Palookaville* and *Lone Star*, too. I mean, I like my work in *Primal Fear*, but I wanted to put it in perspective. Also, I knew that our son was on his way, and I wasn't going to be able to do four movies in a year for a while.

So I got involved with the publicity machine. I sat down and 'strategized', and talked about what I wanted to do, and how much I was willing to do, and what it was going to 'mean' in terms of when I stopped doing it. *Fargo* was never a part of it. I mean, I was going to spend a lot of time talking about *Fargo*, but that was not the one I thought audiences were going to see, nor the one that I thought journalists were going to be interested in. It kind of flipped around on all of us, though, which was fascinating.

During your acceptance speech for the Best Actress Oscar, you made the statement that casting decisions should be based on 'qualifications as opposed to market value'. Did you get any flak for that?
I don't think I have. Nobody's ever said anything to my face. [*Laughs.*] Let me tell you something about that situation. I'd watched the Oscars on television for years, and it just doesn't work as a theatrical event. Never. Because they don't know how to do theatre. It's not TV; it's theatre – it's a huge house with a very specific audience with a massive stage that's empty. I figured if I ended up having to go up on that stage, then I was going to use it as a theatrical moment. If I was given that time to use, I wanted to use it for my own devices. Also, I hadn't worked for six months, so I was raring to go. I did have a script, because I thought about what I was going to say, and if you're going to have that amount of time in front of that kind of audience —

Over a billion people . . .
No, I mean the several thousand people in the house. Really, it's not about television; it's about that group of people. About being in front of a group of, well, not peers, except for all of the people we were sitting around. We were off to the side, in, like, the hooters' corner. It was Joel and me, Ethan and Trish, and Bill Macy, Felicity Huffman behind us. And Holly and Janusz were over in, like, the 'senior high school' section, with Nic Cage and Patricia Arquette. We were in the junior high section.

Anyway, that statement was to honour what was clearly true about the five of us who had been nominated in that category, because the pickings were so slim for we women to choose from. I knew, even though I didn't know any of those other women personally, that they have gone through the same exact things I had been going through for eighteen years. 'Big beautiful breasts.' Too tall, too thin, too short. 'Of course, we have to cast the male lead before we can cast the female part', etc. Playing roles that were only in relationship to the men in the story – basically all the bullshit that goes along with being a female in that profession.

But I felt that that's what people were responding to in the character of Marge. There's the movie, there's the script, there's my work in the movie, but beyond that, there's this character that steps outside all of it, and people get her. People always forget that she doesn't come in until almost halfway through the movie. It's not a huge part. So I guess what I was trying to say in that speech was that I appreciated Tim Bevan and Eric Fellner's support of the story, and Joel and Ethan's decision to cast me. Not that they were necessarily interested in equality for women, or creating only roles like Marge for actresses to play. Of course, if they asked for a lot more money, the way the business works people are going to say, 'OK, we'll give you the money. Now hire somebody people are going to fucking recognize.' But that's the business of it.

But your involvement in a couple of indie projects, post-*Fargo*, has actually brought money in.

Not necessarily that much money. At least one, though, yeah – right after the Oscars, with a friend of ours. I helped him raise the money, but it was only three million dollars, which is basically peanuts. I've found since, though, that it really hasn't changed that much; people can't really get too far with me being in the movie. But I can offer something else. A goal that I always felt I could realistically achieve in my profession was the respect of my peers. So someone can say 'Fran McDormand's read it, likes it', and then someone will at least read the script, or they'll want to work with me, or maybe it's just, 'Oh, I like her work, that means that's what this project is about.'

But on the other hand, it's starting to backfire. I've had to learn to be much more forcefully protective of that, because actors have come up to me and said, 'I did this because you were going to do it. Why didn't you do it?!' And I never said I was going to do it; I just said I liked the script. Then it's like, 'Wait! That's not my goal. I don't want to fuck people around.' And that's a drag, because if anything, throughout the years I've erred on the side of . . . Joel's always giving me shit, saying, 'Oh, is this one another choice for integrity?' But it's the only thing I can count on.

How do you make the decision to work with newer directors, particularly if there's no body of work from which to judge?

It's really specific every time. The largest thing recently I've done with a director whose work I didn't know was *Madeline*, with Daisy Mayer. I hadn't seen her first film, *Party Girl*, but I met with her, and the way she talked about the books – the way she wanted to use them as her bible, essentially – and the way she described the auditions with the little girls, I just trusted her. I looked at her and thought, 'This chick knows what she's doing.' And she really did.

So trust obviously plays an important role.
I feel that it's about judging character. Like working on *Palookaville*. All I knew about Alan Taylor was that I'd seen his short – a producer friend of mine, Maggie Renzi, someone I really respect, had given it to me way before I ever heard about *Palookaville*. So when the name came up again, I remembered him. Also, it was a part – a prostitute – that studios, or what ever you want to call it, the more 'conventional' film world, would never have considered me for. And it was only one day! It was great. You know, our meal was take-out food in the basement of a house next door, I helped pull cable out from underneath my chair – at the time, I really needed to do that. I can't remember what I was shooting right before, but it was like when I worked on *Darkman* with Sam Raimi, and then did Ken Loach's *Hidden Agenda* right afterward – it was a really great antidote to being 'the girl' in an action movie.

Do you find that the roles you choose – whether consciously or unconsciously – create some sort of linearity, or 'narrative', to your acting life?
Well, last year, I did two plays: I played Blanche in *A Streetcar Named Desire*, and Merope, the mother, in a new reworking of *Oedipus*. Those two things felt like the culmination of twenty years of work, and also the springboard for the next twenty. And they followed my playing Marge in *Fargo*. I mean, I didn't fall completely flat on my face with Blanche – my nose was scraped a little on the very tip —

You think so?
Yeah. It was a little bit like being in drag for me. Though I feel like I pulled it off, it was in the same way the best Streisand impersonator can pull it off – you're still aware of the fact that your hands are too big. I was really aware of myself doing it. That's not to say I wasn't aware of myself with Marge – I was – but there was something very contained about it. And there was an ease to it. The same thing with *Oedipus*, which was written by a friend of mine from drama school, who is Pedro's godfather. I mean, we've known each other really intimately for twenty years. There was an ease to it.

But that's not to say it's only there when the roles have been specifically written for me; it just seems to me that, more often than not, transitional work happens for me in the theatre, and then whatever film work I do afterward benefits from that, or is at least informed by it.

Like playing the abused wife in *Mississippi Burning* right after playing Stella on Broadway?

Exactly. That's why I'm really interested in seeing the last two films I did after those two plays. With *Wonder Boys*, the work I did with Curtis Hanson was a *job* for me, in the best sense of the word. I went in, I didn't beat my head against the wall – I had too many other things to deal with. I was quitting smoking at the time, and I was raising my son. So I was trying to negotiate being out of town without him, with him, back and forth. I just wanted to see what I could do if I just went to work, did my job and went home. I don't know if it works. And then I feel like so much of the work I did on Cameron Crowe's movie really is directly related to – although technically on the other extreme from – Merope in *Oedipus*, because the latter is an hour-and-a-half, full-blown Greek drama hurricane monologue about motherhood, and the role I played in Cameron's movie is that of Cameron's real-life mother, basically. A homage to a woman he adores, and who is really a formidable character. But it's a movie, and it's a comedy. We'll see.

So obviously, in film, you're really not sure of how your work is going until you see a final cut.
Yeah. Don't know. Can't necessarily trust my instincts on that.

With theatre, do you know during a performance, or immediately after?
Well, that's a weird one, because of how exciting it is to be working with a live audience. How that completes a circuit, which is something different every night. It's much more tenuous. Also, it's not necessarily a healthy thing for me – or any actor – to talk too critically about performances when you're doing them. You just simply go back in there with too much information every night. It's much easier to talk about it critically later. Whereas with movies, it's always later. I don't have that much ego attached to it. There aren't the same immediate concerns.

Do you read reviews when you're on stage?
I do now. It depends.

Aren't you ever inclined to modify a performance?
Sometimes, yeah. Not even modifying; you just become too aware of it. Even if they say, 'Love the way she delivers that line.' Then you can never say it again; your timing will always be off from that moment forward. The line will never be the same, because there's that *beep beep* in your head – you have to step over that rock every time.

What's your opinion of actors who sign on to a particular project with the proviso that they will have some input on the script?
I'm suspicious of it. I don't think there are many people who simply have the talent and experience to do that. I'm really suspicious of actors directing movies; I'm really suspicious of actors even producing movies. Mostly because I have no affinity for it, or interest in it. The last thing I want to do is to sit around developing scripts. The earliest I want to get involved is talking to designers. I really enjoy talking about my character's environment and wardrobe, stuff like that.

I remember your saying for Marge that you knew exactly what kind of make-up she would wear – a blue eye shadow she would have used since Brainard High School – and that she'd have broken blood-vessels in her face because of constant exposure to the cold.

It's a process of work for me. When I'm not working, I am a voracious reader of women's magazines. I love them. It's my research. So in talking to John Blake about Marge's make-up, for instance – you know, broken blood vessels also happen to make you look really good. [*Laughs.*] They can be strategically placed in a very attractive way – it's better than blush, know what I mean? It's a really specific texture. John can do 'glamour' well, but he's even better at special effects. And special-effect make-up is much better for me than glamour make-up.

But in terms of my research, those magazines are about body image and fantasy – about what's being sold at any particular time. Women are being sold exteriors – 'We can be anything you want us to be.' What's the package? Which mould am I going to pour it into? And I can't fit hardly any of the ones that are in those women's magazines. They don't show me, they don't represent me.

You and 99 per cent of the population.

Exactly. That's what's interesting to me about someone like Kate Winslet, who I adore, because she's completely inside her body. And her body type is not in those magazines except for when she's in them. So along with the interesting choices she's making in her film roles as a professional, by also appearing in these magazines she's reaching an audience that needs to hear from her. She's going to be able to affect twenty-year-old women in a positive way. *I* need to hear from her!

You've occasionally done what you called earlier 'girl' roles, like, for instance, the part of Julie Hastings in *Darkman*. Doesn't that feel slightly problematic to you, considering where you're coming from?

No. Because I'm not on a mission. And I don't think Kate Winslet should be on any kind of mission, either. She should do whatever she wants to do. It's just nice to see somebody doing that – regardless of their reasons – and changing something.

With *Darkman*, by the way, I really missed an opportunity. I could've had more fun, the same way Sigourney Weaver had fun in *Alien* and Kathleen Turner had fun in *Romancing the Stone*. I was taking it too seriously, and also, Sam kind of cast me because he wanted to answer the criticism of not ever having three-dimensional female characters in his stories. It didn't work, though, because I didn't find the dimension of positive silliness that has to go along with the 'damsel-in-distress' role.

Anyway, I don't think I'll be doing any more action movies, unless I can do, like, the Judi Dench thing with the Bond movies. I wouldn't have to pull out the breasts for a role like that. Or maybe I would. I could come back as Pussy Galore in her later years. 'That's *Ms* Pussy to you.'

On the frontier.

Yeah. [*Laughs.*] Pioneer Pussy.

You mentioned that, after *Darkman*, you took the role of the human rights activist in Ken Loach's *Hidden Agenda*. What went into that decision? It was interesting that you once again ended up playing opposite Brad Dourif (who played the husband of your character in *Mississippi Burning*).

That was weird. I had no idea Brad was doing it. But it was much more about working with Ken. Ken had never told me whether he'd seen *Mississippi Burning*, but I'm assuming he did.

I have to be honest, I'd never heard of Ken Loach. I read the script while we were shooting *Darkman*, and thought it was really kind of inaccessible. I said to Liam [Neeson], 'Have you ever heard of this Ken Loach guy?' He almost genuflected. He said, 'Do anything you can to work with him.' He told me to see *Kes*, which I rented, and I thought it was extraordinary. I met with Ken; he came to LA while I was out there shooting the film. When he goes to LA he walks everywhere. He asked me to come get him, because he didn't have a car. I picked him up in my rental car – it was one of those with the automatic safety belts that slide up when you close the door, and he freaked. 'Well, that's very Fascist, isn't it!' I thought, 'I love you. What do you want me to do? I'm there.'

I think the situation for Ken at the time was: 'You want some money? You want to make this political movie about Northern Ireland? How about putting a couple of American actors in there?' My character was originally supposed to be from Germany, and a lot of her background revolved around her guilt as a German. Anyway, he put together a group of international actors, and he took us to Northern Ireland for a week before we started filming to interview different people he had selected from the Catholic community – people who'd been interned, or had family members interned, who'd been searched. We only talked to one RUC guy, also someone Ken chose. And then, the first thing we shot was a press conference with real English and Irish press.

That opens the film. It felt very spontaneous, with everyone jumping on everyone else's lines . . .

Yeah. There were journalists there who had been covering Northern Ireland. And their questions were really being directed at Ken as much as us. 'I have a question – what the fuck do you know about this?!' He basically taught us what he wanted us to know. He manipulated that situation, because I didn't know enough about the political situation in Northern Ireland to defend my own opinion. I chose to serve Ken's storytelling.

That reminds me of something you said about Altman, another improvisation-based director, being a 'master manipulator' in the sense that he made you feel like a collaborator in the process —

You know what it is? It's something that I've been describing in talking about both him and Ken. This whole idea of improvisation, and films that are generated on the 'reality' of an emotional moment with an actor – it's something that I'm seeing in a lot of younger film-makers' work now, and I think that it's being abused, or there's a reverence for it that's ill-placed. They look at Altman's work, or Loach's work, and think, 'Brilliant improvisation. I can do that; I'll just get some great actors together. Give 'em a blueprint and let 'em go.' But you know, never once on either of those sets did I hear a camera operator say, 'We've just rolled out.' You know? These directors knew exactly what they were doing. Improvisational, yes. But they knew the ten different things that could happen, because they'd already thought about it. They were just waiting to see which one came up. They were in control.

Could you talk about your experiences on Mick Jackson's *Chatahoochee*?
I learned a big lesson with *Chatahoochee*, which relates to what I was saying earlier: Never make assumptions about what the final outcome of the movie is. The script I read – the movie I shot – was a dark comedy. And then it turned out to be a very earnest film about a mental-health situation. And I don't think Mick Jackson's intention was for it to be an earnest film. Anyway, I didn't fit; nothing I did fitted into that movie. That's why to this day I refuse to talk about a movie until I've seen it. It's not fair. And it's more respectful to the film-maker.

I took that role for two very specific reasons. One was that my breasts were a big part of that job, because there is a specific flashback scene for Gary Oldman's character when he's in prison – he's remembering having sex with his wife (my character) and being smothered by her breasts. She thought she was sexually titillating him, and she was actually smothering him. So that fact that she had large breasts was integrally important to the development of his character, I thought in a really great way.

Mick had seen *Raising Arizona* – my first use of the prosthetics – so when I went in to audition, it was like, 'I'm sorry. As you can see, I'm flat-chested. But I know I can play this part. I love this part.' I had to find out how he was planning to shoot that particular scene, because if he didn't need these breasts literally coming off of my body [*mimes pulling out prostheses*], 'We've got these to play with!' [*Laughs.*] So to speak. And he cast me, because his intention in that scene was always to have these disembodied breasts, which would amp up the horror of him being smothered. So we got a 'breast double'. I was much more concerned about the poor woman's situation than she was: I insisted on meeting her, and being there on the set the day she worked. She didn't care; she was like, 'Whatever', doing her math homework in between the shots. But it was a victory for me to be cast in that role. And I've always been really – not grateful, but I really respect Mick for making that decision.

The other reason was having the opportunity to work with Gary. We were both theatre-trained, and I'd seen his work in *Sid and Nancy* – I was ready to meet that challenge of *working with Gary Oldman*. I felt like I was ready to be a worthy adversary. I remember at the end of one scene my character breaks down, sobbing, and the dynamic of it was that this would be his character's parting image of his wife. Anyway, before we shot the scene, we were just sitting around talking, and he mentioned some film he'd recently done where, in an over-the-shoulder shot, when the camera was on the other actor, he was doing a really amazing job, but the minute the set-up changed and the camera was on Gary, the other actor wasn't emotionally connected. He said he felt like he was working with a stand-in.

Well, I took that to heart, and was determined to give him as much as I could. I wanted to prove to him that I was not that kind of actor, and that I respected his work. By the end of the day, I was a wreck! My eyes were swollen, I could hardly talk. I learned a big lesson from that. He was not saying to me, 'You have to fucking cry every time.' He was simply relating an anecdote about something I'd never really experienced before in film.

Many of the directors you've worked with have commented on your ability to listen, and react, to other actors. To be 'in the moment'.
What I found out in *Blood Simple* was that it had to be about where you were right then and there, and the people you were with at that moment. Unlike theatre, I couldn't depend on a month-long rehearsal process to establish an emotional or psychological road map. For instance, the whole sequence of events that happens after my character thinks the husband has killed Ray, the lover, and I think I'm being chased. In the middle of it, I go into the bathroom to hide. So that day, you know, I'm hanging out, having a cigarette, a cup of coffee, and suddenly I realize, 'Oh fuck. I have to be hysterical!' And not only that; they were shooting it from all these different angles, so I had to be hysterical *all day*. 'What am I gonna do, what am I gonna do?!' And I remembered a student play I'd done during my last year of drama school. During rehearsal, the director had had one of the other actors hold me from behind until she felt I was at the necessary emotional pitch, and then she'd say, 'OK. Let her go.' It pissed me off so much that I couldn't get away, and I became hysterical.

So suddenly I'm looking around the set at all these guys who were exactly like Joel and Ethan – wimpy, geeky guys, like Barry Sonnenfeld. But then there was Tom Prophet. A forty-five-year-old grip from Austin, Texas. Big old gray handlebar moustache, biceps the size of a ham. I went up to him: 'OK, Tom. I know this is going to sound really weird, OK? But listen: I need you to just stand here and hold me, OK, until Joel says "action". I'm going to fight real hard to get away, but don't let me go until Joel says "action", OK?'

We did the first take and I said 'Thank you very much' to Tom and crawled under a table on the set, huddling there waiting for the next setup. I could hear Joel saying, 'Does anybody know where Fran is?' Jean Black, the make-up woman, whispered, 'She's under that table.' And this is why I'm married to the man today: He got down, crawled under the table, said, 'So, Fran, here's the next scene we're doing. I'll come get you when we're ready.' Didn't ask me why I was under the table, didn't ask me if I was OK. A few minutes later Jean kind of scooted this box of Kleenex under the table. I spent the entire day there.

Anyway, from that point on I decided that I wasn't going to do that every time.

It was stupid. And so now, truly, the best thing for me to do, particularly if I have to be in a place of emotional vulnerability for a scene in a film, is to stand in for myself, on the mark, while everybody around me is setting up the shot. The isolation of that is enough to make me feel – not exactly vulnerable, but it fine-tunes things. It's also very theatrical. That's a pretty grand gesture, to make people deal with the fact that I'm there. I mean, even the guy setting up the light probably knows what the upcoming scene's about, so if you're standing there, and they're having to work around you, everyone kind of knows what's going on. 'Isn't this the scene where he dies? What's she doing out here?' It's all about what's gonna happen right then. Not about sitting under the table crying, or remembering your dog dying, or any of that. You're right there.

It seems very other-directed.
Yeah, because it's not an isolated medium. You can't act by yourself. And you can always tell in someone's performance if they're listening to the other actor or doing it alone. Even in a fashion photo, the best models think. They're thinking, and there's something in their eyes. You can't fake that, just like you can't fake listening.

Do you need to be empathetic to be an actor?
Well, it doesn't hurt. But it's got its limits. Because in the end it's also about self-preservation, and protecting yourself, because I don't want anybody to negatively manipulate me. I mean, I want a director to manipulate me, so well in fact that I don't even think about it until the next day, but I don't want anybody fucking around with me; manipulating me to the point of nastiness, which people can do. So I want to know how to do it for myself.

How did you get involved with *The Butcher's Wife*?
After *Mississippi Burning*, all I ever got offered were Southern white-trash parts. And only dramatic stuff. I'd had it – I couldn't answer one more question in an audition about not being from the South. So I'm grateful that I got to do *The Butcher's Wife*, because I really wanted to do a comedy. But it was so ill-fated. It was a movie that was supposed to take place in New York, and we shot the whole thing on a back lot in Hollywood. There was nothing, *nothing* New York about it.

I was supposed to be a lesbian boutique owner in SoHo – I was psyched. This was, like, mid-eighties – it was about wearing black clothes, having long stringy blond hair, black eyeliner, talking out the side of my mouth – basically, just being really cool 'New York downtown' – this was when SoHo was still cool. But when I get there, I find out the costume designer has a deal with Cerrutti, so she's getting all of these pastel plaid power suits free for me to wear. Very masculine-looking, eighties, big-shoulder-pad things. Well, the point for me of playing a lesbian boutique owner in SoHo was to not be a *dyke*. She's not a dyke. Anyway, at some point, I just threw up my hands and went to work. In the end, though, I shot myself in the foot, because the point was to prove that I could do comedy, but I took it so seriously that there was no joy, no lightness to the character. She was just a bitch, because that's what I felt like.

I believe that if you talked with a majority of the people I've worked with in the last twenty years, hopefully, at least 95 per cent would say that I'm really professional and easy to get along with, and they like working with me. The costume designer from *Butcher's Wife*, however, is one of the five per cent who, if you mentioned my name to her, would say, 'The most horrible experience I've ever had in my life. That woman doesn't know shit.' I made her life hell, because I had a hook for that character, and a real specific way that I could do it, and when it was taken away from me my confidence was shattered. I didn't know how to play the part in a Cerrutti suit. So I made it impossible for her to put me in a Cerrutti suit. But also, what my vanity was doing, since my confidence was shot, was making me think things like, 'OK. This character wouldn't care what she looked like. Yes she would! She'd wear a Cerrutti suit. No, she wouldn't, she's a boutique owner! She knows her butt's big, she would wear something that didn't make her butt look big! But she's a lesbian, so maybe she doesn't care about her body image. Of course she cares about her body image!' And on and on. It was a battle with my own vanity and my insecurity about my own body. And one of the reasons I wanted to play this character was because she wouldn't have that insecurity. She'd wear black because it was *the minimalizer*. Anyway, it's always about the subjugation of vanity.

You know, for all of these characters, Joel is always saying to me, 'I don't think she has to be *that* unattractive . . .' It was the same thing with Marge.

Speaking of *Fargo* one more time, I wanted to get very specific for a moment, and talk about the enormous resonance of your delivery of the 'I just don't understand' line in the police car near the end of the film . . .
Something that informed that moment was my mother; she says things like that. You know, five minutes can't go by without her giving you a list of the people who've died. I was on the phone with her the other day and she said, 'Well, you know, we've got this young girl. They got married, then he left her for somebody else . . .' She just starts right in on this mini-scandal in the community, and her judgment on it. Lasts for about five or six lines – 'Uh, where are you going with this, Mom?' We don't talk that often, but she'll always say, 'What haven't I told you? What can I tell you?' And it's always about death, destruction, drama – offered like a little cup of tea to soothe you, so that a connection has been made. And I think that's what Joel was hearing in Marge – gotta do your job, file the report, everything has to be completed, and then: 'Oh my, that was ugly!'

I actually have to answer something related to that. I allowed something to happen that I have to sort of redeem myself for. Shall I?

Please.
When we were shooting *Fargo*, I had a blast. I really enjoyed it. But I always felt – and I even said this to Joel and Ethan at one point – that Gaier and Carl, rather than Marge, were actually the 'good guys' in the story. And in Joel and Ethan's kind of warped way, they are. We all adored those characters. It was great watch-

ing Steve and Peter work together, and they got really tight doing the shooting. They were great to be around, and there was a real propulsion to their characters. At the end of the shoot, when the costume designer sold wardrobe stuff, all the guys on the crew wanted their things.

Anyway, all of us were always, well, not making jokes about Marge, but Joel and Ethan would say 'cut' at the end of a scene and the crew would just start laughing. And I would also crack myself up a lot. Stuffing White Castle hamburgers in my mouth, that kind of thing. But despite all of the laughing, there were all these moments of . . . well, *terror*. I was *utterly terrified* of her. Then the movie comes out, and I start doing all this publicity, and everybody's in love with her; they adore her. And there was only one journalist, a female journalist from Australia I met while I was doing publicity in London, and she said something like, 'Don't you find Marge really scary?' And I almost went, 'Yes! *Terrifying!*' And then I went, 'No, no . . .' and I played the party line. But, in fact, I never acknowledged what I had always felt about her. There's nothing scary about what she's become in the minds of most of *Fargo*'s audience, but that element is also what's made her so symbolic. So that moment is poignant, but why is it poignant? Maybe it's that she's so naïve, so innocent.

To me, it was her utter imperviousness to evil. Her inability to imagine it, and that somehow allowing her to conquer it. It isn't entirely explainable, which is a good thing.
There's hope there. I have to say, what I appreciate – and of course my perspective is just blown at this point – but what I got from the end of *Fargo*, which I'd been waiting for in Joel and Ethan's work, was an embracing of sentimentality, which they did, and it worked. In my opinion, they backed out of it at the end of *The Big Lebowski*. The whole future thing in that was bullshit, I thought, and *Barton Fink* was bullshit in the way it turned into a horror movie, from my point of view, and didn't really deal with somebody not being able to write. And the whole ending of *Raising Arizona* was like, you know, sappy about them eventually having this big family and going into the sunset in their old age – bullshit sentimentality. Or like a backing off of sentimentality, because they made a comment on it. The end of *Fargo* was *purely* sentimental, and it worked. Of course, Joel and Ethan would just guffaw at that.

I wanted to ask just a couple more questions about New York. First, I would think that anyone with a degree of celebrity can 'blend in' here, as it were, better than most other places in the country. Is that the case with you? Are you ever self-conscious about being out and being observed?
Well, it's only been in the past couple of years that that's happened to me. I had a lot of trouble this fall with it, but mainly because of my son. I don't like having him exposed to it. We don't let it be a part of our life, but it's insidiously a part of his without him having any choice. That being said, at the same time, the natural tendency of

New Yorkers is to respect each other's privacy, no matter who you are or what you do. It's just a given. So when it is there, it's still in a generally respectful way.

We were away all summer, so I felt it a lot more when I first came back, because I was 'home', and I didn't want people to do that to me in my local grocery store. 'This is where I live; this is my neighbourhood.' Also, the more time I spend in the neighbourhood, I'm just somebody else you see every day. So, yes, they know I'm an actor, but I'm in their neighbourhood, so I'm 'their actor'.

There's a clipping I ran across from the New York *Daily News*, basically a gossip item around the time of the Oscars, which consists of a series of quotes from people who live near you, telling their stories of how 'regular' the two of you were. What you wore to the gym, how much you perspired on the Stairmaster, where you shopped, that kind of thing. That seems a little creepy.

Yeah, it is. The problem is – and this is the problem that everybody in New York has – you've always got an audience here. Everybody does. Like when you walk down the street, and you hear a few lines from a knock-down, drag-out fight a couple is in the midst of – I mean, where else do they do it? You're in transit, but you're not in a car, by yourselves, so you're being watched and heard. With Joel and I, now that we have a kid, the times we get to talk are limited. So when we go out alone together to see a movie, get dinner, often the things we're talking about are important, personal things that need to be discussed. But you're sitting at Ollie's Noodle Shop at a table for two with people crammed in on either side of you. And when toward the end of dinner you realize that the people on your right haven't been talking for the last half-hour, you suddenly know that they've been involved in the decision about, you know, which tampon I'm going to use. You've got it anyway as a New Yorker, but there's a certain part of you that can tune out that conversation next door until it's somebody you've just seen in a movie, or somebody you read about in a magazine. Suddenly it's more difficult to do.

Do you ever imagine leaving New York?

There are two instances when I feel like I want to leave New York. One is when the fucking car alarm goes off at 5.30 in the morning, and the second is when my kid has to take a test to get into kindergarten. But I really can't imagine living anywhere else. Although I have to say I can't imagine having to live here for twelve months straight, year in year out. I've never done that in the eighteen years I've lived here. I've always spent time away working or travelling. As a home base, though, there can't be anything better.

Do you have a favourite movie theatre?

Film Forum. It's our date place, because I really don't want to waste my time on most American movies. We went there with some friends the other night – a double date – to see *Mr Death*. The perfect New York date movie. We sat where we always sit, right behind the 'Dedicated in Loving Memory to Karl Mundt' seat. We always pay homage to Karl. We're such geeks.

Carter Burwell

Carter Burwell composed his first film score for the Coen Brothers' *Blood Simple; he has since scored all of their films, as well as nearly fifty others*, including *Being John Malkovich, High Fidelity, Three Kings, Velvet Goldmine, Gods and Monsters*, Michael Almereyda's *Hamlet, Conspiracy Theory, Fear* and *Rob Roy*.

Tod Lippy: You were born in New York, weren't you?
Carter Burwell: I was born in the city. My parents left for Connecticut within a year after my being born, thinking it wasn't a good place to raise a child. But I spent my formative months in a carriage being wheeled around Washington Square Park.

When did you first develop an interest in music?
Well, I don't really remember a first moment; I grew up with music like most children do, and my parents were both interested in it even though they were not really musicians. My mother, when they lived in New York, was interested in the Dixieland jazz scene here, and went to all these clubs. When I was growing up, she had a guitar, and would sing folk-songs to me. I remember thinking – even when the guitar was much bigger than I was – that it was an interesting device. But, you know, all devices look interesting when you're young. I took some piano lessons about the same age as most other people do – I guess I was about ten – and it just was horrible. It pretty much drove me away from the piano until high school, when someone showed me how to play a blues progression so that the two of us could jam together. That was interesting to me. It turned out that the only thing that does interest me is making things up myself. Playing pre-existing pieces of music, whether they're mine or anyone else's, doesn't interest me very much.

Did you get into rock 'n' roll in high school or college?
I hadn't been especially interested in rock 'n' roll during high school; mostly I liked listening to old blues records. This friend of mine who showed me how to play the blues progressions, Steve Kraemer, was multi-instrumentalist – he could play piano or trumpet or harmonica or guitar, but of course he couldn't play them all at the same time, so he needed to convince his friends to play accompanying instruments. That's why he showed me how to play piano. We would haunt record stores looking for old blues records from the thirties on. Steve had taught me to disdain rock 'n' roll as a poor stepchild to the blues – it was just a bunch of rich, white Brits trying to make money off of Black-American culture.

But I met other groups of people in college – in particular, some of my friends who were interested in experimental rock, like Brian Eno, and Roxy Music, John Cale. That was interesting to me – it didn't have that feeling of being derivative; it really felt like a sincere, fresh expression. I liked that; I liked that you couldn't even tell what it was that was being expressed a lot of the time. So my interest started broadening, and then by the time the punk-rock era was happening in the late seventies, we started getting into that through people like Iggy Pop, who was punk rock, but, again, from a sort of ambiguous background. Of course, it was only two or three chords, but it wasn't a 1,4,5 progression the way a lot of rock 'n' roll was. It became more minimal in some way that interested me. And of course, the energy of it, the sexuality of it, was very striking for me in late adolescence.

We went to see Iggy Pop on one of his first of many comeback tours at the Harvard Square Theater. It was senior year for me, and Blondie was the opening band. I don't think their first album had come out yet. A band we'd never heard of, but an amazing performance, of course, and then Iggy, who I'd never seen perform, was quite spectacular. David Bowie was playing piano, and Soupy Sales' sons, Hunt and Tony Sales, were playing bass and drums. It was extraordinary – there was such a rich combination of energies and interests on that stage.

Did you already know you were going to pursue a career in music at this point?
At the time, I was fully planning on going to architecture school. I'd applied to schools, but there was a recession going on, and all the architects I knew in Cambridge were unemployed. I looked in at the architecture school at Harvard, other places. You'd see people up all night, building models – lots of things that would never be built. And then, on the other hand, you're looking at the stage, where it's all happening so spontaneously. These people were making something – who knows what it is, but they were making something – and they were presenting it to the public. And since I wasn't going to get paid in either discipline, I thought I might as well be not paid for something that was a little more fun and spontaneous. So I decided to take a year off before going to graduate school and do other things.

Did you stay in Cambridge?
I did. I hung around, because my other friends with whom I was playing in a band still had one more year of college, so I waited for them. During that year, I tried to learn as much as I could about music. We kind of all agreed that this is what we would do. For myself, the easiest way to get into music was through electronic and computer music, because I knew a bit about electronics, and more about computers, so I looked up the electronic music studio at Harvard, which turned out to be run by this extraordinary person named Ivan Tcherepnin, and he came from a long line of composers and conductors. He had this very broad mind about what constituted music, and not all electronic composers are like that. He really invited chance into his work. When things would go wrong, which they often did with these electronic instruments, he tried to make sure that whatever went wrong would work into the piece. He felt that a piece that can't stand mistakes and meltdowns is the wrong piece.

It sounds very much like John Cage.
Exactly. I realize now that Cage must have been a strong influence on him, but at the time I didn't know Cage's work. So I went and saw him, explained that I was interested in electronic music. Strictly speaking, only graduate students were allowed into that facility, but for some reason he gave me a key to the studio, and

we actually co-taught a class. I had done some film study in college – I'd been an animator, among other things – and he was really interested in music and film, and thought that any contemporary composer should be interested in it, too. He viewed it as a great venue for new sounds, and new structures. So we agreed to teach this class together. I mean, I had no thought that I was going to end up doing music for films; it was just a handy way to get access to the studio, and to interact with a brilliant person. So I spent the year doing that, and then when my friends graduated, we all agreed to come to New York and be a band. Most of them eventually matured and moved on to other things, but I never did . . .

Where did you live when you got here?
Well, when we first got here we really had no money at all. We were living off credit cards. Our first experience of New York was really pretty pathetic, in that we just could not find anything in Manhattan that we could afford to live or rehearse in, so we ended up on Long Island. The first jobs we got basically to feed ourselves were on an assembly line in Syosset. We were rehearsing in some house in Long Island. And then after a year of that, we found a rehearsal space called the Music Building, on 8th Avenue and 38th Street. It's still used for this, but we were one of the first tenants after its life as a garment-industry building. The space we occupied was filled with bolts of fabric. Our deal with the young guy who had just bought the building was that if we converted it into something like a rehearsal studio, he would give us a break on our rent. So we got a three-year lease there.

A lot of other interesting people were taking advantage of this, too, because it was one of the few places where a landlord was actually inviting musicians in – in most places, musicians were the opposite of an ideal tenant. Madonna was there when we were there; this gentleman, Steve Bray, who wrote a lot of material with her, and was her percussionist, her drummer, he also played drums with us. It was a real community. Bands would run up and down the stairs to borrow equipment, or musicians, from each other.

And you were playing gigs at the time?
Yeah, we were playing at CBGB's, the Mudd Club – a lot of clubs of the time. It was great. In a way, I can't really picture how people go through their twenties without that. Most of the bands we were in were co-educational, with women as well as men, and yet there was this bonding element, particularly amongst the guys. I don't know what else to compare it to, except warfare or something. To spend so much time with each other – it was really an extended adolescence. I think that people who didn't ever join a band are the ones who end up at middle age in the woods banging drums and trying to find that part of themselves. We had the good fortune to work it out ourselves in our twenties.

Didn't you also have a job doing DNA sequencing around this time?
Yeah. Whether it's a blessing or a curse, my day jobs – with the exception of the assembly-line thing – were always very interesting. I managed to get a job at Cold

Spring Harbor laboratory, which is a biology lab in Long Island. Just a lovely place – James Watson, who runs the lab, kept it looking like a country club. Tennis courts, and canoes, and there was a bar on the campus. They had these seminars during the summer, and making the physical environment so nice was his way of getting the best scientists in the world to come and spend a few weeks there. I was the all-round computer guy at the lab – my title was 'Systems Programmer' – so I was helping people with whatever required computers: DNA sequencing, neurobiology image-processing of mostly brain scans. My main job had to do with cell biology, and analysing what was called 'gene expression', which means looking at all the proteins in a cell, trying to quantify how proteins come and go as cells change with illnesses like cancer. I mean, I was not a biologist, I was just the computer guy, but again, it was not unlike the situation with Ivan. I've been incredibly lucky; people have been irrationally nice to me a lot of times in my life. James Watson treated me as a scientist, and gave me all the perks they had. I was able to live in this Victorian house on the grounds; our band even rehearsed there sometimes. In the neurobiology labs, they have these big rooms called Faraday Cages, which are completely covered with conductive metal to keep any kind of radio inteference out. When they weren't doing an experiment in one of the Faraday Cages, we would rehearse in there. They liked that; we were the 'lab band'.

How did you first meet the Coen Brothers?
It was from the music scene in New York. A woman who I'd done some recording with, Stanton Miranda, knew a bass player named Skip Lievsay, who was also a sound designer. He was working in film, although I really don't know how much film he had done at that time. But he was working on *Blood Simple.* Joel and Ethan were looking for a musician to do their score – obviously for very little money – and Skip called me one day and asked me if it was something I would be interested in. Generally speaking, if someone asks me if I'm interested in something I've never done before, I'll automatically say 'yes'. So I went by their editing room and saw a couple of reels of the film.

At that point, Joel and Ethan were so young – I mean, we were all the same age, in our late twenties – but they looked like they were just out of film school. And the film looked like it was just out of film school, too, although I couldn't really tell anything about its quality by looking at a rough cut. And I didn't have a demo reel of anything to give them, because I'd never done this before, so I just said I would go home and work up some sketches on the piano, whatever, and bring them in and play them for them. So I went home, did that, and came back a couple of days later and played them some things, from more traditional thriller-type music to stuff that really wasn't like that – stuff that was gentler, more lyrical – to other things. At the time I was playing a lot with tape machines, playing things backwards at different speeds, so I included some of those experiments, too.

I don't think they cared especially for the bits that sounded more like traditional film music, but they liked the other ones. Although they continued talking
to other film composers for months afterwards. I think the people who were
backing the film really didn't want Joel and Ethan, who knew nothing about film
music, to hire a composer who knew nothing about film music.

Did the actual composing come easily to you?
It did come easily, partly because no one was really there to create a sense of
stress. If you meet Joel and Ethan, you'll realize that when you're with them, you
don't feel the pressure of schedule, or millions of dollars, or audience response,
bearing down on you at all. We really just sit around and try to entertain ourselves; it's a very relaxed environment. I think this is what a lot of actors like
about them as well – they really give you the comfort to do what you do best; they
put a lot of trust in the people they work with.

**I recall your saying somewhere that you'll never be able to match the intensity
of writing that first score again.**
There's a beauty to that naïve first moment, when you give no thought, for
instance, to how the music interacts with dialogue, or what happens at the beginning or end of a reel, or how reels change over, or how it's going to mix together,
or what the sound effects will be. I had no knowledge of any of this stuff. None of
us knew even how to synchronize the recording of the music to the picture as we
were recording it. So what we did was, I would have a stopwatch – which was a
very familiar tool for me as an ex-animator – and I'd just say, 'OK, at fifty-three
seconds the music should do this, and at a minute and twenty it should sort of do
this.' I would sit at the piano – it ended up being mostly a piano score, with some
electronics – and I would just try to play it in such a way that it worked out with
the stopwatch. In many ways, I look back on it fondly because the music is more
like *music*, and less like film music. All I knew at that time was how to do song-
oriented music, really, so the pieces are more like songs compared to the music
that I do now, which is finely crafted – contrived – to fit the dialogue and the
moments of the film. We just tried to see where it would go. Even after I finished
recording, Joel and Ethan kept changing where they put it, and played around
with it quite a lot for the year after. Post-production went on for at least a year
after we completed the score.

**Certain points in the score felt very industrial – almost like Glenn Branca's
stuff. Were you using samples for some of it?**
There were samples of a lot of industrial sounds. Sometimes there are tape
sounds. I had some recordings, those Allan Lomax field recordings from Parch-
man Farm prison, which were played backwards very low under one piece so that
you hear voices, but they're totally indecipherable. A lot of things like that.

Were you surprised at how well the film did?

As far as I know, we were all surprised it got distributed at all. We were certainly surprised by its reception.

Did it directly lead to other jobs for you?
Well, it caused Tony Perkins to call me about *Psycho III*, which he was directing. I wouldn't say that I thought of composing as a career yet, but it did result in my starting to get calls.

There are a number of directors you've worked with repeatedly – the Coens, Michael Almereyda, James Foley, Michael Caton-Jones – do you find that communication gets easier with every film?
It is generally easier, because the vocabulary of music is obscure, so someone I've worked with before, we've established our own vocabulary, which usually clarifies things. For instance, during *Raising Arizona*, we had this sound that was the result of blowing down the end of a vacuum-cleaner pipe. And of course, it's time-consuming to say, 'Why don't we try that sound that happens when you blow down the end of a vacuum-cleaner pipe,' so we just called it the 'shofar'. And whenever we needed that sound, we'd get out the 'shofar'.

Generally speaking, how do you approach scoring a film? Do you read the script first, or see a rough cut?
I usually read the script, but that's just a way of deciding whether or not to do the film at all. I wait until there's a rough cut before I start writing music.

Is that something you see on tape?
It varies. Sometimes I'll see it projected, and sometimes I'll see it on tape. But it has to be on tape before I start working on it because I need to be able to try different things in my studio against the film, and I use videotape to do that. There are still people around who use a Movieola – I think John Barry does – but I'm a video man.

How often do you first see the rough cut in the presence of the film-maker?
Well, usually I prefer to see it by myself, because if the first time I'm seeing the film the director or producer is there, then I'm obligated to make some intelligent comments about it as soon as the film stops and the lights come up. That can be a considerable obligation, because often at that point in the process no one outside of the director, producer and editor has ever seen it. They look at me with great expectation, and for that reason alone, it's certainly more relaxing to just watch it by myself.

How long do you normally have to put a score together?
It varies. It's usually something between three and six weeks.

Is that ever not enough time?
Well, that's a difficult question to answer. You know, often one would want more time, but it always *has* to be enough time – it's not as though a film can open with only half of the score done.

Do you compose on piano, or do you use a synthesizer?

I usually begin at the piano, which lends itself to casual melodic exploration. Besides, it takes a half-hour to turn on all the synths and computers, at which point I've either forgotten what it was I wanted to do or I feel obligated now to spend the next several hours working. So I usually begin at the piano and then move to the synthesizers when I've got some basic themes.

How far will you go before you start presenting something to a director or producer?

Well, usually I'll try to have at least one well-developed arrangement of a piece to present. In the old days, of course, people just played piano arrangements, and there are advantages to that, but these days, I think, we all expect to hear synthesized sketches because they give a bit more of a storyboard impression of what the final recording will sound like.

Do you ever present more than one option at this stage?

Usually no, but sometimes I do. If they don't like the first option I play them, it's sometimes good to have others in your pocket. But I like to try to control the process more. So either I present them with one option that I think is really good, or present them with one that's good and another that's so terrible they won't use it. But that's dangerous, because, of course, they might love that second one . . .

Are music cues decided by both you and the director normally?

There's a process called the spotting session, where we go through and make those decisions as to where music should sit. Everyone has a voice in that – sometimes I'll suggest music should be in a place where they hadn't expected it; sometimes they'll want it someplace where I don't think it's a good idea. It's a conversation, and I try not to have preconceptions about it.

At this point in your career, you've done everything from modestly budgeted independent films to big studio projects like *The General's Daughter*. Can you characterize the difference?

The big-budget films tend to involve more people – there's a whole layer of corporate hierarchy that doesn't exist on independent films. I try to ignore those people, but just ignoring them takes a little bit more energy, of course. And the obligation to sell enough tickets to make back the cost of a larger-budget film means that you're also obligated to take the audience into account more often. Whereas with the independent films, we rarely think that much about the audience. Well, I'll refine that: *I* rarely think that much about the audience. I'm sure there's someone there thinking about it.

With the studio films, do you find you have to answer as much to producers or studio executives as to the director?

I kind of avoid that situation by setting a rule: If producers or executives have anything to say to me, they say it to the director, and then the director says it to me. That way I'm only really answering to one person. But there are generally more people who want to be involved in the process. You find a lot of executives want to say at least one thing to you, because if the film's a success then they can go around telling everyone, 'Oh, I gave Carter a few pointers on this.' And of course, if the film's a failure, they'll go around saying, 'He didn't do anything I asked him to do.' But I really try to avoid those conversations as much as possible.

How often do you see a rough cut of a film and say to yourself, 'I've got to do this.'
Well, happily, it happens at least once a year. I see something that's unusual, and feels like the right thing for me. That's one reason why I work as much as I do – recently, people have been showing me interesting films that I really want to work on.

Did *Being John Malkovich* create that kind of response?
It did. I first read the script, and based on that, was pretty sure it was the right thing for me. I think I asked to see some cut of the film, because I didn't know Spike Jonze. He had sent me a reel of some of his music videos, but still, some people who've been very successful in short formats have difficulty making a feature-length film. And he was nice enough to send me a very rough cut. I know, for him and for all directors, it must be very nerve-racking to have someone you don't know well see a work-in-progress like that. So I appreciated that he was that trusting.

Our conversations were mostly phone-based for the first couple of months. I was still working on *The General's Daughter*. Our early conversations were about the general approach he was taking to the film, which I thought was very interesting and provocative: he didn't accentuate the fantastical elements, but treated them more naturalistically – he really downplayed the fantasy. And the one-liners. The original script was much more jokey; there were a lot more scenes that seemed like they were set-ups with a punchline at the end – a little more like television. But they got rid of a lot of that in the process of making the film.

I finally met Spike on the set – they were shooting on the '7½' floor of a building in downtown LA – and I took an instant liking to him. He was very honest about what he didn't know, which is a really nice thing for a first-time director. We agreed that the music should not be fantastical, or over-the-top, but rather just be about the emotions of the characters, and that the whole film would be much more uncomfortable for an audience if all the characters were real and had real feelings – you know, if you really believed John Malkovich was a real person who just happened to have a lot of other people living inside of him. That's much more disturbing than just having some sort of metaphorical conceit. In a certain way, it's a little bit like what I did with *Fargo* – even when comical things are going on, buffoonery, the music always has a straight face; it doesn't realize there's anything funny that's going on. The music believes we're in a true-crime drama, and takes it completely seriously.

Even though Spike was behind that idea at first, the first time that he heard real instruments playing the score, he was really taken aback at how much feeling that injects into a scene. This is a common experience I've had with directors – the first time they hear the score, they think, 'This is just too much feeling. I hadn't expected this much feeling in my movie.' Joel and Ethan are like that, too. The temperature of their films tends to be cool – warmth doesn't really enter into the design, usually – so it's very common for them to react strongly to the orchestration the first time they hear it. That was Spike's reaction, too, but he eventually got into it.

Probably more so than with any other contribution to a film, the music really changes it in a way that cannot be anticipated. It's possible for us to imagine through drawings and language what a set might look like, and through rehearsals to imagine what an actor's performance might be like, but I'm always seeing a look of surprise – whether pleasant or not – on directors' faces when they first hear the music. There's a certain element of ill-ease, because whatever their vision has been up until then, they've had control – hopefully with their actors, but certainly in the editing room. They've manipulated over months the plastic of the film into the form they want, and now someone comes along and suddenly changes it again with music in a way that they really can't undo without hiring another composer.

Unless they're musicians, I guess it's a language they have no access to, right?
Exactly. They *can* say, 'Shouldn't that be an E-minor chord there?', but that won't solve the problem. I've met with Michael Mann a couple of times – I've never actually worked with him – and he really will look at a scene and say, 'What do you think – D-minor?' It could be that he's joking, but I've got a pretty dry sense of humor myself, and I don't think he is; he likes to get into the details. I think his films are often extraordinary – I really loved *The Insider,* and would have liked to work on the film – but I'm not sure what it would be like to work with someone who wants so much control.

By and large, directors are given the music, and the poor folks then pretty much have to accept what it is – or throw it out entirely. It's pretty hard to change it.

In James Foley's film *Fear*, there's a transitional moment where Mark Wahlberg's character sneaks into Reese Witherspoon's family's house late at night, culminating in a sex scene between the two of them. I thought your scoring for that segment was perfect, because it started out completely ominous and gradually built into something vaguely erotic, although still with ominous undertones . . .
Well, I'm glad you got that, because that was the point of that piece of music. I love writing things like that; I love it when the music has to do more than one thing at a time. That also describes the kind of film I try to work on; films that are attempting to do more than one thing. I mean, if you've got a scene in which the only point of it is that people are sad, or things are blowing up, or people are in love, it's not really that interesting to me. I'm amazed that anyone else would find

them interesting. It's the contradiction and the complexity of the emotions we all experience that I think makes life interesting, and I love that level of tension. I think it annoys some of the people in my life that I like to maintain that tension, so that no moment is completely romantic, or completely happy, but we can always remind ourselves that there are other things going on.

It seems that most films are over-scored – I'm so often aware of music trying to amp up certain emotional moments in a heavy-handed way, or to mask certain deficiencies . . .

I think there's a misunderstanding that the function of film music is simply to echo, or amplify, what you're seeing on the screen, so that your experience of that one thing can be as strong and unmistakable as possible, whether that thing is a car crash or two people kissing. And I do look at it differently – I think the function of music is to show you something you don't see onscreen. So, yeah, a large number of scores done for feature films are coming from a different place than I am. I don't want to say they're better or worse.

Also, there are whole styles of film-making which I shy away from that tend to be very loud and abrasive. I guess I've done a couple of films at this point which may qualify as 'action films' – maybe *Three Kings* qualifies – but that's not primarily what people think of me for. Perhaps because even when I do action films, like *The Corrupter*, the score still doesn't come out as just a lot of, you know, sampled drums and what-have-you, pushing the pace along.

To be fair, directors often ask me to do what you described. They see some deficiency – some chemistry is not there between the romantic interests in the film, and they want it pushed. So sometimes I end up writing something that I'm uncomfortable with, because it's pushing too hard. But I want the director to be happy.

You described your music a while ago as 'having a fundamental simplicity to it'. Could you articulate that a little more?

My taste in music – leaving *my* music aside – has generally been towards music that is simpler. What I mean by that is, I have much more admiration for music that accomplishes a lot with simple means than music that accomplishes a lot with considerable means. I've been unpacking things in my new home, looking at my records from when I was in high school, and I've been struck at how some aspects of my taste haven't changed. I love the old records of John Lee Hooker just playing alone, for instance – it's so simple; you can't analytically say what it is about that music that is so striking, but somehow it's very moving, with an utter simplicity of materials. And at the same time I was listening to that, other people were listening to Yes and Queen, which always seemed to me to be taking the backward approach – attempting to ennoble a folk genre by layering on these unnecessary frivolities.

Like a lot of people, I became much more interested in the state of classical music – 'concert music' – when I started to hear what people like Arvo Pärt were doing from the early eighties on, and when those Eastern European composers started moving away from serial music – what academic music had become, especially in this country in the fifties. When other people like Steve Reich or Philip Glass started looking at other traditions in music.

Of course, also, it could just be that my musical tool-set is so simple as an untrained composer. That may have something to do with it as well.

I guess this isn't that uncommon in film music in general, but your scores always introduce a very simple, recognizable musical theme, which is then revisited in different ways throughout the film —
That's very common in film music, and it's usually traced back to Wagner's use of motifs in his operas. He would designate them in a very meticulous fashion not only to characters, but also to situations and subject matter, and then would mix and match them over the course of the piece. So that when someone appears on stage, you might hear their motif, and you would be reminded of what that person's role in the opera might be.

One of the interesting questions that arises when approaching a score is 'What might your motifs be attached to?' Some people have this simplistic view that you attach them to characters all the time, so that whenever you see a particular character, you hear this type of music. While Wagner might have done that, I think if you belabour that point it really does become a comedy, whether you intended it or not. You'll often see it in films from the thirties and forties – the supposed 'golden age' of film scoring – where motifs are used in this assiduous fashion, which I think is ridiculous. I think there's a good portion of the golden age that needs to be criticized.

You employ that in a somewhat ironic way in *Hudsucker Proxy*.
Oh, yeah, we do. And I think it works there because you're talking about a character who takes himself too seriously, so it's all right for the music to make fun of that. But that's a very common tool for film composers. Again, the question is, what might my themes attach to? Will it be something about character? Will it be a story point or a mood? It really can be anything – the semantics of music are wide open.

In some of my first films I really didn't give themes much thought. With *Blood Simple*, for instance: there were a couple of themes in that film whose meaning I really hadn't thought about that much. Same with *Raising Arizona*; it was pretty clear that this theme would work here, and that one there, but we really didn't think about their *meaning*, or how all the associations a theme accrues during a film might pay off later on. Now I think about those things quite a lot, which I guess makes me a professional film composer. But sometimes you can think too much about them.

Your earlier scores weren't orchestrated. When you began doing that, did you find you had to pare anything down musically to mitigate the 'bigness' of the sound?

No, not really. I don't think the size of the orchestra has any relation to this question of simplicity. It usually has to do with the film itself, and the characters. In *Being John Malkovich*, hopefully there's a certain poignancy from the sheer simplicity of the melody. It's not a 'childlike' melody, but there is an impression of simplicity that colours John Cusack's character as innocent, even though he's doing awful things. The music tells us something about why he's doing these awful things – he's not doing them because he's 'evil', he's doing them because he's hopelessly unaware and, emotionally, a child.

But then in other scores, like *The Corruptor*, you actually need complexity. Some of the themes there are more complex and more veiled, because one of the points of that movie is that no one can really tell what's going on. So there has to be something about the music that's a little obfuscating. But I don't think it's a function of orchestration, it's a function of the film.

You use a lot of unusual instruments in your scores. For example, in *The Band Played On*, during the Robert Gallo press conference, there's something like a prepared piano that creeps into the music —
I think there actually is prepared piano in that one. There are pizzicato strings, percussion, and the prepared piano.

Its oddness really adds a sense of menace to the scene. Do you think certain instruments carry particular kinds of emotional weight, or is it all about context?
I think it's context. I don't think instruments, or their timbre, have particular meaning. But there is a harmonic structure that sounds above a note when an instrument plays it, and sometimes those harmonics – there's a mathematical relationship expressed there – mean something emotional. For instance, those prepared-piano sounds create an 'enharmonic' structure. The nature of enharmonic sounds, like large bells, or prepared piano on the low strings, is that they're a little 'off' – they don't fit easily into our ears' understanding of how sounds should sound. So, yes, you could say that those types of instruments do engender a real emotional response that comes just from the mathematics of their overtone structure.

But generally speaking, it's entirely about context. You take an instrument that would normally be disturbing, and use it in such a way that it's insinuating instead, or vice versa.

Do you do a lot of research?
I read a fair amount, so I've learned music theory by reading books on the subject, and looking at scores. Research is one of my favourite parts of the job. Prior to working on *Rob Roy*, for instance, I listened to a lot of Scottish music. Or on *Fargo*, I thought it would be interesting to listen to a lot of Scandinavian music. *Miller's Crossing* was my first orchestral score, and Joel and Ethan knew that I knew nothing about orchestral music so they gave me three months to do it, and I really enjoyed pouring through books about orchestration. Although I didn't orchestrate that – my friend and mentor Sonny Kompanek did – I learned about what

you could do with an oboe, or a cello, and looked at lots of scores. The thing about research is that you're smarter at the end of the job than you were at the beginning. I get this joy from accumulating data, even if I don't know what it means.

My discussion of overtones partly comes from the fact that I sang with a group called the Harmonic Choir for a while, and the particular technique of singing we used was manipulating the overtone series – similar to the type of singing you hear in Mongolian folk music, or Tibetan chants. So just to perform that, or even to speak the language of that music, you had to develop some knowledge of how harmonic series work. And in fact, math is one of the things I studied in college, and it became one of my ways of getting into music. I tend to believe that the universe is mathematical – it's my way of understanding things – so to the extent that music is mathematical, it helps me to understand that, too. Interesting thing about music, of course, it that it's also emotional, so it's a fascinating crossroads between number and feeling.

There's this unfortunate prejudice that numbers are somehow cold and formal and analytical, and feelings are somehow amorphous and undefinable, and therefore the two cannot meet. But of course, music is this wonderful, and very concrete, example of how wrong that view is. Music is extremely emotional, and utterly defined by numbers. I just love that. It's one of those tensions that make life worth living.

Do you feel manipulative when you're writing?

I always feel manipulative. That's why it took me so long to get my wife to marry me – she was sure that I was doing something musically that was manipulating her. It depends on your definition of 'manipulation', but certainly what everyone does in film is manipulative – it's a terrible art because you take people and put them in a dark room, sometimes in the middle of a row so they can't even get away, and turn off all the lights and basically insist that they spend a couple of hours only hearing and seeing what you put in front of them. They're prisoners. And all we're doing the entire time is manipulating their perceptions, and through their perceptions, their experience. But of course, one 'dark side' of this manipulation is when you discount everything that a person brings to the theatre with them – when you just assume everybody is the same. 'Oh, we'll get them to cry by playing solo violin here.' 'We'll scare them by having a loud crashing cymbal here.' It's not even evil; it's just sad, because it underestimates the audience so much. By the time most people go to films, they've already been alive for a decade or two; they know life is complex, so I think it's fair to give them credit for that. Even though film is escapist, I don't think most people go to films to have their understanding of the world contradicted – 'No, it's all fine! Everybody's happy, and everyone will find love', or 'There are good people and bad people'. I really don't believe people go to film for that. Obviously, if you convince yourself that that's true, your job as an executive is much easier – you just find material that fills those preconceptions. But I don't think that's the escape people look for.

Do you think certain films would be better off without a score?
Definitely.

Have you ever declined a job for that reason?
Oh, yeah, sure. I can't remember any specific examples, but I think that's often true. It's really too bad that people don't think that way more often. It's partly that before someone even shoots a film, they've put a line item in the budget for music. Therefore, there is music. When I did the score for *Psycho III*, there was a line item in there for 'orchestra', and I didn't want orchestra – I just wanted to do it on synclavier with some percussion and a boys' choir.

There are a large number of films that work well without scores, and it's often really too bad that they use them. I'm looking at a film right now that Julian Schnabel just shot, called *Before Night Falls*, and he hasn't put temp music into a lot of it yet. That really puts you on the spot as an audience member – you just have no idea how to take what's going on. Also, the film is about a poet, and his words just carry so much more weight, again, because there's nothing there leading you one way or the other emotionally. This poet's particular form of writing has a fair amount of irony in it, so meanings change word by word. Each new word comes and the meanings of all the other words you heard change. So the fact that there's no music keeps the meaning up in the air – who knows where it's going to fall? I think a lot of that film will be best without music.

You've done several documentaries; do you find there's a certain ethical responsibility in scoring 'real-life' material? I've seen certain films where I really felt like the music was working way too hard to colour my views of the situation being documented.
That often happens. If you watch documentaries on television, it's just terrible how much music is used. I guess I can understand it in the so-called 'documentary industry' – the Discovery Channel, or whatever – because they don't want their audiences to be uncomfortable; they don't want you to even think that much. The goal is to make often difficult material palatable. By and large, music in documentaries is a mistake.

In your score for *The Celluloid Closet*, I could only detect several minutes of composed music.
I'm afraid there's more. I confess. *Celluloid* was a documentary, but it is, in a way, a narrative film – it's got a definite point of view, and it's not attempting to stand back from the subject matter. And its point of view is not at the current time a mainstream point of view, so clearly what we were trying to do with the music was manipulate an audience who didn't already believe that, yes, gay culture needs to be represented in the mainstream. It's represented as a heroic journey. I actually wrote the score as a romance – not between any particular people, but I just thought it was the nicest way to approach the subject.

Are there certain scores by other film composers you'd consider to be particularly successful?

Well, there are a lot. When I first got the job on *Blood Simple*, I thought, 'I'd better listen to some film scores.' Since I never really had. I got out the *TV Guide* and *The Birds* was on television, so I set my VCR and recorded it. But I watched it as I was taping, and as each dramatic scene would come to an end, I'd think, 'Damn! I didn't listen to the music!' Then, when the film was over, I rewound the videotape and realized that there was no score. There were some recordings of bird sounds, and some electronically created bird sounds, and that's it.

That was such a perfect exposure to film music. I hope everyone can have that kind of experience. So many of the Hitchcock scores are wonderful: I think *Psycho* is fabulous, but so are *Vertigo*, *North By Northwest* – they're all wonderful. And I love Morricone's spaghetti westerns; I love Nino Rota's Fellini films. Among my contemporaries, I really like Thomas Newman's work a lot. He did a film called *Flesh and Bone*, which not many people have seen, but it's a wonderful score – a prime example of simplicity.

I noticed in *Fear*, for instance, that your score seemed to be mixed down in certain parts —

[*Burwell laughs.*]

A knowing laugh. Do you have any rights as a composer where that kind of stuff is concerned?

No, you don't have any rights like that. They can do whatever they want with placement of the pieces of music; they can edit them however they want, do whatever they want with the levels. That's the way it is. A film mix is a battlefield, generally – dialogue people fight with the sound-effects people, who fight with the music people. In the end, nobody's completely happy, and if you've been to those mixes, you can sometimes anticipate what's going to happen and try to make sure that the music is not too badly bruised. But it's a battle.

Are you interested in doing traditional composing?

Yes, I am. One of the problems that I have with composing for composing's sake is that I really need fairly stern deadlines to get me to work, so I'm probably going to need to go and get a commission of some sort with a deadline attached to it before I actually do it. I'm mean, I'm composing all the time, whether I'm working on a film or not – I'm always at the piano, always writing. But sitting at the piano and writing is not the same thing as a completed piece of concert music, and the distance between those two I find hard to travel. But even if I wanted to, I'd need to find somebody who was going to stand over me with a buggy whip.

Do you have any inclination to explore other areas of film-making?

Well, sometimes I miss the experience of making short films, which I did in and after college. There's a pleasure in the 'auteur' aspect that you certainly don't get as a film composer. With film composing, there's no question that what you're in is, at best, a collaboration. But let's face it, my interest in film-making is not that compelling, or I'd be doing it. Also, I like the solitude of composing – particularly the solitude of composing in New York, where it's not so easy for people to drop in on me, and not so easy for them to ask me to lunch.

Are there other ways in which living here affects your work?
Well, I guess the advantage of it and disadvantage of it are pretty much the same. Being here keeps me out of the day-to-day workings of Hollywood, which is an advantage because it means I don't have to pay that much attention to the industry. When I have lunch with someone, it's not necessarily the subject we're going to discuss – you know, I'm not usually aware of what the box-office figures are for films, or that sort of thing. The disadvantage is, I can't easily go and have lunch with someone in the industry if I should want to. And they can't either, so that gets in the way of my getting work sometimes. But that's about it. I don't find that it's a problem in terms of process, because I can work here or, when my arm is twisted, in Los Angeles. I think it's more that there are moments when you want to have a face-to-face meeting with a director, and that's hard to do if they're there and I'm here.

Thérèse DePrez

Thérèse DePrez was the production designer on *Swoon, Postcards from America, Living in Oblivion, Stonewall, The Doom Generation, I Shot Andy Warhol, Box of Moonlight, Going All the Way, Happiness, Arlington Road, Summer of Sam, High Fidelity* and the forthcoming *Hedwig and the Angry Inch,* among others. In 1997, she won a Special Jury Award for Production Design at the Sundance Film Festival.

Tod Lippy: Where did you go to school?
Thérèse DePrez: I went to Parson's School of Design. That's why I came to New York.

Did you know what you wanted to study?
Clueless. I actually did an accelerated freshman year – a half a year for the year programme, which was very competitive. They review your portfolio at the end of the six months. Every teacher suggested a different area to go into – illustration, fashion design, graphic design, sculpture, fine arts, etc. I didn't know what to do, so I finally decided on graphic design – that's what my father did; I felt comfortable with that. I grew up with typography and design books all around.

How did you become involved with production design?
My brother, who's a year older than I am, was studying film at NYU at the same time, and on weekends, or whenever I had time, I would go work on his films. I did mostly grip and electrics work, but there would always seem to be a position missing on those films – 'Someone needs to hand-paint a sign over there.' 'Someone needs to do the furniture.' So I started doing that, having no idea that was actually going to lead to anything, or even that it was an actual position. And that was really the beginning, doing his student films, which I very much enjoyed.

And then a friend put me in touch with two of his friends who were making a very low-budget movie and needed an art PA – a gruelling, horrible job. Aren't they all? [*Laughs.*] I think we had a three-person art department, and I remember the production designer was crying all the time, but I was happy to do anything. And one of the producers of that was doing a movie right afterward called *The Refrigerator,* and he asked me to design it out of the blue. I was twenty-three, had never designed anything – I didn't even own a camera yet; didn't know how to draft. So I just dove right into that.

***The Refrigerator* was a horror film, right?**
It's a low-budget black-comedy horror film that takes place on the Lower East Side – Avenue D. A young couple from the Midwest moves into an apartment and their refrigerator turns out to be the gateway to Hell. [*Laughs.*] It starred a great group of actors from the Cucaracha Theater who I became very close to; I did theatre work for them because of this film.

So you were doing theatre stuff after this or at the same time?
In between, back and forth, but not any more. Anyway, my brother happened to

do the special effects on the movie. The refrigerator ate people.

Did you build it?
We had two different refrigerators that were completely rigged. The movie cost maybe $300,000 or $400,000. My budget was a few thousand dollars, and I was making $200 a week. 'OK, Thérèse – the gateway to Hell, how do you want to do this?' We did it with garbage bags and seaweed from Chinatown. [*Laughs.*] Up all night with garbage bags and seaweed and lots of fake blood. Also, there are scenes where, in the character's nightmares, people appear in the refrigerator, so I had to build this entire refrigerator set where I hand-painted a huge Aunt Jemima box, a Rolling Rock can of beer, a box of Arm & Hammer, and a milk carton. I kept the four-foot Rolling Rock in my apartment for a long time, and then one day I carried it out and just left it on Houston Street – quite a sight. It was gone in an hour.

What did you do next?
I met Brian Savegar, the art director who did *A Room with a View* and *Maurice*; he knew a graphic designer I was working for. When he came into town, I showed him my little portfolio, which was basically *The Refrigerator*, some MTV work and *The Ben Stiller Show*. He was about to do a low-budget horror film in Wisconsin with the producers who did *Hellraiser* and *Heathers*. They had bought an old boy-scout camp and built a 'quasi-studio', and were just going to pump movies out of there. He hired me as a set decorator. I went out there to do the first one, and Savegar quit – 'This is too low-budget, this is too crazy!' So the art director was bumped up to production designer, and I was bumped up to art director, clueless – again – about what I was doing. I worked so hard – huge elaborate sets, some of the biggest sets I've done, actually – and ended up staying there for almost a year. I did three movies in a row.

When was this?
Early nineties. It's actually not even on my resumé any more. But they're on video.

What were the movies?
One was called *Mindwarp*. And then there was *Children of the Night*, and *Severed Ties*. They all had crazy stars, like Oliver Reed, Karen Black, Elke Sommer, Garrett Morris.

What a great education.
I learned everything that year – construction, budgets, power tools, the hierarchy of the set, how to run your own crew . . .

How big a crew did you have there?
It was fairly large. And ironically, I just worked with the construction coordinator again last year when I was doing *High Fidelity*. Small world.

And then you came back to New York. How did you get involved in *Swoon*?

I remember being in Wisconsin on one of these horror films and seeing the *Swoon* script just floating around – somebody there, I think Jim Denault, was called to be the gaffer – and I remember how well-designed the cover was. Tom Kalin is so brilliant that way. I started reading it and I was very interested. So I called in, and they already had a designer, Neil Spisak – a huge production designer – and I told them I would be glad to just come in and work for free or whatever, and I showed up. They were maybe three weeks out from shooting, and nothing was ready. Neil was used to working with so much money – his assistants were still going out and taking Polaroids of furniture in high-scale stores in Manhattan.

I actually came in being a little bossy-boots: 'Neil, you can't do it this way, this movie is *tiny*.' So he and I spent quite a deal of time together going to all the low-budget prop houses. I remember being in State Supply, which is this low-end prop house – I love them, they've been so great to me. They're in that little grouping of prop houses in the West Twenties. Going to State Supply is like going to somebody's attic. Anyway, when Neil and I got there, I thought he was just going to start to cry, looking at all of the trashed furniture. I remember him calling Christine Vachon on his phone and saying, 'I just can't do this job any more. You should just have Thérèse do it.'

It sounds like you've had one trial-by-fire after another.
I know; it was tricky. I've recently been reviewing portfolios of NYU students. Last year I saw the senior-thesis pieces and this year I saw the junior pieces. And to see what they're doing – beautiful drafting, beautiful rendering. But I wonder . . .

If they have the chops?
I'm one of the few people I know of who's come up a different way, with absolutely no background. I taught myself how to draft, and construction I've done ever since I was a kid. It's just a very different background than what I see the younger people coming up with. And I'm not sure they realize that when they get on a set, it's also going to be about administrative stuff, personality issues and getting dirty.

Was *Swoon* a healthy budget compared to what you were working with in Wisconsin?
No, far lower.

How much did you have to work with?
A few thousand dollars. At that point I luckily was sharing a small woodshop on Ludlow Street, which only had eight-foot ceilings. We had a few sets to build, and I couldn't even stand them up. I always had to keep them on their side. We barely got them down the staircase. I spent many all-nighters in that shop . . .

If I recall correctly, there were a lot of sets in that film.
A lot of locations. I remember one uptown apartment where we did three different sets. A taxidermist's office, a psychiatrist's office, and a house – in this tiny apartment. It was beg, borrow, steal. I called everyone I knew – 'Do you have a

piece of furniture?' 'Do you have a Bank of England chair?' And Tom Kalin, phenomenally supportive, helped me as much as he could. Called his friends, borrowed his furniture, and he always thanked everybody at the end of the day. I remember saying that at the Sundance awards ceremony – he's one of the few directors that every night went around to every PA, every electric, every grip, and thanked us. *Swoon* was a very rough job, too. Tight schedule, budget, we were all young, inexperienced. And the toughest part of it was that it was a period film.

Do you prefer working on period stuff?
I love the research, although I find shooting period films in New York more and more difficult. Which is why doing a movie like *Going All the Way* in Indianapolis – whether or not it was set there – was a smart idea. Architecturally, everything is still intact; you can still find old things. New York is completely different now. Every mailbox, every lamppost, every sign – everything has to be changed, and if you're doing a low-budget movie, you need to go to the Bronx or other boroughs now. Which is what we did with *Summer of Sam*. There are still great old things in those areas. But it's more and more difficult, and every time I see a change on the street, I'm like, 'Fuck, no!'

    Swoon was great in terms of the people that I met as well. Christine Vachon, Tom Kalin, Todd Haynes, Derrick Kardos, who's been my art co-ordinator on seven films I think he was the production-office co-ordinator at that point. And Ellen Kuras, who I've done many movies with.

What film did you work on next?
Dottie Gets Spanked, the Todd Haynes short. Also very low-budget.

How was it working with him?
A dream. There are two directors that I think I'd stay up all night and sketch for: Todd Haynes is one of them and Gregg Araki is the other. They so inspire me with their ideas, and their films are so incredibly visual – as are everyone else's that I've worked for, really. But there's something about their heads that inspire my head. And with *Dottie Gets Spanked*, we built some pretty elaborate sets – again, in my tiny little shop, with a bunch of interns. It was also black-and-white. Luckily I had done *Swoon*, but I was still getting used to how black-and-white transforms on film, the different greys. We had some wonderfully interesting props. I learned a lot from the DP, Maryse Alberti, as well; that was my first time with her.

What did she teach you?
Oh, things I was still naïve about. That wallpaper will moiré. Things moiré on film, or when it gets transferred to TV. I was unaware of that.

You mentioned the grey-scale issue – obviously when you're designing for a black-and-white film, you still use colour props, right?
Yes. And now I've learned what different colours do. Red, for instance – actually

this is something that Tom Kalin and I discovered on *Swoon*. He would have red lipstick on the women, but you actually need to use green lipstick, the opposite of red. Quirky things like that, that through experience you start to figure out. And at that point, you don't have time to watch dailies or reshoot anything, because you're far too low-budget. It was really trial by error.

When you first read a script, how do you determine whether or not it's going to be an interesting project for you to work on?
I try to base things on the writing of the story rather than the art direction. I used to do it vice versa, and that led me into a lot of these horror films – that's when I was a little younger and hungrier. Now I want a really good story. And the first time I read something like *Happiness* – what a crazy, bizarre script. And you would think the art direction/production design wouldn't be that exciting, but actually it was very challenging to make realistic suburban homes with a little twist. I read tons of scripts, and I can tell pretty quickly when it's something I want to do.

And once you've decided that you're going to do a project, what do you do next?
Unfortunately, they're sent to me so quickly – it's like you have to meet the director tomorrow. So I usually get one read-through, which I hate. I like to read a script two or three times. The first time I just read it as story, the second time with 'How will I design this?' in the back of my mind, and then the third time I try to involve both of those. And if I have the luxury of doing that, it's perfect, but normally I don't.

What do you do once you've taken the job? Literally start making lists of furniture, props, that sort of thing?
I actually have the script for *Hedwig and the Angry Inch* over there, which I've completely broken down. First I break it down by locations, then by what we're going to build and what we need to find. And eventually I'll do all the set decoration per location, studying the characters. Then a prop breakdown and a picture-car breakdown – all the graphic design, all the still photography we need to shoot, etc.

And you obviously have a figure to work with regarding how much money you're going to be able to spend.
I have such a great sense of budgeting now. I actually like doing budgets; I was a math/science geek in high school. And there's something about budgets – you have this figure, and you have a list of all the things you need to do; now make them match! And that's tough, especially on a low-budget movie.

You've done both low-budget films and bigger-budget films at this point. Does 'more money' necessarily mean more options?
With the bigger films, what's so difficult is the union issue. I love having union crews, because they are amazingly experienced, but you need to budget for that. They're on their eight-hour day, then they get time-and-a-half, then they get double-time, and that takes a chunk out of my budget. And I hate that my head

has to even go into that vortex. On a low-budget film, we have twenty-four hours a day – we all get into it, we all need to get dirty, we all get it done. It's very different, and I respect both worlds.

What's the largest budget you've every worked with?
I would say *Arlington Road*.

Same issues, union problems?
Yeah, but we were in Texas – that was a little different from working in New York. Spike Lee's budget for *Summer of Sam* was just a little lower than that, but it was tough: 'I need you guys to stay another half-hour to finish painting this wall', but then you have to call three or four people to approve that, and you can't reach them. And you keep wanting to go paint it yourself, and you're not allowed to. Sometimes when they all left I would just do it myself. You just want to get it done. But when it becomes about administrative issues and budget, and I can't get my design done, it gets very frustrating. But not as frustrating as having to go to a cover set . . .

What's a cover set?
If we were planning to shoot on a beautiful day like this, and it suddenly started pouring rain and we couldn't shoot outside, we would have to get inside somewhere so we didn't lose the day. So every day I'll have to have a set standing by, *just about* ready, which is a nightmare because you have to rent things like paint, furniture, props . . .

This is only on bigger-budget films?
It's on every film. Cover sets are a big nightmare for production designers, because you have to have all these things standing by. You spend months doing the research, picking out specific pieces of furniture, and then you can't get them up in time. 'Oh, *Law and Order* wants that prop – it might not be ready.' You get the call at 10 p.m. the night before: 'We need to go to cover, Thérèse.'

What percentage of the time do you actually need to do that?
Depends on the movie. *Arlington Road*, we went to cover quite a bit. We had tornado warnings, rain. Cover sets make me cry. [*Laughs.*] They're like a big, painful tumour.

How did you get involved with *I Shot Andy Warhol*? That must have been your third or fourth Christine Vachon film.
What used to disturb me about Christine, but now I completely respect, is that she always wants to give a director choices. And as much as I have worked so hard for her on so many movies, she'll present the director with three or four different designers. And most of them I know. [*Laughs.*]

That must be anxiety-producing.
It is, but it's healthy for me, too, at this point. I want to hustle for any job – I want

to shine, I want to have a good interview, I want to show them my best work. With *Warhol*, I knew Mary Harron was looking at several people – she had many different people in mind – and I fought for that job. I kept calling her, sending cards; we actually had two interviews – 'Can we have another interview, please?' I don't know how I ended up getting it – I'm not sure whether it was my enthusiasm, or perhaps Christine's not being sure whether these other designers could handle the budget. And I think a good producer should always keep that in mind. You can get a big Hollywood designer to do a little art film, but can they do it and stay in budget? I'm very proud of that movie.

Can you talk about that experience a little more?
It took forever for Tom Whelan, the location manager – who I worked with on *Living in Oblivion* and *Stonewall* – and I to find a location for The Factory, which was obviously the key part of the movie. We finally found a space that is across the street from the Dia Art Center in Chelsea, before Chelsea was 'Chelsea'. No heat, no bathroom, no water. We had to go to the bathroom at the Mobil station around the corner. I remember freezing, it was so cold. We did put in a little plastic sink. And we were pulling hundreds of silkscreens – replicas of the actual Warhol paintings – which we made completely from scratch, with our little plastic sink, running hoses up and down the stairs.

Then we foiled the entire place, as Billy Name had done originally. Our hands were completely black by the time we finished. Alzheimer's! That's why I can't remember anything. And again, tons of interns and assistants. Interns that wouldn't show up when we thought they would. Sometimes there would just be two of us, four of us, five of us, building twenty Brillo boxes, doing all the silkscreens, foiling, etc.

How did you pick the images to be silkscreened?
We researched where Warhol found his images, then had to get those approved by the Warhol Foundation. Then we made the actual screens. Painting all the backgrounds, stretching all the canvas, priming all the canvas, making all the frames. I have a photograph where you can see the entire floor of the space covered with Poppy pictures and the Brillo boxes. That was a huge set, but I had such a wonderfully dedicated crew. My set decorator, Diane Ledderman, was amazing. There's a great place in the city called Materials for the Arts, where artists donate furniture and other stuff which I've been able to use for a few different movies – I actually keep donating back to them. They had a lot of the things we used, and then we went to the depths of Jersey to thrift stores, or even into people's basements. 'We'll clear this all out for you – we'll take all your paintbrushes, your tools, everything.' And we completely filled the space.

I know you wanted every detail to be period-specific, but I'm sure in the second row on the top shelf you could cheat it a little bit, right?
You had your front row, then your filler. And you move things for camera. Now

it's so much harder to find those items. There was something about those particular years where I could still find the junk, the crap, the filler items. You go to the yard sale and say, 'I'll just take your whole garage for $20, just give me all this crap.' That's what I needed to fill the space up. The 8mm projectors, all the things Andy would have had, the old paint brushes. We also built quite a bit from scratch. For instance, he had that very peculiar red couch. Of course we couldn't find that anywhere, so we built it, from just looking at photographs. I remember myself, the decorator and a PA doing that, and we'd never upholstered anything in our lives. We got a hot-glue gun, a staple gun – we had the material, we knew the shape – and we just did it. But through the whole shoot I had to keep going over to it, staple-gunning it back together. [*Laughs.*] 'Ellen, don't get too close to that corner!'

How many films have you worked with Ellen Kuras on?
At least four or five.

Do the two of you have a sort of shorthand communication going on at this point?
It's wonderful to work with a cinematographer who you've worked with before, and to spend a lot of pre-production time with them. A lot of these films that I did with Ellen, I actually sat in on the storyboarding process – 'This is how much of the set we're seeing', 'This is the shot we want' – and that gives me a better idea of what I need to prioritize on. She's incredibly patient, as are a lot of the DPs I've worked with. Very patient, and very art-department-oriented. Ellen will often ask me to look through the lens, and will be willing to change things around if I have suggestions. Her work is beautiful.

I think my biggest complaint about being a production designer would be when I've worked with DPs who, when I'm not on set, have an 'anything-goes' kind of attitude. My on-set dresser – who, by the way, always has to be strong enough to stand up to a director and a DP – will say, 'This is how Thérèse wants it,' and they'll say, 'Get away, we don't care.' And often they're shooting nights and I'm working days, so it can get complicated. But Ellen is one of the most supportive, especially in terms of lighting, which I'm very, very concerned about. Obviously, that's what makes a film. I mean, there's always an issue of fixtures that we may or may not see – if we see them, that's my job, and if we don't, that becomes the lighting department's job. But I'm always anxious to make sure that what they get is OK. That happened a lot on *Summer of Sam*. Because it's a period film and Ellen loves to use fluorescents – she's constantly throwing things up here and there – and I wanted to make sure that if the lighting wasn't period, it was hidden.

Can you describe the typical production designer–director relationship?
It really depends on who you're working with. The personalities I've dealt with are so incredibly different; they really run the gamut. Spike, for instance, didn't spend that much time with me – I usually just sent him sketches in envelopes via

his assistant, and he'd send a little Post-It back that just said, 'OK' or 'Good' or 'Bad' or 'This is better'. We would have very short meetings. Then there's someone like Mark Pellington – or Todd Haynes, or Tom Kalin – but especially Mark, who was just *obsessed* with research and the look of the movie. We would stay up all night together, weekends together, going through books, watching movies. He would always come to see the set beforehand, always look at anything I did, spend enormous amounts of time with me. Actually, almost too much – he's the other extreme. But I prefer that – your life becomes this movie and these characters.

Can you describe the psychological process you employ as you create the environments a film's characters will inhabit? Is there some sort of 'channelling' involved?
Well, having done a decade's worth of films, I've spent a lot of time scouting locations. I've seen hundreds and hundreds of people's homes and workspaces, and I absorb all the different details they each have – the quirkiness of each place. With *Happiness*, for instance, Philip Seymour Hoffman's apartment was completely based on different locations that I had seen in the past. The baseball caps aligned on the wall I had seen in someone's apartment and was amazed by. I remember scouting an off-duty police officer's apartment, where his coffee table was literally the box his TV set came in with a towel over it and some obscure piece of glass he had gotten with a bunch of crap on top – it was the most exciting thing I had seen all day. Sketched it right away – 'I *have* to use this sometime.' That ended up in Philip's apartment, too. Scouting is so visually absorbing to me. It's exhausting, but so exciting. I'm such a voyeur. To go into people's homes and meet them, to poke around, to see these different realities.

Any other examples from that film?
Joy's bedroom is based on my bedroom and all my friend's bedrooms as teenagers. Jared Harris's apartment came from days of scouting interiors in Brighton Beach. I really filled my sketchbook on those trips.

On that movie, was everything shot on location or were some sets completely built from scratch?
That movie was almost all locations. Almost all of them had to be completely redressed, filled, painted, and decorated, though, and were purely based on all the locations I had been scouting for years – I keep really great journals of photographs and sketches based on those locations.

Do you find actors ever have input about sets or particular props?
All the time. The one example I can think of off the top of my head was Lili Taylor on *Warhol*. She came to me and said, 'Thérèse, could we change this around? I don't think Valerie would have had it like this.' And I totally appreciate that, because Lili went so deep into that character – she did so much research – I knew

I could trust her instincts. The only time it can be annoying is when an actor bypasses me and removes something or changes things around without discussing it with me first, just out of respect.

How many films have you done in New York City? *Happiness* was partly shot here, wasn't it?
New York and New Jersey. Which to me was far away. *Summer of Sam, Swoon, Stonewall, Warhol,* Eddie Burns' movie was in Rockaway Beach – kind of New York.

Was *The Doom Generation* shot in LA?
Yes.

Todd Haynes said once that he thought it was much harder to do a low-budget indie film in LA than in New York because there didn't seem to be that surplus of people willing to work for little or no money. Did you find that to be true?
I think that is true. Somehow, though, I managed to find them. [*Laughs.*] I happened to have a great art director, Michael Krantz, who's from New York but who had lived in LA, and luckily he knew a lot of people. There were a lot of sets in that movie. You know, he'd have a carpenter friend who'd come in for a day, and a painter friend who'd come in for a day. But it was yet another film where there were a lot of all-nighters. I was painting everything, and we were building everything together – we had probably a five-person crew. And we had no prop master, so I was on set every day doing props. I was the prop master, the on-set dresser, the production designer – but I love the way that film looks.

Again, it's the low-budget vs the union issue for me. I think there are so many eager people out there. You can call any art school, and if it's the right time, you have these kids just flocking to do anything. Interns are the only way these low-budget movies get made. I just started *Hedwig* and there are so many eager to work on it.

And on larger budget films you can't get them because they expect money?
They don't expect money. It's an insurance problem, which is sad. Studios will say you can't have interns, because if they get in an accident they can potentially sue you. So you have to at least pay them minimum wage, but then they're no longer really an intern, they're paid, and then there's the question of whether or not that can come out of my budget. I remember having a meeting with Spike during *Summer of Sam,* and I was complaining about this. He loves interns as much as I do, and it was like, 'Just hire whoever you want.'

Did you?
Oh, yeah. I couldn't have done that job without interns. We had so much work to do.

Are you generally on set most of the time?
I try to be on set most of the time, which a lot of directors aren't used to but certainly like. And again, it's because at the last minute they want to shoot that other

corner they weren't going to shoot originally, and it's what we will finally see on the screen, and I want to make sure it's what I want to see, too. But it becomes very difficult if they're shooting nights and I'm working days. And there are some directors who want a designer on set all the time. That's just often physically impossible, though.

Do you ever look at a film you've designed and have one of those 'Oops – I missed that one' moments?
Always. I scrutinize every single film. Actually, there's something in Spike's movie that drives me so crazy I can't look at it. There's a scene where John Leguizamo is in his apartment, and all the boys come in and they're fighting, they're wrestling, and he rips the phone off the wall. And there are two black dry-wall screws on this very light yellow wall. No one mounts their phone with dry-wall screws. That's such a 'film' thing to do. And after he tears it off, it's in the frame for a little while. My heart just stopped. That's one of those moments where if I had been on set, that would not look like that. Little things like that. In that film, we pulled off huge riot scenes with cars crashing through store windows, fires raging out of control – you name it. And still, those two damn screws . . .

But it's usually continuity problems. There's a bar scene, and the drinks jump around between cuts. That's the prop master. That can be frustrating. Or really bad scenic jobs. If you have an on-set scenic, you know, if something's too shiny, 'Can you make this more dull?' Or, 'This wall's too white, can you make it a different colour?' They usually have about two seconds – because everybody's watching them – and you can tell they had about two seconds. Even if they're really good, they just are not given the time. And usually, if I'm not there, hopefully a good DP or a good director will give them the time. Especially if it's in the background, and it's a key part of the shot.

You talked about your location scouting serving as a good research tool. What else do you draw on for inspiration? Paintings, photography, architecture?
All of the above. I constantly collect images. Not even for a particular film, just for composition and colour. When I start a job I have stacks of reference books the director, the DP and I will go through for specific shots, composition, colour – it's important to think about the characters regarding colour, and what that means for the characters.

By the way, research is so great to share with the whole crew. One of the wonderful things that Mark Pellington did on *Arlington Road* is he made a big 11"x17" book combining all of my research and his research for each scene, with different texts, different ideas of lighting, etc. And he gave one to the gaffer, one to the key grip, and one to the costume designer so we all had the same information going into a scene, or prepping for a different scene, or even scouting. I thought that was a great idea; that's something I would love to do in every movie from now on. I always have my research on my walls in my office, but to give something like that to a gaffer – 'This is the colour, this is the mood we're looking for' – would be great. It takes a lot of pre-production time to do that, but it's certainly worth it.

How closely do you work with the costume designer?
It depends on the film. Again, with *Happiness*, which had such an eclectic array of colours and locations, I really had to talk to Kathryn Nixon: 'OK, they're in Florida now, what do they wear here? These are the colours of the walls.' I tried to give them all colour sheets of every set. Actually, there's one scene where Lara Flynn Boyle sits on the couch in her apartment with Philip, and her shirt is dark and the couch is dark; she completely disappears into it – all you see is her hand. It's a beautiful shot; she sinks in there and disappears. It's a luxury to have time with any costume designer – in *Summer of Sam*, working with Ruth Carter was great – she is just so talented, and so experienced. And she had so much to deal with. But generally speaking, I constantly try to feed them all the research I've got: you know, here's the period research I'm getting, here's my wallpaper, the furniture, my paint colours, the curtains.

It's different on every job. *Hedwig*'s going to be a curious one. The costume designer is a friend of mine – we did *Going All the Way* together. She does Courtney Love's, Madonna's and Lenny Kravitz's wardrobe. And she did *People vs. Larry Flynt*, *Mod Squad* – she's incredibly talented. And like me, she's obsessed with *Hedwig*.

How's that coming?
Great. I just want it to get green-lit! They want to shoot in Toronto, but I honestly feel I would save more money doing it here. The millions of kids I could get . . . No one has seen *Hedwig* in Toronto.

Here, every disaffected art student would be putty in your hands . . .
Exactly. That's how I got started here. The talent pool in New York – the interns I had on *Happiness* and *Summer of Sam* and all the other movies were so great. And their dedication! For free, just for a screen credit. And now, of course, a lot of them are moving on up. I can't get that when I go into another city or when I do a bigger-budget movie and I don't have access to those people.

But of course there's a 'dark side' to that set-up, right? Some people would call that situation exploitative.
To me, it depends on what stage you're at in your life. I am thankful for what someone like Christine gave me when I was first starting out. I would not be here without that opportunity. Yes, I was abused, and I worked incredibly hard and had to use my own space for either no pay at all or for way too little. But I wouldn't be here without that. Where else do you get that opportunity? You have to make a conscious choice that there is going to be a period of time where you go through that. But you certainly get to a point where you don't want to do it any more.

I get résumés almost every day. I get phone calls out of the blue. 'I love your work, I'll do anything for you.' And I'll call them back and tell them on the next film I'll bring them in and they can help us paste up something. I think it's healthy, but I think the people who are on top need to be aware of the needs of these people. I mean, I really take care of my interns now. I try to support them mentally, buy them lunch, reassure them they're doing the right thing, inspire them. Which I didn't quite have when I started out. It was just nuts and bolts, get the job done. But then again, I was working with great directors who did give me that, and who were behind me.

What's the best experience you've ever had working on a film?
Which film did I get the most sleep on? [*Laughs.*]

It sounds like that would be the worst one . . .
[*Laughs.*] I'd say I was most satisfied with the first few movies I ever did – *The Refrigerator, Swoon.*

Why?
Because I was so completely challenged and my adrenaline was on full-time. And to accomplish something like that – something I had never done before – for basically no money, made me proud. It's just different from my experiences now, where I'll do something, and it'll look beautiful – I mean, of course I'm also proud of that, too. But when you first start out, you go in there and you dive right in with absolutely no clue. And to be able to pull that off – 'Somehow I dragged that piece of plywood off of Canal Street, built that set, and it worked!' Those are the experiences that convinced me to keep doing this.

Spike Lee

Spike Lee's films include *She's Gotta Have It*, *School Daze*, *Do the Right Thing*, *Mo' Better Blues*, *Jungle Fever*, *Malcolm X*, *Crooklyn*, *Clockers*, *Girl 6*, and *Summer of Sam*. Lee's NYU short, *Joe's Bed-Stuy Barbershop: We Cut Heads* (1982), won a student Academy Award, and his documentary, *4 Little Girls*, was nominated for an Oscar in 1997. Lee, founder of 40 Acres and A Mule Filmworks, has also directed numerous commercials, short films, and music videos, and has executive-produced a number of films, including Gina Prince's *Love & Basketball* (2000).

Tod Lippy: I know your family moved to Brooklyn from Atlanta when you were two years old. Did you enjoy growing up here?
Spike Lee: It was a great experience. For a person my age – who wasn't old enough for the Vietnam War, but old enough to know what was going on in the sixties – it was a great time to grow up here. Especially with sports – the Mets in '69, the Jets, the Knicks. New York City is the greatest city in the world, despite the fact that you get politicians – mayors – who try to fuck it up. Or the police.

Why did you choose to come back here to NYU after your four years at Morehouse College? Did you ever consider going to one of the film schools in LA?
I didn't have the grades for USC or UCLA. You had to get an astronomical score on the GRE, and I didn't get it. For NYU, all you had to do was submit a creative portfolio. To this day, I still feel that it's so small-minded to base everything on standardized testing. And it's been proven that that stuff is culturally biased.

But it obviously worked out for me. The way you choose a film school is by looking at the people who came out of there. If you want to make personal, more independent films, I think NYU is a good place. You want to make studio, formulaic bullshit . . . [*Laughs.*] I'll take that back – a lot of good people have graduated from those schools. But people who really want to make standardized Hollywood films, they know that USC and UCLA are the schools to go to, because they plug directly into the studio system. I'm not negating one or the other – it's a personal choice.

Who else was at NYU when you were there?
Ang Lee, Ernest Dickerson, Jim Jarmusch. I tell this story all the time: The biggest thing that happened at NYU while I was there was when *Stranger Than Paradise* came out. When that film hit, all of us really believed that we could make it, too. This was one of our classmates – NYU product. So I tried to follow everything Jim did – go to Cannes, do the film festival thing – with *She's Gotta Have It*.

What did you think of the school?
Well, NYU has its problems, but to tell you the truth, I never really expected the teachers there to teach me. That's not to say that I knew anything – I still don't know everything – but I really thought my education would come from making my films out in the street, and working on my classmates' films. I mean, they could teach you how to read a light meter, but as far as telling a story and that

type of stuff, I never really felt I was going to learn that from anybody. You become a film-maker by making a film, not by talking about it. You get insights from others, but you still have to go out there and shoot that stuff yourself.

Why did you stay in New York after you graduated?
I never ever wanted to live in Los Angeles. There have been models. Woody Allen was here, and Sidney Lumet, Scorsese. So it was not absurd to think that you could be a film-maker and still live in New York.

When did you start working at First Run Features?
I started working there while I was in school. NYU grad school is a three-year programme, and I started working at First Run part-time my second year. When I graduated, I worked there full-time. I cleaned films, ran errands, kept inventory. It was great, because I got to see all the films they were handling. Plus, before we moved, we were right above the Bleecker Street Cinema – that's where I met John Pierson, who was programming there.

So you were seeing a lot of films at the repertory theatres?
Yeah. I went to the Thalia, and to the St Mark's – where The Gap is now. That used to be a regular theatre with two-dollar movies.

How do you think the environment of the city has affected you creatively?
Well, I think that if you live here and you're open, you just come into contact with so many different cultures, languages and races – so many different people – and that's bound to affect your work. It's definitely affected mine.

You know, Woody Allen is one of the all-time great film-makers – and a fellow New York Knicks season-ticket holder – but up until he got with Soon-Yi, I would look at his movies, and I was like, 'Where are the Black people? Where are the Puerto Ricans?'

Where is anyone who doesn't live on the Upper West Side?
But even the Upper West Side! Go to Central Park – every little kid in a stroller is being pushed by a West Indian nanny! Anyway, that just used to perplex me. But he's definitely changed since he's been with her – his films are lot more colourful. [Laughs.] I mean, he's a great film-maker, but I just scratch my head and say, 'What Manhattan is this?' Man, Woody . . . Maybe I'm wrong, but it seems like she has influenced him in that regard. Just look at the films, before and after.

I read somewhere that you got your first camera back when you were in college ...
Yeah, it was a Super-8 camera, in the summer of 1977. I had just finished my sophomore year at Morehouse College, and came back to New York from Atlanta. I didn't have a job, and I'd bought this camera, so I just spent the whole summer running around New York shooting stuff. That's when I decided I wanted to be a film-maker.

Didn't you get some footage of the riots resulting from the '77 blackout?
Yeah. On 125th Street in Harlem, and Brooklyn.

And that was the subject of *Last Hustle in Brooklyn*, your first film?
That film combined that footage with people dancing – in the streets, at block parties, in parks. Shots of DJs plugging electricity into lampposts, stuff like that. That was really the first summer of disco.

It sounds like that film could almost be a study for *Summer of Sam*.
There's definitely a connection there. You know, some things just work their way back in.

Your diaries for several of your films have been published with the screenplays, and they provide a great record of the way you approach a subject. I've also noticed that you occasionally jot down ideas for other films. Do you find that you go back and plumb the diaries for ideas for new movies?
No. I've just been too busy. Basically, we've made a film a year since 1985.

You said at one point you were working at such a high volume because you wanted to 'keep the momentum going'. What did you mean by that?
I'm a film-maker. I like the work. I never ran away from hard work, and that's what film-making is. And I want to tell stories – that's what good directors do. But I'm not going to kill myself. [*Laughs.*]

Is there any difference between directing your own scripts and those you've worked on with other writers?
Even if I don't write something, I'm still very passionate about it. I don't feel like, you know, 'I wrote this, so I'm going at it one hundred and fifty per cent.' Or, 'Ehhh – I didn't write this one; I'm not going to give it everything this time.' Whether I write it, co-write it or have nothing to do with the writing, I'm still going to be passionate about it.

Right after *School Daze*, you said, 'Just because I present problems, people expect me to solve them. That's really unrealistic. It's a burden I won't assume.' That made me think of the two conflicting quotes – Malcolm X's endorsing violence when necessary, King's calling it immoral – you throw up on screen at the end of *Do The Right Thing*. Why is it important to you to leave a degree of ambiguity in your work?
Well, I would say that with ninety-five per cent of the films put out by studios, everything is tied up in a neat little bow. Maybe it's my duty to be that quirky five per cent where everything isn't done like that. Of course, that's going against the grain, and a lot of times audiences resent that. Maybe you're making them work too much, or think too much.

It all really depends on the story, too. I mean, I don't know how I could have ended *Do The Right Thing* any differently. How was I going to give it an ending that suggested a solution to racism and prejudice? I'm not interested in any of that *Driving Miss Daisy* bullshit.

You think it's important for audiences to have to synthesize the differing points of view you're presenting?
Well, as I said before, the majority of films don't do that, especially the films that come out in the summertime. And of course, I'm like everybody else – there are certain times where you want to go see a movie and not think, and that's fine, but I don't think that should be the total content of the films Hollywood puts out. And those films that make you think are getting rarer and rarer, and that much harder to get financed.

Along those lines, most of your films feature at least one scene with a series of compelling characters offering equally compelling – and usually conflicting – views on the subject at hand. Those segments always crackle with energy, because the viewer is constantly being asked to rethink the issue from all these different perspectives. I'm thinking, for example, of the scene with all of the women in *Jungle Fever*.
The 'war council' scene . . .

Your character in the film actually refers to it in those terms.
Yeah. The skeleton of that scene was written, but I knew that the only way it was going to work was if I just told the women, 'This is what the scene's about. Once the cameras start to roll, talk about your personal experiences with the Black men you've dealt with in your life.' And we just rolled. [*Laughs.*] That scene could have been a mini-series. We shot so much footage for that . . .

Didn't you do something similar for *She's Gotta Have It*? I recall reading that you polled a bunch of your female friends when you were writing the character of Nola Darling.
But this was different. This wasn't a survey or anything. We just rolled the cameras.

Another variation on that is the 'racial-slurs' sequence in *Do the Right Thing*.
That stuff carries a risk, though. If I have characters in my films who say terrible things or do terrible things or are just terrible people then there is always the chance, for whatever reason, that people will think those characters are, basically, me. I've been called homophobic because I have characters who say the word 'faggot'. Or if I have male characters in my films who treat women like pieces of meat, people assume those are my sympathies. But you know what? People really pick and choose which directors they do that kind of thing with. I've talked about this with Marty – not only did he direct a film like *Taxi Driver*, but he actually played a character in the movie who's saying all sorts of shit about 'niggers' and what a '.44 does to a pussy', etc. etc. Now, as far as I know, Martin Scorsese hasn't ever been linked to any of that himself – when critics watch his films, they never do that. But if I played a character in one of my films that said some anti-Semitic

shit? That would be the end of me. I'd be 'white-balled'. Because it's not Spike Lee playing a character, it's Spike Lee saying it from the depths of his heart, because Spike Lee is racist, he's prejudiced, anti-Semitic, and he hates white people. But I can't worry about that. You have to let your characters speak.

You talked about how there was no other way to do the ending of *Do The Right Thing* —
That film was set up at Paramount. And the reason why they didn't end up doing it was because they wanted some kind of reconciliation between Mookie and Sal at the end. And we didn't want to do it like that, and luckily, Universal Pictures was there to pick it up.

But generally speaking, it seems like the conclusions of many of your films are extremely open-ended. You know, the movie ends – often with a symbolic image, or gesture – but there is a minimum of narrative closure.
I've always thought that just because the movie ends, and the credits have started to roll, these characters are still alive – they still have life. What's happening to them now? Or what's going to happen? I'm not doing that because I'm planning for the sequel or whatever – I've never done that. But I don't know, I think it's interesting to leave everything open for thought sometimes.

So traditional closure doesn't interest you?
Oh, it interests me. But I don't think films always have to do that kind of thing. That's another one of the formulas – everything needs to be tied up. The movie's over, that's it – you know exactly where everybody is.

When you end with one of those more symbolic images – like Wesley Snipes embracing the young crack addict in *Jungle Fever* – is it something you've already latched on to before you start writing?
It really depends. Sometimes I do know, sometimes I don't. There's not a standard. With *Jungle Fever*, I just felt that – despite the fact that the interracial stuff got the all the attention – the most important story we were telling there was the chronicling of the destruction crack has had on generations of families. In the beginning of the film, you see Halle Berry's character telling another character she'll do him for five dollars, and at the end of the movie you see someone who must be twelve or thirteen, and now the price has dropped to two dollars. The reason why he screams there is because he realizes that in a couple of years it could be his own daughter, selling her body for a two-dollar piece of crack.

In your diaries, you spend a fair amount of time anticipating the reactions – often negative – of people to the different choices you're in the process of making. A lot of your sentences start with, 'If I do that, then they'll say . . .' or 'I have to be careful not to do this, because . . .' Do you find that you self-censor a lot in the writing stage?
Oh, I think every artist self-censors. I just don't know whether everybody writes

it down or not. It's like you've got a checklist of what to do and what not to do. That's part of being an artist; artists make choices, and when you make choices, you're picking one of many options. You know, those other four didn't make it for whatever reason. So, yeah, I do that all the time.

But I also get the sense that you're trying to gauge the kinds of reactions something will provoke in an audience...
Well, I'm not one of these film-makers who say they never think about the audience. You have to – I mean, I don't have the luxury of just saying, 'This is what we're going to do, fuck the audience.' So, yeah, I'm thinking about its effect. But a lot of times, my first question is, 'What will its effect be on *me*?'

It's a balancing act. And despite what people may feel about Steven Spielberg, his gift is that he knows *exactly* what people want. You can't say nothing about that.

A lot of your films tend to have the adjective 'controversial' attached to them. Do you think that's more to do with your choice of subject matter, or is it often just a function of people attaching that tag to whatever you happen to be working on?
Both. I've always said this, and it's true: When I sit down and decide what I'm going to do next, I'm not thinking, 'What controversial subject matter will I choose from this time?' The criterion is, 'What story do I want to tell now? What story do I want to spend the next year or year-and-a-half with?' Or longer – really, it's your lifetime, because that stuff sticks around, it stays with you.

Well, for example, what drove you to make *Mo' Better Blues*?
My father is a jazz musician, and I always wanted to do a jazz film. But I remember seeing *Bird* and *'Round Midnight*, and both of those films were – at least to me – so depressing. I mean, it was raining in every scene. These tragic Black musicians. I mean, come on – Sonny, Duke, Count Basie – none of these guys ever laughed before? They didn't have any joy in their lives? Never smiled? Never loved?

It's sort of the flipside of what you said about Sidney Poitier in *Lilies of the Field*...
When I said that about Sidney, it wasn't a knock on Sidney. It was about the character he was playing. Sidney had to do that kind of stuff because he felt he didn't have an alternative. Because of our history of being betrayed by the media, he had to choose roles like that. He had to be the Super-Negro. I mean, even when he makes a phone call at Spencer Tracy and Katharine Hepburn's house in *Guess Who's Coming to Dinner*, he leaves a dime by the phone. But because he did all of that stuff – because he was a trailblazer – people like me have been able to do other stuff, which is the antithesis of those squeaky-clean characters he played. But his character in *Lilies of the Field* was, I don't know – too pristine. I mean, the minute I get my flat fixed, I'm outta there. [*Laughs.*] I'm not hanging around until these nuns say I raped them, then my Black ass gets lynched.

When I saw Michael Clarke Duncan in *The Green Mile*, I knew he was getting nominated. I knew it. It was that same stereotypical thing you saw in *Driving Miss Daisy*. That's not to say the performance wasn't good, but I think it was the role, more than his acting, that grabbed the Academy. I knew they were gonna *love* that role.

Early on in your career, you talked about being pretty 'hands-off' with your actors . . .
Not 'hands off'. I was scared of actors. The biggest weakness of film school is that they really don't prepare you to work with actors. Technically – moving the camera, figuring out lenses, that kind of stuff – it was fine, but the one thing I was lacking when I came out of film school was the knowledge of how to work with actors. It wasn't until *Do The Right Thing* that I really felt comfortable talking to them. You have to know how to do that, because most actors are crazy. And that's not a generalization. I mean, I understand why they're unstable – it's an unstable business, and they put up with so much rejection. But most of them are nuts.

Can you talk about why you've begun making documentaries? Your first one, I believe, was *4 Little Girls* in 1996, and now you're working on *The Original Kings of Comedy*. What attracted you to the form?
I'm a film-maker. I've never considered film-making to be only narrative.

Weren't you at one point thinking about making a narrative feature about the Birmingham church bombing, the subject of *4 Little Girls*?
In film school.

Why did you decide to do a documentary instead?
Because I thought it was important to hear from the witnesses themselves. The family, friends and foes like George Wallace. The people who were there.

How do you think your work as a director of commercials fits into the rest of your career?
It's all film-making. All of it is about telling a story. A commercial, you've got thirty seconds to tell a story. A music video, four minutes. But they're all about telling stories.

But you obviously approach a Nike commercial differently than you would a film like *Do The Right Thing*, which must have greater personal significance for you . . .
Do The Right Thing took me two weeks to write the script, eight weeks of pre-production, eight weeks to shoot; a commercial usually takes one day to shoot. And I don't know if it's fair to compare a Nike commercial to *Do The Right Thing*. But any film-maker with any pride is going to do their best, whether it's on a commercial, music video, documentary, or feature film.

You once said, 'The most powerful nations are not the ones that have the nuclear bomb, they're the ones that control the media. That's where you control

people's minds.' What kind of responsibility do you feel you have to assume, particularly as you're working in all of these various forms?

Everybody has their own personal code of ethics or morals. Deep down in their heart – whether it's for the money or whatever – they know when they're doing wrong. That's something they really have to deal with themselves. Film is a very powerful medium, and it's just going to get more powerful. At the same time, I don't think *Taxi Driver* made John Hinckley shoot Reagan, or *Natural Born Killers* caused those kids who saw it to commit murder. I don't know where that case is standing now, but it's very important. If a decision on something like that ever goes against an artist, there are some deep ramifications, because no record company, no publishing house, no studio, no television network is going to want to touch anything that they think they may be sued over. And that's going to be the end of free expression as we know it.

Do you have final cut on your films?
Mm-hmm. Since *School Daze*. I'm not going to do a film where I don't have final cut.

My impression is that your control often extends into marketing, merchandising, even design of the posters . . .
Well, I don't have *control*. I have influence. I mean, unless you're Spielberg or Lucas, the studio's going to tell you how many theatres, and when it's going to open, and how much money is going to be spent.

You talked earlier about following the example of Jarmusch. Have you ever thought about owning your negatives, like he does?
I would love to own my negatives. But I haven't had the success Jim's had in markets outside of the US. That's how he gets his films financed. He finances them overseas, and then he just sells the domestic rights.

Your first student film at NYU, *The Answer*, is about a struggling Black filmmaker who is offered the chance to do a fifty-million-dollar remake of *Birth of a Nation*. In one scene, a guy in a Ku Klux Klan robe presents him with the contract – which he signs. It reminds me of the scene in *Girl 6*, when Theresa Randle reluctantly takes off her shirt in an audition for Tarantino, playing himself. This whole issue of compromise is one that obviously interests you as a film-maker . . .
It's something that every artist has had to grapple with. There's always that line they tell you: 'Just do this stuff – we know it's bullshit, but once you become a star you can do whatever you want to do.' But it rarely works out that way. Once they get you, *you're got.* [*Laughs.*] People get trapped. They have kids, they've got a mortgage, a house. I was very lucky – when I was starting out, it was just me, so I could miss a couple meals. And it just wasn't the money – I could be totally focused on the goal at hand: to be a film-maker. I had only myself to think about.

Do you feel you've had to make any serious compromises in your career?

Nothing that was harmful. I'd be lying if I said I never had to compromise in my life. It's not true – the only situation where that could happen would be if I had all the money to finance my movies.

When *Malcolm X* went over budget during post-production, you were able to circumvent the studio by raising your own money from prominent members of the Black community like Oprah Winfrey and Bill Cosby. How did you come up with that idea?
Well, in doing the film, I became a student of Malcolm X, and he always talked about Black people being self-reliant – we have great resources, and we should be using them. So when we hit this impasse with Warner Bros. and the bond company, I made a list of African-Americans who had money, and who could contribute it to tide us over. It's funny, too, because Warner Bros. had absolutely no idea of how we were going to continue to finance post-production – they had fired everybody on the editing staff. So after I raised this money, I thought it would be a great idea to have a press conference announcing it on Malcolm's birthday, up at the Schomburg Library in Harlem. And very soon after that press conference, we started getting funded by the studio again. Funny how that works. [*Laughs.*]

Do you conceptualize your opening credits? They're always so good.
I do, along with Balsmeyer & Everett – there are times when they've thought up the idea, and times when I have. I think that opening credits, besides being contractually necessary, should be creative – they're like an invitation to the audience to what's going to follow. They should be the appetizer. Try to cultivate their minds, prepare them for what's going to happen in the next couple of hours. The best designer in that regard was Saul Bass – he made them an art form.

You're a serious student of film, and I know you've talked before about influences on your work. I was wondering if there was anyone in particular who has had a major impact on your aesthetic?
Martin Scorsese. Billy Wilder. Kazan. Budd Schulberg. You can't do any better, I feel, than *On the Waterfront* or *A Face in the Crowd*. Or *What Makes Sammy Run*. *The Harder They Fall*. Budd's one of the greats. A good friend, too.

I know you like to pay homage to other films and directors in your work, but you're also a great mimic. I'm thinking specifically of the three segments in *Girl 6* which refer to *Carmen Jones*, The Jeffersons and the blaxploitation genre. They're so dead-on.
The idea for that really came from Suzan-Lori Parks, the screenwriter. We just felt it made sense that, you know, here's a woman who wants to be an actress, and those actors are her role models.

They're all playing different parts – different representations of Black womanhood – which is really relevant to the film's subject. Right. She can see herself in each of them. You know, of all my films, *Girl 6* is the one that people dislike the most.

I think it's a great film.

It's the one that's the most misunderstood. I guess the whole phone-sex thing threw people off. Everybody's like, 'What's up with you with that film? What the hell were you thinking about?'

I love the fact that Theresa Randle uses a monologue by Nola Darling for her audition. And like *She's Gotta Have it*, I think it really explores the dynamics of power in gender relations – the shiftiness of the whole thing.

And it explores the choices you have to make – how far you're willing to go – to achieve your goals. That character gets so hooked up, so tangled in the phone-sex world, by the end of the movie she's forgotten why she even took the job in the first place, which was to get enough money to move to LA to jumpstart her stagnant acting career.

And the music, too – all the stuff by The Artist Formerly Known as Prince . . .

Speaking of homages, wasn't that scene with the falling telephones near the end referencing *Sid & Nancy*?

Yeah. [*Laughs.*] That was a fantastic scene in that film, when that garbage started falling when Gary Oldman and Chloe Webb were kissing.

You made a note in one of your diaries about how you hate 'preachy' films –

Well, I'm sure some people would find that ironic, because I'm accused of being preachy sometimes. When did I say that?

It was around the time of *Do The Right Thing*. You also said, 'I can't have too many of these speeches. This is cinema, not theatre.'

Well, you're always going to walk the tightrope, and sometimes you slip off. I guess that's the thinking behind those statements.

You mentioned somewhere that you find New York actors less into the 'star thing'.

Well, that's not necessarily the case any more. All the actors I was talking about who've become big have probably moved to LA. [*Laughs.*]

Do you use a lot of theatre actors in your films?

Yeah. If there was no theatre here, there would be little reason to shoot films in New York. You've got the locale, but the talent pool is what New York is really about. It's the only place in the world with this kind of abundance of good actors.

Do you ever find walking around the city to be a problem?

Nah. Taxi drivers blow their horns, stuff like that – especially during the playoffs.

Do you think New Yorkers are generally pretty low-key about celebrity?

It depends on who the person is. Michael Jackson can't walk the streets of New York. Neither can Michael Jordan. People recognize their faces and go crazy, which doesn't happen with me. It really depends who you're talking about.

You live on the Upper East Side now. Didn't you get a lot of flack when you moved out of Brooklyn?
There really wasn't that much. I thought it was going to be more.

But you're living in a pretty conservative, somewhat segregated neighbourhood.
When Tonya and I decided that we had to move out of SoHo – because we needed more space – we realized the space we needed we just couldn't get there. Not in a residential building. And I didn't want to be in some kind of illegal real-estate situation, so we started looking at houses, and it just so happened that the best deal we found was on the Upper East Side. It wasn't by design, though, because we wanted to stay in SoHo.

I know you're working on a new documentary, *The Original Kings of Comedy*, but there's a new feature, too, right?
Bamboozled.

That was shot on digital?
Mini-DV. That's was a first for us. Ellen Kuras, the DP who shot *4 Little Girls* and *Summer of Sam*, hadn't used it yet, either, so it was a learning experience for all of us. And then we were able to utilize that knowledge for *The Original Kings of Comedy,* which was also shot in Mini-DV.

What was the budget for *Bamboozled*?
Ten million. Rest assured, ten million was not the original budget – we had to cut it down. It was a risky film, with a risky subject matter. We had a long list of 'nos' with that film. But Mike DeLuca, Bob Shaye and Michael Lynne at New Line stepped up.

Why is it considered risky?
It's a satire about television. But it addresses stereotypical images of African-Americans throughout the history of cinema and television.

I know you've been trying to make the Jackie Robinson biopic for some time. Do you know when that's going to happen?
I've just got to get the money. One day, I will.

Do you feel like you're at the top of your game right now?
Gotta keep getting better . . .

Tim Robbins

Director, writer and actor **Tim Robbins** has had starring roles in such films as *The Shawshank Redemption, Arlington Road, The Hudsucker Proxy, Jacob's Ladder* and *The Player*, for which he won the Best Actor award at the 1992 Cannes Film Festival. He wrote, directed and produced *Cradle Will Rock* (1999) and *Dead Man Walking* (1995; nominated for four Oscars, including Best Director), and wrote, directed and acted in *Bob Roberts* (1992).

Tod Lippy: You grew up in New York, right?
Tim Robbins: Well, I moved here when I was three years old, from a pretty quiet neighbourhood in California. In a lot of ways I think it's defined who I am, personally and professionally and creatively. I think the wonderful thing about New York that's unlike any other city in the country as far as I can tell is that it celebrates diversity. It's a given that different races, different nationalities, different languages are all going to intermingle in this huge, wonderfully complex experiment of democracy. So many cities are segregated, but it isn't that way here – and it's always been that way. I'm raising my kids here for that reason. I want them to see and experience this diversity.

I often see you out and around here. Is that ever a problem?
Generally, New Yorkers are pretty cool about that kind of thing. They'll say that they like your work and that's it. Also, I think if you keep moving – you don't linger around – it's OK. I walk fast, I keep moving. But, unlike LA, a lot of people are not living here to be in show business, so you don't get the 'hey-I've-got-a-script' thing. Everyday kind of life is so much more about this kind of conglomeration of ideas and professions and different kinds of personalities. It's a much more interesting environment.

How has it affected your work?
Well, I think it lends itself to less judgement of people – and the less you judge, the more you're able to write them honestly and act them honestly. There are deep complexities in human nature, and oftentimes what you hear coming out of people's mouths is not the obvious, not the stereotypical. People who do write that way probably have blinkers on, and live off of prejudices and stereotypes.

From my impressions, you had a very liberal upbringing.
We knew at the time about the civil-rights movement, and we were encouraged to ask questions about it. We knew who Martin Luther King was, and we had friends who were different colours. We were basically living in an artistic community – and with creative people, you find a lot less bigotry and racism.

I recall reading something about your mother proudly announcing to you that your sister had been arrested in a Vietnam protest march . . .
Yeah. That was really very cool the way she presented it. I'll always remember that. I think that my parents believed from a very early time that that was an

immoral war. They were in California when Nixon was senator, and they had a track on him from a very early age – they were at UCLA at the time.

Didn't you become involved with theatre here as a kid?
Yeah, my sisters worked at a place called the Theater for the New City, which started out at Westbeth, then moved to Jane Street, and ended up on the Lower East Side. A very off-off-Broadway, experimental theatre. I worked in their street-theatre programme, mostly. I think the first year I did it I was twelve – it was a summer job and I'd act in these little street plays with songs in them about various neighbourhoods. Then they'd turn into more political vaudevilles – Watergate-era stuff. It was 1971 to 1977 when I worked there.

Had you decided on an acting career at this point?
I was coming around to it. I wanted to be a director and an actor. I started directing in 1973, at Stuyvesant High School. My second year there I directed my first play; after that I would do one every year. When I got to UCLA I wanted to study directing, not acting – I'm not even sure you could study acting. I think there are some very good acting teachers – I was certainly influenced by Georges Bigot, an actor with Théâtre du Soleil who was doing a workshop in LA – but the danger with acting teachers is the frustration factor – why are these people teaching? Because they really want to teach or because they can't get jobs as actors?

Basically, the one rule I kind of lived by was that no one knows for sure about anything in acting. I still believe that. It's a mystery, really. I'm sure there's validity in all the theories, but it isn't a fucking religion, and you don't have to give up who you are to follow a way or a person, like some kind of cult. Any time I saw that happen I just kind of ran the other way. I remember a fine actor the first year I was at UCLA who I used in a play. He was really funny – instinctually funny, a natural clown on stage – and then he got into a Method class. By the next year he was taking himself so seriously that he'd lost it. That was tragic to see.

Why did you go to UCLA?
Well, I wanted to get away; you know, it's a good growth thing to get away from home. It's part of the reason you should go to college, to live by yourself for a while in a safe environment. I chose UCLA because I had family in Los Angeles – a brother and his girlfriend lived there, my grandfather and my grandmother lived there. I didn't have much money, so I had to find a place that was realistic. I went out there and worked for a year in a warehouse to establish residency so I could afford to go to UCLA. I got in – didn't get in to the theatre department, but I went anyway – and started taking courses.

When did you start up the Actors Gang?
At the end of my time there. We did a production of *Ubu Roi*, and it was quite successful at the school, and I decided to take it out into the real world after I graduated. There was a group of us who were calling ourselves the Actors Gang,

so that became our first official production. It was pretty successful.

The Actors Gang aesthetic, with its emphasis on works in the Brechtian or Surrealist tradition, has been characterized as a 'Warner Bros. cartoon come to life'.
We were doing stuff that was so un-Hollywood. It was interesting, too, because most theatre in Los Angeles is what actors do to try to get agents, or work; casting directors and agents come to theatre there. Our thing was, we're not doing that; we're doing *theatre*. We wanted to create fantastical experiences, not reality-based stuff. We didn't have any living-room sets, you know? Wherever our imagination would take us was where we would land. Plus, the whole point in playing characters onstage was to try and create someone who was completely unlike yourself, so we'd wear make-up and costumes and wigs – really change our appearance – which also doesn't help with casting directors.

But what has happened over time is that casting people and agents have come to realize that there's a breadth of experience to actors who come out of the Actors' Gang – a lot of the members have been working in film regularly in the past few years. About five years ago I built a theatre as a kind of lasting place for them to work out of. We'd been kind of an itinerant company up until then. We're almost at twenty years now. We're going to do a revival of *Ubu* in 2002.

In the mid-eighties, you wrote a series of plays with Adam Simon for the Gang. Was that your first writing experience?
I started writing in a course at college. It was great, because it would only accept six or seven writers, and they would all get their plays done. So you really saw how it worked. And then after *Ubu* I wrote a really terrible play, a musical. A total disaster. Then we did a German Expressionist play, *Methusalem: The Eternal Bourgeois*, written in 1922 by Ivan Goll. Adam Simon came to that, and we started talking about working together, and then came up with the idea for *Slick, Slack, Griff, Graff*, our first play. We did three together: that, *Carnage* and *Violence*.

Did you feel like it was swimming upstream to do experimental theatre in LA?
Well, no. We would get pretty decent audiences. We weren't trying to fill a huge house, though; we were just doing ninety-nine-seat houses. Sometimes, the places we were at were difficult to get audiences to come to. We did a play off Skid Row once – the theatre stunk so bad, drunken guys pissing . . .

When did you start getting acting roles?
Well, I graduated in '81, and let's put it this way: I was still delivering pizzas in 1984, OK? [*Laughs.*] I did get jobs, but I didn't get a lot of jobs, and I wasn't really making a living for a while. Part of the reason for that, though, was that I would take four or five months off every year to do Actors Gang stuff, which drove my agents crazy. But it was the only way I could stay in Los Angeles and stay sane, I think. I always had an outlet, a place to go create and experiment and challenge myself.

I think that's a way to survive in Los Angeles. There's so much sedentary time there; so much down time in show business. And you're not interacting with people generally, on a day-to-day basis, and if you are, they're probably all in your industry. So you're constantly reminded whether you're working or not, what your position in the industry is, what your last job was, what your last hit was – it's everywhere you go, whether it's a restaurant or the cleaners.

What would you consider your first significant film role?
Well, I thought my first significant film role was going to be this George Lucas thing, *Howard the Duck*, but that didn't work out that well. Right before *Howard the Duck* came out, I'd gotten this job in *Five Corners*, and that was really the movie that signalled a change for me because it was a lead role, and it was a good project, with good actors – coincidentally, in New York City. It was huge for me, because up to that point I had been so distrustful and cynical about show business. I mean, I'd had a couple of nice parts, like in *The Sure Thing* – it was great to meet John Cusack, and to work with Rob Reiner – but for the most part, I was doing stuff like *Hardcastle & McCormick*. It was a great way to make a living, but I didn't take it seriously.

As a matter of fact, when I was starting out I very nearly lost my agent because I was so flippant about it. Actually, I did lose my commercials agent. I went into an audition where they wanted me to tell a joke, and I knew what that meant – something quick to look at the actor, hear what their voice sounds like and then move 'em out. I'd been on things like that before, and I was fed up. I'd had it. So I told the longest joke I knew – it was like seven minutes long – and I just wouldn't stop, because I knew they were trying to get me out of there. And the end of it is this terrible punch line – it's one of those jokes where you go on and on and on and then you're like, 'Why did you tell me this joke?' That's the whole point of it, that it's a groaner. Anyway, I got to the end of it and I left. By the time I got home, there was a message from my commercials agent on my machine, saying they'd dropped me. [*Laughs.*]

Did you ever consider someone like Cassavetes, who used his acting work to supplement his own projects, as a model?
I think he is a much purer example of an independent than I am, in that he really used his own money to finance his films. I've been able to finance my theatre that way – and I've put a considerable amount of money into the Actors Gang – but as far as my films go, I've had other financers for them.

When did you come back to New York?
I moved back here in 1987, after *Bull Durham*. I'll tell you, coming back for *Five Corners* really made me miss it a lot, and made me want to get back. I always felt like I was going to wind up back here, but when you're starting out as an actor, and the jobs are starting to come, you really don't want to leave Los Angeles. Also, as I said, I had this creative outlet. But I decided to come back for a couple

of reasons. First of all, Susan lived here. But also, career-wise I was able to, because after *Bull Durham* I started getting scripts, instead of having to go audition for everything.

You did an interview right around the time of *Bull Durham* with Joan Lunden for *Good Morning, America*. It never aired, but it was on an in-house 'bloopers tape' I came across while working at ABC News. It was actually with you and John Cusack, your co-star from *Tapeheads* —
You saw that? [*Laughs.*]

Yeah. It's clear why they never aired it – you both were so hilariously resistant to her questions, particularly regarding your private life.
I remember that. I can't believe you have that. I remember she said to me, 'Well, Tim, all the gossip columns are talking about your relationship with Susan Sarandon . . .' And I said, 'That's a really interesting choice of reading material for a journalist, Joan.' [*Laughs.*] Listen, man, it was set up beforehand. It was not something I wanted to talk about. It was oil and water, boy. And John was right there behind me the whole way: 'I'm with Tim; let's talk about the movie.' [*Laughs.*]

A lot of the press we did for *Tapeheads* was painful. I remember we'd gone through this whole junket in LA, and this guy from *Rolling Stone*, I think, interviewed John and I. We just got punch-drunk, and we started talking about our shoes and hair – that's all we would talk about. We said that all acting was about was shoes and hair. [*Laughs.*] I thought it was pretty funny, but we got written up as being the worst interview of the year or something.

That was probably one of your first experiences with hardcore publicity. Over time is it something you learn to navigate better?
Well, at first it's very difficult because you want to punch people who ask you personal questions. Then you get more philosophical about it, and more tolerant of the idiocy. You don't give in to it, you just figure out better ways to deflect it that are less confrontational. But the bottom line is that these people are strangers to me, and I would never talk about my personal life with someone I don't know. It's like if someone comes up to you on a bus, and says, 'What's it like to be with one of the sexiest women in the world?' You want to say, 'Get the fuck out of here.' Anyway, you just figure out how to deal with it.

Do you find that you can 'use' publicity to promote other agendas, particularly political ones?
Usually when I do publicity I'm talking about it in relation to the film I'm doing, and not bringing things up out of thin air. I remember doing a junket for *Nothing to Lose*, and there was a question about what its political message was, and I was like, 'Are you kidding me?' That wasn't why I was doing this movie, and it wasn't why I was doing the press. They were trying to draw me into a political discussion about this comedy.

When did you do the 'Bob Roberts' short film for _Saturday Night Live_?
It was actually during the trip to New York for _Five Corners_. That's what inspired me to write it, because I'd come back to my old neighbourhood – I was living on LaGuardia Place, and I'd grown up about four blocks from there – and I was shocked to see how gentrified the Village had become in such a short period of time. That kind of early-eighties explosion of wealth. Franchises had hit the Village in a big way. So I started thinking about the concept of a yuppie folk-singer out of that experience.

Was the _Bob Roberts_ feature your first screenplay?
Yeah. It was the first thing I wrote. Everything I've written so far for film has gotten done.

That's a pretty good track record.
Well, it's more just perseverance and stubbornness than anything else.

I know you'd utilized a lot of improvisation in your theatre scripts; did that play a role in _Bob Roberts_ at all?
Well, you can't really do that with a film because you have to give a script to a respective financer. You can do it when you're filming, and I think the best example of that with _Bob Roberts_ is Gore Vidal waxing poetic about the state of the Union after his character has lost the election. That was a situation where we stole two hours out of the schedule with a makeshift desk we found on one of the locations. We just let Gore talk about America. It's really great.

There's a marvellous moment – I believe it's his first appearance in the film – where we see an image of him on a local nightly news broadcast with blueberry pie dribbling down his chin. It's a subtle reminder of how the media presents its subjects in such a way as to bias us one way or another . . .
Right, right. [_Laughs._] And Bob, of course, had much more control over his image. I just saw this thing last night on _Nightline_ about George Bush complaining about the 'left-wing conspiracy' that's being fomented by the Democrats to ensure that McCain is the Republican opponent. Sour-grapes stuff. Right behind him, though, was this backdrop with 'A Reformer with Results' or something like that, repeated like a hundred times behind him – just the visual image. So as you're watching George W., you're getting this image, and then, finally, he actually says it, 'I am a reformer with results.' [_Laughs._]

Did the success of _Bob Roberts_ give you a sense that you'd hit your stride as a film-maker?
I'm not one of these people that . . . I've never been really content with what I've done. I mean, I know I've done a good job, and it's been well-received, but I'm always looking to the next thing. I should probably enjoy it a little bit more.

That's the last time you acted in one of your own films. Is that too difficult?

Well, I didn't want to do it with *Dead Man Walking*. Sean was my first choice, and, you know, he's such a great actor, I don't think I could have done it as well. And with *Cradle Will Rock*, it was just so complicated, with so many different things to worry about, I didn't want to have to worry about a performance on top of it.

How did you come across the book for *Dead Man Walking*?
Susan found it. She met with Sister Helen in New Orleans when she was doing *The Client* down there. They got to talking, and she brought it to me and asked me if I wanted to do it. At the time, I was really hoping to do *Cradle* next – I was in the midst of writing it, and coming to the end of a draft – but finally she just asked me if I was going to do it or not, and I decided to do it. I wrote the first draft in September, and we were shooting by January. So it came really fast, unlike *Bob Roberts* or *Cradle Will Rock*.

Were you always committed to the flashbacks to the actual murder? That kind of relentlessness has a lot of integrity – just when the audience is sufficiently sympathetic to Sean Penn's character, they're reminded once again of his brutality.
Well, when I first met with Sister Helen, I wanted to be sure that she was OK with the fact that the guy was going to be clearly guilty, because there were two people in the book, and one was probably innocent, or at least did not commit the actual murders. I didn't want it to be one of those movies where an innocent man is going to die. The other thing we changed was that it was an electrocution in the book, and I didn't want to get to the end of this journey and have the audience be able to say, 'We should never electrocute anyone, we should do something more humane, like lethal injection.' I wanted to present the most sanitary, white-washed version of execution that they have come up with now: a cold and calculated, anesthetized version of killing someone.

It was meant to be a meditation in a lot of ways. It had to bring people to a meditative place where they could make their own decisions, and see a human life, however flawed, extinguished. And I think that movie had a huge effect on a lot of people; it changed a lot of minds. Most importantly, if you're against the death penalty and you haven't considered the victims' families, then it took you to a place that was uncomfortable and made you really examine why, and maybe even if, you were against it. If you were still against it at that point, you were against it after having walked in the victims' families' shoes – a much stronger opposition. And on the other side, I think it took people who were for it and showed them specifics that they were uncomfortable with. Sister Helen has told me that it's had a tremendous effect on her work. She would give talks before where twenty people would show up, now there are 2,000. She has sensed a 'sea-change', as she puts it, as far as people's perceptions of the death penalty [are concerned].

You said you'd already started on *Cradle Will Rock* when *Dead Man Walking* came along. When did you first decide to bring *Cradle* to the screen?
I first heard of the story in, I think, 1992. As soon as I learned of it, I immediately

knew I had the ending; I just had to figure out how to arrive there honestly, and earn it. As I started to do the research I discovered these other stories as well that were just as compelling, like the funeral march of the dummy, which was a real thing. It was actually a Pinocchio puppet. They were doing a production of *Pinocchio* as Congress was in the midst of these cuts, and as an act of protest the cast – a bunch of circus performers – took the dummy of Pinocchio out on to the streets of Broadway in a mock funeral procession with the audience following behind.

So I thought that would be a great image for the end as well, but I didn't want to do *Pinocchio*, so I thought up the idea of having a ventriloquist instead.

Why did you decide to tie in Diego Rivera's destroyed mural for Rockefeller Center?
I guess the connection was Rockefeller, really, because I'd read that when *Citizen Kane* came out, Rockefeller or someone had cancelled the film at Radio City Music Hall at Hearst's behest. Also, Rockefeller was the one who suggested Welles leave the country to help the war effort in Brazil by doing a documentary on Carnaval. It was a kind of cultural exchange programme between North and South America that our government was doing to make sure that it didn't go Nazi, so they were sending artists down there. Rockefeller was the one who called and got Welles involved in the debacle that became *It's All True*, which basically wound up ruining his career. Because as he's out of town, they're recutting *Magnificent Ambersons* after test screenings and completely tearing him apart in the press when he wasn't there to respond. So by the time he gets back, he can't get a film made in Hollywood.

So something was sort of fishy about Rockefeller, and I started doing more research on him and discovered this mural thing that happened about four years before *Cradle*. So I decided to write that into it as well.

You wrote several hypothetical scenes between Rockefeller and Hearst, where they discuss somewhat schematically the power they wield, particularly relating to cultural patronage and their support of Fascism.
I got some flak for that. That's an embarrassing chapter in the Rockefeller family's history that they'd rather have forgotten, and don't want to be reminded of, especially since they're so connected with modern art. And I know the Hearst people didn't like the way he was portrayed. But you have to remind people of these things. It's conveniently forgotten how supportive we were of Hitler and Mussolini. The powerful and the élite were in bed with these guys because they were decidedly anti-Communist – and we feared Communism more than anything as a threat to our capitalist system – so they buoyed Hitler and Mussolini, helped them build their war machines. We're supposed to forget all of this.

And you see these World War II movies that have absolutely no mention of this, which glorify our involvement in that war as saviours. I think it's intensely political when you ignore things like that. It's propaganda. You notice we aren't seeing any Vietnam war movies glorifying war, or glorifying soldiers. We've conveniently skipped back a few wars to World War II again and again – I mean, look at the History Channel – it's like the World War II Channel.

Are you happy with the critical response to *Cradle*?
Well, it was pretty well reviewed. It just wasn't thoroughly embraced by the critical community in a way that would have propelled it into award consideration and that kind of thing. And ultimately, that's what drives the box office on a movie like this. It either needs to get this groundswell of incredible support to find its audience, or it dies on the vine. If it doesn't have that, it can't make that next step. That says nothing about the quality of the movie – I mean, I know it's a good film – and over time, I'm sure more people will find it. But coming out when it did, and being released the way it was, there were so many things going on at the time, and it was difficult for it to find a mass audience.

Do you read reviews?
Mm-hmm. Sometimes I wish I didn't.

Are you ever inclined to respond?
I was on *Cradle*. Particularly because I thought there was this very unfair thing happening with the Orson Welles situation. People seemed to think that I'd defamed him in some way; some people mentioned that in their reviews. I didn't really write anybody back, I just felt like I wanted to. Because I think they missed the point on that.

It's difficult when you're dealing with an icon. It's very hard to please people. And with Welles, what we created was accurate to the descriptions I had read about him: He was pretty wild, he was a drinker, he was a genius. Genius doesn't come in a pretty package with a bow on it, you know? It's messy; it's uncomfortable. Groundbreaking artists make people around them uncomfortable, and that's what we were trying to do with Welles. We were trying to create a character who was controversial and possessed an incredible genius, but who was also prone to demonstrative behaviour, who did drink, who did burn the candle at both ends, and pushed the envelope. I could have written scenes with him ruminating as he puffed on a pipe, you know, having a genteel conversation with someone, but I just didn't think that would be honest.

I knew there was something up in Cannes. You know, we had these incredible screenings there – fucking standing ovations for five minutes. All three of the screenings were met with this amazing public response. And the day after the screenings, I was doing an interview with a French journalist and she said, 'Orson Welles is a character in your film; why isn't the film about him?' I said, 'Well, it could have been, but I didn't want to do that. That's not what this is about. This is an ensemble thing. He was one person in a group of many creative people at the time.' And she said again, 'Well, still, shouldn't it have focused on him?' I kind of started to understand what would eventually become part of the problem, which was that Welles was such a large character in life and in death that to portray him as anything less than a visionary whom the world centred around was going to be met with a response that was either controversial or uncomfortable. That same day I saw this incredible ecstasy of these screenings and then I saw the intellectualization of it – which I also read in some of the reviews of other French critics – all within twenty-four hours. And they didn't match at all. It was mind-boggling to me.

So you felt like these 'gatekeepers', as it were, were going to somehow limit access to the film?
I don't know, it's hard to analyse. There are many different factors determining whether or not a film reaches a mass audience. How much the studio's behind it, which other movies the studio's releasing at the same time – I think Disney had nine or ten on release at the same time – how much energy is put into it. Who knows. It's always been a mystery to me. *Jacob's Ladder* came out a time when it was just not right for that movie to be seen. We were about to go into the Gulf War, and the country did not want to see a movie about a Vietnam veteran involved in drug experiments when, as the movie's playing in theatres, we are inoculating Gulf War soldiers with anthrax. I got a letter from one guy who resisted – he got put in a brig because he would not take the drugs. He said, 'Thank you, because I saw *Jacob's Ladder* before I left, and it gave me the strength to resist.' And now they've found out that a lot of these soldiers got sick from these vaccines, with this Gulf War Syndrome.

That movie found its audience in video and cable, and it was huge. You see movies that somehow hit the *Zeitgeist*, make tons of money, are huge hits, and then you see them a few years later and you go, 'What? What did I see in this? Why is this not working?' Certainly you can't judge the success of a film based on its initial box office. You have to wait ten years, see it again. If it still works, it's a great film. There's a lot of great films that didn't do well in their initial release. *It's a Wonderful Life* was a bomb. *Citizen Kane* didn't do well. *Shawshank Redemption*.

You'd said after *Cradle Will Rock* that you wouldn't be directing again for a while. Why the moratorium?
It was a huge project, and I'm exhausted after it. You know, something'll come up in a few years, but I'm not going to direct for a while. I'm going to start paying more attention to my acting career.

Of the scripts you get as an actor, what percentage do you actually end up turning down?
Actual offers?

Yes.
I don't get a lot of actual offers. I mean, I probably don't see some of them. I wish I did. I can't really say, because to tell you the truth, in the past four or five years I've had windows of time where I can work in between directing, so I really

haven't been able to be as selective as I have been in the past. When you've got a two-month window and you say to your agent, 'I need to work in those two months; I need money to pay the mortgage,' they come back to you with, 'OK, here's a movie that's shooting, and there's an offer on that.' I'm not really in a position to turn that down.

So choosing to direct has adversely affected the acting career?
Yeah. If you consider the amount of time you put into writing a film, trying to set it up, shooting it, editing it and then publicizing it, you're talking about a good two to five to seven years of your time. And the actual shooting process, where it takes you off your mark as an actor, is about a year and a half. So your earning power or 'heat' is highly diminished. And your momentum as an actor is also kind of stalled – who knows, maybe that's a good thing.

Anyway, I'm not going to direct for a while, and will concentrate on being more selective with my acting roles. I would like to start having a little more control over that, because I don't feel like I've paid enough attention to it. But your question was, what percentage of scripts are good?

I guess that's the hidden question.
You also have to understand, I'm on a list – I'm not sure what number I am, but there's a certain echelon above me that the movies go to first. So the really good scripts often don't even get to me.

You don't know which number you are?
Oh, you know, it's pretty obvious who the top echelon are, and that's good, that's OK, because they deserve it. If you can open a movie, and you can deliver a product of quality, then you deserve that. I've been directing – that's where I've been putting my creative energy – so I never feel wanting, or jealous, or competitive in that sense. I get the scripts I get; they get the scripts they get. To worry about it – to spend time complaining about it – is wasted time and wasted energy, and it's all negative. So I've got my own stability career-wise. I would like to up the quality a little bit, but I think that comes with time and with dedicating your energies to that.

Once you've accepted a role, are you ever compelled to rewrite your part?
It depends on the script, and it also depends on whether they want that from you. But when I'm an actor, I tend to just be an actor. It's difficult when you come into a project, you've read it once, twice, the director and producer have been living with it for years, and you give notes and maybe some of them are good – but maybe some of them are bad, too. You have to be able and willing as an actor to say, 'Listen, I may not know what's right here.' At some point you just have to give over your trust and faith to the film-makers and hope that they pull it off.

I mean, you can change lines and make them a little more interesting. Little things like that. But I don't get involved in the structural problems, or the visual style, or anything like that.

Any favourite roles so far?
Five Corners, Bull Durham, Shawshank, Jacob's Ladder. Also *The Player, Short Cuts.*

How have you drawn on your own experience as an actor when directing?
Well, you just know what your actors are going through, and you know what kind of space they need, and what kind of protection they need, and you try to create an environment that is about them. It's not about the technical stuff. We did a lot of ambitious technical things with *Cradle,* but it all started with, 'How do we capture what the actors are doing?'

You said at one point that you hated having to do auditions for *Cradle.*
I just don't like it. It's a necessary part of the process, but it makes me uncomfortable because I don't like passing judgement, and I don't like disappointing people, especially actors. The truth is, there's really very little that separates the people who get it from the ones who don't – it's just an intangible something you know when they walk in the door, or after they've read. A spark, a magnetism, chemistry – you know it's right. It has nothing to do with 'being the best'. It's not a race.

That's the difficult thing about making movies. It is a collaborative art, and it's very difficult to be an actor and audition – constantly putting yourself and your emotions on the line and expose yourself to judgement – because ultimately there is no gauge you can read that will make you feel better about not getting a part. Unlike in some kind of athletic competition, you know who wins the race, or who scores the most goals. You can't look at any kind of scoreboard, though, when you haven't gotten a part. It's all so intangible.

Are there any movies you particularly liked this year?
I liked *Boys Don't Cry* a lot. It's typical that the Academy wouldn't nominate that for best picture. That's by far the best picture I've seen this year. So good. I liked *Three Kings* a lot, thought that was really well done.

Incidentally, did you know that there is a dialogue reference to 'bleeding-heart liberals' in every one of your films?
Oh, yeah. There's also another line that's in every film as well: 'Are you a Communist?' [*Laughs.*] It's in *Bob Roberts* when he asks the newscaster; it's in *Dead Man Walking* when someone asks Sister Helen if she's a Communist, and it's in *Cradle Will Rock.*

Is that intentional?
I don't know what it is. I guess it's that kind of twentieth-century obsession with a tactic that's been used by people on the right to define as a 'Communist' anyone who disagrees with them. If you're going to accuse, accuse big.

Are there any directors you'd like to work as an actor with that you haven't so far?
Tim Burton, Wes Anderson, Paul T— what's his name?

Paul Thomas Anderson?
Yeah. Wait – is it Wes Anderson?

There are two —
Two Andersons? My God! [*Laughs.*] I didn't realize that, but I know I like both of those guys. I like Spike Jonze very much, and, as I said, I love David O. Russell. And Alexander Payne, I love his movies. And I'm sure there are others, but those are the ones who come to mind immediately.

On the more hypothetical side, are there any directors who are no longer with us whom you would have particularly liked to work with?
Orson Welles. I'd love to screen my movie for him, and tell him that people got really pissed off about it. I'd love to see what he thinks. [*Laughs.*]

Stacy Cochran

Stacy Cochran wrote and directed the forthcoming *Drop Back Ten* (featured in the dramatic competition of the 2000 Sundance Film Festival), *Boys* (1995), and *My New Gun*, which was selected for the Directors' Fortnight at the 1992 Cannes Film Festival. She made the short documentary *Richard Lester!* in 1998.

Tod Lippy: When did you move to New York?
Stacy Cochran: I came after college. I grew up in New Jersey – eleven miles from the city, but a world away . . . [*Laughs.*] As soon as I finished college I moved to New York and lived in somebody's broom-closet for six months. When my boyfriend, Eric, finished school – he was a year behind me – he came down, we got married and started to have children. [*Laughs.*] No, that's not really true. We did get married right away. And then I worked for a while at Children's Television Workshop.

What were you doing there?
I wrote for a magazine for six- to ten-year-olds. It was sold on the newsstand, so we had to have a media cover. It was usually Michael Jackson and Ewoks or something and I'd have to make up some kind of feature story appropriate for six-year-olds, and then a game to go with it or something. I'd make up puzzles and contests.

When did you start making films?
I started writing scripts on my own while I was at CTW, and then when Eric got a job, I quit and started shooting little things I had written.

You were writing feature scripts?
I wrote one and I showed it to a friend, who said, 'Why don't you write something shorter so we can shoot it?' So I wrote a ten-minute thing called *Cocktails at Six*, and we shot that.

How did you find a crew?
A friend, Adam Merims, got the crew together with Tony Jannelli, a DP that I like a lot. I knew Tony. I had been volunteering at the IFFM the year before – cutting cheese and pouring wine at a reception for something he shot – and I met him and we stayed friends. Between Adam and Tony, we pulled it together. We shot it in my parents' apartment. The first day everybody showed up and there came this moment when all these people – well, there weren't that many people, but to someone who had never shot a movie it looked like a lot of people – had crammed into my mother's dining-room. All these guys standing there, waiting in total silence for me to direct the movie, I guess. It's not that Tony and I hadn't decided how to shoot it, but there's still that performance moment. The movie was about a six-year-old, and she was standing there waiting, too, and I figured, 'She's the one I can deal with here.' So I went over and whispered to her. And she did what I said to do, and then everyone was working and it was fine. I still whisper to actors.

That seems so respectful.

I just hate that screaming across the room. The other thing I don't like is talking to more than one actor at once.

What happened with the short? Did you show it anywhere?
I showed it at the next IFP market. I can't really remember what else I did with it. I had a little distributor and she sold it to a couple of places and it showed at some other festivals, too. I remember it showed in Uppsala, Sweden.

So you got a sense of the whole film-making thing.
I also got a sense of what I didn't know. So I thought, 'Well, maybe I should just go to film school, because I don't know what to do next.' I couldn't afford to keep buying film for myself to learn, so I decided to go to Columbia.

Why not NYU?
Why *not* NYU? It was right across the street from my apartment. And the thing about Columbia, at least at that time – I started in the fall of '88 – was that the facilities were shitty. But I kind of liked that, because I knew I wanted to be a writer, first, and then direct.

And Columbia is known for its emphasis on writing.
Partly because they don't have the facilities to teach you anything else. The thing is, at NYU, I would've had to spend a lot of time working on other people's films as boom operator or camera person or sound recordist – really long hours on other people's movies. Which is OK, in theory, but I was pregnant at the time – I've always been pregnant. [*Laughs.*] So I knew that I only had a couple of months before I was going to have a teeny, tiny baby, and the deal at Columbia was they didn't really care how technically proficient you were. They wanted you to write a lot and then to shoot – even with a camcorder – and then cut it yourself on tape, and do that over and over. Time was, as usual, very important to me, with the new baby and all of that, so I just bought a little VHS camcorder for myself. I couldn't even deal with the equipment room and waiting on line or scheduling. We had these little directing assignments, and I could just go shoot it, cut it, and hand it in the next day. And for me that was better.

Who was teaching when you were there?
Ralph Rosenbloom, Romulus Linney, Chris Kazan.

Milos Forman wasn't there then, was he?
He was there the year before me and the year after I left. But Emir Kusturica was there. At the time, I was out of my mind with excitement, because I had just seen *When Father Was Away on Business*, which I thought was one of the best movies I had ever seen. I really scrambled to get into his class. And he didn't give a shit about me. You know, as much as you adore your teacher, at some level if he just looks right through you, your interest in him has to fade a little bit, self-centred as that sounds. It didn't make me like his movies less, though, and I must say that

he did tell me one thing that was very constructive. We had to shoot a thesis film, and he looked at all our scripts. I wrote this ten-minute movie about a guy who gets hit by lightning while he's washing his car in the driveway. And Emir said, 'Just make sure when you shoot it that the characters always have their feet floating a little bit off the ground.'

That's great.
Yeah. And he was so right. And that was probably the only thing that anyone could have said that would actually mean something to me. I thought about it when I was shooting, and I still think it's good advice. So, in a way, I guess it was worth all the frustration of being a complete nonentity in his room for a year and a half, because he actually contributed something beautiful to the whole process.

And this was *Another Damaging Day*?
Yeah.

Were you happy with it?
I don't know. I can't look at it. I get palpitations watching anything I've ever done. And Ralph Rosenbloom was such a sweetheart – he got mad at me over that movie because he had suggestions that I ignored, and he never really forgave me. It played at the New York Film Festival, which was kind of fun, and he was standing on the sidewalk afterwards, still mad at me.

What did it play with at the festival?
The Sting of Death. A Japanese movie.

Was it a good match?
[*Laughs.*] No, no. It was a very, very long poem of a movie. All of my family came, of course, and when my brother came out, he said, 'There are some things even a dog won't eat,' which was a line from *The Sting of Death* that he read in the subtitles. That really said it for him, the whole event. He still says that to me on occasion when the subject of my fabulous career comes up. Anyway, I had to write a feature script for school as well, so I wrote *My New Gun*.

I remember you said once you couldn't believe how fortunate you were in getting your first feature made.
Spoken like somebody on a motorcycle as they approach a wall at ninety miles an hour. [*Laughs.*] 'I'm so lucky!' – BOOM!! Yeah, it was lucky. I was taking this producing class that Leon Falk taught. He would occasionally bring in people from the industry, whatever 'the industry' means – people who had paying jobs – to talk to us about different aspects of becoming film-makers. And he brought in an agent from William Morris to teach us how to pitch movies. So when it was my turn, I talked about *My New Gun*, describing it in great detail, and the agent said, 'Wow, that sounds great. You should write that.' And I said, 'Well, I did write it, because if I hadn't written it I wouldn't be able to pitch it to you.' So she

asked to read it, and she really liked it. She wanted to know if I had an idea for casting Debbie Bender, and I said, 'No, not really.' And she said, 'What do you think of Diane Lane?' And I just couldn't have been more excited about the idea. It was a beautifully perfect idea. And Diane read it and she liked it and that was that. IRS Media and Columbia Tristar Home Video had decided to make the movie and they liked Diane. I went out and met with her and loved her – there's nothing not to love about her; she's fantastic.

Was that your first LA film-world experience?
Yes, it was. I'd been to LA a lot because my mom is from there, but never for my own work.

And how did the meeting with Diane Lane go?
I was a little nervous meeting her. She's so beautiful – one of her eyes is a little funky. She got hit in the head with a tennis ball, I think.

And she was obviously into it.
Yeah, but she wasn't like, 'Oh my God, I have to make this movie!' She said, 'I like it, I'll do it. Do you really want me to do it?' I said, 'Yeah.' She said, 'OK.'

How did the production go?
It was fun, and it was very quick, although I didn't learn what quick – or cheap – was until *Drop Back Ten*. But we had to go fast and be efficient, and I like that. I like to be precise about what you're going to do, and go in and do it.

You like to have a 'spine' in place?
More than a spine. A very specific idea about what to shoot and what not to bother shooting. The idea is to be direct in a way that's not simplistic. To be casual in a way that's not lazy. It takes an enormous amount of work, in a way, to be prepared enough to be casual when you're actually shooting. Everybody in it was so focused on the same thing. Stephen Collins said to me, 'You'll never have this much fun again.'

Were you pleased with the response to the film?
I came out of the first screening sobbing: 'This is the stupidest piece of garbage I've ever seen and it doesn't even make sense. I can't even tell if it's been written in English or not; what are these people saying to each other?' But it turned out well, and I thought at the time that it had taught me a lesson: if you just know what you want and you're focused and your goal in shooting a movie is to make sure everyone is moving in concentric circles, it will be something in the end. But it's a lesson that turned out not to be completely true – you can make that effort· and have it not turn out right at all.

Did you go with the film to Cannes?
Yeah. It was the first time we showed it, at Directors' Fortnight. So it was exciting. We all went, and decided that instead of getting a couple of hotel rooms we'd get

a house and then anyone who wanted to go could go. So a lot of extra people came who worked on the movie, and we all stepped into this great little house on a hill.

What was the response like?
Great! It was really great. And then from there I got to go to a lot of other festivals – it just toppled its way on to the festival route. Boy, that was a long time ago.

At that point, were you already beginning to write *Boys*?
I don't think so. I tend not to be able to think of two stories at the same time. I kind of have to have something really, really finished before being able to even get into that dream state where you decide what you really want to write about.

You likened the writing process to 'walking around in traffic with your nose in a book'.
When you're actually writing something it's not so much that you have an idea, it's that you're consumed with something that's more than an idea – it's kind of like a cloud that's surrounding you.

So when did you start writing *Boys*?
I met the producers Paul Feldsher and Peter Frankfurt and they said, 'We really liked *My New Gun*; let's do something together.' Peter said, 'There's this James Salter story that I've always wanted to make a movie from – an eight-page story and I don't know how to approach it as a feature; do you have any ideas for it?' I'd never read any of Salter's stuff before, so I read it – it's called 'Twenty Minutes' – and it was phenomenal. It's very brief, which I always like. You know, there's this thing I just read in the *New York Review of Books* – it was Tom Stoppard saying something about writing as the compression of language for the expansion of meaning. Which is exactly what is so much fun about making movies. Compression of language and action. Keep it down to the barest minimum so the meaning expands as much as possible. Of course, most movies are exactly the opposite, expanding the action to the point where the meaning has completely disappeared.

Anyway, 'Twenty Minutes' is about a woman who is riding a horse, and she falls off the horse because its hoof tips the edge of a fence in just the wrong way – just enough to topple the horse and change everything. So she falls off the horse and she's lying in the meadow in the story, dying, and in that time, she goes back and forth between being acutely aware of the meadow that she's in and having everything that's gone before floating through her mind, mostly in terms of her unsatisfying life with men. I thought that maybe there was a way of changing the details of her story without changing that essential moment. And in the first draft, we were so successful – I think I somehow managed to change everything and still maintain the heart of it. Not so clearly in the final film, though. And I was sad to see it change so much. The horse barely exists in the final cut! There are still things from the story that survive, but you've got to be a pretty careful observer to pick them up. I still think the movie is beautiful. I love Robert Elswit, the DP, so much. And there are scenes that I like and many implications in it that I like, which turn the standard elements of movies on their head a little bit.

But the thing that was mostly lost from *Boys*, in the end, was its sense of humour about itself. It really was meant to be funny, as hard as that is to believe looking at the movie now. Originally, the idea was that the movie would start out being about this woman, Patty Vare – you're trying to get a handle on who she is and you're making assumptions about what the movie is going to feel like that become incorrect as soon as the horse's hoof hits the fence. You weren't meant to realize how melancholy the film is until you got to the end of the movie – you were meant to be diverted from the melancholy aspect of the story for the body of the movie, so when it comes back to you, you realize it's been there all along. That was the idea, to make a movie that is floating over the top of this bedding of grief that's underneath it all. When the studio decided to take the most melancholy aspect of the story and chop it up into little pieces of confetti and drop them everywhere in the movie, you never got a chance to step away from it so you could feel it when it came back. It was just always in there, putting you in a cranky mood when you were supposed to be watching a funny scene. And for me, that was, well, 'disappointing' doesn't really say it as well as 'excruciating'.

How did you become involved with Interscope, which financed the film?
Peter and Paul thought it would be a good place to go because it was big enough to be studio-like – the movie would be distributed pretty widely if it got made – but small enough that you weren't just dealing with levels of bureaucracy that went on infinitely. So we showed a first draft to the Interscope executives first, and they wanted to do it. They wanted me to change it pretty dramatically, but I actually liked the idea of having to rewrite for someone. I had basically shot the first draft of *My New Gun*. Believe me, I'm grateful for that, and *My New Gun* feels like it is just what it was meant to be – it wasn't over-thought, but then on the other hand there are places where I felt I could have done more for it. I kind of liked the idea of being forced to rethink what I had written this time.

So I enjoyed the writing process on *Boys*. I would go back and forth between New York and LA, constantly complaining. They'd say, 'We really like it, just come on out and we'll have a meeting and talk about a few things,' and then there would be a note on every fucking page, and I'd get on the plane ready to kill myself. But by the time I got back to New York six hours later, I'd have an idea how to do what they were looking for that was completely different from what they had asked, but which would actually solve their problem. I found that the best way to endure picky little notes on every page was to take as broad a view of the problem as possible, and be willing to rethink the whole point of the script every single time. It kept me from getting bored with it, from getting cross-eyed.

Despite the fact that you thought Interscope would be less of a studio presence, the whole experience sounds very 'studio-ish' to me.

It was, but I had never done that before. And I would get a kick out of coming up with a whole new animal every time.

So you never felt like it was out of your control?
No, not while I was writing, because I felt like it kept getting better – not in the ways they were anticipating it would, but we all agreed that it kept getting better. And I was getting paid for it. [*Laughs.*] It was a weird kind of puzzle that I'd never come up against as a writer before, and I liked that. Then there came the time when most of us were happy with the draft – but not all, which became the crucial problem. Interscope said they'd really like to make this with Winona Ryder, and I said, 'Good. Let's send it to her and see what she thinks.' And we did and she read it and within a day she decided to do the movie. Unfortunately, it was a draft that someone at Interscope didn't consider to be a final draft – in a way, I agreed with him, because there's always more work you can do. And Winona agreed that there were a few things that could be improved, but she said let's not let it get completely turned on its head.

I'm guessing that she had the clout to say 'enough' to Interscope, since her attachment to the movie pretty much secured the financing.
You just put your finger on the appendicitis. I don't know. The thing is that the draft that she agreed to do was pretty good, but could have been better, and so I wrote another draft that I thought *was* better, and it was the first one that every single producer in the ever-growing list of producers associated with the movie was really happy with. And then – well, Winona didn't like it. And so the question became, do I help her to understand why I think this draft is better, or do I just go back to the draft she preferred? I really wanted to make a movie with her, but I felt that the best thing to do was discuss it with Interscope and make a united decision and either say, 'You know, Winona, we're so much happier with this that maybe we should just work with someone else,' or, 'We want to make this movie with you so badly that we'll go back.' My instinct was to simply have a brief, focused conversation with the people I was in business with, which would end in a clear decision. But it didn't. We got caught in the middle, and it somehow morphed into you say black, we say white between me and them. And it just became totally insane.

By the way, this all happened after the sets had already been built and we were two weeks away from shooting.

So the production wasn't as smooth as *My New Gun* . . .
No, it wasn't. It's so crazy that it wasn't – there was no reason why it shouldn't have been. The executives would say, 'Just tell us what you need, because we don't want to leave Baltimore' – where we were shooting – 'without shooting something that you feel you should've gotten.' So I said, 'Well, thank you, I appreciate that. Before I answer I just want to think about it for a minute.' So I did that, and I came back and said, 'This is what I think we really need that we're not getting.' And they said, 'Hmmm, let's think about that – we'll get back to you tomorrow.' And they'd

call back and say, 'No.' [*Laughs.*] My favourite thing was not getting the editor I wanted to work with approved until we were a month into shooting.

What about dailies?
They were cut by someone who I wasn't working with, so when the editor I wanted to hire finally started she was really behind the eightball in terms of schedule. So we called and said, 'We have ten weeks to cut, but we're starting a month late. Could you give us an extra two weeks?' And the answer was, 'No, and we're taking two away.'

I love that scene in *Heaven Can Wait,* where Warren Beatty is the quarterback and all of a sudden his own team turns on him. That was my perception of the whole thing: 'Wait a minute, guys!'

What happened when you delivered the first cut?
The 'eight-week cut'. It was good. We were all excited and everyone was laughing. And one of the executives said, 'OK, let's work together now to make the ending work' – because the ending was not good.

The original script had a different – much darker – ending than the film, right?
Well, we ended up shooting the version of the script Winona wanted, not the final draft. Part of this thing was a casting issue. Dermot Mulroney, who was originally going to play the baseball player, had to bow out at the last minute, and Skeet Ulrich got bumped up from playing one of the cops to playing that role, which was a complete reversal of what the casting should have been. It really shifted the balance of the movie. I wanted to fix it, but I never got an opportunity to. And the studio, rather than addressing that problem, just decided to reassemble the entire piece. I had originally wanted Skeet to play Baker, the kid who falls in love with Patty Vare. Skeet was unknown at the time, and I wanted him to be the one who sneaks up on the movie, who, as the movie progresses, takes over the story.

Why didn't the studio go with him?
They didn't know him. And they felt he was too old. Of course, two years later he went on to play a high-school student in *Scream* and it didn't seem to bother anyone.

So you went with Lukas Haas ...
Which everyone was happy with. He was a sweet kid, and he had sort of a delicacy which was interesting.

And I also thought he had a sense of awe around Patty Vare, which was nice.
Yes, that was probably one of the best things about the movie. So that was fine. But the reshuffle of actors was just the beginning of things really changing all the time.

What happened then?
Well, they did a preview screening of the first cut, and the audience didn't seem to 'get' the part about Winona, and did get the part about Lukas. So, of course, the studio's instinct wasn't to make the part with Winona compelling – which was my

goal and would not have been hard to do. Their instinct was to throw the whole first section of the movie away and put Lukas in the first frame so the audience didn't have to wait for him. That's kind of like saying 'I've got a headache' and chopping off your head to fix it. And it's not that I didn't understand the problems that the audience was having – that this one audience had – but their problem was sort of isolated. In my opinion, it's valuable to hear what's not working for them, but it's not necessarily valuable to hear what their suggestions are for improving it.

It seems ingenuous, of course, but you would expect the studio to have a certain amount of trust in the instincts of the person who wrote and directed the film.
Or in themselves, for that matter. I mean, Interscope made me write a new fifteen-page wraparound after they saw *Bridges of Madison County* – they thought it might be a good idea to do the whole movie as a flashback, like that movie did. I thought it actually exacerbated problems that we had, but I did it – I didn't have a choice, because I felt that I had committed myself to the movie, and I was happy that they weren't hiring someone else to do it. So we shot it, and they loved it. Then they decided to do another preview. I didn't even go. I said, 'I'll write it, I'll shoot it, I'll cut it in, but I'm not flying out to see what they say, because I don't care what they say. If they liked it, fine, you've got what you want.' If they didn't like it, I'd say, 'So what else is new?'

They called me from the car on the way home from the preview: 'The kids don't like it, it's out.' I mean, you just spent a half-million dollars on a reshoot that you're going to throw away because fifteen kids didn't like it. It seemed silly to me. Then they brought in another editor to make mincemeat of the thing.

You were taken off the movie?
For a while. And I was troubled by two things. One was the structure. I love structure, and when they scrambled the structure it was very sad. It made me feel like, in *Toy Story*, where the mean kid, Sid, disassembles toys and puts them back the wrong way so they look like really gruesome freaks. But also, the grammar of the scenes was off. It felt clumsy, and I was embarrassed to have a movie that – whether you like the movie or hate the movie – was just clumsy within scenes. So they let us come back and work on it some more and repair things so it moved better, and we were able to minimize some of the freakish nature of the structure. [*Laughs.*] It made a big difference, and it does sort of survive in a way. There are things about it, attitudes about things, that returned. And somehow or other, by the very, very end, we kind of liked it again. But then the reviews were so bad that everybody turned tail.

Do you think that the studio was behind it until there was a bad critical response?
No, the studio wasn't behind it. I remember my agent at the time said, 'It isn't going to make money, and the studio isn't behind it, and it's got problems, but we like it and we think the critics are going to like it and you'll be OK.' And then the critics hated it.

Not all the critics. Terrence Rafferty, for one, gave it an extraordinary review in
The New Yorker.
He has an uncanny ability to feel the film-maker that is inside a movie – any movie. But the studio wouldn't even have screenings for the critics before it came out, so most people were poised to hate it.

Rafferty even mentions that in his review.
He does, yeah. I have a friend who at the time was working on a small paper in Texas who called me and said, 'I think you may have a problem.' She had wanted to do a feature story on Lukas Haas for *Boys*, and when she called the studio to set it up, they said, 'You know, don't do it. He's got another movie coming out for somebody else in the fall, do it for that one.'

That must have sent shivers down your spine.
It was not so good. And of course, I was nine months pregnant at the time. [*Laughs.*] My agent was sending me lots of scripts in that little window of time before it was released, and then the minute that we got a dumpload of bad reviews, they were, like, talk about etherized – they disappeared, they were just gone. Then I went into labour, my favourite thing to do when times are hard. [*Laughs.*] That's what I like about the pain of childbirth. It's distracting.

How many years did this whole process take?
I started writing it in '93, and it was released in '96, I think. It was a long time – three full years of work on one movie. But when was the right time to walk away from it? Never. I kept feeling that if I just worked harder, and thought harder, I'd come up with a solution that would make it all make sense again. And we sort of did save it enough times that I started to believe I could always do that. And the fact is I couldn't.

Why, after directing a relatively high-budgeted studio picture, did you make
Drop Back Ten **– a small, self-produced independent movie – next?**
Because I didn't have a choice. I read a lot of scripts after *Boys*, but it seemed that somebody else had always been hired by the time I finished reading anything – the day I got it, another director was already attached. For instance, I loved the idea of doing a movie of *Madeline*. I wanted to do something kind of cool and floaty with it. And right about that time I met Isabelle Adjani, who is one of the most beautiful things that the earth has ever come up with, and I thought, wouldn't she be an incredible Miss Clavell? She'd be so graceful and different from the book in an interesting way. But someone else had already been hired. Nobody would even talk to me on the phone about it.

So I decided that I was just going to write something that I would like to shoot, and see what happened. And I wrote *Drop Back Ten*.

I'm assuming you went the New York indie route?
Well, my agent showed it to some of the New York independent companies and

they didn't want to make it. We did find a producer who wanted to invest in it, then at the last minute – literally just a few weeks before we started shooting – he backed out. And – this may come as no surprise – I was pregnant. [*Laughs.*] I know from reading this you'd think I have twelve children, but the three I've had just seemed to come at prime moments. So he dropped out and my agent starts saying, 'Why don't we just regroup and try to plan for early spring.' And I was, like, 'He doesn't know that I'm going to have a two-week-old baby in mid-February.' I didn't want to tell anyone that, but I couldn't postpone anyway, because I was already climbing the walls that I hadn't been able to shoot anything for so long. So I just decided I would cobble together loan after loan after loan.

It's ironic that it was your third, rather than your first, feature where you actually fulfil the indie cliché about 'maxing out your credit cards', to make a film.
Is that humiliating? I'm not sure. It was interesting because I was able to produce it myself in a different way than I would have been able to pull off right out of film school. But on the other hand – I don't know, I guess there is no other hand.

Can you talk about the 'different way' you produced it?
Initially, I thought I had two choices. The budget was so tiny – it was a quarter the size of *My New Gun* – that the film could only be made by either not paying anybody, which I wouldn't do – I can't work that way – or shooting on DV or something. And I decided that I wasn't going to do either one. I hired Spencer Newman to shoot it – his first movie, but he has a beautiful eye. And we thought we would just try and be smart about it. Any problem that we had in terms of time and resources, we were just going to think of a way to outsmart the problem somehow, and just force ourselves to have a good idea. So I had to make decisions like, 'We will never use a dolly. Ever.' Of course, on set, everyone would say, 'We've got this little doorway dolly, it's nothing, it's in the truck, it's just like a platform on wheels. It's not a real dolly track. . . .' And I was like, if we start that, then it's going to mean reconceiving everything, and it's going to change the way we approach the day too much. Let's just say that we can pan and tilt, but the film is going to be a series of snapshots that sort of move and sort of don't move. And it's going to be about the rhythm of the snapshots in a way.

OK, we did use one dolly when we were shooting the movie-within-the-movie, the scene where Pamela, the director, is shooting a football game. We thought that would be fun – Pamela gets a dolly shot, but we don't. I don't think people sit there and go, 'Why are there no dolly shots in this movie?' But there's a sort of smallness that a decision like that gives the movie that is at least a consistent smallness, better than cutting corners randomly.

It must have felt like the ultimate vindication when the movie was invited to Sundance.
For a few weeks, we really were excited. Everybody felt great. To say that there were no other producers on our side is not to say there weren't allies. I mean

Nancy Novack, the editor, and Spencer, and the cast, of course, and Todd Thaler, who cast it so beautifully and helped me produce it. I couldn't have asked for anything more from all of them, and I wouldn't want to trade them in for anything.

Did you find being invited to Sundance problematic, in that it meant you had to rush to get your movie in some sort of shape – however unfinished it might still be – in time for the festival?
I can't say anything negative about the festival. I was so grateful for their support and enthusiasm. When Geoff Gilmore called and talked to me about it, the way he was talking about the movie made me feel that he and the rest of the committee understood it in the way we had all hoped that someone would understand it. The fact that it was shown in Park City in a somewhat imperfect form, well, it negatively affected some people – namely the distributors who passed on it – but there were a lot of people who saw it who were enthusiastic about it.

I guess once they took it at Sundance, I started thinking to myself, 'If we can just get a decent print there on time, we'll pick a distributor and work with them to finish it.' Pick! We're finishing it now on our own, and of course I've got a new baby, which is tricky. I said, 'We just have to do it.'

You've said that *Drop Back Ten* isn't autobiographical, but there is an element of the film – particularly the scenes involving the movie-within-the-movie, where Pamela, the director, is at odds with the producers and her lead actor – that at least hint at your situation on *Boys*. Did it feel kind of cathartic to write it?
No!

Writing shouldn't be therapeutic?
Maybe it should be, but then it'd better be pretty abstract therapy, not just trying to get your gripes off your chest. This movie is meant to be funny, but it's also about a culture of cruelty. In a sense, James LeGros's character is figuring out how to penetrate that and do the right thing. But he's also trying to get what he wants!

Your films are all always informed by a very considered subtlety – that compression of information you talked about earlier – and I think certain reviewers who take things more literally often miss the point.
Well, it would be really easy for me to take a bad review and start trying to explain it away.

What are you going to do now?
I don't know, I have to finish this movie and see what happens to it. Maybe part of the reason I can't think seriously about the next thing while I'm working on something is because I think I'll never do anything else.

Do you think that every time?
Kind of, until I'm really finished with whatever I'm making, and then suddenly I know what I'm thinking about and then I start writing that. But it's not like I was

ever confronted with a three-picture deal, so it's a little bit of a problem of having to reinvent the wheel every time. Not reinventing the structure and the story and the characters – that's the joy of it. I wish I had the ability to say, 'I want to set up this movie,' and that meant it was going to be set up.

You made a short film about Richard Lester in between *Boys* and *Drop Back Ten*. How did that come about?
Somebody called me to tell me they were doing a series of ten-minute pieces called 'Directors on Directing' for Italian TV. They asked some directors to choose someone whose work meant a lot to them and then shoot a little piece about them in their own style. So I said I'd like to do Richard Lester, but I didn't want to do it in 'my style', because, first of all, I don't think I have a style, and if I do, let's hope I'm not aware of it. I'd rather do something that kind of plays on things about his style, both in terms of surface details and the underlying sense of the way his things are put together. So they said 'OK,' and they helped me track him down – he still has an office at Twickenham – and he said he'd be happy to do it, just pick him up at 8.00 in the morning on the scheduled day and whatever we wanted to do that day, he'd be happy to do.

Of course, a week later, the producers called to say, 'You know what, we already did five of these segments, and you were number six, and we're just going to stick to the five.' So what was I going to do? Call Richard Lester and say I wasn't coming? I decided I'd just do it myself. Robert Elswit was going to be in London, because he had just shot *Tomorrow Never Dies*, and he said, 'Sure, let's do it.' So I rented a Betacam there, and Robert brought his little Super-8 film camera, and we shot the whole thing in a few hours, and God, it was fun. I was a nervous wreck, completely in awe of my subject. And we made a half-hour film and it showed in a bunch of festivals. And Bravo bought it, so that was good.

Do you think the DIY aspect of that encouraged you to go ahead with *Drop Back Ten*?
No, I think it was just the same problem twice. I had no intention of doing either myself, but it was a matter of 'Do it yourself or don't do it at all.'

Quite some time ago, you said you were very suspicious of the New York independent film tradition of getting people to do crew work for free, or for very little money. You mentioned your aversion to that here when discussing *Drop Back Ten*; can you elaborate on it a little more?
Well, things have probably changed. Back in the eighties and early nineties, the 'independent' thing seemed really gutsy, but many of those East Village projects actually depended on the commitment of a lot of poor saps that wanted to be in the film business. You could always find kids and make them work like hell for you for nothing, because maybe if they spent three years doing it, they'd move up a notch. Meanwhile, the film was for some film-maker's glory. I was always sceptical – these people presented themselves as being so different from the 'careerist

assholes' of Hollywood, but in fact, a lot of them were very careerist, too, not particularly nice, and selfish, selfish, selfish.

Do you have any particular influences? Everyone always mentions Raymond Carver when they talk about your films.
They do? Because they're slim? I like Raymond Carver a lot, but for me, his stuff – maybe because he was so prolific without changing very much – eventually digs a deep groove in one place. Lately, I like Philip Roth better, because it's more complicated and unpredictable. But neither one of them has anything to do with what I do. I'm a big fan of William Eggleston, the photographer – he has a way of being so precise that it feels completely offhand, and the way that works can be very exciting to me. But I don't ever compare myself to anyone.

Would it be appropriate to describe your experiences as a sort of cautionary tale about the young indie director who goes to Hollywood only to get chewed up by the 'system'?
You mean the 'cautionary tale' about the first-time film-maker who wasn't as smart as she thought she was? [*Laughs.*] No. Regardless of what happened to me, I wasn't left with the feeling that I didn't want to make bigger movies if I was given the opportunity. I'm sure you know that there are a lot of people who have commercial failures but just keep getting opportunity after opportunity. I don't know why some do and some don't . . .

You were featured in a piece in the *New York Times* last year about the large number of acclaimed female directors who have had a long lapse between films – The 'Whatever happened to —?' piece.

Do you think it's completely off the mark to say it's a gender issue?
I don't think it's off the mark, but I also don't think it's the whole story. No matter what business you're in, some things work and some things don't work.

Can you talk briefly about how you feel about living and working in New York?
One thing about living in New York as opposed to California is the diversity you find here – and not just racial or cultural diversity, although that's certainly a part of it. New York has a genuinely diverse population, and my friends have genuinely diverse concerns. That's not to say you can't find diversity in LA, but it's harder for me to be able to benefit from it there. You're encouraged to drive where you're going, so you're often alone in your car, and more importantly, I guess, you're encouraged to be around people who work in the movie business. It's like politics in Washington. It's not that it's necessarily a bad thing – the centre of an industry does need to coalesce somewhere – but for the work that I want to do, I need to splinter off first, and then get together with the DP, and the AD, and the casting director, and the actors that I'm going to work with. But I don't need to come together with the whole industry – in fact, it would do more harm than good if I did that on a regular basis.

Wes Anderson

Wes Anderson has directed and co-written (with Owen Wilson) the features *Bottle Rocket* (1996) and *Rushmore* (1998), which garnered Anderson both a Best Director Independent Spirit Award and a New Generation Award from the Los Angeles Film Critics Association.

Tod Lippy: When did you first come to New York?
Wes Anderson: Well, probably four years ago I started spending about half the year here. I'd wanted to live here since I was about fifteen or so. But only in the last year did I really move here permanently. We're working on a movie that's set here now, so part of the thing when we put together the movie was for me to come here and set up an office. And we arranged a travel thing, also, since Owen's living in LA and I'm living in New York, and we both go back and forth. But there's a lot of research stuff I wanted to do for the movie here, too.

What kind of research?
Well, the visual idea of the movie – the setting – is that it's a kind of imaginary New York. Conceptualizing it at this point is a little shaky, so this will sound kind of vague, but the ideas are very specific. Basically, I would say that we're using a historical New York, and combining things from a lot of different periods. Things that I'm just interested in about New York, kind of from a New York literary world. So it's set in the present, and it's set in New York, but we never say New York, and the street names are all changed, and there's a lot of anachronism – not in a way that should be very self-conscious, but in a way that creates a slightly different world.

Which is the same thing we did with the other movies. In *Rushmore,* the school itself is sort of a dream version of the school it was shot at, and when Max gets kicked out, he ends up at the public school which is kind of like a prison. It's the same thing with New York in this film – it's kind of exaggerated – you know, there'll be phone booths on the streets, the kind they don't have here any more. Things like that. Rotary phones. So I've been visiting lots of places.

Where have you been going?
The one thing I've been trying to see is a lot of the clubs that are around. I went to Racquet and Tennis, and the National Arts Club, where I think they shot a little bit of *Age of Innocence.* Also, I want to see the Century Club, which I haven't been to yet. The architecture here – it's the only place in America, except maybe for Philadelphia and Boston and a few other places, that has this kind of history behind the architecture. The places where I grew up, it doesn't exist like that. This is more like Europe.

What other kinds of research are you doing?
I guess it kind of depends on what happens in the script. There were certain places we wanted to visit, but I don't even know if some of the stuff is going to be in the script. We've gone to certain places thinking that they're going to be part

of it and then dropped them again. One thing is Forest Hills – but I don't really want to go into it too much. The script is so unwritten at this point.

This has been a fairly long writing process – I remember reading something well over a year ago about your having begun work on the screenplay.
I know. *Rushmore* came out about one year ago, and there was a lot of stuff to do through to the point when the movie came out. But I've definitely been working on the script for a solid year. Probably more intensely in the last couple of months.

Is Owen Wilson here now?
Owen was here until a few days ago – he was here for the last month. And I'm going to go out to LA for a short period of writing out there.

I've read that you do a lot of note-taking as you're walking around, observing things. Do you find that those notes actually lead to ideas which drive the script, or are they simply embellishment for a storyline you've already come up with?
The former. It comes from a collection of ideas and characters. I had a whole history for this family that we're writing about – we had all the characters, the setting, little episodes – but we had no story for a long time. It was really a backwards way to do it. But at a certain point, I'm just going with what I feel is automatic. And writing about this subject and this group of characters is what I keep wanting to put my energy into, even though it seems like it would sure be a lot easier if we just cooked up a plot or something. But apparently we don't work that way.

Isn't Salinger's Glass family an inspiration for the family in the script?
Yeah, I guess so. Really more than being an inspiration, it was an easy way to communicate to people something more or less similar to what we're doing. I don't know how much it resembles the Glass family, but there's stuff like that.

They're all genius types?
Yeah, a family of geniuses. But they're not geniuses in the same way as the Glass family was. They're geniuses where you would probably think some of them were not so smart.

The Glasses always seemed so sad.
Sad and superior. And Buddhist. We don't have that.

You talked about the literary angle. Are there particular things you're reading? I see a set of bound volumes of *The New Yorker* over there –
For some reason, I'm completely obsessed by *The New Yorker*. Ever since high school; I started reading it in the library there. So a ton of the things I've been reading lately are from *New Yorker* writers like Liebling, Wolcott Gibbs, Joseph Mitchell – people who, you know, wrote about New York. And then, also, playwrights from the same period, particularly Kaufman and Hart. I read this Moss Hart autobiography, called *Act One*, which is a great one. I also just started this

book about this theatrical producer named Jed Harris, which is interesting. I don't know how all this stuff is tying in.

Are you reading any plays?
Yeah, reading plays. I don't know how all of this stuff is feeding into it, but somehow it is, I think.

Any stuff from the Algonquin Round Table?
We screened some Robert Benchley shorts. A movie like *Twentieth Century* kind of ties in, and that's Ben Hecht. I don't know, it all overlaps, anyway – Harold Ross was part of that. So it's definitely all that period – but a long period, like forty years or something.

It also has to do with the seventies – especially visually. I don't know, it will all be distilled into something, hopefully.

Are you looking at other New York-based films? *Everyone Says I Love You* **sounds sort of vaguely up the alley of what you're doing . . .**
Well, we've done some screenings over at Disney, and the stuff we've screened is kind of tying into it. One thing in particular was this Lubitsch movie I'd never seen before, *Cluny Brown*, with Jennifer Jones – I think it's the last movie that he completed. There's something about Lubitsch that definitely ties in to all of this. And we screened *Murmur of the Heart*, the Louis Malle movie. There's another one by him I want to screen over there, too, that fits in to all of this, called *Le feu follet*. And then that ties in to Fitzgerald and other things. And then we screened *Hannah and Her Sisters*, which I love, and which has got something to do with this movie, as well.

I always thought of that as Woody Allen's take on the Glasses.
In a way, yeah. I have no idea how that movie makes any sense, really, because it's got so many different little threads which connect for a while and then don't connect for a while, and somehow it hangs together. Like, Woody Allen's story really has nothing else to do with the rest of the movie. I mean, they tied him in: he was married to Mia Farrow, he becomes involved with Wiest at the end. In the movie, it just works, but if you start to talk about it . . .

When you say you're 'screening' things, does that mean Disney locates and projects the prints for you?
Well, we took a cheaper office in order to be able to screen movies. This office, a sublet, costs less so that we can do these kinds of things.

Where are you living? I remember you saying at one point that you wanted to live in Nick Nolte's character's loft in *Life Lessons***.**
Right. I ultimately was unable go with a 10,000 square foot loft. I mean, he's got a whole building in that film. Somewhere along the line I switched from wanting to be in Tribeca, or whatever's the one that's beyond that, to wanting to be in,

like, the Dakota or something. Anyway, I'm living on the Upper East Side, which I didn't plan to move to. But I knew a guy whose brother had moved out of a place across the street from him, and it was a great apartment for me. I guess that's the way people get places in New York.

Do you and Owen Wilson always write together?
We try to figure things out together, and then sometimes we write scenes on our own that we show to each other. And then, sometimes, we kind of make up the scene while we're together. We don't necessarily put it on paper together, but we'll 'talk' the scene together. Sometimes we'll just have this conversation. But really, it's never with a plan.

Do you find that one of you is stronger, say, at dialogue?
It's probably pretty meshed in together. It all kind of overlaps. It could just as easily be that one of us writes a scene, gives it to the other one and he says, 'Oh, that's good.'

How many drafts do you tend to write?
Well, we don't really work normally in drafts. We focus on a part of the movie for a period of time, reworking it. There's a million versions of twelve pages, and then that's kind of set aside for a while and we go with another segment. So there aren't really finished drafts.

When do you show something to the studio? Do you have a deadline with Disney for this next script?
I don't know what the deadline is. We're probably pretty close to it, though, I would think. We're not tied into a release date or anything, and I don't think the shareholders are counting on the returns on this project. Hopefully we'll finish it soon.

Do you write with actors, or at least specific individuals, in mind?
Quite a lot. I just like to get a cast, mentally, because it makes me feel closer to making the movie. But then there are some parts for which you have absolutely no idea. There was a kid for Max I always thought of, but he was much, much older than the character.

You said you imagined him being a very young Mick Jagger.
Yeah, that was what we really thought of. Unavailable, in this instance.

Can you talk about having Jim Brooks as a mentor during your rewrites of the *Bottle Rocket* script?
With Jim Brooks, we went through what seemed at the time to be a year of work, which in fact when I look back on it was only three or four months. But three or four months of really intense scrutiny, which we weren't prepared for, and which forced us to learn how to make a screenplay. We were really overconfident about the material – we were set in our ways after having written one screenplay. Sometimes I really don't understand how Jim saw that we could make a movie out of

it. The first thing he heard was a *five-hour* reading. For a caper-comedy. That's something that probably shouldn't be so epic.

But he was a combination of patient and properly aggressive to get us to figure stuff out. Especially with me. And now, when we're writing, that's what we think of, this stuff we learned from Jim. He'll often say, 'Well, the way I learned it was like this' – I mean, he probably invented the way he says he learned it – but that's kind of the thing we do now, we often think of the kind of 'rules' that we learned from Jim. How to make the story work, and what you need to do as far as the audience is concerned.

Do you think of an audience when you write?
Well, maybe not so much. But at a certain point, you think of communicating. You know, making something clear, and engaging somebody about certain things. Our whole approach to that stuff came from working with Jim.

Do you still go to him for advice, send him pages, that kind of thing?
Well, with *Rushmore*, once we had our script he was the first person we showed it to, and then he gave us some notes. We actually added a scene based on our conversation with him.

Which scene?
Well, it's a scene where Max has a big confrontation with Miss Cross. It came out of something he felt we needed. And then he was the first person I showed the finished movie to. He told me to work on pace, which I did. I took out several minutes. As long as he's available to us, he's our best first audience. I mean, you can show it to a friend who's kind of tuned into everything you're doing in the movie, and they may or may not know how to critique it – it's hard to be the first person watching something. Jim *knows* how to be the first person watching something, because he's looked at so many things in progress. His experience with that is broad, because of all that he's produced, as well as directed and written.

I noticed when I was reading the *Rushmore* script recently that there were a few scenes there that didn't end up in the film. It was mostly expository stuff –
Yeah. What did we cut? The scene with Miss Cross and Mrs Guggenheim?

Yeah, exactly, where they discuss how each of them finds Max intriguing, and we get some backstory about Miss Cross's late husband.
That scene we cut on the day we were going to shoot it. I was never sure whether we needed it or not, and assumed we'd probably end up cutting it. The day we were shooting it I basically got obsessed with a certain part of a shot – which I ended up not even using in the movie – so I dropped the scene.

One of the great strengths of the movie is that you don't need a lot of explanation; you're compelled from very early on just to accept its logic.
Whatever explanation you give is probably not going to be sufficient, really. So

you've got to just get on with it. But I think most of the other stuff we cut was pretty minor. There's one little thing of Bill Murray talking to his wife on the telephone, and one thing of Max taking his books out of a locker after he's been kicked out. He's throwing them in the trash when Bill Murray appears. Those were the only other scenes we cut, and two of them were non-dialogue scenes. That locker scene we cut because it made for a more dramatic transition from his getting screamed at by the headmaster to a curtain that says, 'October', and he's suddenly in the public school.

Other than that stuff, it's mostly just bits of dialogue that are pulled, basically to make it faster.

There's some significant dialogue cut from the kite-flying scene —
'The child's become the father of the man.' Right, that's gone. Couldn't get it right, in a way. I'm not sure I knew how he needed to say it, and it somehow had to be exactly perfect. Also, it's a long scene, and a lot of that stuff you've just got to get through so you can save the scene. But with *Bottle Rocket* there was tons of material that we cut.

If the first draft engendered a five-hour reading, I'm almost afraid to ask how long your first assembly was.
Not long. The first cut was probably an hour and forty-five minutes. Maybe 100 minutes. The movie that we released was just under ninety. But we also added a whole new opening scene, so the actual thing we had was probably cut down to eighty-five minutes or something. The script was not a long script. On the set of that movie, I was sort of thinking of myself as a Cassavetes-style director. So even though we had our scenes and stuff, I would never let the scenes stop. We would always add more stuff and extend it at the end.

All improvised?
Some of it. Also, the thing is, we rehearsed that movie for two years. So when we rehearsed it we would work out lots of business and things that became part of the scenes. Also, it had lots of scenes that were pretty repetitive – I mean, every possible variation on a certain scene was done, because there aren't that many events happening but there's lots of stuff among the characters. Also, the structure of the movie is kind of peculiar – it reaches a certain point and then goes into something completely different, and then reaches another point and goes somewhere else. So it was looser, I guess.

How much rehearsal did you do for *Rushmore*?
Well, I rehearsed with Jason Schwartzman, because I had him. But not a ton with other people. Seymour Cassel came to visit us, and we spent a couple of days rehearsing with him, and Brian Cox came to visit and we did a couple of days with him. We had little sessions with different people, very informal. Then we would sometimes rehearse at our hotel, things like that.

I feel, though, that you don't need a lot of rehearsal for some of the stuff. When you're doing a play, you want to rehearse a lot because you need to get it set, and then duplicate that over and over. With a movie, you work on it a little bit, then all you have to do is get it right once, and then that's it. Also, with a movie, when you're close on someone's face, you're obviously looking to capture a different kind of moment from what you get on stage. A kind of documentary accident, whatever it is.

Do you figure out your shot lists well in advance of shooting?
With *Bottle Rocket*, some stuff was worked out way in advance, like the robbery where they're in their yellow jumpsuits, or the one where they rob the bookstore – certain scenes where there was this strong idea, visually, with lots of staging and all that stuff. And I always felt like those were the scenes which worked the best; the stuff I didn't really have a great plan for was where I felt like I didn't do as well as I could have. So with *Rushmore*, I just tried to make sure, if I didn't have an idea that I'd spontaneously gotten for a scene, to spend time and figure out some approach to the scene where the staging and the shots were going to add something to it, and help the actors to play it and put some extra spark into it.

I would think that would be particularly important when you're shooting in widescreen.
Yeah. We wanted to do *Bottle Rocket* in widescreen, too. It's great just for photographing actors, I think, because you can have three guys in the frame in close-up and you don't have to cut between them to see the moments that happen on each person's face. You're there for it, and the other guy's there, too. I really prefer that.

Do you do a lot of takes?
I guess I would have to say yes. The thing is, thirty takes of a master with moves and several pages of dialogue is a lot; that's a big deal, and the better part of a day, and I've done that, and I don't enjoy it. I feel that if you've done a certain number and it's not happening, then it's probably not going to happen.

But, sometimes fifteen or something is good, and it's what it takes. Maybe twelve; somewhere in there. The best is where you do four or five takes, and you have a range of choices from that. It's different if it's a scene where cutting is possible, like the scene where Bill Murray has gone to see Miss Cross and he's standing on her step. It's a shot of him and then a shot of her, going back and forth. A scene like that, I feel like I want to have quite a bit of stuff, because we'll use stuff from eight different takes since they'll be different moments, especially with someone like Bill Murray – you never know what he's going to surprise you with. If you're going to take the time in the editing room, and study the material looking for little moments, you know, then you want to have a variety.

But on the other hand, a lot of stuff in the movie are scenes which are going to play in the master, in which case you do the twelve or fourteen takes and get it perfect, because once you've got it, that's it. I know I got very obsessed with time

– the script supervisor would give me little readings on it. I wanted to get all the lines, all the material in there, because I knew when we were cutting I was going to be very aggressive about it, and if it wasn't happening at the right pace, we'd have to cut off that whole part of the scene and possibly lose something that might have been good in the movie.

You didn't go to film school, did you?
I almost went to film school, but I didn't. It would have set me back two years, I think, if I'd gone. But I think I would've liked it, too. Probably quite a bit.

Your use of the frame really rewards careful viewers – like the scene in *Rushmore* where Max orders the dynamite, and in the foreground you see the wooden box with just 'DY–' on it.
Well, it's really just getting the right tone for it. Or the right little flavour. With that, I just didn't want to read the whole word 'dynamite' – I thought it was too much of a cartoon. This way, it's something that you kind of pick up on the edge. I mean, it's right *there*, but at least it's obscured. By the way, that's my editor, the guy who's selling him dynamite.

You know, there's a kind of simplicity to the shots in a way. It will sound ridiculous, but with this movie, I tried harder. I've said this to people before, and they tell me it sounds crazy. But with *Bottle Rocket*, you know, you're in the middle of the shoot, you get really tired, and you've really got to finish some stuff, and the movie suffers for it. Not often, but a few things. With *Rushmore*, I never permitted myself to do that. There's one chance for everything.

Also, I draw the shots. A thing like that, we've kind of constructed a setting – you know, half the shot is inside, half of it outside, and here's where the box of dynamite goes. And if you know what you want, then everything can be built for it. This might sound like overkill as a description of a shot of a kid buying a box of dynamite, but maybe it says something about the whole approach of the movie. How 'undocumentary' it is in some ways.

You also show a lot of restraint, particularly where it involves the withholding of information until the last possible – and most rewarding – moment. Like the scene in the library, where we start with a shot of Miss Cross reading, and Max's hand suddenly comes into frame with the lemonade.
I like that thing of withholding something in a narrative way, which is kind of almost a theatrical device, when you reveal something after the fact through dialogue. Like in *Bottle Rocket*, the way you learn that he actually robbed his own house is over the course of several scenes. You sort of puzzle out what's happening, and then you understand. And I'm not sure you fully understand the movie until that point. Especially in the short that we made. At that point you realize that these guys are not serious criminals.

Withholding is good, then.

Withholding is good. Isn't that a Hemingway thing? Or is it omitting? 'As long as you know what you're omitting.'

As far as directing actors, do you prefer to give direction privately to each person?
I usually just talk to one person at a time. I mean, there's some stuff, when you stage it and everything, you're all together. But when it comes to adjusting things, the thing I'm more comfortable with is having it be very private. I don't even really like to have people around when we're rehearsing; I don't like to have anybody watch us as we figure it out; I prefer to wait until it's all done, and we can show them, like, a rehearsed scene from a play. But that's not really the way people are accustomed to being on a movie set. I don't know if crews love it; I think they like to be there for that stuff. Maybe that's something that will change over time; maybe I won't feel so protective or uptight about that stuff after doing a couple of movies.

But I think most actors prefer it. Although some don't care. Like Bill Murray; he has fun with the crew. But at the same time, when you're figuring it out, I think he'd just as soon it was quiet.

You got a wonderfully restrained, nuanced performance from him – something you don't always see in other films of his. Did that involve any wrangling on your part?
No, it wasn't wrangling. I think a lot of the movies he does, he knows that's what he's there for; that's what they're paying him to do. With this, he just believed in the script, and believed in what we were doing, and there wasn't really a struggle to find what kind of performance he was going to do, because he knew what kind of performance it ought to be.

I'm struck by the agelessness of your characters – the sense of 'equality' between the older and younger characters in your films. For instance, Grace in *Bottle Rocket*, who, while sitting in her school's playground, gives very adult advice, in very adult language, to her older brother. And then obviously the relationship between Max and Blume, and even Max and Dirk, in *Rushmore.*
The Grace thing is probably not so hard to spot as being a little bit of a Phoebe Caulfield thing. In that case, the borrowing probably verges on stealing. But I don't really know where that theme comes from. I don't know why we do that. For some reason, it seems to appeal to us. Like with Max and Blume – them being equal, and Max being slightly the dominant one in some ways – was one of the ideas behind that whole relationship in the movie.

You really puncture that bubble for a moment in *Rushmore*, though, when Miss Cross, out of exasperation with Max, finally 'pulls rank' on him with her line about him 'never having fucked before'.
Right.

***Rushmore* is a 'high-school movie' in the same way *Election* was a high-school**

movie – in other words, not really for the broad population of high-schoolers. Right. Both of those movies might fall into the category where they can't find a 'demographic' for the movie: it doesn't exist, because it's a personality type rather than an age group or anything else. There's no way for the marketing people to break it down, except that if they go to a certain bookstore, or comic-book place or something, they might find a bunch of people who would respond to it. So I don't know. There are high-school kids who do get into that stuff, but it's a little sliver of the high school. So I guess it makes a problem for whoever's going to release the movie, because they've got to find the audience. There's not something preset.

But, you know, with the Coen Brothers, they can say, 'Well, we'll just sell it to the people who like the Coen Brothers,' because it's kind of like a brand name at this point. If we can ever get to that, we'll be in pretty good shape. But then the Coen Brothers are not going to make a $100-million-dollar movie. But we've never even broken twenty.

Do you get impatient with people who don't 'get it'?
No, no, no. I don't feel surprised. Sometimes when we're writing the thing I think, 'God, what are people going to make of *this*.' The only thing that bugs me is when people think something is really stupid, or not funny – because there's no way to defend it. I remember this review of *Bottle Rocket*, where the writer said, 'In the movie, their getaway driver is named Bob Mapplethorpe. *Ha. Ha*.' I mean, what are you gonna say to that? '*We* thought it was kinda funny . . .' I certainly couldn't explain what was funny about it – probably nothing.

Of the two films you've made, do you think one is better than the other?
I don't really know. I feel like *Rushmore* is more 'finished' for me. It's more carefully made, and the film-making – whatever that is – is maybe better. But, you know, I don't want to sell the other one short. There's definitely parts of that where I feel like I wouldn't have done it any differently from the way I did it – most of the movie I feel that way about. There's just stuff that, if we'd made a movie before, we would have solved certain problems before we were shooting. In *Rushmore*, we had a movie that could work from what we shot; we didn't have to go reshoot things, or rewrite things after we wrote them. Or spend a year in the cutting room. I think we cut *Rushmore* in two months or so. Also, some of the visual ideas of *Rushmore* are more complicated, maybe a little more ambitious. You know, he's putting on these plays, and certain things like that. *Rushmore* is personal to me in a way, from stuff growing up, but *Bottle Rocket* is personal because it's about the stuff that we were doing right then, six months before we were shooting the movie. And it ties a lot into my whole friendship with Owen; that has a lot to do with what went into the movie, and making the movie. Also, getting further away from having just finished *Rushmore*, it's not like there's one I'm still 'with'. I'm with something else now.

When *Rushmore* was released, were you surprised at the critical response?
I think so. I don't know, was it that great? It was pretty good, I guess. I still don't really know what it's like to have a movie that's a big hit. That's probably a lot better.

Sometimes, though, if it's a popular success, it seems that less attention is paid to the film-maker, and more to the stars.
Maybe so.

When the critics like it, they tend to focus more on the 'auteur'.
I'm being a little glib about it, anyway. Compared to what happened with *Bottle Rocket*, we were ecstatic about the way the movie was received. *Bottle Rocket* got good reviews, but everything was low-key. Everything was quiet. Nobody had heard of the movie, because Columbia never got into it. To this day, they don't consult with me about anything to do with the movie; I don't think they're even aware of it. I really want to do a Criterion Collection version of it, because there's tons of material that's related to it that might be of some interest. I guess the DVD of it is fine. Also, I really don't like the art that went with any of the releases of the movie.

Do you read reviews?
I read everything. I wrote this thing about screening *Rushmore* for Pauline Kael that was in the *New York Times* –

I was going to ask you about that.
What happened was, I went to visit her, I really liked her, and thought she was a real character. I respected her very much, and, you know, I sent her the piece that I wrote before it was published, and she made a couple of changes to it. And then, after the piece was published, I got attacked by some people.

David Edelstein wrote a letter to the *Times* saying you were 'making sport of her infirmities'.
Which I feel is idiotic. I mean, the piece begins with her forgetting who Bill Murray is – not a terrible crime – but then I explain in the piece that she's on medication which can cause a memory lapse. But the story I was trying to tell was what my experience was in approaching her, which was funny, because I was convinced that telling her Bill Murray was in it was the one piece of information that was going to get her into it. And then she had no idea who he was. I mean, it's well known that she has Parkinson's; I wasn't the one who 'broke the story' on that. And also, she's a character; she's not someone who's this sweet, gentle old lady. She's someone who's very tough, quite prickly. I don't feel it's wrong to write about her in a way that shows some of the edges, because otherwise, what's the point of writing about it? As far as Edelstein and David Denby's reaction to the piece, I don't know. I mean, she suggested I show the movie to Edelstein, whom I'd never heard of. The next thing, he's attacking me. What were your thoughts about the piece?

Well, I'll tell you, I came across Edelstein's response first, which frankly biased

me against it. But when I finally read the piece, I thought it was very funny, and that you'd covered your bases, as it were. You must have gotten your fill of the media when you were doing press for *Rushmore*.

Oh, God, yeah.

As I read through some of the articles, I noticed that you'd answer the same question differently: For instance, to the old saw about whether or not the character of Max was autobiographical, you answered in the San Francisco *Chronicle* that 'Max is like me, except that he's not shy', but in *Newsday*, a month or so later, you said, 'He's not me'. Was this a case of having a little fun with the whole process?

No, not having fun. I'm sure I was contradicting myself, but I didn't ever want to make it too much of an autobiographical thing. I mean, there's some stuff that's obviously going to be, but it's really a made-up character, something Owen and I invented. And then, I guess, depending on my mood, I either tried to qualify it or to distance myself from it in different ways. But you know, Schwartzman and I went on this bus – we went all over the country for a promotional tour on this insane bus. We just went crazy. It's like, my whole focus became how to make sure we were in the best possible hotel as quickly as possible. How many of the interviews can we not do, or get through, before we can go to the hotel? It was just insane.

How did the whole bus tour thing come about?

I don't like to fly, so we ended up on the bus, which, in itself, was good; they got us this great one. It's just that it was incredibly boring out there. But once we got to DC, we switched to good hotels from then on, and it was OK, basically.

Do you feel like part of a film-making community here in New York?

I didn't know any movie directors or anything until quite recently. Now there are several people in New York – Peter Bogdanovich, Noah Baumbach, who's a really great guy. This director James Gray, who did *Little Odessa*, comes here a lot. And I've met other people, like David Russell and Vincent Gallo. So yeah, in a way, kind of, I guess.

Are you out a lot? Premières and that sort of thing?

No, but I have these screenings, and a lot of those guys come to those. I don't like to go to premières; it's a weird way to watch a movie. Big crowds and things. Sometimes it's fun, but it's not really the greatest to me.

Are you going to shoot the next movie here?

I would like to. The only creative reason – meaning not having to do with the money – not to would be if we decided to build a lot of the movie, which is a possibility. One idea I have that could be a way to go with it is that it's snowing throughout the entire movie, in which case it would probably be best to just build it. Most of the snowing would be outside windows and stuff, but still, it probably has to be built. To snow for the entire movie is a tall order, a big hassle.

You once said, 'It really doesn't matter where you make your movies, it's who you know in Los Angeles.'

I said that? It sounds like a *Speed the Plow* line or something. Not a memorable one, though. I don't know exactly what I meant by that – I mean, I know what I meant by 'who you know in Los Angeles'. But that's just about getting money for movies.

Are you planning on staying here?

Yeah, this is the city where I want to live, so I don't have any plans to leave. I've got to go to LA sometimes because Owen prefers to be there – he comes here to write with me, and I've gotta go there to write with him – but this is where I like to live. I've got all my stuff here.

Jonas Mekas

Jonas Mekas, director and co-founder of Anthology Film Archives, is a film-maker, poet, critic and long-time proponent of avant-garde film. He founded the influential journal *Film Culture* in 1955, and wrote the 'Movie Journal' column in *The Village Voice* from 1958 to 1976. Mekas was also instrumental in the creation of the New American Cinema Group, the Film-makers Coop, and the Film-makers Cinémathèque in the fifties and sixties. He is the author of a number of books of poetry and prose; his films include *Guns of the Trees*, *Scenes from the Life of Andy Warhol*, *Lost Lost Lost . . .* and *The Brig*, which won first prize in the documentary section of the 1964 Venice Film Festival.

Tod Lippy: You arrived here from Europe in 1949. Was there much of a film scene at that point?

Jonas Mekas: Half a century ago, New York, amazingly, was pretty busy film-wise. People today think that everything began in the sixties, but that's not really true. The very first evening I arrived here I went to the New York Film Society, run by Rudolf Arnheim and somebody else – they had monthly screenings somewhere in the West Twenties – and I saw a double bill of *The Cabinet of Dr Caligari* and Epstein's *Fall of the House of Usher.*

As I began to get to know New York better, I discovered there were many places to see films. Of course there was the Museum of Modern Art, which was basically a university of cinema, where you could see all the old silent films, the European avant-garde from the twenties and thirties. And if you were more avant-garde-oriented, Amos Vogel's Cinema 16 was the place to go. They were screening films at the Needle Trades Center on 24th Street between 7th and 8th, and on Sunday mornings at 11.00 at the Paris Theater on 58th. That was our church. If you were of the left persuasion, a Trotskyite, you went to the Club Cinema on 6th Avenue, near 10th Street, and you could see *Kameradschaft*, or documentaries displaying solidarity, etc., and meet other people of the same persuasion after the film. There was music, dancing, even some cookies . . . [*Laughs.*]

Then there was somebody by the name of Peter Hollander, who ran a little distribution company for independently made films – 'experimental' they called them in those days – which was called Kinesis. He's now in Boston, working in television. He was across 47th from, you know, 'Where Wise Men Fish' —

Gotham Book Mart?

Right. He was on the second floor. Emile de Antonio also had his first office there, and so did Lewis Jacobs. Then, if you wanted to see silent films of all different formats – not just 35mm or 16mm, but things like 19mm, which they were using at the beginning of the century – you went to the Theodore Huff Society, run by Bill Everson, Herman Weinberg and Bill Kenly, who was also a manager/programmer of 5th Avenue Cinema, where I first saw *Blood of a Poet*. He premièred Hans Richter's *8x8* there in 1956. Anyway, all the old-timers were at the Theodore Huff Society, as well as some younger people – Bill Everson was still very young, he had just come from London. That was on Tuesday nights, usually.

So it was already very busy, as you can see. And I could probably think of others. For instance, Gideon Bachmann started his Film Study Group around that time. I met him there and began helping him with programming, writing notes. We showed things there like von Sternberg's *Salvation Hunters*, with Sternberg present.

In the Spring of '53 I started my own screenings series at Gallery East, which was right around the corner on Avenue A and First Street – I did not move very far, as you can see. And that fall, my brother Adolfas, George Capsis and I started Film Forum, and that continued for a couple of years. And if you go to 1954, Richard Leacock, Sidney Meyers, Lionel Rogosin and Shirley Clarke were all starting to buzz around. Some of them were still making documentary shorts, but others were making their first features.

Maya Deren was quite active in this period, too, right?
Maya Deren's most productive period was already over, between '43 and '46. By 1950, she already had her classic works completed. But, she got very involved in other ways. In 1953, film-makers in New York decided to organize themselves, create their own association. Meetings took place once a month or so among twenty or so film-makers, where we'd discuss how to organize ourselves. We'd also show at least one film each time. After six or seven meetings – and a lot of arguing – an organization was created, called the Film Artists Society. It was created and basically ended at the same time. In the last meeting, Maya Deren showed one of her films, and Lewis Jacobs jumped on it, tore it to pieces. She was so angry, she stormed out. And it's strange, because Jacobs had been one of the first to write about her seriously in a very important catalogue edited by Frank Stauffacher and Hans Richter for the San Francisco Art Institute. But then he attacked her.

You had an antagonistic moment with her early on as well, didn't you? You'd written a piece criticizing the whole experimental movement in a 1955 issue of your magazine *Film Culture* —
Yes, yes. I heard from her lawyer immediately after it came out.

What was the piece about?
It was in *Film Culture #3*. I need to say that I was at this point still pretty naïve; I'd arrived from post-war Europe and had seen nothing before I got here because you really couldn't see avant-garde cinema in Europe at that time. So I did this survey in 1955, where one of the points I made was that American avant-garde cinema was totally pervaded by homosexuality. [*Laughs.*] I didn't realize I'd touched such a sensitive spot. Later, you know, when I began seeing more, understanding who was doing what, meeting people, of course it all became very, very normal to me. But in that essay I presented it as something negative, instead of just making an observation, or presenting it as a fact, which it was.

I recall you likening this moment to 'St Augustine before his conversion'.

Yes, I had my conversion and then recanted, so to speak. But for a couple of years after that, Maya and I definitely avoided each other – you know, we'd move to opposite sides of the street when we saw each other. [*Laughs*.] But then, my brother and I had a jeep, and very often we'd help her move her equipment around, and help her set up, and eventually we ended up being very good friends.

There's a very funny sequence in your film *Lost Lost Lost*, which starts with a title card reading 'Raising Money for *Film Culture*', and then cuts to an image of you with arms outstretched, a hat in each hand. How did you finance the magazine? People have continually remarked upon your ability to miraculously come up with funds . . .
Parker Tyler once told me that some people thought that because Adolfas and I came from Eastern Europe, we must have been paid by the Soviets to spy here, and that's where our money came from . . . Anaïs Nin thought so, too.

Andrew Sarris said there were rumours that you were actually funded by the CIA —
Oh. [*Laughs*.] Very few people realized that I had a series of full-time jobs, working steadily since a week after I came to New York. I started working in factories, places like that. Between 1952 and 1959, when I decided to become really independent, I worked at Graphic Studios on 22nd Street, where we did the preparation for the Spanish-language version of *Life* magazine. So I was quite well paid. But for the first two years I was a delivery boy, so I found out everything about the city. We also did some work for *Newsweek*. I knew all the girls there, I mean, all the secretaries. That's one good thing about being a delivery boy.

Did that give you the knowledge necessary to produce a magazine?
That experience I already had. When I was eighteen, I was the editor of a weekly provincial newspaper in Lithuania, and then a year later I was editing a weekly literary newspaper. So I had a lot of experience already. But my work at Graphic Studios gave me money, which all went into *Film Culture*, and filming, and other projects.

What inspired you to start the magazine?
Well, there was nothing much in the way of film publications. At that time, the only serious one was *Sight and Sound* – we'd get all the back issues at Gotham Book Mart. There was also *Sequence*, also from England. And of course there was *Cahiers du cinema*, and occasionally, the University of Southern California would put out *The Hollywood Quarterly*. But in New York, there was only *Films in Review*, which has improved over the years a little bit, but at that time their interest was only in the most conventional commercial cinema.

When did you recruit Andrew Sarris?
Very soon – the second issue, I think. His first review was of *The Country Girl*, which he didn't like. Roger Tilton, who made *Jazz Dance*, a film with Richard Leacock, was teaching at Columbia, in the School of Journalism, I think, and he

said to me after he'd seen the first issue of the magazine, 'Oh, you must need more writers. I know two crazy students. One, Eugene Archer, just demolished *Battleship Potemkin*, and the other, Andrew Sarris, just demolished *Cabinet of Dr Caligari*.' So I met them and I liked them both, and immediately engaged them.

What was the circulation of the magazine?
At that point I don't think we published more than 1,000 copies. Our highest circulation, probably in 1966, was 4,000. We got a distributor in New Jersey, Bernhard DeBoer, who helped small magazines like ours, and he planted it all around – in university bookshops across the country, that kind of thing. My brother was the businessman of the magazine.

And of course in 1959, the New American Cinema group began their meetings, and we became the voice for them.

How did 'The Group' come about?
It was in the air; it came from thin air, really. All I know is that Lewis Allen and I called the first meeting. I remember clearly how the film-makers cooperated. Lew was working for the Whitehead Theater, and he had an office in midtown, so that's where we had our first meeting. It was Shirley Clarke, Lionel Rogosin, Emile de Antonio, Dan Talbot, and somehow that meeting originated among us.

Bogdanovich was also involved, wasn't he?
Yes, Bogdanovich, also. Actually, that reminds me of another one of our 'universities' in this period, which was of course 42nd Street. In the fifties, 42nd Street from one end to the other was full of movie houses. I mean, there were something like twenty theatres. You could watch movies all night, see five or six different Westerns, or anything – if you didn't like one you'd go into another. And that's where Andrew Sarris, Peter Bogdanovich and I spent a lot of our time. There was a Horn and Hardart cafeteria on 42nd between Seventh and Eighth, and you could sit and have coffee and eat cheap doughnuts. That's where Peter told me about his first script, which became *Targets*. His original idea was a film about a movie buff who just went to see movies, and was always fantasizing – there was very little plot there.

Wasn't he also a camera operator on your film *Guns of the Trees*?
No, I wanted him for my lead actor. I actually have screen tests of him; I still have the footage somewhere. I don't remember why I decided against using him.

Right around the time of the founding of the group, you wrote a rather infamous attack on Cassavetes' second version of *Shadows* in your 'Movie Journal' column for *The Village Voice*. What motivated that?
It's difficult for people who have not seen the first version to understand my reaction to the second version. In truth, even in its second version, *Shadows* is still quite a remarkable film. But I can see it only with the memory of the first one. What he did with the second version is due in large part to Niko Papatakis, who

saw the first version and got the idea that if John could just make it a little less 'amateurish', edit out some scenes to 'shape' it more, he would be able to get a distributor. He managed to persuade Cassavetes to do that, though I think Cassavetes accepted that, because from his other work that followed you can see that was more or less what he wanted, anyway.

But the first version was much more open. It was like jazz. The second version introduced completely new scripted scenes, like the one at the Museum of Modern Art, and morality sort of creeps into it. I was so disappointed, because the first version was more free, more contemporary as an experience, and it had so much more poetry.

Cassavetes dismissed it by saying he'd fallen too much in love with his Arriflex. After that, we didn't talk for about ten years. The last time I saw I him, I asked him where the footage for the first one was, and he told me he had sent all the materials, the work print, to some film school for the students to fool around with. I contacted the university, but they had nothing left by then.

While you were in the midst of editing *Film Culture*, writing your 'Movie Journal' column for *The Village Voice*, and organizing the New American Cinema Group, you were also programming at the Charles Theater, right?
Yeah. We showed a lot of *auteur* kind of Hollywood films, like later Fritz Lang and Edgar Ulmer. Also some more rare Hollywood films, like those of Douglas Sirk. And we opened Ron Rice's *The Flower Thief*, Stan Brakhage's *Anticipation of the Night* —

Which Amos Vogel had rejected for Cinema 16 distribution.
Right. That led to the founding of the Film-maker's Cooperative, in '62.

The Coop was founded by you and who else?
Mostly with my brother, Adolfas. I mean, let's face it, a good number of us discussed the need for it already in 1960, '61. We felt there should be another distribution venue besides Cinema 16 and Kinesis. Brandon also distributed some avant-garde films, by Harrington and Markopoulos, for example. And there was Radim, run by Rosalind Kossof – she distributed Tim Davis and Ellen Bute. But all these distributors were very choosy, and limited, and some film-makers were very unhappy that they weren't taken by any of them. And why? Because the content was changing, improvisational styles were coming in, and neither Brandon nor Amos Vogel, nor any of the existing distributors, felt that this was 'cinema'. So a point came where we decided – myself and my brother took the initiative – to do something about it. We called a meeting specifically to establish our own distribution centre. In a way that came out of the New American Cinema group. Several people – my brother, myself and Emile de Antonio – were appointed to investigate distribution possibilities. There was another committee to explore production possibilities, and one to explore censorship. As a result of our investigation, we suggested at a meeting of the Group that the only solution was to do it ourselves.

So on January 7th of 1962, we called a meeting at my loft at 414 Park Avenue South, and about twenty film-makers attended. Amos Vogel was there, too, and tried to persuade us not to form our own distribution centre because it would 'destroy the avant-garde'. 'There's no place for two distributors,' etc., etc. [*Laughs.*] But the decision was unanimous. I mean, at this meeting he was facing a dozen film-makers whose films he had refused. But even with ones – like Brakhage and Markopoulos – he did distribute, he only handled some of their films.

So that is more or less what happened. Film-makers' Cooperative was created. My loft became the Coop office for the next three years. I was sort of pushed into the corner in my own place. We published a catalogue, and it grew very fast.

And there was absolutely no exclusion?
No. None at all. We established three or four basic principles: no films would be rejected. The film was your membership card to the Coop. In the catalogue, all of the films were listed alphabetically; none would be preferred. The Cooperative would be governed by film-makers themselves, and the actual administrative work would be done by a person who was hired by the film-makers. All decisions were made by the film-makers, and all income – except for the percentage needed to run the Coop, also decided by the film-makers – would go to the film-makers. So everything was by the film-makers and for the film-makers.

It seems like this policy of non-exclusion carried into the 'open screenings' you spearheaded —
Yeah. At the Charles Theater, in 1961, I began doing these open houses for film-makers – that's where it all started.

What was the atmosphere like at them?
They were quite well attended. We also started midnight music concerts. Sun Ra gave his first New York concerts at the Charles. Bob Downey – we screened his first films there. Stanley's Bar was around the corner, where everybody gathered before and after. It was a very active, exciting period.

Did you literally have people coming in off the streets with cans of film?
Yeah. There were actually several people who ended up in Hollywood who first showed their films at an open screening. Brian De Palma was screening there, and bragging about being the only good film-maker – 'Brakhage is nothing; he doesn't know how to make films.' He was very pompous.

But for the Charles Theater, a lot of credit has to go to two young men, Walter Longsford and Edwin Stein. Stein was a psychiatrist, and Longsford is still around, working in publicity, I think. They had rented the theatre as a commercial place for, like, two years, but it didn't do well in that neighbourhood. Now it's some kind of Adventist Church or something. Anyway, they were very open to all kinds of film. They had people like Jack Smith selling tickets, and the guy who later became one of the biggest people in that humour magazine, you know, 'Who, me?'

Mad magazine?
Yes. He used to write his stuff in the ticket booth; he was our ticket-seller. Forgot his name.

When did you first see Jack Smith's films?
Well, in 1961, on Avenue A and 9th Street – or was it 7th? – there was a movie theater that had recently closed, and one could climb up on the roof of it. That's where much of *Flaming Creatures* was shot. But we didn't see the footage until the next year, when Tony Conrad strung all the rolls together. And we screened it first one midnight at the Bleecker Street Theater, which Lionel Rogosin had opened, I think, in 1957. When we created Film-maker's Cooperative we used Bleecker Street for some of our midnight screenings. And that was where we screened *Flaming Creatures* for the first time.

That wasn't the screening at which you were arrested?
No, it was after that. The Bleecker's managers threw us out after that screening. I still have the letter; they told us they would lose their audience if we continued our series there. [*Laughs.*] So then we made a deal with the Gramercy Arts Theater on 27th Street, which became Film-maker's Showcase, an offshoot of the Coop. That's where we screened all of Andy's early works, like *Sleep*, *Kiss* and *Eat* – all the early ones opened there. Also Kenneth Anger's *Scorpio Rising*, and Markopoulos's *Twice a Man*.

Can you talk about the *Flaming Creatures* incident a little more? It seems like such a defining moment in experimental film history.
Well, in those years – 1961, 1962, 1963 – every film shown publicly had to be submitted to the State Education Department's Division of Motion Pictures, which, in reality, was a board of censorship. And if they didn't like something, you had to cut it out. We decided that we were not going to submit our films to them. This is right around the time Lenny Bruce was arrested – that kind of thing was happening everywhere. It was a very, very touchy period for a couple of years. And it was only because of Lenny Bruce and the *Flaming Creatures* case that everybody began talking and writing about it, and all of those restrictions gradually faded out over the next several years.

Which screening caused all of the problems?
It was at the Bridge Theater on St Mark's. The place was used mostly for theatrical performances, but occasionally some film screenings, or mixed-media events, took place. That particular evening we screened a Kuchar film, Andy Warhol's footage of Jack Smith filming *Normal Love*, and *Flaming Creatures*. It was raided by the police, and all three films were seized; we never got them back. Ken Jacobs, his girlfriend, Florence (now his wife), Jerry Sims and I were arrested.

And then you were arrested again several weeks later for showing Genet's *Un Chant d'amour*, right?

After the *Flaming Creatures* arrest, everybody said, 'Why would you let yourself be arrested for such a "bad" movie as *Flaming Creatures*?' So I thought to myself, 'OK, I'll permit myself to be arrested for something else that you might not be able to say is a bad movie.' I mean, at that time, *The Balcony* was playing – this was Genet we were talking about. So two weeks later, I made arrangements for a screening of *Un Chant d'amour* at the Writer's Stage on 4th Street. That time I had packed a sandwich in my pockets, because I knew I was going to be arrested. A chicken sandwich. And of course I was arrested, and of course at the trial the prosecuting attorney was also smart: He dismissed the second case – the Genet – because he realized he had a much better case with *Flaming Creatures*. Anyway, I ended up with a two-month suspended sentence.

But I had my chicken sandwich in my pocket. They took me to the Tombs, and there was a Black guy in the next cell, and I started eating, and he looked hungry so I gave him half of the chicken. Later – like two years later – I was walking somewhere and this guy ran into me, remembered me. 'You gave me a chicken sandwich in the jail!'

How did you meet Andy Warhol?
Well, as I said, my loft became the Film-maker's Cooperative office for a couple of years. It was a very, very busy place. Film-makers would come by to screen what they'd shot the day before, that kind of thing. It became so talked about that everybody was there. Salvador Dalí, Allen Ginsberg, Robert Frank – everybody. And most of the time I didn't even know who was there; they were just sitting on the floor and watching movies and laughing. And then one day, Naomi Levine, a film-maker and painter, said to me, 'Come to my birthday party. There'll be lots of interesting people there, like Andy.' I said, 'I don't know Andy.' And she said, 'You don't know Andy? But he's been sitting in your loft for months watching movies!' Then of course when I met him, I recognized him. So my loft was Andy's first movie university. Of course, he also saw Hollywood movies. Soon after I met him he shot his first film, *Sleep*, and a series of three-minute *Kisses* which he called 'leaders', or trailers. I showed them all at the Film-maker's Showcase.

I was looking again the other day at your film *Scenes from the Life of Andy Warhol*, and was struck by the sequence of close-ups of all the people around a table at a bar at one point in the film – Barbara Rubin, Ginsberg, Gerard Malanga, all the others. Everyone exuded this sense of entitlement – in all the best senses of the word – as if they were absolutely certain of their significance at that particular moment in time.
Well, there was energy in the air. We were just very, very busy, each one in our own area. We were obsessed, possessed. We didn't think we were in a particularly unique period. We couldn't step out of it and look at it from the side; that came later. But we were very busy, and there was a lot of intensity and energy, and that's it.

In the later sixties, when you began organizing Anthology Film Archives and

spearheaded the 'Essential Cinema' collection, you got a lot of criticism from film-makers for going against the non-exclusivity implicit in both the Coop and the open screenings...

In some of its principles, Anthology went against the Coop. We got a lot of flak. But, in a sense, there was no other way of doing it. Back in 1960, there had been only a dozen or so universities with film departments, but when in 1970 the AFI published their first guide to universities and colleges offering film courses, there were 1,200, with over 20,000 courses – in one decade, that's how much it grew. You can imagine, then, how students at all of these places were insisting that they see not only Hollywood films, but also the current avant-garde. There was a lot written about it at this point in the press. So P. Adams Sitney and I would get calls constantly: 'Who should we show?', 'What should we order?', 'We have money for two programmes; please prepare something for us.'

So we prepared once, we prepared twice, twelve times, thirty times, and finally we said, 'OK. That's enough.' It was a waste of time. It wasn't only that you were preparing the programme; you were writing the notes, everything. That was when the decision was made to review the whole field and to prepare a list which we could then send out, and say, 'Any film on this list has something unique and something special, and will indicate to you where the cinema is going.' So that is how the Essential Cinema collection came about – it grew out of a concrete need. And we decided we should include not only avant-garde, but general cinema that related to the concerns of the avant-garde – that's how Eisenstein, Cocteau, Vigo and a few others came to be included as well. And it would have continued to expand if our main sponsor, Jerome Hill, hadn't died in 1973. All funds were cut off, and the project froze after we had chosen about 330 or so films. We planned to continue to infinity, but that didn't happen. It remains a very sort of heroic, unfinished attempt.

That's where the most dissatisfaction came from. Many of the film-makers who didn't end up being included had actually been postponed for later sessions, but then the project ended, and those film-makers were left out in the cold.

Who was involved in making all of these decisions?
It started with P. Adams Sitney, Stan Brakhage, Ken Kelman, James Broughton and myself. Then after a year or so there was a clash between Brakhage and the rest of us, because he insisted that we all have veto power, which meant that we couldn't make any progress. After several meetings, we'd ended up with, like, ten titles, and films were being excluded for ridiculous reasons, like one bad cut. Curtis Harrington's film, *On the Edge*, was excluded for one cut. I mean, it was a bad cut, but the film is still a very fine film. *Flaming Creatures* was another one. So Brakhage left, and that's when Peter Kubelka came in.

Did you have a space at that point for Anthology?
Yes, that's why we went ahead. Again, it was Jerome Hill's doing. An army buddy

of his, Joseph Martinson, was chairman of the Public Theater, and they got the building the Public is still in, 425 Lafayette. There was one end on the ground floor that they had no money to do anything with, so Martinson asked Jerome, knowing he was a film-maker and was very familiar with the avant-garde, if he thought he could use the space for a cinema. Jerome contacted me, and we discussed it and said, 'Why not?' Jerome had inherited part of his parents' railroad fortune, and his foundation, Avon, put up the money.

At that time, Peter Kubelka was in town. He was in charge of the United Nations film division. He had dreams of a very special 'invisible cinema' theatre, which I'd known about for a long time, so we arranged for him to design the 'ideal theatre' – egg-shaped, all black, and where each viewer could see only the screen. Jerome put up the money and it was built.

I was already determined to devote more time to my own film-making, so I'd decided not to run Anthology. I invited P. Adams Sitney to be the director of it, and he returned from Europe to supervise the construction and preparation. We opened on the first of December, 1970. But the job of running Anthology and dealing with all the temperamental personalities involved soon proved to be too much for Sitney. He couldn't take it. He decided to just handle the library. He took care of all the paper archives – and he was there for many years. So I had no choice but to take over the directorship. I thought it will be only for a few years. But here I still am.

And then, a few weeks before we opened, Martinson dies. It was a rental situation, and it became immediately complicated with the Public. Although Joe Papp was very friendly, a very nice guy, he didn't care about cinema. And then in 1973, Jerome dies. The people in charge of Jerome's foundation thought the whole project was some kind of weird whim on Jerome's part. So their support sort of trickled down to nothing. We moved out to 80 Wooster Street to the premises of the Film-maker's Cinematheque, which I had purchased in 1967. It was the first SoHo cooperative; it was there, really, that SoHo started.

In the seventies, you became much more interested in archiving —
Not interested in it. Pushed into it, because of necessity. As soon as we opened Anthology, students would come and want to do research on the films, so we had no choice but to collect materials on all the films and film-makers. P. Adams went to Rome, London, Paris, spending days and days in bookshops picking out rare books on film. Some of the books we have in the library here now from the twenties and thirties are so rare we have to be careful who we let into the space. Even so, some of them have disappeared. And usually they've been stolen by scholars, not by students. They consider themselves 'authorities' on this and that, and 'if anybody should have it, it should be me'.

When did you get involved with the preservation of films?
Preservation began when we decided that if we voted a film in, then we had to get

the best possible print to show it. That involved a lot of searching. For instance, it took us two years to find an acceptable print of *Man of Aran*. We went to London, everywhere, and then we discovered that the negative was right here in New York. Then for other avant-garde films from the forties, you'd have to locate the artists' families, etc. National Endowment was just taking its own first steps, and Chloe Aaron in '71 mentioned to me that they were thinking of film preservation and suggested we ask for money. So that's how the film preservation programme began.

Have you collected mostly negatives?

Well, we have everything, positives and negatives. A lot of 16mm labs have been forced to close during the last twenty years, so we dragged a lot of material from them, mostly negatives. I don't know, I thought we had like 15,000 films, but now we're in the middle of indexing everything and counting, and it looks like we may have 20,000. Some of it is here, some in New Jersey. Maybe only one-third is indexed or catalogued. The rest we don't know what it is at all. We have no archivist. All work is done by volunteers, under my supervision. And I have no time, so the indexing is going very slowly.

And we've discovered among the materials we've dragged from the street – from dumpsters, practically – originals of Yvonne Rainer, Robert Breer, Joan Jonas, Robert Frank. The labs just threw them out, and the film-makers didn't know. The same thing happened with *Flaming Creatures*. For years, Anthology kept the originals. Then Jack Smith took them back, and took them to some lab. Then he forgot which lab. [*Laughs.*] Whichever lab it was, it went bankrupt, and they dumped all of their materials into some film stock house, and it just so happened that the film-maker Jerry Tartaglia was working there, cleaning stuff. He was working on one reel, and he started looking more closely at it – 'This looks familiar . . .' – and he realized it was the negative of *Flaming Creatures*, so he took it to Jack. For years Jack kept telling people that I had stolen the film, and had it hidden in my 'lobster' closet. [*Laughs.*]

When did you move to this building?

We opened to the public in 1989, but it took us practically ten years to fix it up – we'd bought it in 1979. As soon as we purchased the building from the city – it had been a courthouse before – and began the renovation, other people started to do the same. We were surrounded by ruins here when we bought it.

What are your facilities like?

We have two theatres, one seventy seats, one 200. Mostly the avant-garde goes into the seventy, because it attracts smaller audiences. We have video in both the theatres, so it's very open, and very flexible. A lot of variety.

One crucial element here is that, unlike, say, MoMA – which, due to their particular financial set-up, has to programme far ahead of time – we're very open. Since we don't have any money, and nobody's funding us in any more substantial way, we *can't* make plans. We only schedule two months ahead, so we can very easily accommodate anybody who's passing through town, for instance. You know, whether it's a particular film-maker or a national group from Algeria, or Turkey, who decide they'd like to have a little festival here. We can always accommodate them.

The way programming works is we always have the Essential Cinema repertory going, but then we also have one or two little festivals. For instance, next March and April there will be a Greek film festival, and there will also be a Cuban film festival. And there's something else. There are outside curators who come in, some for one-night or weekend shows, some who take one night a week for several months. New film-makers, documentary film-makers, various special-interest groups, and of course, the avant-garde. I know of no other such place where all the branches of cinema are represented. We try not to permit ourselves to be focused on any one thing.

What is your role these days? More supervisory?
I'm sort of like a conductor. I orchestrate, I coordinate. I have different curators, different helpers. I still supervise all the people who are involved in programming; it's still my responsibility.

You've talked about how much you've managed to do with little or no money —
Yeah. We still owe about $330,000 to the banks for the original loans when we renovated the building. That's $30,000 in interest alone every single year. You know, we could put that into programming, preservation. We get around $15,000 from National Endowment, but that's peanuts. [*Mekas takes a phone call; after he hangs up:*] You see, that's part of my hunting for money. I went to this place on Park Avenue for some occasion, and there were all these paintings on the walls, and stacked against the wall, and I said to the woman who owned it, 'Is there one here that you don't like?' [*Laughs.*] And she said, 'Yes, to tell you the truth, there is one I'd like to get rid of, because I can't show it to anybody.' She pulled out this George Grosz drawing from his erotic series, and gave it to me. I gave it to Sotheby's to sell, and they estimated it at $8,000. But at the last minute they decided they couldn't put it in the catalogue, because it would offend some of their buyers. Anyway, the woman I just talked to found a buyer who will pay $5,000.

Speaking of money, I was interested to hear a comment of yours about how you thought grants were actually damaging, rather than improving, experimental film.
Yes, the grant system has destroyed, or at least contributed to the destruction of, the American avant-garde. I used to meet Paul Sharits, for example, and ask him, 'What are you doing?' and he would tell me what he was working on: 'Oh, I'm making this film, and doing that . . .' And then, when the grants started flowing in, around 1970, I'd see him and ask the same question, and he'd say, 'Nothing. I didn't get any grants this year.' Film-making became dependent on money.

If you take the American avant-garde cinema at the point of 1966, when the grants first came in, the whole body of classic avant-garde of the fifties and sixties was already there, with no grants, no money, nothing. Kenneth Anger, Brakhage, whoever you want to name – it was all there. And then after '66, the field was flooded by all those who make films solely because they can get money. So it's very questionable whether it was a favourable development or not. The democratic distribution of grant moneys – so much to Blacks, so much to Whites, so much to Asians . . . I'm not so sure I believe in democracy in art. Unless we are talking about 'applied' film-making.

Many years ago, you made a comment about democracy and art not going together. Do you still believe that?
Yes. You can't plan art; you can't institutionalize it. I'll give you an example – I received a catalogue recently from a contemporary art museum in Lithuania, in Vilnius, and there were statements by some artists and the director. 'Our main problem remains the limited support we receive from the Ministry of Culture.' They're blaming the mediocre art on the Ministry of Culture! [*Laughs.*] I mean, not to say that institutions like the NEA, or state arts councils, haven't allowed more people to be exposed to certain things – for instance, allowing orchestras to be created all over the place, or things like that. But you can't subsidize the creation itself. Like the movements: nobody planned Dadaism, or Cubism, or Pop Art, or Fluxus.

Do you think that there has been a significant decline in experimental film here in the US since the late sixties?
There has been a revival in the last five years, mostly in Super-8 film-making. There's a lot going on, not only here but in Europe. It's like the last gasp of Super-8; I'm not sure people are even making the film stock any more. I think it's because with Super-8 one can still be irresponsible and do and try anything, thus something fresh happens.

Don't you feel the same about video?
Video is so unpredictable; I think the problem with video is that videomakers are still too inhibited by cinema – they're still making 'films' with video.

So many of the motifs, gestures – even technical innovations – of experimental film have been strip-mined by mainstream culture for everything from MTV videos to TV commercials to narrative film-making. Don't you find that depressing?
But it's like using a dictionary. The vocabulary is there, and it's used on television and everywhere else. It's like with other vocabularies. You either write a poem with it or you write a press release. When you read a poem, you're elated; you read an ad and you throw it away. This argument began in '65 and '66; I remember Gregory Markopoulos storming into the Coop one day after seeing some-

thing on TV: 'They're stealing from me! They're stealing from Kenneth Anger!' I said to him, 'They can't "steal" from you – no matter what they do, it won't be the same.' He wanted to sue them. [*Laughs.*]

Well, you have to assume that part of his frustration had to do with knowing the kind of audience the television programme was getting was infinitely larger than the audience for his films. Do you think avant-garde cinema can ever hope for a broader audience?
No. No. No. That's a dream. It's like the difference in readership between poetry and prose. Prose is published in millions of copies, and poetry – even the most popular – never goes over 5,000. The content and the form determines the number of those interested in it.

I mean, Markopoulos and Brakhage both had Hollywood dreams. They wrote scripts, and Markopoulos even went there. He came back. Shirley Clarke persuaded Roger Corman to produce a film of hers. She went out there, and lasted, I think, two days. She wanted to do it her own way and she clashed with Corman. He didn't fire her; she just left because she couldn't work in that kind of environment. And that's it. Brakhage made one paid film for promotion – an educational science-fiction film about somebody travelling inside the bloodstream. I can't remember the title. He doesn't distribute that one. It's not such a bad film.

There are film-makers in the past several decades – Bette Gordon, Lizzie Borden, Todd Haynes – who seem to have successfully negotiated between avant-garde practice and more traditional narrative cinema.
Yeah, but even if you go back to the sixties, you could say *The Flower Thief* or *Queen of Sheba* do the same. I think Ron Rice did it better; he didn't 'negotiate'. Or, as you say, you can look at the later work of people like Bette Gordon or Yvonne Rainer. All of this work gradually approaches more and more Sundance, and then Hollywood, but not quite – it still sort of remains within its own New York school of film-making. [*We are interrupted by librarian Robert Haller, who pops in to tell Mekas that Lucasfilm has purchased an ad for the Anthology's annual film-preservation fundraiser brochure. As Haller leaves, Mekas laughs:*] That's where Hollywood comes in . . .

In any case, there was, and still is, this 'middle' kind of cinema, which doesn't fit into the avant-garde, and didn't fit into Hollywood, 'public' cinema because of its techniques and content. There were people like Shirley Clarke, Lionel Rogosin, my own brother, Adolfas, working at the same time as others in the New American Cinema Group. But when the Film-maker's Cooperative was created, only the avant-garde stuck to it. De Antonio said, 'No, this may be too limiting. I'll look for bigger companies to distribute my films.' The same with Shirley Clarke, Rogosin and a good number of others. As the time went, and the Coop grew and developed and became known, they all said to me, 'Hmmm. Maybe we should have joined the Coop . . .' I told them they made a horrible mistake. If they had joined at the very beginning, they could have succeeded. Now, gradually – individually, like lone sharks – they've all been destroyed by time. That generation is lost. I mean, De Antonio continued with limited distribution, but those who wanted to reach wider audiences, and make more narrative films, sort of destroyed themselves by not joining the Coop.

Actually, three days or so before Emile De Antonio died, he, Rogosin and I met at the Second Avenue Delicatessen, and we were planning to do a festival and catalogue of that whole middle cinema. Then when Antonio died, Rogosin left for London . . . Some day it may still happen.

Do you have your own personal Essential Cinema list?
I don't. At the end of the millennium, I had a request from four or five publications to give them lists of ten or one, or whatever. I refused. I cannot reduce cinema – or music or literature – to one or ten. I'm much more open. I can maybe reduce the avant-garde to ten film-makers, sort of, as a game, but not to ten titles. Absolutely not.

How does one look at an experimental film?
I think that one thing I should say about people who do surveys on, or write books about, the avant-garde, is that they all often make one similar mistake. They pay too much attention to the length of the film, what kind of techniques were used, how much money it cost. They don't look at it from the formal angle. Cinema has to be taken like music or literature or any other art – as an art with different formal directions. Each form has its own content, and requires its own techniques – and in time it changes. Of course, even within narrative cinema, there are many subdivisions, many genres. But non-narrative forms – whether documentary, journalistic, or whatever – they all have their own histories. Cinema is a big tree. And it has to do a lot with form. There is not enough discussion of forms and styles in cinema.

To make clearer what I have in mind, we could go to music. There are different forms: symphony, quartet, song, etc. Schubert, for instance, is not put down for writing songs: actually, his songs are among the greatest of musical songs. But his symphonies are discussed and appraised within the form of symphony, not song. Same with quartets. If one writes a quartet and it comes out like a symphony or song, then something is wrong. All forms have their own rules, histories, etc., etc. Same in literature.

Only in cinema we still have a mish-mash. I mean, in the discussion of cinema, or even in the viewing of cinema. No film is discussed within its own form.

If you had a choice, would you rather be remembered as a film-maker or as a figurehead/organizer, sort of a Clement Greenberg for American avant-garde film?
I do not have much choice. It depends on the group of people talking about me. For instance, to the Lithuanians, I'm only a poet. In fact, I have a book of poems

coming out there this week. To the historians of cinema, I'll probably be remembered as an organizer or inspirer of different directions. To independent/avant-garde film-makers, again I will be something else. So it's not up to me. It's very simple – even now, in the US, mostly I'm a 'maverick organizer' type. I'm not a film-maker here at all. In Europe – like in France – in the first place I'm a film-maker. It depends on the place and the time. I can't push it; it will be what it will be. I'm too busy to think about it, especially now.

In *Lost, Lost, Lost*, a film about a feeling of displacement both specific – your experiences as a Lithuanian refugee – and general – the notion of the poet/artist as outsider – you ask in a voice-over as you're driving a car, 'What am I doing here?' After a moment, you say, 'The landscape doesn't answer me.'
Yes, that comes from the period when I was still pretty lost.

Do you still ever feel that way?
No, no, I just don't ask those questions any more – I learned they can't be answered. And of course, I am not an outsider. I am totally in. Totally in cinema. Cinema is my home and my country.

Christine Vachon

Christine Vachon, co-founder of Killer Films, is an independent producer whose films include *Boys Don't Cry*, *Velvet Goldmine*, *Happiness*, *Kiss Me Guido*, *I Shot Andy Warhol*, *Stonewall*, *Kids*, *Safe*, *Go Fish*, *Swoon* and *Poison*. She won the Independent Feature Project-East's Gotham Producer Award in 1999. Her book, *Shooting to Kill*, was published in 1998 by Avon Books.

Tod Lippy: Did you enjoy growing up in New York?
Christine Vachon: I loved it. I think I had a lot more freedom than my counterparts did in the suburbs. I was fairly independent and mobile from the time I was eight or nine years old. And one of the cool things about growing up here was that you could walk to the movie theatres. So many of my friends who grew up in non-urban environments had to constantly arrange to be driven from one place to the other. It's like me when I go to LA, because I still can't drive – I guess I'm having the suburban experience in my later life. [*Laughs.*]

Also, I grew up at the time when the repertory theatres in New York were really at their height. My family lived on the Upper West Side near the Thalia and a cinema called the Olympia, where your feet stuck to the floor. When I was eleven, me and a schoolfriend wandered into *Cries and Whispers* at a theatre on 42nd Street. There were theatres on 42nd Street where you could go in and see movies for a dollar – and it wasn't a pornographic movie, you know? So we would go see movies just because they were there.

Didn't you go see *Patton* when you were seven?
Yeah. I loved it. Also, when I was seven or eight, my older sister was told to take me to see *Oliver*, which I was dying to see. Once we got outside of the building, she said to me, 'You really don't want to see that stupid kid's movie; let's go see *2001* instead.' So I saw a lot of movies very young.

Did you go to any of the more experimental stuff?
Well, my older sister was actually one of the founding members of the Collective for Living Cinema, and she made experimental movies. I remember going to one of her screenings – I must have been eleven or twelve – and afterwards telling her how dull I thought it was. Actually, it may not have even been something that she had made, but it was in that vein. She said, 'Uh! Why do you think that something has to *happen* in a movie?' It's funny, because now I make movies that most people would consider wildly experimental, but in my family's eyes, I'm very mainstream.

When you started Apparatus Films with Barry Ellsworth and Todd Haynes in the late eighties, wasn't one of your goals to meld narrative cinema with a more experimental approach?
Totally. And to some degree, we were successful. But I also discovered a snottiness in the New York so-called experimental or avant-garde film scene that was very unwelcoming when I first came back to New York after college. I remember that *Superstar* was turned down by several venues who wouldn't show it – it was

considered crassly commercial. *Superstar!* That film, in a way, crystallized what we were trying to do. It was relentlessly entertaining, but at the same time, incredibly provocative and interesting on so many levels. And it still holds up – I mean, it's almost twelve years old. It's still amazing how fun that movie is.

Around the same time, I remember reading the application for the Gay & Lesbian Experimental Film Festival – you know, the one founded by Jim Hubbard and Sara Schulman – because I had done a short film and was hoping to submit it. It said something along the lines of, 'The movie must have some *other purpose* than to entertain.' And I was like, 'What's wrong with entertaining?' Anyway, it kind of blew my mind how closed that world was. And in some ways, it forced me more towards mainstream film-making.

But you must have been quite aware of the critical theory that informed that kind of attitude from being a Semiotics major at Brown. And didn't you also study with the film theorist Christian Metz in Paris?
I did, and I'm glad that I did all of that. When I first got out of Brown and people asked me my major, and I said 'Semiotics', I was either met with a blank stare or a 'Who do you think you are?' look. Those were the years when Deconstruction wasn't so prevalent – I mean, now it's everywhere. Sometimes it was easier just to tell people I was an English major.

When you returned here after Brown, what did you do?
Well, for about four years, I bounced around doing PA work, and assistant editor work. I also did a little bit of location managing, and music videos, which were just starting.

What were some of the films you worked on?
I worked on Jill Godmilow's *Far From Poland*, Bette Gordon's *Variety* – a bunch of them.

Can you talk a bit about your experience on Bill Sherwood's *Parting Glances*?
Well, in films it's all about ignorance being your best friend. What you don't know kind of can't hurt you in a way. You take experiences as they come, and you use them as you will. Bill totally operated that way on *Parting Glances*. He really had no idea how it was done, he just knew what he wanted it to be. And that approach got that movie made. One of the things about film-making – which is kind of a drag – is that it's so stanched in a 'This is how it's done' mentality, especially when you get into the union shit. You know, that kind of 'old-school' stuff. And it's very refreshing to work with people who are just coming at it completely sideways.

When did you and Todd Haynes get together?
We met at Brown, but we weren't really friends there. He took a little longer to get through school than I did; he took some time off. I didn't, because I was subsisting to a large degree on social-security checks, which at that time – because my father was dead – meant I couldn't stop my education for a second or the

money would disappear. So I had no choice but to go all the way through.

We re-met in New York a few years later. I saw *Superstar*, and I realized what somebody like Todd could do. The luckiest thing that ever happened to me was that we met each other at the beginning of our careers. So that was kind of the beginning for me of doing what I really wanted to do.

So *Superstar* was made after Apparatus had started?
It was being made. Though a lot of people give me credit for producing it – which I didn't do – I did help Todd a lot with finishing the movie, because I had worked as an assistant editor, and there was a lot of that process that Todd was not familiar with. So it was a good entree into the movie.

Can you go into the specifics of the founding of Apparatus?
Actually, Barry Ellsworth approached Todd and me separately. At that point, he was friends of both of us, and we weren't really friends with each other yet. Barry was from a reasonably well-off family, and had made a decision to use some of this money to start an organization. The three of us met several times, and figured out what kind of company we really wanted to start. It was a tremendous amount of fun. It's so stupid that it doesn't still exist, and what I really was angry about was that we were doing something so original, and so interesting, and it just didn't fit into any grid. It was, like, if you were giving grants, grants were supposed to regard the film-maker as this kind of pristine artist who can't be interfered with, but of course all the movies that the NEA and NYFA and NYSCA were financing were falling apart because there was nobody there steering the ship.

So what we were saying was that we would offer grants where we would actually produce the movies, helping the film-makers make them in the best possible way. But the funding organizations were, for the most part, not interested. NYSCA gave us some money one year, and then the next year took it away. It was frustrating. And we also hit the bad grant time – after all the NEA stuff in the late eighties. I think Barry got cold feet and thought, 'Am I going to spend the rest of my life begging for money?' It's too bad, though, given what we accomplished in three short years. The body of work was really interesting. We gave a lot of technicians their starts – people like Ellen Kuras and Maryse Alberti and Thérèse DePrez. We used it as a launching pad into feature films, but we would have kept it going if we could have.

How did you select projects?
People submitted stuff. The first year, we got forty or fifty and we selected the three that we wanted to do. And we played by the rules – I mean, we participated in deciding what the movies would be, but it wasn't solely our decision; we brought in a committee or panel or whatever you call it – I'm so unused to grantspeak now I can barely do it any more. And then, the second year, we were like, 'Wow. Is it that nobody wants to make movies, or are we just not getting them?' So we made a huge effort to get new projects, and then, something like thirty or forty per cent of our applications were from women, or people of colour, and that was really cool.

And it ended in, what, 1992?

Something like that. I made *Poison* – and got a taste of feature film-making – Barry got sick of it and Todd was clearly going in a direction of making his own movies. It just kind of lost steam.

Jonas Mekas told me in his interview that he felt grants were causing the death of the independent film.

I don't disagree. I can really argue both sides of the case. On the one hand, I see these mealy-mouthed producers who basically aren't dealing with anything I have to deal with – foreign-sales, and this actor as opposed to that actor, and this union deal, and should we shoot it in Toronto, etc., etc. – and they're just filling out their application and mailing it in, you know? I met this Canadian film-maker a while ago who'd just gotten a million and a half dollars to make his first feature, and he said to me, 'I don't really care who sees my movies.' I mean, I do believe in a certain degree of art-for-art's-sake – some of my film-makers, like Todd Haynes and Todd Solondz, should really just be given the money to do whatever they want, because they're national treasures – but I also *do* care about who sees my movies. If you make a movie for the right budget, then you will probably be able to get it to a place where it's not devastating anybody financially. And that's part of the trick – it's a commercial art form, and that's part of the process.

You know, a 'low-budget' movie is under two million dollars. Well, two million dollars would immeasurably improve my style of life, and I'm sure it would improve yours, but you hear people say, 'Uh! We've *only* got two million.' These numbers are insane. I'll read a script, and say to Pam Koffler, my partner at Killer, 'What do you think. Ten, twelve?' She'll say, 'Ten, maybe nine if we shoot it this way.' And we're *little*! I mean, if you want to express yourself, be a modern dancer.

How did you and Pam meet, and when did you decide to form Killer Films?

Pam did some work for me on one of my least-seen films – *Postcards from America* – and then when I did *Kids*, she was our line producer. Then I had this sort of extraordinary period where I did three features back-to-back in New York City.

By the way, it's getting harder and harder to shoot in New York. It's such a drag, because I hate not shooting here. I hate having to go away.

Why is it harder?

Because you used to be able to work non-union here, and you really can't any more because the deals are so tough – they include certain kinds of deferrals that a lot of studios and distributors just don't want to assume, so you end up having to make your film for significantly less. And then there's the border; there's Toronto. So you show your budget to your film-maker, and they're saying, 'Must stay in New York, must stay in New York', and you tell them, 'Or we can go to Toronto and you can shoot for an extra week, or have this much more money for your art department.' What do you think they choose? I hate it; I feel like I put in my time here – I *trained* a lot of these people – and I should be reaping the rewards from the fact that they're finally moving up.

Do you see any solution?
Well, although I'm not as close to it as, say, a line producer is, I think there needs to be a real redress of the kinds of deals unions can make with the kinds of movies that we make which allow them to get made. Because in my movies, things really aren't out of whack. I understand if a movie comes here and Travolta's getting paid twenty million bucks, or what have you. But with my movies, there's always a certain parity across the board. The director's not taking an outrageous amount of money, and there's a certain passion involved. I don't know how you can measure that, and I'm sure the union would say, 'Well, cry me a river.' But there has to be a way to redress it so that those under five million can be made.

The way you put it, it almost sounds like a moral issue.
Well, maybe it is. Maybe it's back to the old 'Certain movies have a right to be made' argument.

I imagine it wouldn't be so easy to convince the Teamsters of that one.
But what if its members aren't working? No one likes to leave their home, unless you're, like, nineteen, and you want to go on vacation and get laid.

Anyway, Killer was founded because Pam and I did *Kids*, *Stonewall* and *I Shot Andy Warhol* in the space of a year. It was great – a lot of continuity, and we built a team. At the end of that, I said, 'I want to keep this together,' and asked Pam to stay with me and she did. We called it Killer Films from the Cindy Sherman movie we were doing at the time, *Office Killer*. I just really liked the name.

What draws you to a project?
Three things. The script or the concept, depending on how it's being pitched to me. Is it interesting, provocative, original? Is it something that gives you that feeling in your stomach you get when you're reading something really good? That's number one.

Number two: the director. Is he or she a psychotic? We've had a few along the way. Are they collaborative? Killer is tremendously director-driven, and we never impose our will on a movie, but we try very hard to make the movie as good as it can possibly be. Sometimes that means protecting it a little bit from the director – especially first-timers, who get terrified to cut their films down, for instance. Sometimes it's just about working somebody through that process until they feel confident enough to go to that next step. And most directors continue to come back to us – or they go away for a film and then come back and say, 'Oh my God, I didn't realize how good I had it.'

And also, are they somebody who is going to be able to articulate their vision in a comprehensive and efficient way to a film crew, or production designer, or DP? They don't have to have ever done it before – we work with a lot of first-timers. And I'm not saying I need a director to sit there and go, 'Yes, I know the difference between a grip stand and a flag.' Who the hell cares? Somebody else can do that. But I do need them to have a sense of what it's going to look like, and how they're going to accomplish that – they need to be able to communicate their vision. So that's number two.

The third thing is, can I sell it? And that's not so obvious, because, you know, sometimes something can seem like the most anti-commercial movie in the entire world, but it has a part in it that a great actress will make her own, or there's something about it that will appeal to a particular group. Some of that's just gut. Sometimes, the director is somebody who's incredibly impressive, who will be able to get great talent into his or her movie. Those kinds of things.

It's hard to put your finger on it. Sometimes things have come to us that we've turned down. We turned down *You Can Count on Me*, for instance, because I didn't see it in the script. It was a beautiful lesson to me. I loved the movie when I saw it at Sundance. It just shows you that a script is just a piece on the way to the movie, and that with the right things – beautiful casting, beautiful direction – it all went to a completely different level. Sometimes I see it, sometimes I don't.

How did you first hear about *Boys Don't Cry*?
What happened was – this was around five years ago – Rose Troche called me and said, 'I met this girl, she's really smart, and she's going to give you a call.' So Kim Peirce came by the office, and she'd shot this short as her thesis film at Columbia, based on the Brandon Teena story. The film was at DuArt, and she couldn't get it out because she didn't have any money. I paid to get it out. And it was good, but it wasn't like, 'Oh my God, this is the next Bertolucci.' It was a competent film, with some spotty performances, but some surprisingly strong ones as well. But Kim is what impressed me the most.

So we started out thinking, 'Maybe we can take this footage and make it into a feature.' But after talking to her over a period of time, and seeing her grow so much in leaps and bounds – she went from point A to point Z and then back to point A again – it was clear that the footage just wasn't good enough any more. Her vision was expanding and growing, and the movie needed to, too. So she started a long process of working on the script. We went through many drafts with her – she worked with a couple of different writers, one of whom is suing us right now – I guess it's a sign of success, right? Anyway, it kept getting better and better. And actually, what happened to it was, it started out that she wasn't sure about the legalities of using real-life characters – she'd begun with made-up names and fabricated situations to a certain degree – and as she started delving deeper and deeper and deeper and getting to the heart of what really happened, the reality of it – as always – became the most fascinating thing.

And no, we didn't see the documentary film, by the way. Those film-makers really treated us like we were trying to steal something from them.

They started up around the same time you did?

I don't really remember. I think they might have. I remember I wanted to see their footage at one point – I figured in the best of all possible worlds we'd help each other – and I think we've actually helped the documentary quite a bit. At some point, though, I read some nasty things they'd said about *Boys Don't Cry* on the web, which sort of stunned me. I thought, '*Man*, I only ever go out of my way to say nice things about your documentary.' Which is dull —

Nice things up until now.

Up until now. [*Laughs.*] Anyway, Kim went to Nebraska; she spoke to a lot of the people there, hung out with the kids. Meanwhile, I was trying to get it financed, and having no luck. I had it set up and it fell apart three times. Arrow was going to do it at one point. Lakeshore was going to do it at one point. I couldn't get it over that last hump. Finally, the script was better than it had ever been, and I submitted it to MGM as part of our first-look deal, and they green-lit it. Kim quit her job. We started up, we cast, and we set up the first day of shooting for November 15 or whatever it was. I remember Kim was experiencing a syndrome fairly common among first-time directors: '*Oh my God, I'm not ready!*' And I suddenly had this little bit of a vision: I was hearing that there were other Brandon Teena projects in the pipeline – there was a Fox Searchlight movie with Drew Barrymore, and New Line had a Neve Campbell one – and I was just like, 'Kim, I don't care if you're ready or not, it has to happen *now*.' She was really kicking and screaming.

And then, MGM un-green-lit the movie. I had this conversation with them where they told me, 'We really wanted a more universal story' – I couldn't figure out what had happened. It was awful. The train had already left the station: that's always my metaphor. The great thing about film is that there's a certain point where it's just too late – 'Can't stop it!' It's like an army marching in to conquer a territory. So we were kind of at that point – or maybe I just wanted to make us feel like we were at that point; it's always hard to tell in retrospect.

Across the hall from us, Hart Sharp had put together equity financing for *You Can Count on Me*, which was supposed to go into production, but there were some problems with the script or casting or something, and suddenly it looked like it was going to be put off for another six to ten months. So the financing was sitting there without a movie. I went in and told them about the film – which I had pitched to them, like, ten times – and they bought it. They got into it. So we were off to the races.

What was your budget?

A little under two million.

You mentioned a lawsuit from one of the writers. Weren't there others as well from the people whom the characters were based on? I guess it's always sort of tricky dealing with real-life situations . . .

Well, basically, when you commit a crime, or are the victim of a crime, it kind of becomes public property. Aphrodite Jones had written a book about the incident which Diane Keaton optioned, and which was going to be the basis for the Drew Barrymore script, and I think they sued Fox. Everybody was suing everybody, basically, and accusations were flying. Also, I really think everybody else thought our movie was going to be bad.

Why?

Well, I think that there was a perception that, you know, Drew Barrymore wants to be in a Brandon Teena movie, and then there's this little indie film with a first-time director happening. I mean, which one would *you* back?

Did the others cease and desist once you went into production?

No. The New Line one was being produced by this guy Don Murphy, who bought the rights to the documentary for David Veloz, who did *Permanent Midnight*. When they caught wind of our movie, Don Murphy proceeded to harass my movie. I don't know to what end, except to make my life miserable, which he succeeded in doing. But the fact of the matter is, we did have Lana Tisdale's signed release. Lana has since chosen to forget, perhaps, that she signed it, but we have affidavits from the people who took it to her house and watched her sign it: we're covered. Did she sign a release for somebody else? She may well have. I wouldn't be surprised if she gave her exclusive life-rights away more than once. But we have them.

Anyway, Murphy started sending threatening letters, and got a lawyer involved. In fact, he was the one who got Lana into coming after us, as well, which in a way is the biggest shame of all. At the Toronto Film Festival, where the movie was having its North American premiere, he threatened legal action against the festival. Literally an hour before the premiere, I had the festival people saying to me, 'Unless you indemnify us, we won't show it.' I should have been drinking champagne with Kim and the actors, and instead I'm sitting in a stinky hotel room with my lawyer and the festival's lawyer, waiting for some stupid paper to get faxed that I have to sign to indemnify the festival.

You personally?

Yeah. It was just so ridiculous. I mean, how dare he do that to me? But the worst thing he did regarding Lana was that he ruined what could have been such a wonderful experience for her. She could have joined in the celebration of the movie, and instead, it became a source of stress and discomfort and litigation. Litigious people are always bad.

How did the production itself go?

You know, it was tough. I wasn't there the whole time. Eva Kolodner was really the on-set producer. I spoke to her and to Kim practically every day. It was hard, but in a way, even though every movie's different, they're all kind of hard in the same way. The same old stupid story – 'Blah blah blah . . . but we got the shot. 'Blah blah blah . . . but we made the day.' It certainly wasn't the hardest one we've ever done.

Why did you choose to première the film at Venice?

Well, we were clearly not going to be ready for Cannes. The guy who runs Venice now, Alberto Barbera, used to run the Torino Festival, which showed some of our work early on. I've known him for a long time, and always liked him a lot. I was in Cannes, walking down the street, and I saw Alberto and congratulated him. He thanked me, and said, 'So what have you got?' And I told him we had this movie called *Boys Don't Cry* – actually, it still might have been called *Take It Like a Man* at that point – and he said he would have his New York person call me. She did, she saw it and it was in. They showed it opening night of their Directors' Fortnight-y kind of thing. And it was a wonderful experience.

Venice is so different from Cannes. It's easier for me – particularly that year before at Cannes, with *Happiness* practically opening the Directors' Fortnight and *Velvet Goldmine* at the end. I was just herding in one load of actors, directors and parents through all the paces and then the other. I've never been through anything so stressful. It was horrible; I was pulling my hair out. It was like planning a wedding in four days. Of course, I guess I would temper that by saying, 'Well, on the other hand, I hope I have such problems every year.'

The 'wedding-planner' analogy is a pretty broad definition of the producer's role, isn't it?
A great producer needs to produce everything about the movie, from the very beginning to the very end. For me, the experience that a director has at that stage is definitely part of it – helping them deal with how the film is perceived, all those kinds of things, are part and parcel of what I do.

Do you feel like you've carved out a certain position of power in the film industry?
Well, it's always yes and no. I get my calls returned a tiny bit faster, but I don't necessarily feel like much has changed. I still back the movies I've always backed. People say to me, 'Now that your track record's so good, won't people just get behind you and say, "It's a Christine Vachon movie – I want to be a part of this"?' But the same problems are still there: 'I don't know, I've never seen a film like that before', or 'But who's in the lead?', or 'Has this director done anything before?', because most of the movies I make tend to fall into the dreaded 'execution-dependent' category.

While you've produced a number of unconventional, challenging films like *Swoon*, *Postcards from America* or *Poison*, you've also been involved with what many would see as more 'mainstream' fare, like *Kiss Me Guido*. What goes into your decision to make a film like that?
I've never made a movie because I thought, 'Oh, this will be commercial.' The criteria are pretty much the same for every film. I thought *Kiss Me Guido* was hilarious, and I still do. I've been criticized for it by the gay community, who said it was an obvious attempt to be commercial – except that it wasn't particularly successful. [*Laughs.*] When it came out, it was competing with films like *The*

Birdcage for audiences. The gay niche market had already been created, and people at that point seemed to want material that was more sophisticated.

And then other people were critical of it because they found it 'offensive'.

Why?

Oh, I get that on every film. I don't think we've ever made a movie that somebody hasn't been offended by. On *Boys Don't Cry*, a female producer who I won't name, but who is very well-established in Hollywood, was at a screening of the film at CAA. I really wanted to meet her, but I couldn't find her afterwards. Somebody told me later that she was 'really offended' by the rape scene, and was so pissed off that she left immediately afterward. I was, like, 'Man, you cannot win.'

What would you say is your most successful film?

Financially?

Actually, I was curious to hear how you would define 'success' in your answer.

Well, I can answer it in two ways. I would say that the most successful film I ever produced would probably be *Safe*, because it was incredibly difficult to do – it was a movie that somehow, against all odds, got made – and looking back now I truly can't figure out how we got those people to give us money. And it's an extraordinary film that will live way past its makers. If you get one of those, then you can die happy. Financially – in terms of how much it cost in relation to how much it made – *Go Fish* was probably our most successful film. Maybe *Boys Don't Cry* will give it a run for its money.

I mean, I think all our movies are great. But when other people think so, too, it's fabulous. As Pam said the other day, 'The Oscars don't mean anything until you win one.' Then you say, 'Wow – these awards are the be-all and end-all!' – because, of course, they are. In a way, the fact that *Safe* didn't get those accolades when it came out was really difficult, but in another way, we still got it made, and it's living on.

There's all this revisionist history going on with that film. It really came to a head last year when it topped so many critics' 'Best of the Decade' lists.

Right. All those people who now say they 'knew the minute they saw it' how great it was.

In your book, you say, 'I know that my reputation is more in the direction of being a bitch than a fount of niceness.'

I do have that reputation, but I feel that at a certain point in my career I made the decision that I wanted people to earn my respect – I think that's important. And it's not so much that I'm a woman in a man's business, you know, so I need to show everybody how tough I am.

It's not a popularity contest. Ultimately, when you are only ever making decisions for the good of the film, you're gonna piss people off. You've got to get the shots that you need to make the film as good as it can be. And the summer-camp atmosphere that prevails on film sets these days really gets on my nerves. You know, who cares if the crew gets ice-cream?

Do you feel a part of the indie film community here, if such a thing still even exists?
I feel a part of it, definitely. I find it very small, though – there's very few of us. Ted Hope and Larry Meistrich and I really began our careers around the same time – Larry actually worked for me on Larry Carty's *Oreos with Attitude,* one of the short films Apparatus produced, and Ted and I started AD'ing at the same time – we were often up for the same jobs.

On *Happiness,* when the crew was being really obstreperous about the hours and all of that, Ted was waxing sentimental about the 'old days', and I remember being a little dismissive about that. But I see what he was getting at, and he's right: There was a certain spirit from the mid-eighties and early nineties in New York City independent film-making – a real sense of camaraderie. You were making really cool movies that had a right to be seen; there was a sense of mission. You know, everyone on the crew read the script.

A lot of crew members will tell me what a great experience *Poison* was for them, and they think it was because of something I did, but in fact it was because of something *they* did, and now they're not doing that any more. They cared about the work they were doing, and cared about the director, and cared about how good it was going to be. Now, they're like, 'Ha! We're running over – meal penalty!'

How do you account for that attitude?
Well, to be fair, people grow up, and they have to start thinking about doing stuff for more than just the joy of art. I think that's definitely part of it. And I think also that film is perceived differently now. One of our hardest problems on *Happiness* was that there was a perception that there was an endless fountain of money because *Welcome to the Dollhouse* had been a financial success. So when we said, 'We're making this movie for *so* little money' – which we were – people didn't believe us. There was this feeling that *somebody* was making money. And besides, you can really only ask somebody for that great favour so many times.

Killer Films recently made a deal with John Wells, the producer of the television series *ER*. Could you talk about the specifics of that?
Well, we had a great two years with MGM/UA – that sounds like a sound bite for *Variety,* but it's true. It really allowed us to stop worrying about how we were going to pay the rent, and we were able to really concentrate on development – we could think big-picture, long-term, etc. And we actually made a movie with them, too – *Crime and Punishment in Suburbia* – which is pretty unusual for these kinds of first-look deals. Usually that means they're the first people to say 'no'.

Anyway, at the end of that, this fall, Killer suddenly found itself in a position it had never been in. Maybe I'm being a little disingenuous – we've got a great reputation, and directors love us, and we're talent magnets – but suddenly *Boys Don't*

Cry put us on the radar in a way we'd never been before. We really could have made a deal with anybody. And we decided to sit back and think about what we really wanted. We had recently decided to get represented, which we did, by CAA. Kevin Huvane thought, 'This is totally off the wall, but why don't I put John Wells and Christine together?' John's a fabulous guy; he's really smart. It's an equity investment in our company. We're completely free agents. It's fantastic.

Are you spending a lot of time in Los Angeles now?
I go there a lot, but I still can't drive. We actually have an apartment there now – the 'Killer bungalow'.

Is there anyone there full-time?
No, not yet. I actually think it's better for us to stay New York-centric. Pam spent a lot of time there doing *Crime and Punishment*; I think we'll continue to be out there several days a month. Laird [Adamson] was just there for the AFM, and Brad [Simpson] goes out to do agent meetings every two or three months. But New York is really where it's at for us.

Is there a particular producer–director relationship you've used as a model?
I don't really have any role models. I mean that in the sense that you never really hear about producers, except the ones who are big meddlers, or assholes, or enemies of production. The producer as *auteur*, the producer as creative force, is sadly maligned. John Waters once told me I was the Ross Hunter of independent production, which was a wonderful compliment. Dan Minahan, who just did a fantastic digital feature for us called *The Contenders*, wanted to do a Ross Hunter show for AMC, and he found out a lot about him. He was an amazing producer, and really let Sirk do those incredible things. So maybe he's a role model, without knowing a whole lot about him. But if I could die with a body of work like his, I'd be happy.

I think, though, that the relationships I've developed with directors I've kind of invented myself. And now, interestingly, that's looked on as a model. It was reported back to me recently that some ego-swollen film-maker I've never heard of, who was getting badgered by some company to cut his movie, told them, '*Christine Vachon* doesn't make her directors do this.' I guess that's a good thing . . .

I think of preview screenings as being associated with more studio-generated films, but I was wondering if you also use them.
We do previews constantly. But not NRG screenings – I'm suspicious of those. We do our own kind – we bring in an audience, have them fill out question-naires. We do it fairly rigorously, and we make – no, we strongly encourage – directors to use that as part of their process. Todd Solondz does, totally; Todd Haynes does, totally. Kim became a total convert, also. You have to start with the supposition that the movie's going out there to be in front of an audience, and to work for an audience. And if it isn't, then you aren't doing something right.

So what better way to find out?

Does that mean that we sit there with the results and say, 'Well, Kim, this questionnaire says that the rape scene's too long'? No. But it means you take on a sense of what the general *Zeitgeist* of the screening is, and you act accordingly, if you want to. Usually what happens at those screenings it that something you never, ever would have thought was confusing, or was a stumbling block, or got in the way of what you wanted somebody's experience of the movie to be, becomes apparent, and then you say, 'Thank God we did this.' Or you realize you could make it so much more affecting if one little thing changed, you know? Or you find that nobody's liking a particular character, and it's interfering with their ability to process something else.

NRG screenings are about 'the numbers', and our movies never test well in that way. With *Velvet Goldmine*, those NRG screenings were probably the last nails in the coffin. I just remember this poor person from Miramax – can't remember her name, but she had an Australian accent – saying to us over and over, 'And thees score is beloy ehvrage.' And I was like, 'Yes, but if you took *Last Tango in Paris, 400 Blows,* whatever, and subjected it to that, of course it would be *beloy ehvrage.*'

What do you think happened with *Velvet Goldmine?*
It's the tragedy of my life – it broke my heart. When a movie doesn't work, it's easy to blame the distributor, and I really don't want to do that. I do have to say that at a fairly critical point, I felt like a lot of confidence was removed. I don't know what would have happened if 17 times as much money had been spent; I can't make that assessment. The critics were more split than anyone had originally anticipated. I was so angry at some critics who said it was 'too ambitious'. I mean, in this day and age, when a movie is actually about something, actually tries to do something, to slam it for that? I'm not saying it's unflawed, but I think it is one of the richest experiences you can possibly have in the cinema. The last time I checked, there were seventy-five websites dedicated to the movie alone – basically all teenage girls!

I was wondering if you find any cross-pollination between the indie world in New York and the more established film-makers who live and work here.
Absolutely not.

Olivier Assayas said something similar about the divide that separates most of the New Wave directors in Paris from his generation . . .
Boys Don't Cry was the first little chip of bigger-deal people telling me, 'I've admired your work for so long.' About four years ago, I went to do a meeting with Jean Doumanian – they were looking for somebody to line-produce Woody Allen's movies, and they brought in everybody. I took the meeting as a sort of 'Why not?' kind of thing. But when I got in there, it suddenly dawned on me that she had absolutely no idea who I was; she didn't know anything about me. I mean, at that point, we'd made *I Shot Andy Warhol, Kids, Stonewall, Safe* – but she had no clue. Actually, I only went in because I wanted to see the office.

John Pierson

As a producer's representative, **John Pierson** has been instrumental in bringing a number of seminal independent films to the screen since the mid-eighties, including *She's Gotta Have It, Working Girls, Go Fish, Roger & Me, The Thin Blue Line, Slacker, Clerks* and *Crumb.* Pierson is the author of the 1995 book *Spike, Mike, Slackers & Dykes*, and creator and host of *Split Screen*, a series on the Independent Film Channel.

Tod Lippy: When did you move to New York?
John Pierson: I moved to the city in the summer of 1974 – the summer prior to starting at NYU film school. But I had moved up to the New York area in '67 – I went to junior high and high school on Long Island, in Huntington, and I started to come into the city then. I remember one time we were supposed to have a high school social-studies class trip to see *Lenny* on Broadway – you know, we had one of those hip liberal American History teachers – and, instead, I sort of wandered off to see a bunch of movies. *Last Picture Show* had just opened, plus there was an Antoine Doinel triple bill at the Elgin. I'll never forget that – it was a red-letter day for two reasons: I saw four great movies, and I got in trouble for bailing on the Broadway show. Normally, I was an obedient child, so I'm still not sure what compelled me to do that.

So you obviously already knew about the Elgin Theater.
I knew about it. Can't remember where I saw the listing – was I looking at *The Village Voice* at that point? Probably. Again, this very same teacher probably told us to read the *Voice*, so it's really his fault.

So you started at NYU in 1974?
Yeah. I got there after the 'two Martys' – Scorsese and Brest – were already finished. In fact, *Mean Streets* had opened, and I remember that the NYU Film School had a sort of unofficial holiday on its opening day. It was a big moment for NYU to celebrate – the first real triumph of an alumnus. But Marty Brest had also just passed through the programme. He made a short called *Hot Dogs for Gauguin*, which ends with the Statue of Liberty being blown up – it was frequently screened around the film school.

Were you doing production at NYU? Or was the Cinema Studies programme – the more critical/theoretical division – already up and running?
It was, and I was basically a Cinema Studies major, but I also did TV production work and film production. Annette Michelson was teaching there.

When I was at NYU, she was credited with causing at least one student breakdown in every seminar.
I think I touch on this in the book – the screenwriter Larry Gross was there, also, and he was, like, the smartest kid in school. He took her on, and I thought he actually got the better of her, which was pretty amazing because she was so formidable.

And Bill Rothman was there, teaching Hitchcock over and over again. He later ended up at Harvard – teaching Hitchcock. [*Laughs.*] Bill Everson was there. Actually, when Janet and I got married we showed *Seven Chances* at the wedding, but the first place I saw that was not at one of the Buster Keaton revivals at the Elgin, which Ben Barenholtz did every February, but in a Bill Everson class. I'll never forget, he introduced the film by apologizing for the fact that it had a slow start. 'Don't worry, it builds.' I couldn't believe this guy was apologizing for Buster Keaton.

Were you also looking at a lot of New American Cinema stuff – Brakhage, Michael Snow, that kind of thing?

Yeah, actually, Brakhage taught one summer, and I took his course, which was kind of legendary because at the end I think he didn't feel like having to grade anybody, so he took the 'temperature' of the room and gave everybody a B+, which really pissed off the students with A averages. And again, there are a lot of Brakhage films that I think are great, but people thought I took a potshot at him in the book because I told the story about the day he was feeling besieged by unwanted questions, and he did one of his Two-Thousand-Year-Old Man routines. He took the word 'question' and said, 'Examine the roots: it's "quest" and "shun". You're shunning the quest, therefore you're not thinking for yourself. So stop asking.' I was, like, is this a comedy act?

Did you start working for the distributor Bauer International right after you graduated?

There was a little pause; I probably did some travelling. I was out in January of '77, and I answered an ad in the *New York Times* for Bauer. 'A. J. Bauer' it was called, but it later became 'Bauer International', because it sounded more like a conglomerate. It was basically just three guys sitting around an apartment. But the two Cuban émigrés who started that company were both in their early twenties, and were able to convince Wim Wenders to let them handle his films up to and including *Kings of the Road*. They got involved with other New German Cinema stuff as well, like the Syberberg film, *Our Hitler*. That was in the catalogue, but they could never actually afford to pay for a print because it was so long. [*Laughs.*]

Those guys also started a movie theatre. Before I arrived it was on Second Avenue and then, when I got there, they moved into the Actors' Playhouse on Sheridan Square. Other people who worked at Bauer were Tom Prassis, who's now at Sony Pictures Classics, and Donna Gigliotti, who, after a long, very successful career – including an Oscar for producing *Shakespeare in Love* – is head of production for USA Films. And Kevin Lally, who writes for *Film Journal*.

One of the two guys, Ray Blanco, eventually got involved with Spanish-language TV, I think – I can never quite keep track of him. But neither he nor the other guy, Ken Edwards, ever really became indie film mavens. They had to keep moving out of town to avoid their creditors.

When did Dan Talbot start New Yorker Films?
Oh, long before. He was everybody's – well, I don't want to say 'mentor', because it makes it sound like he was out to help everybody else. We basically looked up to him as the guy who really did it first.

It seems like New Yorker Films was a training ground for so many other New York film people . . .
Yeah. The people who worked for New Yorker were Reid Rosefelt, Jeff Lipsky, and, years later, Bingham Ray. Suzanne Fedak, Mary Lugo were there. That was kind of the core group.

What about Ira Deutchman?
He was at Cinema 5, Don Rugoff's company.

Another distributor/exhibitor . . .
Yeah. In the early days, there was a real connection between those two sides. Rugoff, Talbot, Ben Barenholtz . . .

How do you think working in that context affected the people who ended up becoming the major New York indie distributors – like Ray and Lipsky at October, Deutchman at Fine Line, *et al.* – in the eighties and nineties? Did it create a uniquely 'New York' mindset?
I think a lot of people learned how to be entrepreneurial, number one – even if you wound up being a division of a larger entity, like Sony Picture Classics. Because people like Tom Bernard and Michael Barker were working at places like Films, Inc., they just got this more entrepreneurial instinct than a lot of the LA people might have had. Out there, I think it may have been more about plugging into a pre-existing system rather than making something up from scratch.

I think the other thing – sort of the trademark of independent, specialized art film – was that nobody was shy about having opinions about what they liked, and what they thought was good. And in those days, anyway, you could really get behind something you believed in – you didn't have to draw a line between, 'Well, *I* like this, but who else would? Is there an audience for it?' It was more like, 'I like it. It's good. We're gonna do something with this.' And with certain people it's carried over to the current day.

Like with whom?
Well, most of the time with Sony Pictures Classics. I know they're always talking about it. I mean, whenever I hear Michael Barker mentioning 'demographics' it kind of makes me think the pods got him. I'm not saying they shouldn't think about things like that, but when your roots are in the realm of personal taste, and a belief in quality, it makes a difference over time. That's not to say that people in LA don't have personal taste, or don't believe in quality, but I think it's more pronounced in New York. Everybody has an opinion, and stands by it. I mean, you've got Bingham Ray, a year after *Blair Witch* premièred at Sundance, saying,

'I don't care if it grossed one hundred million dollars, it's shit.' So it goes both ways – it's not just positive, it's also stuff like, 'That director's no good, that film's no good. Fuck it, I don't care if people do go to see it – it's still crap!' You know, in LA, if it grosses four hundred million dollars worldwide, it's not shit any more.

Did any of the New York distribution companies have a West Coast presence, other than UA Classics?
Not really, besides those guys having to report to the studio in LA, I think it was New York through and through. I mean, there was always Goldwyn on the West Coast, and then later, for a brief span of time in the mid-eighties, Island Pictures was dominant. But two years later, Miramax was on the rise, and that was that.

You talk in the book about 1979–80 being a very important period for independent film in New York, what with the founding of the Independent Feature Project, the 'American Mavericks' festival which you helped programme –
Also, UA Classics was formed. At that point, I was programming 'American Mavericks', which happened in January of '79, and then afterwards, Sam Kitt, who was director of that festival – and who now runs 40 Acres – set me up to program a little theatre called the Harold Clurman, which is still there over on Theater Row.

What kind of stuff were you programming?
Well, there were three years of it, and we did some of everything. We did a very popular series called 'Road Movies', which was an attempt to define this genre of film that various people were beginning to write books about. That was very popular with the critics. And we made a ton of money doing rock 'n' roll movies, which was a first love of mine. Nobody was really doing that in any kind of systematic way circa 1980, 1981. Stuff like *The T.A.M.I. Show*, which is one of my all-time personal favourites.

So then I got another distribution job that overlapped with that, at a company that had been called Tri-Continental Films. They'd gotten a huge settlement to move out of that triangular building on Sixth and Cornelia when it was turned into condos. They moved to Park Avenue South – when it wasn't so fashionable – and changed their name to Unifilm. They were known for being the major importer of political films from Cuba and other Third World films that wouldn't have gotten in here otherwise.

Like *Memories of Underdevelopment*?
Exactly. Then they had a sort of crossover hit with *Pixote*, and New Yorker had *Bye, Bye Brazil* right before that, and all of the sudden, it seemed that there were other possibilities besides the college market, or institutional market. But, like many companies before and especially after, as soon as there was sort of a semblance of 'Oh boy, we can have hits here', people started spending too much money, and it kind of went *kaboom*.

Then I formed a corporation called Roadmovies, out of homage to Wim

Wenders' production company back in Germany – he wasn't happy we stole the name, by the way – and the people in that group were Anne Thompson, who's now at *Premiere*, and Sam Kitt, Tom Prassis, Arthur Silverman, who went on to produce *Parting Glances*, and my NYU roommate Larry Altschuler. And there was a PMK publicist, too, Eric Myers. We came together because we liked certain kinds of films, and we had a theatre to show them in. We did it at the Clurman for a couple of summers, and then we did it at the Bleecker. But then Sid Geffen, who owned the Bleecker and the Carnegie, asked me to just do it by myself, and, to the dismay of some people in that group, I ended up doing it. That's how I wound up programming on my own.

How and when did you decide to become a producer's rep?
It evolved right out of what I was doing in that same span of time between 1979 and 1985. I was programming film at the Clurman and the Bleecker, then I formed Roadmovies, worked at Unifilm, worked also at UA Classics in its last year – 1982. I also went to Films, Inc., which was upping its catalogue profile. We re-released catalogue items like *Once Upon a Time in the West* and *400 Blows*, and Warner Bros. Cartoons, and made new prints of lots of Paramount and Fox titles, because that's what they had. And while I was there we got involved with programming the second screen of Film Forum, because Dan Talbot stopped doing it.

So in other words, I've been around the block around twelve times. And if you've done that enough, a lot of people are going to bump into you.

How did you get involved with *Parting Glances*, which was by all accounts your first producer's rep gig?
The guy who pulled me into the film was Arthur Silverman, who I'd mentioned earlier. He was going to law school, and he had a third year clerkship in Alaska, and he was like, 'Hey, can you help me out selling this film?' We sold it at IFFM to Cinecom.

I guess the reason Arthur thought I was ready to be the rep on *Parting Glances* was that I knew the players, such as they were then – of course, they're the same people now. Go figure. And when he asked me to do it, I realized to myself, 'Hey – he's right. I do know these people, for a variety of reasons, and I do know how their system works.'

Can you define exactly what a producer's rep does?
Well, there was no job description circa 1985. The zen part of the job was being a kind of a translator between the business interests – mainly distributors – and the film-makers. And obviously it's helpful in that kind of situation to have a working familiarity with how exhibition works, and marketing, and publicity. That would be the overview.

What you need to do if you're going to rep a film is you need to help get it finished – whether it's with your own or other people's money – and into a state where it's showable to distributors, oftentimes at a festival. But not always back then; not always. You could go direct – there were not that many films – and say, 'Hey, I've got one for you to see', and just screen it for somebody.

The psychological skill you need is the ability to make a film look as good as it can, or maybe better than it is. The business skill is to then try and parlay that into the best possible deal. There has been much said over the years as to whether 'the best possible deal' means a bigger advance or more control over the release of the film, with greater participation in the back-end, or net profits. I used to give that kind of rhetoric a certain amount of lip service myself until over time I realized that you should get it up front. [*Laughs.*] You do need to get big advances wherever possible. That's what locks in your relationship with the distributor – if they have more risk, they're going to do a better job.

So then you have to be able to negotiate all the aspects of the deal which are to the benefits of your film-maker, without creating a complete breakdown in understanding between the two sides. You don't want to drive things so hard that you have an alienated distributor.

Do you think your knowing a lot of these people socially worked to your advantage in negotiating?
I think it put everybody more at ease. And I think that everybody knew that I was familiar with their work. But again, you don't want to have too much trust, because there's an element that needs to be a little bit adversarial – because, of course, they always like to pay less. Having said that, though, in my experience, I've found that everybody wants to do best by the film. I never had a case where I felt like a film got in the hands of the wrong distributor who really messed it up. I remember people saying to us when we sold *Working Girls* to Miramax, 'How could you sell a film to those guys? They're rock 'n' roll crooks!' – those were the very early days for them. But they ultimately paid more money than the three bidding companies, and they did a great job on the film. After that, I never really listened too carefully to 'Don't do anything with this one or that one – they're terrible!' You just want to try to stay away from companies that appear to be on the verge of going out of business.

After you do a deal, you still want to stay involved in a partnership with the film-maker to make sure the right ad campaign is being developed, and the right trailer is being made. Like on *She's Gotta Have It*, the fact that you could make a trailer where Island had the idea for the meat of it, and then Spike, of course, had the left-over idea to use Mars Blackmon selling tube socks as a frame – that was great. So you want to help things like that to happen.

Have you ever found yourself turning down a movie because of concerns about the film-maker's personality?
Well, I've been lucky, because the films that I've liked, with the exception of *Amongst Friends*, have been made by people who, if I haven't loved them – and in many cases I have – have been very open-minded. I mean, the Michael Moore situation – where

he had all of these sort of impossible demands – was part of who he is and the film he made, so that was kind of fun. I might feel differently about it now . . .

But it was a good ride.
Yeah. That's exactly right. That's a case where there were, with and without my prompting, page after page of deal demands which we were able to get because there was such a hot pursuit of the movie.

What was the oddest demand he made?
It depends on who you talk to. The one that wound up being the politically weirdest, I think, was just this issue about which theatres it could or couldn't show in in Israel, and whether they did or didn't admit Palestinians after curfew. [*Laughs.*] I mean, funnelling money back to the five families who are thrown out of their homes in the film, that was a really smart thing to do – especially after you get three million dollars.

Can you quickly sketch out the typical financial arrangement you make with a film-maker?
Well, agents generally work off this ten per cent figure. When I started out representing films, I thought, 'Well, that's too much; let's make it five.' And there were cases where, of course, I even bent lower than that. Then once I started helping to find money for people to finish their films, it went to seven-and-a-half per cent. And in cases where I was able to invest my own money or money from a company I was involved with, like Island World, then that money was treated as any investment money would be treated – with an ownership interest in the film, and generally some kind of premium on the repayment of the investment itself.

There are fewer of us sixties types left, but there used to be huge, raging debates about who should get their money back first if a film made something. There was generally a lot of derisive behaviour towards investors – 'Oh, they just invested money; people with deferments should get paid first.' It used to be endlessly debated, but now I think it's become clear to people that money is money, and money gets returned first. But those issues were very much alive in the eighties. There were times when I felt I was being attacked for thinking that when you put the money in to finish a film, and then expect to see a return on that investment, there was something wrong with that.

That strikes me as a very New York indie attitude.
I think you're right. And it was prevalent in the early days of the IFP in New York, with somebody like Sandra Schulberg, who was the forefront of certain issues like that. So even institutionally, there was a real concern about that kind of thing.

There was a similar attitude toward distributors. Film-makers would say, 'That distributor made money off that film – it's obscene that we haven't gotten anything back.' And I'd say, 'Well, that's what they do: they distribute films. They get a fee for doing that.'

I remember in your book you talked about the friction around *Go Fish,* when the film-makers were suspicious about where all the money from the advance had gone.

In that case, I just think that four hundred thousand dollars wasn't that much, even for a sixty-thousand-dollar film that had additional completion costs. And when it's being split between me and Christine Vachon and the film-makers, of whom there are two, that's just arithmetic. But that's another case where, you know, if you invest money, you get certain rights. If you want to pick on somebody, pick on Christine, because, yeah, she helped you get the film done, but we invested the money, and we should get our money. You have whatever opportunities you have because of that.

They seem to have stopped doing this, but Ted Hope and James Schamus used to say, 'Oh, John makes really hard deals.' In the meantime, their whole theory was that they wanted a piece of the action in future films from people. I think asking for participation in somebody's future can be the hardest deal of all.

Obviously, the business of independent film has changed enormously in the last several decades. Generally speaking, do you think things are better or worse?

This is a very long, long answer to what seems like a simple question. We used to think that a film in the early eighties that grossed half a million dollars – with a much lower ticket price than we have now, by the way – had disappointed us. Hey – for all the acclaim and wonderful attention to *American Movie*, it's huffing and puffing and chugging to try to get to a million-dollar gross now. So I'm not really sure if that's a now vs then proposition. There are so many films now – *Slam* is another good case in point – that get so much attention and *oomph* behind them now that actually don't do business. And those two are relatively successful; there are literally a hundred films that opened last year in New York that basically couldn't draw a fly.

So in the eighties, for instance, when less films were being released, I actually think that the films, on a case-by-case basis, got more attention. But having said that, I think it's crucially important within film culture to realize how incredibly influential a Fassbinder film in the seventies was. Or, in the eighties, a Todd Haynes film like *Superstar*, which for legal reasons is basically unshowable. Their influence vastly exceeds their box-office performance. So people who are trying to apply the rules from the top down, Hollywood-fashion, are crazy, and that's where at the end of the nineties, when you look at *Brothers McMullen*'s gross – even though I swore to Ed Burns I wasn't going to pick on him any more – you go, 'Wow. That's a ten-million-dollar film.' That's great. But when you look at it as some sort of independent-minded breakthrough, well, it's a struggle to come up with some kind of explanation for how that might be challenging people. Not to take anything away from him, because I'm sure he made it from the heart. But I don't know why anybody would be impressed just because it performed. On the other hand, if you talk to the audiences who were seeing that film, they enjoyed it. So you've got the same problem. The people who are so adamant about how audiences want something better than what Hollywood is offering, well, they're wrong. The so-called independent audience is happiest at *Life is Beautiful*.

Or *Shakespeare in Love*.
But I liked *Shakespeare in Love*, so I'm not going to pick on that one. [*Laughs.*]

Yeah, but like it or not —
All I'm saying is, in a recent poll *Life Is Beautiful* was voted the favourite foreign-language film of all time. That is so much more troubling than a six-hundred-and-fifty-million gross for *The Sixth Sense*. Nothing could be worse for film culture than that, because it shows that you can market anything, and Miramax has. Even if I liked the film, I'd be suspicious. Even if I didn't know that Roberto spoke pretty good English.

So which kind of success do you think independent film-makers would rather have?
I think people want both. I mean, maybe in New York, if you're not really talking about the old, old school, I think you're really dealing with people who want to have it both ways. Someone like Kevin Smith, or a New York-area born-and-bred guy like David Russell – he's managed to have it both ways. That's impressive to me. His three-film arc is amazing. Forget about John Sayles this and John Sayles that – David is my model. From an ultra-low-budget film to a modestly budgeted Miramax film to a studio film that really is, using Manny Farber's term, a 'termite movie' – completely subverting the system from within. It's great. That's a model of a person trying to go both ways. And I feel the same way about Kevin.

The indie film atmosphere here is generally described as 'collegial', but I know you've previously cited Lynn Hirschberg's article about Miramax in *New York* magazine from several years ago, where she talks about how 'spiteful and fractious' that world can be.
That whole article was basically going to be her taking down Bob and Harvey. She went to all of their competitors, and they all railed against the two of them, thinking they were taking part in an article that was going to be extremely critical, and then, basically, it turned into a love letter to the Weinsteins. Harvey ended up looking like the truly talented person that he is, and the seductive person he can definitely be. And next thing you know, Lynn Hirschberg is in negotiations with Miramax to start the magazine project they were supposed to launch before *Talk* . . .

You recently stated the current independent film scene has become 'all about marketing'.
My theory is that Miramax has led the charge here, and everybody else has figured out how to copy them. Although, in some cases, there have been innovations coming from elsewhere. I know Tom Bernard and Michael Barker are very sensitive about the idea that Miramax started it all. The point is, Miramax mar-

kets the high end so well – you know, taking a film that's crossing over, that's breaking out, and taking it steps and steps beyond. So if it took all these years to get a film to go to fifteen or twenty million dollars, like *Kiss of the Spider Woman* did back in the mid-eighties, then you get to *sex, lies and videotape*, and suddenly you can go to twenty-five million dollars, and it's like, 'Wow, this is great!' And then you just count the steps on the way: *The Piano, The Crying Game*, and then you get to *Pulp Fiction*, and finally to *Scream*.

And then to *The Blair Witch Project*.

Well, that's obviously in a category all by itself. And that's an area where somebody else, namely Artisan, really does deserve credit for not merely copying a Miramax model, but going into a new area and trumping them.

But do you think this emphasis on marketing has had a detrimental effect?

Well, going back to the example of *Life is Beautiful* – thanks to the marketing, you have everybody in a little town like Cold Spring sitting around and talking about it, and that's great, because if they didn't see *Life Is Beautiful*, they wouldn't see anything, so you can't really let that bother you. But hey, the people who are all flocking to one film in Manhattan, for instance, when maybe they could have broken up their votes into three, four or five different ones – experimented, you know, seen a Todd Haynes film – that to me is not a positive. That's a bad development.

Also, you want to think better of New Yorkers. You would almost expect them to be a little more adventurous – you know, searching out the tiny Film Forum ads in *Time Out*.

You have to get so microcosmic on a certain level. You look at, for instance, the Hank Greenburg documentary. There are baseball fans; there are people really into Jewish issues. If you can mobilize these two forces, you will have a far, far, far better run in a few weeks at Film Forum than you will for the highly touted, very well-reviewed *American Movie*. Go figure: it's because there's a real targeted audience. There's a handle; you can motivate people to get out there. I mean, they've been on *The Today Show*, they've had lots of coverage in the *New York Times*. For a little movie opening at Film Forum. That's a good thing. So on the one hand, you have these little sub-niches, and on the other, you have these breakout hits that go through the roof. The question becomes, what happens to the middle ground? It gets harder. One reason for that is that there is no shortage of theatres, no shortage of openings – you'll see thirty non-Hollywood films running on any given weekend. How could anybody possibly say that Hollywood movies are crowding these films out? The fact of the matter is, in New York or anywhere else, if a movie isn't performing, whether it's an indie film or a blockbuster, it's going to get bumped.

Where did anybody come up with the 'let it run three months and see what happens' rule? When did that ever work? Oh, I know: *My Dinner with Andre*. Everything is about *My Dinner with* fucking *Andre*.

What about *The Marriage of Maria Braun*? That had a year-long run at The New Yorker in the seventies . . .

That was a huge hit, though. It came off the New York Film Festival and opened with a bang, and just stayed. I mean, it was Dan Talbot's theatre, so he might not have played it for a year if he weren't distributing and showing the film. Now there's an incentive for somebody. And that's why when Sundance opens their theatre chain, they're going to have to think about becoming distributors.

You've said that if something catches fire in New York, it will give it a much better shot nationwide.

It will give it the possibility of getting booked all over.

When I heard that I was thinking about Sandra Bernhard's paraphrase of the Kander and Ebb song: 'New York, New York – If you make it there, you'll fail everywhere else.'

Well, that could be true also. I'll qualify it: it will get you play dates elsewhere. I mean, who's going to go see *Hank Greenberg* in Dallas?

Any thoughts about the New York press, particularly the influence of the *New York Times*?

Well, Janet Maslin's gone now. I would say the impact of the *Times* has been declining – and I'm not blaming it on her, I'm actually very fond of her – since the end of Vincent Canby era. Janet couldn't necessarily make a movie. Now what's interesting is that, even after that sort of dwindling of influence with Maslin, you've got this troika of critics at the *Times* who will have equal weight – which means less weight for all three.

But on the other hand, even though there were other good reviews for that recent Indian film, *The Terrorist*, I would bet it was the A. O. Scott review in the *Times* which led to a thirteen-thousand-dollar opening at the Screening Room – the likes of which they've never seen. So in that limited a run, I think the *Times* can still matter.

Reid Rosefelt says – and I've come to believe him – that it's not just having a rave review, it's how the review actually describes and characterizes a film. Because there are certain films, like *American Movie*, again, that no matter how much you try to twist and bend and talk about how it's so much more than just a movie about a guy trying to make a film, basically I think that's all that people could read. Could Vincent Canby in his heyday singlehandedly have done for *American Movie* what he did for *Roger & Me*? I don't know.

It wasn't even about grosses; it was more in terms of authority. And you can say that authority's bad – I mean, the whole idea of the Internet is a breakdown of authority, a democratization. And that's what everybody wants in independent film – they want everything to be democratized: 'Let's not get stuck in traditional distribution thinking; let's think Internet.' 'Let's not get stuck with these three critics having all the power – anybody can be a critic!' 'Let's not get stuck thinking that all movies need to come from Hollywood – or even New York. Let's have movies from Austin and Milwaukee and Flint.'

And digital video is playing into that even more.
Right. 'Let's take over the means of production.' But in an age of more authority, you could pick up *The Village Voice* and read Sarris doing the more mainstream stuff, Hoberman being Hoberman and Tom Allen doing the genre stuff. And then Canby at the *Times,* and of course, Pauline Kael. I mean, you could really sink your teeth into what they wrote, and you could generally sink your teeth into the movies they were writing about. But again, as an old dog, I have to say that in many cases they were, in fact, writing about better movies. I think that a lot of younger critics now are like, 'Stop glorifying the seventies with this rosy nostalgia.' But, you know, I think they're wrong. I think it was better.

Do you think that stems from a lack of interest on the contemporary audience's part for that kind of more challenging material?
I can't really put my finger on it. I think in independent film, though, in the current twenty-year era, it becomes harder and harder to break new ground. Even if you start to look closely at movies from twenty years ago, it's hard not to say, 'Well, that's sort of like that movie from forty years ago.' If you wait long enough, it's new again. Everything's happening in a tighter cycle now. I think it's really hard as you get to the end of a two-decade span to look at a film and say, 'Wow. That's a true watershed, pace-setting movie.'

A 'masterpiece'?
Not even that. I mean, few people would call *Blair Witch* a masterpiece, but you can't deny its impact and meaning. I wouldn't pick on the film as much as a lot of people have.

Well, you have a slightly vested interest.
That's true. But I have to say that *Blair Witch* doesn't mean to me what *She's Gotta Have It* did, or what *Slacker* did, or even what *Clerks* did.

Of the films you've repped, which would you characterize as being the true 'watersheds'?
I think *She's Gotta Have It* for sure. And I think *Parting Glances* over time, you know, played a huge historical role in the rise of gay cinema – and obviously launched Steve Buscemi's career as well. But *She's Gotta Have It* is a great film, and it launched Spike's career and brought back Black film-makers. *The Thin Blue Line.* There's one of the few films that actually changed history. *Roger & Me.* I'm sorry Michael turned out to be a sort of one-trick pony, but that was a really good one trick. In the context of that Reagan–Bush decade, it's a very political film. I think *Clerks* has just launched literally hundreds of other film-makers, for better or worse, like *Slacker* did before it. Those two link up in my mind because Kevin saw the former before he thought he'd ever be able to make a film. But again, they're so

different, because *Slacker*, even though it doesn't seem so, is actually very stylish, and *Clerks* is just not. To this day, Kevin is really not a film-maker, but he's a great writer, and very provocative and funny as shit. And then I'm a complete Chris Smith fan, but I can't really tell what his two films thus far have done in terms of influence on other people. That's a case where you're just falling below a threshold.

How did you first get involved with *Blair Witch*?
Dan Myrick sent me a copy of the trailer they'd done for investors without telling me it was a fake, and I went for it. He got a big laugh out of that. I just waited a day and then said, 'We should put this on "Split Screen", and then have you guys talk about what you're going to find when you look through the footage' – the whole investors' trailer just said that the duffel bag full of stuff was being turned over to Haxan Films. Then I said, 'We have to take this a step further. Next spring, come back on the show to tell us what you've "found".' So we gave them ten thousand dollars for those two segments. That was a third of their budget.

I loved the play between 'Is it or isn't it real?'; 'Do you or don't you believe it?' I'm amazed to this day that so many people bought it. Needed to buy it. I'm a big *X-Files* fan, and it just makes you wonder how many people sit around at the end of each episode going, 'Yeah! That really happened!' [*Laughs.*] That was the ultimate nineties urban legend show. One of the things that was really amazing about *Blair Witch*, and this is the sad thing about it, was that it mobilized this demographic – teenagers – that everybody always thinks they might be able to get for an independent film but never do. You know, maybe *Pulp Fiction* got some of them, or *Clerks* on its video run, but *Blair Witch* was *so* teenage.

And this is the audience you *have* to worry about getting for independent film, since it's the generation that will eventually grow up and become independent film's potential audience. One of the reasons you've got a falling off of general support for everything is that the core audience is an ageing audience. And it's an ageing audience that is less able or apt to go out.

And there's video and cable, especially for people with kids.
Right, and this audience is acutely aware of making those calls now. 'Is this one to see in the theatre, or rent, or should we just catch it if it ever shows up on cable?' It's almost unconscious, it's so quick.

You've spent some time in LA; you talk about your trip there to sell *She's Gotta Have It* in your book —
I find LA a very pleasant place to visit, especially on days like this, when I have to shovel snow off my porch. I spent an entire seductive month there during *Roger & Me*.

Do you think you could have done what you've been doing anywhere but New York?
In the nineties, I started getting interested in some really non-LA and non-New

York film-makers: Rick Linklater was from Austin, Michael Moore's from Michigan, Rose and Guin were from Chicago, Chris Smith's from Milwaukee. But I still feel like New York was a better base than any of these other places, because, for one thing, I just got the sense that these film-makers really had a better time visiting New York than they would have had going to LA. But I never got involved with an LA-based film-maker.

You're not repping anything any more; what are you up to? Are you still producing?
We spun off a movie from last year's show, a documentary called *How's Your News?*, which I co-financed with Matt Stone and Trey Parker, which may be a movie or may be an hour-long TV special. That will be done later this year, and we'll figure out what's going on with that. The director, Arthur Bradford, has been a camp counsellor at this place called Camp Jabberwocky, for mentally and physically challenged people. He picked five of them, and they went across country to interview people on the street.

What do you see your role as being these days?
That's a stumping question. I feel like, on a certain level, the parade is sort of passing me by. But I'll willingly let it go right now. I enjoy a kind of 'elder statesman' role. I feel like Ben Barenholtz must have felt ten years ago. [*Laughs.*] I think I can provide some perspective at times. I'd particularly like to find a way to cash in big time with those Internet bucks, based on what I've done and what I know. But as for being a productive member of the film community, I'm a bit perplexed right now. I'm having a crisis. I liked more films in 1999 than I have in years. It was a great year. But, as I'm fond of pointing out – *Blair Witch* and *American Movie* aside – Sundance had little or nothing to do with it. American independent film had little to do with it, except that the David Russells of the world grew up through the ranks.

So I'm not sure how my part of the world fits in with that part of the world. I'm a little confused right now. But I'm thinking about opening a snow-shovelling business . . .

Sidney Lumet

In 1993, **Sidney Lumet** received the D. W. Griffith Award for Lifetime Achieve-ment from the Directors Guild of America. His film-making career spans nearly fifty years, and includes the films *Twelve Angry Men*, *Long Day's Journey Into Night*, *The Pawnbroker*, *Fail-Safe*, *Serpico*, *Dog Day Afternoon*, *Network*, *Prince of the City*, *The Verdict*, *Daniel*, *Running on Empty*, *Q&A* and *Night Falls on Man-hattan*. Lumet has been nominated for a Best Director Oscar four times, and was the author of the 1995 book *Making Movies* (Knopf).

Tod Lippy: I know you've made over fifty films, but I'm not sure of the exact number...
Sidney Lumet: I'm not, either. [*Laughs.*]

Do you know, percentage-wise, how many of those were shot in New York?
The only ones not shot in New York were *The Morning After* and then the ones I did in Europe. I don't know quite how many of those there were – at the most, ten. Seventy-five per cent of them, then.

You said somewhere that you found the city to be 'character-rich geographically'. Could you elaborate on that a little bit?

New York can become whatever you want it to become. It can be ice cold – I'm talking about emotionally – and it can be as warm as can be. Just architecturally, in terms of the feel of the city. So it's an endless palette for whatever story you want to tell.

You've also talked about the access to actors here —

The acting is really the best in the world. It's amazing. So many American actors start here, one way or another. Eventually, some of them wind up in LA doing various TV shows or whatever, but even that's breaking up a little. There are more and more TV shows being done here, so the talent pool is enormous.

Does that go for technicians as well?

When I started, you could literally put one crew together, and slowly it grew to three crews . . . Now it's an enormous pool of technicians. We almost came a cropper several years ago when unions were having problems with studios and couldn't come up with a new contract, and studios just stopped making movies here.

This was in the mid-nineties?

Yeah. And the problem there was that the infrastructure collapsed. The camera-equipment houses, the lighting houses, the sound-effects studios, they all took a severe beating. But that's all been restored now.

I remember you writing a letter to the Union right after you wrapped *A Stranger Among Us* – it was quoted extensively in Jimmy Breslin's column in *Newsday* – vowing that you wouldn't make your next film here.

And I didn't. I went up to Toronto.

How was that?

I love working in Toronto. It's a wonderful city, and a very different atmosphere from New York. If you want modern architecture, it's one of the best cities in the world. Beautifully laid out – and the control that they've had over construction has been marvellous. Also, because of the weakness of the Canadian dollar, by now I think they're getting much more work than New York.

In your book about film-making, you talk about the difficulty of shooting the diamond-heist scene in *A Stranger Among Us* on 47th Street – basically, having to do on one Sunday (the only day the shops closed) what would normally have been spread over several days. Do you think working with the restrictions inherent in a city of this size and density has made you a more creative film-maker?

I'm a great believer in need, you know? Not having everything easily presented to you. Obviously that's got its limitations, because when you're doing certain kinds of pictures you need everything at your disposal. But in general, without doing *Titanic* or Lucas or Spielberg movies, I think deprivation is good for the imagination – it helps.

You wrote a piece in the *Times* a while back about the importance of location shooting. You were responding to George Lucas – who had mentioned not long before that location work could soon be made obsolete by digital technology. I believe your point was that one can't really approximate the energy that comes from shooting in an actual urban environment – its effect on the actors, in particular.

Lucas is a marvellous movie-maker, a wonderful director, and *American Graffiti* is one of the really magnificent American movies. But it's very easy, especially if you're as interested as he is – and as I am, by the way – in all of the technical advances that Lucasfilm has been involved with, to get yourself into a little isolated box up there on the farm and end up with a very narrow focus on the kinds of movies you want to make. I'm sure that at some point very soon one will be able to digitally create any background one wants for any sort of location. But I don't know what that will do to actors, particularly in highly emotional scenes. What's it like playing that in front of a blue screen, with the light all wrong for what you're playing? Knowing all the other adjustments that actors can make, I would imagine that down the line they'll adjust to it – but for a while it's liable to be a little rocky.

Well, to be completely cynical, I guess one could just digitally 'correct' their reactions.

[*Laughs.*] Right. Put a tear in their eye.

You said once that you didn't move to LA or work there because you felt that it was an 'inorganic' place.

I don't want to get pretentious about all this – it's not that important – but the history of art is the history of cities, and cities have always had another purpose – they've either been the major seaports or the geographic centres of the country. And that's where art has always gone – like a camp follower, to where the money is. LA had no reason for being. It's not a port, and the farmland has been eliminated, not that there was much there to begin with, so it had no reason to *be,* other than the fact that land was cheap. Now, maybe all of that doesn't matter – maybe movies have finally given the city an organic function. Which is fascinating, considering how impossible they make it to shoot in Beverly Hills. It's one of the worst cities I've ever been in to shoot.

Why is that?

They're terrible people. They're rich and they don't want to be inconvenienced and have their parking spaces taken up and all that sort of stuff.

Why do you think New York became a centre for so much independent film-making in the last three decades?

Well, there's a great deal of – the word 'entrepreneur' always amuses me, but I hate it, so let's call it 'hustle'. [*Laughs.*] You've got more hustlers here. And I don't think it's at all coincidental. There's a level of energy. I shouldn't really say, because I don't know what the UCLA film school is like these days, but I do know that it's gotten to a point where your worst nightmare here is running into NYU film crews. They're all over the fucking place, it's unbelievable. It's adorable, but Jesus, God, enough already. [*Laughs.*] Harvey, thank god, has shifted the whole thing downtown – way downtown – so as long as it's below Canal Street, that's fine with me. [*Laughs.*]

Weren't you born here?
I was born in Philly, but I came here when I was one or two.

I know you got involved very early in acting in the Yiddish Theater and then later, on Broadway. How did that come about?
Well, there was almost no choice. My father was an actor, so I just got thrown into it, and I loved it and was good at it and it kept me off the streets. It was a very good childhood that way.

And you did some film work as well?
Only one, a picture called *One Third of a Nation*, with Sylvia Sidney.

Why only one?
I was a 'theatre person'. A theatre snob, at that. In those days, movies were not serious work – you went to movies to make money.

How did you get into television?
Sheer luck. I was good friends with Yul Brynner, who was working for CBS. I'd been teaching at the High School of Performing Arts, where I had set up the drama department. I was in my second year, and it was not fun any more – there's a limit to teaching for me; it's the law of diminishing returns.

You were teaching acting?
Yeah. So I was talking to Yul one day about this TV thing and he said, 'C'mon in, nobody knows what the hell they're doing, and we can have a ball.'

What year was that?
It was '49, '50, something like that – maybe '51. There was a wonderful guy at CBS by the name of Charlie Underhill, who thought that the best way to get directors for the television dramas was to take people from the theatre, because they knew scripts and they knew acting. And then they could teach us the technological end of it, which they did. And he hired Marty Ritt, he hired Yul and me and Johnny Frankenheimer and Bobby Mulligan. He got himself quite a group of people that he put to work.

You were directing episodes of *Danger* and *You Are There*?
Right. And then, after the CBS contract, I did some freelancing, mostly on the hour-long shows.

I know that you were involved with Walter Bernstein, among other 'off-limits'

writers, during the blacklist period. Do you think there was any difference between here and LA with regards to the industry's dealings with blacklisted writers?

I thought – although I'm not absolutely sure about this – that we were better at getting blacklisted writers working under the table than they were on the Coast, but I don't really know. I know in movies there were instances of people like Albert Maltz being hired and so on. There was certainly a real underground of blacklisted writers.

And if the writers found fronts, you would hire them?

Yeah. It was complicated, because there was the income-tax issue. And there always had to be someone at the studio who knew. It would always be someone quite high up, because their influence had to spread over a lot of departments – payroll, for instance, because these shows were CBS packages, not outside packages. You had to be very careful who you picked. In this case, it was a wonderful guy by the name of Bill Dozier, who ran RKO for a while. And of course, if Bill were alive today, he would say, 'I didn't know a thing about it' – but he knew and he took very good care of us.

Didn't you start up an actors' workshop on Irving Place around this time?

That was where I had started directing, actually. I was in the Actors Studio, and I had had a quarrel with Bobby Lewis, who was conducting the advanced class, and got thrown out, so I went down to the Village and formed my own workshop.

Why were you thrown out?

My quarrel with the Studio was that I thought we were the best realistic actors in the world, but realism is only one style. I thought that it was very important in a workshop atmosphere to work on other theatrical styles as well – to work on high comedy, to work on Shaw, to work on Chekhov, to work on Shakespeare, to work on the Greek writers. And there's a very organized way that one can go about it, and that's what we did over the course of three years. It was wonderful.

Who was involved with that?

Yul was there, Richard Kylie, a wonderful actress named Mary Welch, Annie Jackson, Ruby Dee – that's who I remember at the moment. It was a good professional group.

When you started working in film, was it a fairly easy transition for you to make from TV?

Yeah. No problem whatsoever.

Were you shooting in film for TV, too?

No, everything I did in TV was live. I didn't do any film work for television, because it was the worst of both mediums – you didn't have time for the perfection of film, and you didn't have the spontaneity of a live show. So the fortunate thing is – and I've said this so often – that the laws of optics are constant: a 35mm lens is the same whether it's on a movie camera, a still camera, or anything. So the amount of live work taught you everything you needed to know about lenses and editing, especially, because you were editing as you went. There is no substitute for live TV in terms of training.

Is that why you've attached such importance to the rehearsal process in your films?
Yes, I'm sure. I got a tremendous value out of it.

One more New York question: Before John Lindsay became Mayor here in the mid-sixties, didn't film crews have to pay off policemen to 'guarantee' a problem-free shoot?
It was serious enough that you'd have to pay off all three shifts. The shifts in those days were 4–12, 12–8 and 8–4. So on a normal movie day starting at 6.30 or 7.00, you'd hit all three shifts. [*Laughs.*] And there was a standard rate for the sergeant, a standard rate for the patrolman and a standard rate for the lieutenants. But Lindsay knocked all that out – he really did a tremendous amount. He assigned tactical-force policemen to you, and these guys wouldn't take a cup of coffee. The corruption literally disappeared overnight – it wasn't even weaned away, it just disappeared. He is responsible as much as anyone is for the amount of movies being made in New York.

Was that your first exposure to police corruption?
No, because I grew up poor in New York. [*Laughs.*] If you grow up poor in New York, you get exposed to it.

You have to be one of the most prolific directors in film history – can you talk about why you've made so many films?
I don't know that I can tell you accurately. I love doing the work. I get a tremendous amount back from it. So despite all the energy that it takes, I'm being filled up at the same time that I'm emptying out. I don't feel that everything has to be a masterpiece. There are many reasons for taking movies. Sometimes I've taken movies because I wanted to solve certain problems. One time – I wrote about this in the book – I was having tremendous colour problems, and I knew that Carlo Di Palma would get me past them, so I took a movie just so I could work with him.

Is it ever an issue of money?
Sometimes I've done it purely for the buck. Absolutely. When I got married and knew we were going to have children and I wanted us to live in a house, I took a movie to pay for the down-payment on the house. To me, a very good reason to do a movie.

Do you remember which film that was?

Yes, it was a movie called *Child's Play*, for David Merrick. I took a movie recently just to set up a trust fund for my grandchild. But also, the thing is, you can always find terrifically interesting problems to work on so that you're expanding your technique all the time, even on those films. And I am interested in the long haul. Again, not to get pretentious about it, but nobody's career is made from one picture – well, maybe it is for something as extraordinary as *Citizen Kane*, but that's the exception.

Also, I never joined 'the club' – not just in terms of not working out there, either. There's a whole kind of movie existence that one can lead – you can lead it here, too – and I have never been a part of that. Because of that, I knew that if I ever didn't work for a period of time, I'd be very rapidly shunted aside. So, to sort of to keep my oar in, it was important to keep going, keep going, keep going. If there wasn't a magnificent script, I'd take a very good script. If there wasn't a very good script, I'd take a good script. I never knowingly took a bad script, but as I say, it wasn't important that they be home runs every time, critically or commercially.

Can you talk about who belongs to that 'club' in New York?
It depends on the decade. First of all, when I began, there wasn't a club – Kazan worked here and I worked here, period. That was it. [*Laughs.*] Now I guess it's represented by the Weinstein group, and before then, it was that first wave of Hollywood refugees – the ones who had broken away from there and come to work here. This would include a lot of actors, by the way. I can't really analyze it for you because I don't know enough about it – I'm that detached from it. I know it exists and I know I'm not part of it.

Some of these projects you've taken on for 'ulterior' motives – how often do they turn out to be better than expected?
It happens all the time. The good ones turn out surprisingly bad, and the ones that are loaded with problems turn out to be superb. It's by no means an axiom. The thing is, no one really knows. Maybe Steven Spielberg knows, and he's the only one since Disney. For the rest of us, that's why the process is so important – all we can do is work well and then hope for the best. And I'm not being falsely modest here. Good work is an accident. Now, there's a reason the accident happens to some of us and will never happen to other people. You have to know how to prepare the groundwork. But whether or not it happens is an accident. There are too many elements – too many people, too many techniques. Who can depend on that?

Can you see some sort of pattern to your career?
No. It's partially because I've never worked from any preconceived notion of what the work should be. I would take something because it interested me. And sometimes I would look back and see a pattern over the years: 'Oh, I was interested in that during those years – look what I picked, and the way I did it.' But at the time I didn't see it, and now, looking back, I don't see it.

The seventies were a pretty extraordinary decade for you – *Serpico, Dog Day Afternoon, Network* **– do you feel like you were working with stronger material?**
No, I think it has to do with being in tune with the times. Because in my view, I did some work in the eighties that was wonderful, but totally rejected. *Daniel*, for instance. [*Laughs.*] And I thought *Running on Empty* was a very good movie.

Were you surprised by the negative response to *Daniel*?
Stunned. Amazed. Commercially, I didn't expect it ever to be anything – we all did it for minimum, and nobody took any money or expected any money. But I was amazed at the critical reception, because I think it's a startlingly original movie, and I find it deeply moving. I generally don't look back at my stuff at all, but the few times I've seen it since, I just – if I come in and see two minutes of it I can't tear myself away from it.

I remember a couple of the reviews for the film seeming almost hostile – as if the movie had more of an effect on the reviewers than they cared to admit.
I wish I felt that. I felt they were just hostile. I know there was a campaign against it. The *New York Times* worked very hard to defeat it. I remember that year, after the reviews came out, I was so shocked by the response that I began to really think back on the period before the film was released. And I remember, for instance, that twice that year the Sunday *Times Magazine* section published articles by Judge Irving Kaufman, who presided over the trial of the Rosenbergs. I'm pretty sure this was part of an attempt to rehabilitate him – I mean, I'd like to know when the *New York Times Magazine* has ever published two articles in one year by the same author.

Particularly a relatively obscure one.
Right. Then I remember when we were getting ready to open, I was really surprised that there wasn't even a request for one of those boring Sunday articles in the Arts & Leisure section about the movie. And we're talking about E. L. Doctorow, one of the major American novelists – not to mention the fact that it was one of the few instances, possibly even the first instance, of a writer of his stature adapting his own book. But the *Times* didn't even inquire about it. Also, that Sunday before we opened, there was a very prominent review in the Book Review section about a non-fiction book that had come out by somebody named Ronald Radosh, an historian, and another person about the Rosenbergs. The two authors were very right-wing people, and the book tried to establish the guilt of the Rosenbergs. And then, finally, on the last page of that same Book Review, Walter Goodman wrote an article – I still haven't forgiven him – the essence of which was 'A plague on both your houses – those of you who say they were innocent, those who say they were guilty. Let's just drop it, already.'

But in *Daniel,* **the Isaacsons – the couple based on the Rosenbergs – are never shown to be innocent.**

The movie never said innocent or guilty. For all I know, the Rosenbergs *were* guilty. The movie – in my view and certainly in Edgar's – was not about the Rosenbergs; it was about the consequences to children when parents become deeply committed to anything. Who pays for the parents' commitment? That's what that piece is about thematically. To me, the book was about that, the movie was about that. But with *Daniel*, people said, 'Oh, you're just trying to avoid the politics of it.' Avoid the politics?! How can you do that movie and say you're avoiding the politics, when you show the FBI storming into these people's apartment and ripping everything apart? Anyway, I'm quite convinced that the reason for the *Times*'s campaign against the film is related to that old German–Jewish vs Russian–Jewish fight. I think the Ochses and the Adlers were embarrassed about some Jews who were vulgar enough to make such a fuss. I could never prove it, of course, but I'm absolutely certain that it was a decision made above the level of the editors. I don't know which member of the Ochs or Adler family it was, but I'm sure it was decided on that level.

How often do you think politics has played a role in reviews of your films?
Never. I think that was the only time it ever happened. Because it's a horrendous thing to do, and you save your shot for when you think it might matter.

Don't you think *Daniel* will eventually be reconsidered critically?
I don't know, because in all honesty, I don't pay that much attention. One can always be surprised. You know, they just had this live performance of *Fail-Safe* on CBS. According to all the publicity surrounding it, I got some of my best reviews on that picture. [*Laughs.*] Everyone keeps talking about the 'classic 1961 film'. The only thing is, I don't remember that picture getting very good notices. Go figure.

One more review question: I recently read Pauline Kael's piece on *Network*. Do you remember that one?
Oh, yeah. The pits.

I really felt she missed the point of the film on that one.
She's so bright, so you know when she misses it's deliberate. And what she could not stand – because she was a very good writer – was, number one, another really good writer. [*Laughs.*] Her attack on Paddy Chayefsky in that review is unspeakable.

All the directors she loved continually did, in my view, dumb movies. I think De Palma is a wonderful director who has done one bad script after another, starting with *Carrie*. But she liked that. She liked crap surrounded in elegance. She, like so many critics, was in a real power struggle. What she wanted out of her career was the *Times*, and when she didn't get it, she was going to attract attention whichever way she could. But she never did affect the box office of a movie; the *New Yorker* doesn't do that.

She also had a perennial pattern of falling in love with a director and then destroying him. She did it with me. When she was still on the *San Francisco Quar-*

terly – that's where she began – she sent me her review of *Long Day's Journey into Night*, comparing it to Carl Dreyer – it was that kind of review. And then, after *The Group*, and after a personal meeting between us, things kept getting worse and worse.

I can't believe how prophetic *Network* was.
Oh, absolutely. News as entertainment.

Not to mention corporate ownership of the networks, live TV news, 'Reality TV' – you can just go down the list . . .
He was prescient, Paddy. He was nuts. You can say the same thing about *The Hospital*, too.

Peter Finch's character keeps making these incredibly pungent observations about the dangers of what he sees happening around him, and even as the 'spectacle' of his tirades is applauded by the rapt audiences, absolutely no one is listening to his message. I guess you could argue in some sense that the same situation occurred with the film, which attracted enormous attention, but which obviously failed as a cautionary tale, since virtually everything depicted in it happened anyway . . .
That's right. Well, it's my old belief – art never changes anything. [*Laughs*.]

I was wondering, why did you use a voice-over in the film?
Because Paddy wrote it. It never occurred to me to question it. That's not as naïve as it sounds. Clearly, he wanted to set this picture at a distance from you. In order for him to say what he wanted to say, he wanted you to laugh, and the nature of the laughter had to be from outside. I think that's why he used a narrator – he wanted a certain amount of detachment. The only one that you really lock in with, and that takes quite bit of time, is Bill Holden. Everybody else is 'over there', including Peter Finch.

Do you think of *Prince of the City*, *Q&A* and *Night Falls on Manhattan* as a 'trilogy'?
I never set out to do that. People do lump them together.

Perhaps one reason for that is the fact that, as far as I know, they're the only three scripts you've had a hand in writing.
Right.

Why those three in particular?
Well, starting with *Prince of the City*, the minute I read the book, I knew how to do the movie. I knew it. And I wanted Jay Presson Allen to adapt it, but she was working on another picture, so she said, 'Sidney, why don't you do the break-down?' – which is when you take from the novel what you'll keep and what you'll throw out. I finished in two, three days, and she read it and said, 'This is great. Why don't you start writing while I'm finishing up this other picture?' And there

was no fear in it, because a lot of the book was simply transcriptions of the tapes, so that provided an awful lot of good dialogue – like, 'I'm going to clip him', I mean, 'clip', what a word! That's right off the tapes. Then when Jay finished, she came in, did a polish on it, and very generously said to me afterwards – she didn't have to do this – 'Look Sidney, I think you should get screenwriting credit on it because you've really done the donkey work on it.' So I said fine.

Then, because I know the life of cops so well – not just from that but from *Serpico* – when I got to *Q&A*, it was just quicker and easier to do it myself. I didn't have to explain it to a writer. And the same is true of *Night Falls on Manhattan*. I read the galleys of Bob Daley's book – he wrote the original book of *Prince of the City*, too. *Night Falls* was not very good, actually, but it began with a recounting of this big dope dealer in Harlem who took out five cops when they came to get him, and escaped. He was eventually caught and William Kunstler defended him. The nature of Kunstler's defense was he didn't kill the cops – it was self-defence, because a number of them who were themselves involved in the drug trade had come up there to execute him. And then the book went on to some cockamamie romance between the detective and a lady DA – you know, a totally conventional book. But as I was reading the galleys, I thought, 'Well, what if this were true? What if the cops were really on their way up there to kill him? What if Kunstler was right?' – I mean, he was right about an awful lot of things. So the script was really my own development of the first three or four pages of what had happened in that novel, and it became easy to write myself.

All three films share themes that I know are important to you, particularly that whole personal/political dissonance that occurs when an individual's ideals are challenged by his or her position within an institutional framework —
And can you hold on to them? The endless problem.

Of course, more specifically, all three share the backdrop of corruption in the NYPD.
But in a sense, for something like *Night Falls,* that's just the propelling incident. By the way, I'm so happy for Jimmy Gandolfini.

His performance as the 'fallen' cop is astonishing in that film.
He's marvellous, isn't he?

He had a much smaller role in *A Stranger Among Us*.
That was his first job. We stayed close because I gave him his first job. But in *Night Falls*, when he got up from the couch and went, 'I got caught with my hand in the cookie jar', I mean, ahhh, that smile on his face . . .

In *Prince of the City*, there's that wonderful moment when Treat Williams's character, standing in the elevator, says to his partner, 'Don't hate me, Joe,' and, as the door begins to close, his partner responds, 'I could never hate you, Danny.' And we see Williams's pained reflection in the closing elevator door.

How many takes did you do on that one?

One, I think. On something like that, when you know how much the actors are putting out, you want to be certain before you start calling about the mechanics of where and when the door hits. Of course, you need a little bit of luck, but I knew I had it right away.

You always had that image in your mind?

No, not until I got there. Because you never know in those city buildings, sometimes you can find gates that close in the elevators instead of doors. And a gate would have been just as good.

But you'd already used gates to great effect in *The Pawnbroker*...

[*Laughs.*] Right. No, it was right there on the set.

It's interesting to think of *Prince, Q&A,* and *Night Falls* almost as one film – each one as a sort of variation on a theme. Many images – motifs, almost – repeat themselves: ruined policemen sitting in cars, revolvers in their mouths; characters being patted down for wires; bodies being dredged up from the East River. There are even repeated bits of dialogue, like where the somewhat naïve protagonist is complimented, and is then caught blushing. There's a scene like that with Timothy Hutton in *Q&A* —

Right, and it's in *Night Falls*, when Dreyfuss says it to Andy Garcia.

And there are always clandestine meetings taking place in some abandoned lot by the river.

Usually it's noisy there, that's why. And of course, it's so strong, visually. When Phil Rosenberg, the production designer, found that location with the burnt-out pier for *Night Falls*, in the scene with Gandolfini and Andy Garcia, I could have kissed him. It was great, with that twisted pier behind them.

Why did you chose to open *Q&A* with the crane shot of the traffic light going from red to green? It's such a great analogy for a movie starting.

I don't know, from the minute I got on to that location I knew that was the way I wanted to do it. I did think it was a marvellous shot. On the pictures that you feel the closest to, that kind of thing happens extremely often. You know the opening shot and/or the closing shot – you don't know anything else, you don't even know what you think about the picture, but very often you know what those two are.

I was wondering how you got involved with *The Morning After*?

I had been dying to work with Jane Fonda all my life, because Hank and I were so close and I had known her since she was seventeen. Loved her work, always have – she's a marvellous actress. She had been after me for years to do that script, but the beginning wasn't very good. Anyway, she kept working on it and making it better and better. I was getting older, and she is very persuasive. So finally we said, 'We'd better get it done, because there may not be that much time left . . .' [*Laughs.*]

It's a basic thriller in some respects, but it still manages be layered with all of the themes that run through so much of your work – how prejudice poisons relationships, the unfair advantages of the privileged classes, etc. Were those elements that you brought into it?
No, that was all there.

That film really 'got' LA in a visual sense. I was struck by the use of saturated colours, for instance, like that crimson façade of the building where the murder takes place.
We were reinforcing all of it with filters. You know what's interesting? When you're a resident of a place, everything becomes ordinary, because you see it all the time. When you're not, it's all exotic. Johnny Schlesinger once told me that I shot London better than any British director. And I remember telling Sandy MacKendrick that he did more with the Orange Julius stand on Broadway in *Sweet Smell of Success* than I had ever done with the city in a lifetime of shooting there. That's because it comes at you absolutely freshly.

You've had final cut on all of your pictures since when?
Murder on the Orient Express.

But I'm assuming you're still often asked by a studio to go back and do cuts?
Yeah. And in those instances, it's like anything else – if push comes to shove, you just put your feet down.

I would guess you're more inclined to recut something if it's a film you're less emotionally invested in —
Absolutely. If it's something that I've done for commercial reasons because I think it's time I had a hit, sure, I'll try it. I think I talk about it in the book, but the whole thing now of screenings and focus groups and so on is so hopeless. I don't know what's going to be done about it, because we'll never know how many pictures it's ruined. And I don't believe in the whole process, because I think people change their minds as soon as you ask their opinion about something. The minute you're told your opinion matters, something changes – just look at political polls, which are so often wrong. So I think that those cards are useless and hopeless. They never helped me and as far as I know, they never helped any movie – except for the classic story of, you know, the Glenn Close movie where she boiled the rabbit. It's going to get worse, too. We see movies now deliberately made for, and by, focus groups. And that's despite the fact that it's been a wonderful year for American movies.

In an interview right before *The Fugitive Kind* was released, you said, 'I hope it's a hit . . . because it'll make the next four much easier to do.'
The next four flops. [*Laughs.*]

Do you find that still to be true?

I do. It's important to get a one hit out of every four just to keep going.

Are there any recent films you directed that you suspected would be box-office draws?
I thought *Critical Care* had a very good chance of being a major hit – although I didn't do it for that reason. Unfortunately, the company that I made it for got sold between the time I made it and the time it was released, and that's death – you're finished when that happens. Believe it or not, it's always very important for the new owners to make sure that the previous management looks bad. That's happened to me three times. It happened with a very good picture called *The Deadly Affair*, with Simone Signoret and James Mason. Marvellous movie. It got caught in that kind of a meat grinder and so did *The Hill*, a picture I did with Connery. And there's nothing you can do.

Why did you decide to remake *Gloria*?
Not a very good decision. [*Laughs.*]

You mean because of the inevitable comparisons to Cassavates' original?
The original is a lousy movie – it's really not good. It doesn't even make sense from a plot point of view – it was made because John wanted to give Gena a job. I did the remake for two reasons. First of all, I wanted to work with Sharon. I think she's talented – a fine actress. And second, I needed a big chunk of dough for a reason that will remain nameless. And I had them over a barrel because there was another director who had been on it for months and hadn't picked one location. They were six weeks from shooting and Sharon was sitting on top of a big salary, so I could hit them for a lot of money. But I did want to work with Sharon.

Have you ever gone over-schedule or over-budget on something?
On *The Wiz*, I think I went over-budget and over-schedule because there was no budget and there was no schedule. [*Laughs.*] It was also frantic. But that's the only time.

That must make you all the more marketable.
It's helped me a lot.

What are you working on now?
I can't tell you, because I don't like to talk about it until it's on the verge of happening.

You said earlier that you 'got a lot back' from film. What exactly did you mean?
It's an enormously, incredibly satisfying way to work. First of all, it's never lonely. There's constant contact with other people, and life all around. You are constantly communicating with and dealing in feelings between yourself and others. There's a sense of energy. There's enormous reward. And it's sheer fun – actors are fun, great fun, and always interesting, endlessly interesting. I guess I've

worked with as many if not more actors than any other director working today.

Are there any you haven't worked with that you'd like to?
So many. And the time is going, going. I've never worked with Meryl and I'd love to. I've never worked with Michelle Pfeiffer – I think she's marvellous. And Julia Roberts is wonderful. I love Matt Damon – God, we've got so many good ones coming up. Jude Law, wow. Russell Crowe, wow. De Niro – I've never worked with De Niro. Not to mention the older ones I keep seeing all the time, like Paul Newman, for instance. I'd love to work with Pacino again. I send them stuff, they send me stuff, but we've never been able to mesh and want to, desperately. Sissy Spacek, I've always loved her work. Holly Hunter, love her work. There are so many good actors. I would have loved the old studio days, I tell you, with the stock company. I really would have.

Do you feel that you're still at the top of your game?
I don't know. Again, I don't think in those terms. I know I'm brighter now than I ever was. And I think I'm hipper. [*Laughs.*] But I'm an old man now. I won't know until I go back to work, simple as that. I haven't wanted to work now for well over a year. Very unusual for me. I don't know why. Maybe I got tired – I have a right to have gotten tired. But now I'm slowly starting to gear up again.

Ulu Grosbard

Ulu Grosbard directed *The Subject was Roses, Who is Harry Kellerman . . .?, Straight Time, True Confessions, Falling in Love, Georgia,* and *Deep End of the Ocean.* His work for the theatre includes the New York premières of Arthur Miller's *A View from the Bridge* and *The Price,* Woody Allen's *The Floating Light Bulb,* Beth Henley's *The Wake of Jamie Foster* and *Family Week,* and David Mamet's *American Buffalo* and *The Woods.* Grosbard has been twice nominated for a Best Director Tony Award and won an Obie for his direction of *A View from the Bridge.*

Tod Lippy: I know that in 1942 you fled with your family from the Nazi occupation of Belgium, and, after spending most of your adolescence in Cuba, came to New York in 1948. Where did you live when you got here?
Ulu Grosbard: We moved to 77th Street and Riverside Drive. When we got here, I spoke English fairly well, but not completely fluently. I was fluent in terms of reading and comprehension, but I was largely self-taught, in the sense that I was an avid reader ever since I was a child. Anyway, I wanted to go back to school, because I had had no high school – I had gone to work when I was about fourteen.

Didn't you train as a diamond-cutter when your family was in Cuba?
Yeah, diamond-cutting. So I had to get some high school credits. There was this private, sort of preparatory school called Morningside, and I went there for about six months. I didn't quite finish, because in the meantime I had decided I would apply for college. It turned out, of course, that these credits wouldn't qualify me at places like Harvard or Yale, but I'd discovered that the University of Chicago didn't require an actual high school record; they would give you a battery of their own tests. So I took them, and they accepted me, and I was able to catch up – I got my bachelor's there in about a year. And then I went on and got a master's in English, with a minor in Philosophy. After that I went up to Yale Drama School for one year – which I felt was basically enough time there. This was during the Korean War, and I had been drafted, so I left Yale and went into the Army for a couple of years.

Did you end up in Korea?
No. The armistice was arrived at while I was in basic training, so by the time I finished, it was over. I ended up in Fort Bragg attached to the 82nd Airborne in a military intelligence unit, basically marking time. And then I came back to New York. So really, before that, I'd only spent about six months in the city, right after we'd first arrived.

Had you been interested in theatre all along?
No, it wasn't really until college in Chicago that I thought this was something I would want to pursue.

When you came back to the city, how did you get involved in directing plays?
What happened was, when I came back, I took a part-time job teaching English,

oddly enough, at Berlitz. And then I ran into an acquaintance from Yale, and he and his father had a summer theatre in Bellport, Long Island. He had just been drafted – he'd done the full three years at Yale, and had gotten a series of deferrals to do so. And he was supposed to direct the second half of the season, but obviously wasn't able to, so he asked me if I would do it for him. That's really how I came into my first full-fledged directing experience. And that's where I met Duvall and Hackman – they were both in my first production, which was Arthur Miller's *A View from the Bridge*. It was the first time the full-length version – which had been directed by Peter Brook in London – had been staged here. The one-act version, in conjunction with *Memory of Two Mondays*, had been done in New York on Broadway, and had failed. So Miller rewrote it and had a successful staging in London, but nobody would do it in New York, so it was released as a summer-stock production.

You also directed the first off-Broadway production of the play some years later, didn't you?
Yeah. It must have been six or seven years later. By then I had done *The Days and Nights of Beebee Fenstermaker,* and I had done *The Subject Was Roses*, and I couldn't find anything I really wanted to do – after *Roses*, I was being offered this, that, and the other, but nothing I was interested in. So I went back and did *Bridge* with Duvall, Jon Voight, and Susan Anspach.

That must have been one of Voight's first appearances.
I think he had been in a musical on Broadway, but *Bridge* really made his career – it established him. He was wonderful in it.

When did you begin assistant-directing for films?
That happened around this time, too – in the late fifties. And again, it was totally by accident. I ran into another classmate from Yale, Eric Bercovici, on Cornelia Street in the Village, where I was living. I asked him what he had been up to, and he said he was working for a small movie company in New York. I can't even remember what he was doing, but I asked him how he got the job, and he said, 'Well, I looked in the Yellow Pages.' [*Laughs.*] I thought, 'My god, what a brilliant idea.' And that's exactly what I did. There must have been a hundred and fifty listings for this and that – I systematically made my way through it, one by one, knocking on doors. I ended up at a stock-footage company on 57th Street. In the meantime, though, I had made contact with a guy who was doing a half-hour, non-union series they were shooting in Yonkers.

This was for television?
Yeah. He didn't have anything for me initially, but told me to keep checking back. And about three or four months later, he said to me, 'Do you know how to drive a truck?' I'd never driven a truck in my life. [*Laughs.*] They'd just lost their equipment-truck driver, so he told me to show up on Monday morning. I said,

'Sure', and I get into the truck and start driving, and sure enough the truck breaks down on the Henry Hudson Parkway. [*Laughs.*] The carburettor or something. So that was the start of my movie career. I ended up driving the truck for a couple of months, and I became an assistant to the guy who was production manager. He was then kicked upstairs, and he offered me his job.

So I was production manager for four or five more months, and became very friendly with the First AD, Joe Manduke. Joe got a job on *Splendor in the Grass* as a Second AD, and within the third or fourth week, was offered a First AD position on another picture, so he recommended me for the Second AD job. I interviewed with Charlie Maguire, who was Kazan's production manager, and he gave me the job. And once I did that, I really had my pick. It was a wonderful situation, because I had joined the union, and could make enough money to then go four or five months living off my AD's salary while I tried to find something to direct off-Broadway. So I would do theatre work – like *The Days and Nights of Beebee Fenstermaker* – in between film jobs. I worked for Kazan, for Arthur Penn on *The Miracle Worker*, for Robert Rossen on *The Hustler* . . .

Didn't you work on Lumet's *The Pawnbroker*, too?
I was actually location manager on that. That's sort of a complicated story. Eli Landau was doing two pictures at once: *The Heart Is a Lonely Hunter*, which Sidney was going to direct, and *The Pawnbroker*, with Arthur Hiller. I had been hired by Sidney and Landau to be the production manager for *The Heart Is a Lonely Hunter*. They had cast Montgomery Clift, but about three weeks out from shooting, the insurance company told Landau that they wouldn't insure Clift. Landau almost took the risk himself, but then he got cold feet, so they cancelled that production and moved Lumet over to *Pawnbroker*. They already had a production manager on that picture, so I moved over as location manager – I did all the scouting in Harlem for the movie.

At that point I started getting production manager offers on other features, but my main concern, my main focus, was still the stage. I remember I had turned down an offer to do three pictures as production manager – it was a big deal – and then Frank Gilroy offered me his play *The Subject Was Roses*, and we were able to get it financed. It wasn't until several years later, when Frank and Edgar Lansbury, the play's producer, got an offer from MGM to do a film adaptation of *Roses*, that I directed my first film. The studio was offering a fair amount of autonomy for us, so I did it. The irony of it is, after Sidney fell out of *The Heart Is a Lonely Hunter*, they came with it to me. I decided against it for some reason – I think it was a matter of casting.

What initially attracted you to directing, both for theatre and film? It almost sounds like you backed into it . . .
I didn't back into it; it was a conscious choice. I was always interested in human behaviour in crisis. Part of that obviously has something to do with my

background, having gone through World War II. That experience left a profound impression on me, and I think it clearly had something to do with my fascination with the theatre. Whether I would be any good at it or not I really didn't know until I went to summer stock. It was then that I really got into it – I thought I had a feel for it. So it was a long period of time between when I made a decision to try and pursue it and when I was able to actually get my hands dirty.

As you mentioned, your first film was an adaptation of a play you'd already helmed on Broadway. Could you talk about some of the differences between directing for film and directing for theatre, particularly in that case, where you were working with the same material?
Well, in doing the film, I found that it became more of a craft-learning experience. I used two of the three original actors: Jack Albertson and Martin Sheen had been in the play, also. The problem in that case was – and fortunately the play had closed by then, so some period of time had elapsed – to make sure they didn't go back to remembered stage performances. They needed to keep it alive, and keep it fresh. I needed them to work moment-to-moment, and not rely on what they had done before, or what had worked for them in a particular scene on stage. And when you have good actors, they will spark off of each other, and certainly Sheen and Albertson did. And Patricia Neal was a new factor – for her the part was fresh – so that wasn't a problem.

You know, the stronger the play, the more it resists adaptation to the screen. So what you're really trying to do is not to lose the point of the play – not get trapped into false attempts to translate it to film.

You mean the old cliché about 'opening it up'?
Opening it up, exactly. Which can really weaken the tension created by the structure of the material. The structure of a play is a very different animal than the structure of films. There is a sense of sequencing to good film material – you go from sequence to sequence, not from the beginning, middle and end of each scene. So when you're filming, there's almost an organic resistance there, in a funny way. It can be done, and done well, but you find yourself, for instance, sometimes wanting to go with a camera in a way that you can't, because it would be at the expense of the tension of the scene. When you see this done with some adaptations, you realize the movie doesn't work even though the play has worked beautifully on stage. I understand the instinct, which is to try and make it into a movie, but you're better off trying to be faithful to what made the play work, even if it means to some degree photographing some of it. Better to err on that side and retain what made the play work in the first place.

You've often been characterized as an 'actor's director' – can you talk about the director/actor relationship a little bit?
Well, when you get hold of a good play or screenplay, you want to bring it to life,

and it's essential to work with actors that are capable. The paradox of good acting is that, on the one hand, the actor knows his lines – knows where the scene is headed – yet on the other hand, he has to work moment to moment: in a sense, *not* know where he's going. It isn't that dissimilar from a great athlete, except that a baseball player or tennis player has the advantage of being faced with a fresh situation every time. For an actor, he knows the scene, but at the same time, he has to be able on some level to act spontaneously. It's a curious paradox, and yet good actors will give you the impression that those lines are totally new to them. And they themselves feel like they've never heard them before, that it's never been said before. When you can achieve that, it's very exciting.

What I'm looking for in an actor's performance is true behaviour – the way people really do act, do behave, and do think. Not an actor's idea, or a director's idea, of how people act. And I think good actors have the same instincts, and work on the same wavelength. Any real first-rate actor goes for that sense of spontaneity. That sense of real life.

Have you ever used non-actors?
I have on movies. Non-actors don't work out that well in theatre, because they have to repeat. But you can get wonderful performances on film, because you only need to catch them once. And if you find someone who's not self-conscious, and who has a strong presence, I think you can get terrific stuff. Particularly in smaller parts, where, for example, the profession of the character is important. If you're casting a waiter in a small speaking part, you're clearly better off using a non-actor, because there's no way you're going to get a day-player actor to learn how to handle the tray or put the plate on the table in the way that a man who's been doing it for ten years will. The trick is to find someone who's not frozen by the camera. It's not that hard, though, because if you give the guy something to do that he knows how to do, he'll feel comfortable with it.

You mentioned the importance of spontaneity – I recall reading that for a scene in *True Confessions,* you purposely neglected to tell any of the extras that there was going to be a physical confrontation between Duvall and Charles Durning in order to get the most authentic response from them.
That's absolutely true.

Is that something you've done often?
It depends on the situation. That scene was kind of a roll of the dice, because we didn't rehearse it, either – we couldn't rehearse it without giving it away. So we basically just walked it through once for the cameras. We were obviously covering it as much as we could. And it was wonderful – the extras literally didn't know what was going on. But you can't always do that; it depends on the situation, and who you're working with. And, of course, the luxury of time. On that picture, I had terrific producers – Bob Chartoff and Irwin Winkler – and they gave me a great deal of latitude. I didn't have to worry about the studio at all. And I had a

wonderful cameraman, Owen Roizman. But you're very often at the mercy of the situation in which you're shooting.

Right after *Georgia* was released, you said in an interview that you had 'assured Jennifer Jason Leigh that her intuition was so strong that she would land on her feet, and if she didn't, I would always be there to catch her'. Can you elaborate on what you meant by that?

Well, I think it's important for an actor to be able to trust his director, and that trust comes out of working together. The actor gets a sense that the director knows what he's talking about, in terms of the story and the individual scenes, in the kinds of directions he gives, and in his understanding of the character. And, of course, in his command of the set. Once an actor develops that trust, it's easier for him to take risks. He can be bad in a take and trust the fact that the director can tell the difference between that take and one where his performance is truer, so, in the cutting room, he will end up on film with his best work on screen. It creates an atmosphere of being able to go for something, and not being concerned that you're going to pay the consequences if you fail.

I wanted to ask you about a few specific scenes from your films, particularly with regard to the actors' performances. One that has always astounded me is Barbara Harris's post-audition monologue in *Who Is Harry Kellerman, and Why Is He Saying Those Terrible Things About Me?* It's one of those moments you were referring to, where there's absolutely no 'performance' – she's completely embodied this character who's living through this particularly defenceless moment. What was that like to shoot?

I remember that well, because at the time Barbara had a great distrust of the camera. It took a lot of shooting to get to the point where, in that one take, she suddenly dropped all her defences – in fact, it was probably the most film I shot in that movie. She was also able at some point to make a very personal connection with what she was saying. But it happened one time, and that was it. The others had shadings, but there wasn't that marriage. Moments like that – well, it's like with great performers on stage, for instance. You can look at somebody in that kind of situation and say, 'He's inspired – he can do nothing wrong.' He knows his lines, and he knows where he's going, yet he is experiencing total freedom. And of course it happens with improvisation, but it can happen with written text, too. It's joyful.

Speaking of working with an existing text, I thought the scene in *Georgia* where Jennifer Jason Leigh sings Van Morrison's 'Take Me Back' was another moment along those lines.

That's true. And the airport sequence, too.

All of the concert footage in *Georgia* was filmed live, wasn't it?

Right. I was very concerned about it at first. Barbara Turner, who wrote the script and was another one of the producers on the film, was the one who kept pushing me to do it, and I finally agreed to it. All the music supervisors I spoke to, though, thought we were nuts. The only guy who really encouraged me was Robert Altman, because he had done it in *Nashville*. He gave me one very simple suggestion: 'Shoot the close-up first.' In this instance we used multiple cameras, but I realized what he meant. We shot the close-up live, and then for the wide shots, you recorded it live, and you used that as the playback. So you didn't have playbacks done in the studio before you started shooting. You used the best close-up take, and then, once you moved back, the musicians who'd just played it – and all of the band members in the film were pros, except for John Reilly, who was an amateur musician – could do it again. It wasn't like having actors fake it to music that another set of musicians had recorded months before in a studio. It was very easy.

How many cameras did you have?
Four. I had two on Jennifer, and two recording the other guys. It is one take.

Almost the first half of the song is one continuous medium shot of her from the side. One could imagine a million ways to shoot and cut that together, but the very, very slow tracking shot provides this unblinking, almost cruel, perspective on a moment of absolute vulnerability.
Well, I decided to shoot it this way when I saw it in rehearsal – to just go for broke. Originally I'd thought of not even cutting at all. But then I did eventually put in that cut halfway through, where you switch to the other side. There was very minimal cutting to the audience, also. Before I went into it, I felt I had to depend on the fact that I would not try to cut it down: that I would stick with the eight-and-a-half minutes that the song runs. I didn't know whether it was going to work or not, but doing anything else would have violated my sense of what the scene required.

It's almost like an endurance test.
Yeah, it is. It's hard for an audience, but it holds.

What about the scene near the beginning of *Straight Time*, when Dustin Hoffman's character, who's just gotten out of jail, goes to visit his ex-con friend (Gary Busey) and the friend's wife (Kathy Bates) and son? By the way, was the son played by Jake Busey?
Yeah, he was the little kid.

You shot that dinner-table scene from one set-up, taking in all four of them in a continuous take which must run four or five minutes, and the emotion just bounces out of it. How long did that take to get right?
That wasn't a lot of takes. Actually, the most takes I did in that movie was in the first scene with the parole officer. Emmet Walsh came in and was very tense, and was really playing into the guy being a 'meanie', you know? I thought what he needed to do as an actor – because he has an edge as a person – was to go com-

pletely against it; to genuinely try and be a nice guy. It would still come across, but it would be much more subtle. I shudder to think of the amount of footage I spent on that. It was something like thirty thousand feet – it was crazy. But I thought, 'If I don't get this guy right *right now*, I'm dead for the rest of the movie.' Normally I don't shoot a lot of footage.

Do you have long rehearsal periods beforehand?
No, no. It depends on the actors, but not really.

Do you spend a lot of time with actors just discussing the character with them?
No. Again, it depends on the actor, but with most of the people I've worked with, once you're on a wavelength with them, there's not a lot of talk. The references, the discussion – there's something intuitive going on between myself and the actors. The references are mostly concrete, and as simple as possible. I am very leery of intellectual discussions about the character. I think it tends to make it cerebral – there's a danger of taking the life out of it by talking about it too much. Good actors really don't require it; they have an instinct about the characters. First of all, they made a choice to play the part, so already going in they have an affinity for it.

With plays, it's a little different, because you can go into depth more. The whole rehearsal process is different, because you have to repeat it so many more times, while at the same time keeping it alive. You can't always totally rely on instinct. In a play, you need to get into it more, because at some point that instinct is going to disappear, and then you have to find a way back to being fresh with the material. It's hard: getting back to that instinctual depth takes some figuring out sometimes, and can be an arduous process.

You're known to be meticulous in your choice of actors, both for film and theatre —
I think casting is most of it.

My impression is that there have been times when a project you were interested in died on the vine, so to speak, because you couldn't secure the actors you wanted.
Yes. That's true. You know, the excitement and the joy of a project has to do not only with the story – the quality of the material – but who you're going to be working with, and how right they are for the material. If they're not, and they're miscast, they may be a good actor, but as far as I'm concerned, forget it – you'll never get what you're after; it's not possible. You need to marry the character as written with not only the actor's ability, but with whatever it is in his personality that will enable him to create the character.

You've talked before about your choice of De Niro for the role of the priest in *True Confessions* – I recall your saying you wanted him not only because he was a great actor, but because he had a somewhat similar background to the character.

Also because I trusted completely that if he felt he wanted to do it, and saw something in it, that it would happen. At that time he was very careful about the choices he was making – he was coming off *Raging Bull* – both in terms of the kind of character he wanted to play and who he would work with.

He created that character in the course of our making choices about the costume, the shoes, the cufflinks, you name it. You saw him define the character for himself as he made those choices. He came into the shoot about four weeks into it – I started shooting all of Duvall's scenes, because of the way the screenplay is structured – and in the meantime, my associate producer, Gail Mutrux, had set it up so he could spend time with a priest, who taught him Mass in Latin, which is how it was delivered in 1948. I went to watch a couple of rehearsals, but most of the time he was on his own, really just learning how to perform the mass. By the time we started shooting, the character was totally there.

Do you find that most of the actors you work with are research-oriented?
Yes, particularly in this kind of situation, where a very specific knowledge of certain rituals is required. On that film, Duvall spent a lot of time hanging around homicide detectives. Again, there's no substitute for reality. When we were shooting *Straight Time*, for instance, the way the original jewellery robbery was written in the screenplay and the book it was based on was that they went into a manhole and cut the alarm wires to the store. Sheer nonsense. I mean, these guys were not electrical engineers. Not to mention the impossibility of finding wires in a manhole. So again, I asked Gail [Mutrux], who also worked with me on *Straight Time*, to call the cops and find out how thieves actually rob jewellery stores. And she came back to me and told me that what was currently in fashion is what's called 'smash and grab'. They know they have three minutes before the police will get there, so they just break into the cases and grab as much as they can, beating the alarm. So we rewrote the scene, and that's how we did it.

The irony of it is, we shot the scene at around noon at a store on Wilshire Boulevard in LA, and we had cops hanging around to control traffic, that kind of thing. At one point, my AD came over to me and said, 'The police have to leave; they're not going to be able to control traffic.' He told me they'd just had a robbery around the corner, on Beverly Drive. So I called lunch. And it was true – two guys had broken into the store around the corner in an absolutely identical way. We checked it out – the glass cases were all smashed, exactly like the ones on the set. It was uncanny to be walking from a movie set to an identical real-life situation.

We were originally going to use candy glass for the cases, but when you get into close-ups on candy glass, it looks phony. It has a slight colour to it, and it breaks in a different way than real glass does. In rehearsal, it was clear to me that it wasn't going to work. But there was a danger to the actors if you used real glass, which is very unpredictable. That's how we came up with the gloves and the protective goggles he wears.

That brings up another subject – how much input you have in the writing process before shooting begins. Herb Gardner said that you were a terrific director for a writer because your hand is invisible: 'He just seems to be doing your work for you.' I know there have been times when you've gone with a first draft, like with *Georgia*, for instance —
Right.

But with a film like *True Confessions*, there was a rather protracted rewriting process with Joan Didion and John Gregory Dunne. First of all, if you don't feel a script is 'ready', what attracts you to it anyway?
The basic premise of the story – whether it's something that's credible to me, and moves me. It's not anything preconceived, really. I mean, different directors are interested in different kinds of stories, and one's not necessarily more valid than the next. But my own interest has been in always trying to find material that I feel has some genuine relationship to my experiences in my own life and my friends' lives – life as I know it, so to speak. In the case of *True Confessions*, I'd read Dunne's novel first.

After you were given Didion and Dunne's first draft, didn't you ask them to restore some more material from the book?
Yeah, that's true. John and Joan had been much more drastic with the screenplay than I would have been, and I felt there was stuff missing. For one thing, we ended up altering the structure to conform much closer to that of the book. When I first met them and Chartoff and Winkler, I went into the meeting really thinking I was wasting my time. I mean, here they had already written their own screenplay, and I was about to make suggestions that really would change some of it considerably. It was an ironic situation, though, because everything I wanted to change was in John's book. Anyway, I said my piece, and the next day they called and said they wanted me to do it.

Since you're not a writer, do you find it frustrating to have to wait for the good material to come to you?
Well, ideally, you write and direct your own stuff. The only possible drawback with that situation is that as both writer and director, you can sometimes get so close to the material that you lose a certain perspective. They're different talents, to some degree, but if they're married in the same person, it's a great advantage.

Would you say that has anything to do with the fact that you're not a particularly prolific director? You've said before that you find it hard to go into a project just for the sake of working.
I want it to excite me. It's hard to come by, given my taste, or wavelength, or whatever it is I function on. I wish it were easier – I would have worked a lot more.

What percentage of the scripts you read do you turn down?
I can't really give you a percentage, but it's pretty high. And a lot of them are

legitimate movies that are made and are quite successful – they're just not my cup of tea. I feel that way even about the stuff I read that I'm not offered a lot of the time. I think you get to work a lot more if the wavelength you function on is a more popular wavelength – it makes life easier, and it's certainly legitimate. It's just a matter of where you feel you function best.

You're also known to spend a lot of time developing many of your projects. I know *True Confessions* took something like two-and-a-half years, and I remember reading that *The Wake of Jamey Foster*, the Beth Henley play you directed in 1982, was a several-year process ...

Well, we staged that originally in Hartford, and then it was another year before we did it on Broadway. I don't think that amount of time is necessary, though. It's a matter of circumstance: when the cast is available, how ready the material is, all those things. *Deep End of the Ocean* we actually jumped into and began production on without a screenplay, because we were committed to a timetable. Stephen Schiff, the writer, and I had first met on Memorial Day, when Mandalay gave us the go-ahead, and we had to go into pre-production three weeks later. Michelle Pfeiffer was available at that point, and because of the rains and weather conditions, we couldn't go any later; we'd get trapped. In fact, we just finished when the rains hit.

Is that a somewhat problematic way to work?

Well, we had the script by the time we started shooting, but we had to scramble somewhat. And the structure was there because it was based on the book. But quite often that's not that uncommon a situation, because the availability of the star is an issue. And of course, with big action movies, they're locked into the release date.

And there are other reasons. With *Straight Time,* we basically improvised most of the script. We had a draft of Alvin Sargent's screenplay —

Weren't there several writers on that?

Well, Jeffrey Boam did some stuff because Alvin Sargent wasn't available – he was already working on *Ordinary People.* The problem was, Dustin had committed to a crew, and there was this full crew just sitting there, not doing a thing. So I literally went back to Alvin's first draft and cut it down with him – it was 180 pages long. But then once you cut out chunks, you have to figure out how to reconnect everything, and that's when Jeffrey Boam came in. And did a really nice job, by the way.

But a lot of it was improvised. We'd improvise it the night before, type it up, and I would edit it, then we'd stage it the next morning. We really flew by the seat of our pants on that movie.

Dustin Hoffman was originally going to direct that himself, wasn't he?

Absolutely.

Weren't there some conflicts between the two of you on the set?

No, the conflict between us came at the very tail end of the movie, when it was almost finished. It had to do with his wanting to come into the cutting room. It was a matter of time more than anything else. We knew how to end it, with the final scene of him in the car, driving away, intercut with the successive mug shots – which had been in Alvin's first draft. But we still had to figure out how to get from the scene where he kills Gary Busey to the last image. So we actually stopped shooting for a week or two while I did a quick assembly to get a sense of the arc of it. At that point, Dustin wanted to come into the cutting room, and I felt that it would slow us down terrifically. That's when he got angry. During the shoot, he was high-strung, but I thought we worked very well together.

Has that ever been an issue for you on other films?

Not really. At some point on *Deep End* Michelle wanted to go over some stuff in the cutting room, and I told her to just give me her notes, which she was really good about. Good actors have good suggestions – there's no question about it. The thing about making a movie is that the cliché about it being a collaboration is completely true. If you have no ego about it, you take contributions from wherever you can get them. From actors, from everybody. And it makes a better movie. You have to be open to it – you pay for it if you're not.

You already touched briefly on the kind of stories that interest you, but I wanted to go into depth on that a little more. One theme, in particular, seems to reappear in your work: 'The difference between what we are and what we wishfully believe ourselves to be', which is how you described the situation of Eddie in *A View from the Bridge*. It plays off of something you mentioned in relation to *True Confessions*, about 'why things come easily to some people and not to others'. One can certainly see how that disparity between self-perception and reality informs the sisters' relationship in *Georgia*, for instance.

That's true. I don't know that it's a conscious, articulated view, you know? I think it's something I respond to on a spontaneous level. Looking back, I realize a lot of the things I've been attracted to are family stories, dealing with the ambivalences in close relationships, whether it's *Roses*, or *True Confessions*, or *Georgia*, or *Deep End*. They all have in common something that I remember reading in Arthur Miller's introduction to *Salesman*, where he talked about how family members can turn into strangers overnight. That aspect of relationships, I think, has always fascinated me, and there's something that resonates with me when I come across it in material that captures it. It's the mystery of the relationship between work and grace: the basic theological Catholic view of Thomas Aquinas, or the Prodigal Son theme: the one who it comes easily to, and the one who, no matter how hard he or she works, will never get to it. It's certainly there in *Georgia*, and in *True Confessions* as well: the wonderful irony of the cop who seems to be the corrupt brother, and the priest – supposedly the pure one – whose salvation comes from his downfall brought about by the corrupt one, who's actually purer in spirit. But I think those paradoxes do attract me.

Kent Jones made the observation that 'subtraction is central' to your work, which is absolutely true – several critics, in fact, have mentioned the appropriateness of the fact that you trained as a diamond-cutter. Where do you think that kind of reductive minimalism come from?
I'm trying to get to making the point of the scene in as simple a way as I know how. Primarily, I think it comes from wanting to not move the camera for its own sake. On the other hand, I admire people like Brian De Palma, or Spielberg, in terms of their innate sense of being able to use a fluid camera. But it's a question of being true to what you see in the scene, and how you feel you're going to make the point of it. And not trying to do something that doesn't feel right for what you're working on.

Well, for instance, close-ups are so often resorted to in many films to hammer home a point —
No, I have a real aversion to punching. [*Laughs.*]

In *Falling in Love*, there's a scene on the train when De Niro, sitting at a window seat, is trying to find Meryl Streep's character. When she finally walks by, the audience sees – and feels – him notice her, but because you don't cut to a close shot of that moment of recognition, we also get to see her miss him, which adds a layer to the scene that otherwise wouldn't have been there. Very subtle, but ultimately very important, I think, to the truth of the moment.
I think less is more very often. Sometimes, obviously, you need to come in. But I think I do trust my own sense, when I'm in an audience, of not wanting to be hit over the head, or spoon-fed. Let me find out what is happening on the screen without being punched.

You've made a couple of real 'New York movies': *Who is Harry Kellerman* and *Falling in Love*. In *Kellerman,* I was intrigued by how well you captured the manic energy of the street, particularly in the scene where Hoffman's character leaves with his guitar to go see his shrink, with all of the cutaways to street musicians, vendors, people getting into cabs, etc . . .
Well, Herb Gardner has a real sense of New York – he's a true New Yorker. A lot of that was in the script. I'll tell you the craziest thing that happened on that movie – probably the craziest thing I ever did on a film. There is a shot at the end where Georgie is in his plane, flying over New York City, and he dives into the Empire State Building. At that time, Mike Nichols was shooting *Catch-22* in Mexico, and he had literally requisitioned all the planes with the equipment necessary to do motion-picture photography. We finally located a plane in England – the one he hadn't managed to find – and brought it over. We met the pilot at

Teterboro Airport, and it was this B-29 from 1946: multicoloured, obviously can-nibalized and reassembled from other airplanes. But it had the plastic bubble in the nose of the plane – the little compartment with a camera mount. So the cam-eraman and I crammed into this tiny compartment with the camera. We went up at the crack of dawn – we didn't even dare apply to get permission to do this shot – and as we flew over the Empire State Building the pilot went into a dive. Let me tell you something – when we started to dive toward the building, the plane shud-dered and groaned like nothing I've ever heard, and I thought to myself, 'My God, this is insane.' It was even worse when the pilot pulled up out of the dive – it was shaking so violently – but somehow we made it back up.

The problem was, I knew immediately that the dive had been too slow – it just didn't give one the sense of a real dive. So we did it a second time. [*Laughs.*] When we got back and looked at the dailies, we realized it was still too slow. Eventually we ended up hiring a helicopter and doing it with a zoom. But it was an insane thing to do. When you're making a movie – I'm sure any director can tell you this – you feel like nothing can happen to you in the course of your mis-sion. You have to get that shot. [*Laughs.*]

Falling in Love **really explored the fact that New Yorkers are often forced to play out their private moments, good and bad, in crowded public spaces, whether it's Grand Central at rush hour or a packed store on Christmas Eve.**
That's true. Michael Christofer wrote that screenplay, and making the film sort of quintessentially New York was something we really aimed for. That was a terrific experience, I must say. Shooting in New York can be great; at that time it was cer-tainly easy to do. I don't know if it's still true – I haven't shot a movie here in a long time – but people were not jaded. Even when we were shooting on Fifth Avenue – like that shot of Streep and Dianne Wiest walking down Fifth between 56th and 57th – the people on the street were incredibly co-operative. Great crews, too.

More generally, what kind of influence do you think the city has had on your work?
I don't know that it influences my work directly in any way. Indirectly, it's a place where I feel at home. There's certainly a different feel to daily living here than there is in LA. If you're in the movie business, LA is a company town. In New York, the minute you step onto the street you're part of a larger sense of life, a life that has nothing to do with making movies. It's not that I don't like LA; I've spent a good deal of time there, and there have been occasions where I thought, 'Some day I'll wake up and my feelings will have changed overnight.' But it never happened.

David Picker

David Picker, currently President of Worldwide Production at Hallmark Entertainment, served as the Head of Production of United Artists from 1962 to 1972, where he shepherded into production such films as *Tom Jones*, *A Hard Day's Night*, *Midnight Cowboy*, *Bananas* and *Last Tango in Paris*. He has since held top positions at Paramount Pictures, Lorimar Pictures and Columbia Pictures, as well as working as an independent producer on such films as *The Jerk*, *The Saint of Fort Washington* and *The Crucible*. In 1998, Picker was awarded the Gotham Producer Award from the Independent Feature Project-East.

Tod Lippy: You've been described as a 'show-business blueblood' – can you talk about your family's history in the industry?
David Picker: My grandfather came over from Russia in the 1890s. After going bankrupt in the textile business, he borrowed a few dollars from his brother and opened a nickelodeon in the Bronx in 1912. Built it up into a chain of eighteen theatres, merged with Marcus Loew and worked with Loew's Theaters until his death in 1928. He had four sons, and they all went into the movie business. My father, Eugene, his oldest, was president of Loew's. I was born in 1931, and of course I went into the movie business. So I had uncles, my father, my grandfather. My sister, Jean Picker Firstenberg, is head of the American Film Institute, and my daughter, Caryn, is a vice-president of Miramax – fourth generation. I don't have any sons, but four generations ain't so bad.

Joining United Artists must have felt like an inevitability.
I grew up in the movie business. I grew up going to movies, hanging out in my father's office, watching movies in a projection room that he used to screen everything in. So really, it was a question of where in the movie business I wanted to go. I worked at different summer jobs. One of those was at UA, and of all of the companies I was at, it seemed the most exciting, so I started there in January of 1956.

And you began as an assistant in the ad department?
Well, you could call it that. I was kind of a gofer in the ad department, and a liaison between advertising and sales. After two years, I became an assistant to Max Youngstein, who was one of the partners, and head of both marketing and production. In those days, it wasn't called marketing, it was called advertising, publicity and exploitation. And at United Artists, everybody was required to train junior staff who would hopefully become their replacements when they left. I worked with Max from 1958 to 1961, when he chose to leave as a partner and went into business for himself. The fact is, he left a lot sooner than anybody thought he would, so when he left, I got the job. I was, what – twenty-nine or thirty years old. I stayed there another ten years or so, eventually becoming president, and opted not to continue because it became part of Transamerica, and was no longer the company it had been. Arthur Krim and Bob Benjamin eventually came to the same conclusion when the two of them spun off to form Orion. Arnold Picker,

my uncle, who was the fourth partner, and who was the international expert, had left before Arthur and Bob because he felt that this was no longer the company that he had been a part of. He didn't continue in the motion picture business.

But it was the single most exciting company anybody could have ever worked for.

Could you talk about UA's corporate culture a little bit?
Quite simply, it was a company that was operating without any agenda other than the financing and distribution of motion pictures. There were no politics – the company was owned by the principles, and the basic philosophy of the company's operation was advocacy and efficiency. As head of production, my job was to convince Arthur and Bob that the pictures I wanted to do were the ones we should do.

You had a phenomenal track record.
Well, they were terrific films. The very first picture I said we had to do was *Tom Jones*. After the fact, the partners admitted they weren't that high on the project, but they felt that since my enthusiasm was what it was, and it was the first film I had advocated as strongly as that, they should encourage my enthusiasm.

How did *Tom Jones* come about?
The way it happened was very simple. Arthur and Bob didn't read the script. I went over to London to meet with Tony Richardson, and I called them from a restaurant there and said, 'We have to do this project.' They said, 'All right. But make it a two-picture deal and cross-collateralize it with another movie in case it doesn't work so we'll have another shot.' I said, 'That's easy,' and the deal was done, just like that. There were no boards to deal with, no hierarchy; just four men – Krim, Benjamin, Arnold Picker and myself – who talked to each other every day. I read the scripts – occasionally Arthur and Bob did, but Arnold didn't very often – and decisions were made.

Basically, because of the simple tenet by which we worked, which was that film-makers had final cut as long as they stayed within the budget parameters in the script we had approved, we were able to attract every major film-maker in the world, from the most esoteric, classiest 'art' film-makers to the most commercial. It was an incredibly exciting place, where advocacy carried the day.

Was that final-cut policy partly a function of economics? I remember reading somewhere that, at least initially, UA was not able to spend the kind of money that some of the other majors could on projects.
The reality is that the majors didn't know what we were doing; they basically ignored us. It wasn't that we were doing one thing and they were doing something else. Krim and Benjamin had bought the company in the early fifties, and it was years before the other majors realized that it wasn't that we were making pictures that much less expensively, but that we were attracting film-makers because

our philosophy of doing business was completely different. It took years and years and years before they caught on.

Did being on the East Coast have anything to do with it?
Well, really everybody was in New York. I mean, the studios were in California, but in those days all the home offices were still here.

Did you have a lot of contact with that community?
No, I wouldn't say it was a 'community'. But we certainly knew each other. And there were very, very respectful relationships. There were several instances, for example, where another company and ourselves would have motion pictures with the same background, topic, something, and you could pick up the phone and work it out.

Really?
Absolutely. This is a fact: there was no piece of information in the business at that time that I could not get a truthful answer to. I could call a friend or a colleague or somebody I knew and get information. If they didn't want to give it, they would tell me that honestly, or tell it to me off the record and I would respect that. And in no respect are we talking about collusion – like, 'Are you going to pay more than this amount?' – I'm talking about 'When are you releasing the movie?' or 'Is it true you're negotiating for this?' or 'Are you going to do that, because if you are, I'm not going to do this.' Ted Ashley, who was running Warner Bros., had a picture at one point that was on the same subject as one of ours, and I said, 'Look, either you go first or I go first.' And he said, 'Okay, why don't you go first.' It was as simple as that.

Not to say that there weren't people who were dishonest – there were – but the business has evolved from one of trust to one of distrust. When I was at United Artists, we would finance a picture, borrow money from a bank, pay the bank a loss or pay out the profits without a signed piece of paper – today, you can't do a screen test on an actor without a signed piece of paper, a deal memo.

How involved were you in the actual production process?
We didn't look at dailies. I visited sets occasionally, just to visit friends or whatever. But the film-maker delivered the finished print. Most of them brought us into the process, some didn't.

It sounds like you weren't as likely to be perceived as adversaries.
Well, sometimes we were. [*Laughs.*] Especially if there were budget problems.

You mentioned having a strong response to Richardson's script for *Tom Jones*. What is it that attracted you to it, and, more generally, to others?
I can't tell you what. I read scripts, and I don't really look to anybody's response but my own visceral response. But you have to be familiar with the film-maker; you have to have a feel for what they intend to do with the script. Yes, movies

were far, far less expensive to make then, but so was their grossing potential. So everything is a risk. And I don't envy people in the towers of Los Angeles today who have to make decisions about one-hundred-and-fifty-million- or two-hundred-million-dollar movies. But I will tell you that a four- or five-million-dollar movie was just as important to us. And there were times when we got in trouble, but thankfully many more times when we didn't.

It wasn't always easy, and there were personality problems, but that's the nature of the business. You're dealing with creative people who have very strong feelings about their work and how they feel they have to deal with people who get in their way. That's the fun part of it.

How did you come across *Midnight Cowboy*?

It's very simple. There were a lot of film-makers we were in business with, and several we were not in business with, and one of those was John Schlesinger. I'd seen *Darling* and *Billy Liar*, and I was in London – as I was often – and I made an appointment to see John. I said to him, 'Here we are: we want to make movies with you.' He said, 'Well, there's only one thing I have at the moment that I'd like to do, but you'll never do it; it's very dark.' And he told me about this little book by James Leo Herlihy called *Midnight Cowboy*. So I read it, and agreed with him that it was very dark, but told him that if he could make this picture at a specifically negotiated price, we'd develop it with him.

So he and Jerry Hellman, the producer, agreed on the price, and we all agreed on a writer. We hired Jack Gelber, a New York playwright, and for a year they went off and worked on it. They called me after some time and said, 'The script simply doesn't work.' I said, 'Well, what do you want to do now?' 'We'd like to hire Waldo Salt.' I said, 'Okay, hire Waldo Salt.' Another year went by, and when they came in two and a half years after our initial deal, the budget was not the same as it had been before. It was a very, very difficult situation, because we'd committed to doing it on the basis of a certain number, and they weren't close to it. I was very emotional, because I really wanted to make this film and I felt that John and Jerry, you know, had not lived up to their end of the obligation. I remember Bob Benjamin saying to me, 'Relax. Sit down. It's only a movie.' And I said, 'It's *not* only a movie. It's a great project,' etc., etc. . . . So we explored different options and, to make a long story short, we found a way to do it, painful as it was, and we approved a higher number. And they went off and made the movie. I went by the set once, when they were shooting outside of what is now the Peninsula Hotel – it used to be the Gotham Hotel, on 55th just west of Fifth Avenue. Didn't see any dailies or anything.

When it was finished, John and Jerry called and said, 'We're ready to show you our cut.' I asked how complete it was, and they told me it had everything but John Barry's theme, which he hadn't composed yet. They were using a temp song. So they said, 'Why don't you come on over?' And I said, 'Well, you know what? I'm going to take a chance. I'm going to bring everybody.' So I had the entire marketing, sales and executive team of United Artists – about forty of us – go over to the theatre on 54th Street between 11th and 12th to see the first screening of *Midnight Cowboy*. And when that movie ended – in my career, it was probably the most extraordinary response to a motion picture I'd ever witnessed. Nobody could move, nobody could say a word; we just sat there, stunned. Finally, Arnold Picker turned around and said to John, 'It's a masterpiece.'

The temp song that he'd laid in was 'Everybody's Talking', which he planned to replace with the John Barry. And we wouldn't let him do it – it was just too perfect. So we bought the rights to that and left it in. John and I have been friends ever since, and subsequent to that he brought two other projects to me, neither of which I wanted to do. It was difficult – a man makes *Midnight Cowboy*, and he comes in with *The Assassination of Trotsky*, which I didn't want to do, and *Day of the Locust*, which he eventually did make. But I didn't want to do it. And then he gave me Penelope Gilliatt's script to *Sunday Bloody Sunday*, and I said, 'OK'.

What about *Last Tango in Paris*?
That was a phone call from Alberto Grimaldi, the producer. That had been at Paramount – just like *Tom Jones* had been at another company. I'd been involved in the Clint Eastwood Westerns with Alberto, and he said, 'Bernardo's got this project. Here's the cost, I can send you the treatment. It's Brando, and Paramount doesn't want to use him.' I asked him to send me the treatment. And we made a deal based on the treatment and, of course, the director. I was a big fan of Bertolucci.

When you're able to move quickly, give answers quickly, and when you're known for being sympathetic to the creative process – it's still not easy, but you have access to everything. And you know, we were tough businessmen. We didn't roll over and play dead. But, they knew there was enormous respect for the creative process. And we were in business – it was kind of scary – with everyone. Fellini, Bergman, Truffaut, I worked with them all – although to call it 'work' is sort of ridiculous. And then you add on the top of that the Beatles, the James Bond franchise . . .

How did the Beatles' films come about?
They came to us because the head of our music publishing operation in London had been contacted by somebody – I don't think it was Brian Epstein – involved with the Beatles saying that they'd be interested in doing a couple of low-budget rock 'n' roll movies. This was before anybody knew who they were; they were still based in Liverpool and they hadn't exploded yet. When that idea was passed on to me, I thought it was great, so we made a three-picture deal with them. Between the time we made the deal and started to think seriously about what kind of low-budget movie we could make, they exploded. And we had them under contract. Now that it was clear that we had something major on our hands, we had to figure out who to put them with. I determined that the logical person was Dick Lester. He'd directed a sequel to *The Mouse that Roared* for us called *Mouse on the*

Moon, and Walter Shenson had produced it, so I called Dick and said, 'Look, we've got the Beatles, I'd like you to work with them, and Walter to produce it,' and he agreed, and that's how it happened.

Had you heard their music before you made the deal?
No. Didn't make any difference. The fact is, conceptually, I liked the idea of doing low-budget music films, and we obviously had an involvement in the publishing and the soundtrack, and we had a record company that was starting to happen, so it just made sense. Subsequent to the Beatles, we did other deals, with groups like Jerry and the Pacemakers. As you know, music-oriented films and soundtracks are valuable assets to a company.

Do you think your being unusually young for the position you held had something to do with your interest in these various projects?
I never looked at it that way. Don't forget – I was brought up in the business. When I joined UA after the Army in '56, I basically knew as much or more about the motion-picture business than most of the people I was working with. I'd lived, eaten and breathed movies my whole life, and it was all I cared about. Everybody approaches their vocation a different way; mine was total – not for ambitious reasons, just for love of what I was doing. Seven days a week, twenty-four hours a day – it didn't make any difference to me. I saw every movie made that I could see. You pay a price for that in your personal life, but I rationalized that in my own mind.

It just strikes me that your breadth of experience and knowledge – something one would normally gain only after working years in the business – made for a particularly potent combination with the enthusiasm and energy of youth.
I guess that's why they gave me the shot. I mean, obviously I had no 'track record' to speak of.

How did you get the James Bond franchise?
I had tried to buy the rights to James Bond before we were able to make a deal with Broccoli and Saltzman. Fleming was not an easy man to deal with – I couldn't get them. They were there to be taken, though, and when Saltzman secured them, and then Cubby joined him, we wouldn't let the two of them out of the office until we had a deal. Other companies had their shots at it – Columbia turned it down, twice – but nobody else stood up. And obviously, although we thought it might be a franchise, nobody anticipated the enormity of it, because that would have been foolish.

And your relationship with Woody Allen?
It was simple, again. Woody and Sam Cohn came to see me – actually, Sam the first time. He said, 'You want to make movies with Woody?' I said, 'Absolutely.' And we worked out a deal where within a specific fixed amount of money, the only obligation Woody had was to come and tell me what the idea was. We had a

number. The fun part of it was that the first idea he came up with I didn't want to do, because it wasn't funny. I looked at him when he told me this idea, and I said, 'Woody, I'd be very happy to do this as the fourth or fifth movie, but the first time it's got to be a comedy.' This was a Thursday or a Friday, and he said, 'Oh. Okay.' Monday he called me with another idea and I said fine – that was *Bananas*. That's the way that deal was structured.

Here's a difference in the business. In those days, I was only interested in one thing: how much we could lose. Ok? So if the picture was a flop, you'd lose X million dollars. That's not the business we're in today. We're in the business of 'How much can we make?' And I will tell you that I don't think there's one person who's ever been in the motion picture business who can tell you with any degree of certainty what any movie can make. But you always know how much it can lose. So we were prepared to take risks based on protecting the downside. Today, it's very different. You need insurance policies, so you make things over and over that have already succeeded, because that means they may succeed again, as opposed to looking for things that maybe haven't been quite done a certain way before. Very different, and nowhere near as much fun. Ask anybody.

After the Transamerica deal in 1972, you left UA to do some independent producing.
I did a deal with UA where, in fact, I could do three movies of my own choice within a certain budget.

And you stayed in New York?
Oh, yeah.

***Lenny* was one of those films, right?**
Lenny was a deal I had made at UA before I'd left the position I had. Bob Fosse asked if I would produce the movie. The producer by title was Marvin Worth, who had owned the property, but Fosse had total control over it. So I became the executive producer of that. And then I did *Smile*, and *Juggernaut*, which was a script we had developed at UA with a producer and director who had not gotten the movie going.

This was your first foray into actually producing films?
Yeah. *Lenny* was the first movie I'd actually produced. Bob had creative control of the movie, but we were friends, and my function as producer – which I have always believed since – was to enable Fosse to make the movie he wanted to make while at the same time keeping it within certain economic parameters. And collaborating to the extent that Bobby would get what he wanted and needed. It was an extraordinary first film to work on. I couldn't have had a more complex, challenging, creatively exciting or personal relationship with a film-maker. I adored him, respected him – he was brilliant. And we were able to talk shorthand. I

instinctively knew what he was thinking, and I was there for him – he permitted me to be there for him. So I learned a lot.

I'm not a producer who can just sit back and be a functionary. I have to feel like – not that I get my way, 'cause that's not what it's about. But I have to feel like I can contribute to the project on a creative as well as economic-control level. If I can do that – if I have at least the ear of the director to listen to what I have to say – then I feel like I am fulfilling the function that I need to fulfil. Working with Bobby, working with Michael Ritchie, and then with Dick Lester on my first three movies was terrific because they were three totally different personalities, all talented in their own way.

I'm always attracted to the director and the writer; those are the people I love spending time with, and working with. Everything else has flowed from that. It's never been the deal, or the economic benefits. I've always obviously been comfortable, but it's never been the dollar; it's always been the experience.

You moved to LA in 1976 to become head of production at Paramount —
I actually moved to LA for personal reasons before that, and lived there for eight or nine years, during which I was president of Paramount.

What was it like moving into the studio system in LA?
Well, it was a different world. It's not a world I'm nearly as comfortable in. I had enormous respect for Barry Diller, and I still do – he's one of the smartest men I've ever worked with – but we had totally different personalities, and after two and a half years it was clear that my personality and his were not really compatible, and in the nicest possible sense he lived up to all the understandings that we had, and I just went off on my own and produced a couple of movies for them. But the results of my time there, which included, you know, *Grease*, *Days of Heaven*, *Up in Smoke*, *Saturday Night Fever*, making a deal with Redford for *Ordinary People*, just proved, at least as far as I was concerned, that I was able to bring something off with my own style. But clearly, my style and the studio style were totally incompatible.

Can you elaborate a bit more on that difference?
Well, again, I'm talent-driven and content-driven as opposed to insurance-driven. Barry and I acknowledged that the kind of projects I was drawn to were not as high-profile, big-name projects as perhaps the studio would have liked. I remember when *Heaven Can Wait* came along – it was a package with Warren and all the other elements and it was expensive and Barry knew how far he wanted to go in making the deal. It was more about the deal than the film. Those high-profile movies were more 'studio-style' than the ones I was doing. That's where my style differs – I believe in my own reaction to content and talent, and if I have a long enough opportunity, I always trust that it's going to come through. To succeed within a year or a year and a half is impossible, unless you're very lucky. But you need to establish an atmosphere where film-makers want to work

with you, and that takes some time. And, of course, a number of those films went on to be quite successful. But there were other people in place at Paramount after me, and a lot of credit went to them. But that happens all the time.

Also, everything in the industry at that point was starting to change. Ancillary markets were getting larger, negative costs were getting larger – it was really starting to be a different world. And I really am a New Yorker – I do not like living in Los Angeles. I just don't. I'm not comfortable there. The business is different. Again, it's a place where terrific things happen, and there are wonderful film-makers there – certainly in the UA years, we were involved with many of them – Billy Wilder, Blake Edwards, John Sturges, Norman Jewison, you name it. That isn't the problem. The problem is it's a different lifestyle. It's more about perception than reality in some ways. I don't know any other way to say this, but I have no particular interest in seeing my name in print, or being talked about in a particular way; I'm not competitive in that sense. I really prefer to just operate with the people I prefer to operate with, and to be left alone. So it wasn't the easiest place to be comfortable. And as the costs began to escalate, it became more and more different.

Yet after Paramount you spent several years as President of Feature Films at Lorimar . . .
Yeah, that was probably – even though we did some interesting movies – a mistake. And it was a mistake because I was led to believe that it was going to be one thing and it turned out to be something else. I hoped that maybe there was a United Artists lurking there somewhere, and there wasn't. Once Jack Schwartzman and I realized that, it was time to move on. I had perfectly decent relationships with Lee Rich and Merv Adelson, and like them, but I didn't go there to be just an executive. It was OK, because I'd just produced *The Jerk*.

You had one more relatively short gig at a major in the late eighties at Columbia, serving as David Puttnam's President of Production. Did you also see that as another potential UA?
Well, maybe. It was swimming upstream. The movie business had changed dramatically. David had told Coca-Cola what he was going to do, and they supported everything that he wanted to do until he got there and started to do it. It was an unfortunate series of circumstances that David found himself in. But we did some interesting movies.

You picked up the negative for *School Daze*, right?
Well, it was more than that. Tom Rothman, who was Spike's lawyer, called me and we made the deal over the phone because it had fallen out somewhere else. We did some good movies there, but it was never going to work.

You knew that right away?
Shortly after I got there. David had clearly been led to believe that he was going to

be supported, and Coca-Cola probably believed it when they said it. But once the community didn't respond well, they kind of disappeared, too.

What do you mean by 'not responding well'?
The fact is, David and I are both people who are talent-driven. When David was a producer and I was running Paramount, he brought Alan Parker and Ridley Scott to me, and we did their first movies. That's a long-range policy for a studio, and it's a policy where a lot of heavyweight players in the Hollywood community can get bent out of shape if you don't respond to their muscle. Many establishment producers like Ray Stark, for example, didn't like having their projects rejected by David. It was as simple as that. It was more about people whose noses were out of joint, like Mr Cosby, who produced, starred in and later publicly rejected a picture he made for the studio. He also didn't return the million he was paid to make it.

So after all of this you returned to New York?
I'd actually returned to New York before Columbia; I'd moved back in the early eighties, after Lorimar. I just went back out for the year and nine months I was at Columbia. So yes, after that, I came back to New York and made a whole bunch of movies. Some were good; some were not so good. I guess my favourite was *The Saint of Fort Washington*. It took me nine years to get it made, and it got hurt for a number of reasons, but it's a movie I'm very, very proud of.

And then in the mid-nineties I made another deal with Paramount. And in two years, I had fourteen scripts in development and no movies, so when Fox called and asked me if I would consider producing *The Crucible*, I went to Paramount and said, 'Look, I'm just sitting here doing nothing. Let's just end it now.' And we did, amicably. When *The Crucible* was over, my friends the Halmis asked me if I would consider helping them at Hallmark. I said I'd try it for a while, just as a consultant, and I had a great time. Under this arrangement I'm free to develop some independent films as long as it doesn't interfere with what I'm doing. I'm having a great time here. You know, the fact is, we do the best of this kind of stuff. There's a production of *David Copperfield* that Peter Medak directed which I think is just stunning. To be able to have the fun I'm having here at Hallmark, and be able to come up with ideas that push the envelope a little bit, or go into arenas we haven't seen before in television, while at the same time developing the kind of personal movies that I respond to – at this advanced stage of my career it's pretty nice.

And also, talking to my friends who are out there in the middle of it all – I don't know of anybody who should be envied. You know, there are huge amounts of money thrown around, and when something is successful, it's nice. I've certainly been asked to produce some very big movies, but doing a hundred-million-dollar movie just doesn't interest me. When a studio invests that kind of money, it really is their movie; it's not the producer's movie. Or if there's a major star in it, it's his or her movie. This is not to put down the producer function, because I think guys like Jerry Bruckheimer do a brilliant job of making a certain kind of movie. But that's not my taste, and it's not material that particularly interests me. And if it doesn't interest me, I'm not going to do a good job. The kinds of stuff I want to do are much more personal things, whether they're funny or dramatic or whatever. It's really more of the kind of independent film mantle that Miramax inherited from the UA of the sixties. I grew up with films being made by independent film-makers, even though we did them at a major, and it's what my instincts are always driven by.

You were given a Lifetime Achievement Award from the Independent Feature Project a few years back; do you find that independent producers here often consult you for advice?
Actually, not that many. I don't know probably sixty-five per cent of the directors today. I don't know seventy-five per cent of the younger agents. That's just natural, and I don't have either the desire or the interest in doing it. When I was running studios, I knew every film-maker, every writer, every agent in the business. But you evolve, and I've evolved to a point where I love what I do, and I'm still developing films, but my interests have prioritized in a different way. I used to see every movie within reason that was made. I pick and choose now. I just don't have the interest or the patience.

What are some films you've liked this past year?
My favourite movie is Almodovar's *All About My Mother*. It's so extraordinary because he does a very difficult thing, which is to humanize without sentimentalizing – a talent that not a lot of people have. But I liked *The Green Mile,* and I liked *The Cider House Rules,* and I liked *Magnolia*, and I liked *American Beauty,* and I liked *The Insider*. I liked *Hurricane* – a movie I worked on for three years, but never got a script that I could get made.

In 1987, you were on a committee for the Imagen Awards – given yearly to the entertainment industry for positive portrayals of Hispanic-Americans – and made a statement to the press that only one award, as opposed to the usual three, would be given because of the dearth of non-stereotypical roles for Hispanics in film and television that year. Do you think that film has some broader function than simply to entertain?
Well, it is an economic reality that the movie business is based on profit and loss. But I think that there needs to be a certain responsibility to the audience to help insure that there's a future to the business. That's not to say you don't do things that may offend some people, because I totally believe more than anything else in freedom of expression. But I think there's an obligation to represent – both within the craft and within the audience – the broadest possible spectrum. And that means the recognition that in the United States the makeup of the population has changed, and African-Americans and Hispanic-Americans must be given opportunities. One of the problems we have in our business is that unless

somebody mandates it, it doesn't happen. On *The Saint of Fort Washington*, I had to mandate in our crew that every department be integrated. Unless somebody literally says, 'This has to happen,' it just doesn't happen, and it's kinda sad. When I was at Paramount, we hired Joan Darling to direct *First Love* – the first film there, as I recall, to be directed by a woman. I wish things happened naturally, but they don't.

I think a lot of the movies I've done have entertained, but I think a lot of them also have something to say about the world in which we live, and I think that there's kind of an ethical obligation and a responsibility to enlighten and broaden the potential audience and the potential workforce. I don't mean to get fancy, but you either think that way or you don't.

Do you have any opinions about John Grisham suing Oliver Stone over *Natural Born Killers*, which Grisham claimed led to a copycat murder of friends of his?
I think something like that might occasionally happen, but I think there's a lot more to it than that. I don't think there's any *quid pro quo* for any of these things. What offends me more is the hypocrisy of entities who say they have no impact when they do. For instance, I've had television news executives say to me, 'This programme is untouchable' – this was *60 Minutes* – and then you'd look at the fact that a golf tournament was on CBS, and somehow two weeks before they'd done a profile of Tiger Woods or something. There's a lot of hypocrisy; I find that offensive. But I don't think you can point a finger at any particular movie, novel, broadcast and say it was the direct cause of something.

You've had an enormous number of successes as a producer and executive, but also, as you mentioned, some failures. Is there some point in the process where you tend to know which of the two a film is going to be?
It's so complicated. It depends on who you are and where you are at any given point in time. You can convince yourself of just about anything.

I would think the emotional investment a director has in a project might make it more difficult for him or her to be objective than, say, someone on the studio level.
But as an executive you can pretty much convince yourself you're going to have a success, even though an objective point of view might be that you're not. And I don't think there's any one moment when you know that. There are always surprises. That's what's so extraordinary about what we do; it's totally unpredictable. An awful lot of things have to come together to make anything happen, and nobody really knows. At UA, we did what we thought was going to be one of our biggest movies, called *The Greatest Story Ever Told*. Until several days before it opened, we thought we were going to have a big success, and of course we had a disaster. One of our top people thought that a movie we had with Stanley Kramer, *The Secret of Santa Vittoria,* was going to be a huge success, and almost negotiated a buyout of Stanley's profit position. Fortunately, the deal fell apart, because nobody went to see it.

I made a movie called *Won Ton Ton: The Dog That Saved Hollywood* because I wanted to do an homage to old Hollywood movie stars. I remember we had an enormous one-hour break on Merv Griffin's television show – and then the movie opened and nobody came. I made a bet with the head of Universal on *The Jerk* about how much film rental we would earn. He had a much clearer vision than I did, and I ended up sending a very big contribution to his charity because I had underestimated what it was going to do. You know, Billy Wilder once said to a group of us, 'There's three kinds of movies. Musts, maybes and nevers, but the problem is, you don't always know in the front which is which.' After the fact it's really easy to see.

There are four times in my life when I was absolutely, positively convinced that the movies were going to be successful, and I was only wrong once. That group was *Tom Jones, Last Tango, Midnight Cowboy* and *Where's Poppa?* I thought *Where's Poppa?* was going to shoot through the roof, but it just offended a lot of people, and nobody seemed to see in it what I saw.

What's your feeling about test screenings?
Oh, I have a big problem with them. I mean, it depends where you screen the movie. Anything within fifty miles of downtown LA is idiotic. I think the only thing that really works is the actual screening itself, as long as it's an audience that's kind of unadulterated. We actually did it recently with one of our shows here. My problem is what happens after the screening, when you turn that audience into critics. I don't feel comfortable with that. It's one thing to listen and watch, because at that moment I think their response is authentic – they're either interested or they're not, they're responding or they're not. But once you put a piece of paper in front of them, and then you have a focus group, I don't necessarily trust it, because people are being asked to give opinions. One person makes a comment, and it's something that none of the rest of the group would have ever thought of. Maybe I'm old-fashioned, but I don't take as much from them as some people do. But the reality is that studios use them. Those top two boxes carry a lot of weight.

It's a version, really, of readers. I mean, how many people at studios at the highest level actually read scripts any more? Now what you have is a group of seven or eight people sitting around a table, and every creative executive is pushing their particular project, trying to – this is probably the best way to characterize it – get projects made that they think their boss will approve. That's not what we used to do. I would try to get projects made that I believed in, that I would then try to convince my boss to do.

There's a famous old joke, about the woman who goes into the butcher shop and buys a chicken. The fellow puts the chicken on the counter, and she lifts up the wings and sniffs and she says, 'Take it back, I don't want it.' And five times he puts a new chicken on the counter, and five times she rejects it. Finally, he says to the woman, 'Excuse me, Madame; can I ask you a question? Could *you* pass such a test?' I don't know how a script can pass some of these tests. It is a different business, and the movies reflect it.

You've had a lifelong on-again, off-again relationship with the studio system, and by extension, Hollywood —
I don't think it's on-again, off-again; I think that what my career reflects is love of motion pictures, and I certainly have never been able to adjust to what I think you have to do in Hollywood, which is not only understand and care about movies, but also play a certain kind of game. With me, what you see is what you get.

Do you think the film business, which most would argue has changed considerably for the worse in the past several decades, could ever change again for the better?
I have no idea. The fact is that most movie companies today are only one small part of the companies that own them. I grew up in a world where the movie companies were in the movie business, period. That was their *raison d'etre*. Now they're a marketing arm of a larger entity. I'm not grousing about it, it's just the reality of the way it is.

I don't know, maybe the saviour will be the proliferation of information on the Internet, where there will be other ways of receiving information. On the other hand, I would not be happy with the day when I can't go into a darkened theatre and see a movie on a screen. But maybe the audiences for all these things are being chopped up a little bit – although obviously the big hit movies do better than ever, and the others do worse than ever.

Hopefully, there will be outlets for the kind of creative film-making that we respond to as individuals more. There were a lot of good movies this year, made by companies that were owned by studios, as well as studios themselves. I just hope that the independent spirit prevails, so that movies aren't just a reflection of these giant companies, whose basic use of film is to market products. I don't think we can live on a diet of such rich desserts. The calories will put us into shock.

Would you ever go back to Hollywood for another studio job?
Anybody who would hire a sixty-eight-year-old New Yorker to run a studio today should be fired.

Nora Ephron

Nora Ephron, who began her career as a journalist and essayist in the late sixties, has directed *This is My Life*, *Sleepless in Seattle*, *Mixed Nuts*, *Michael*, *You've Got Mail* and the forthcoming *Numbers*. Her screenplays (which have earned her three Oscar nominations) include *Silkwood* (with Alice Arlen), *Heartburn*, *When Harry Met Sally*, and *Hanging Up* (with Delia Ephron). Ephron is the author of *Wallflower at the Orgy*, *Crazy Salad*, *Scribble, Scribble* and the novel *Heartburn*.

The following interview with Ephron, who was on location in Los Angeles at the time, was conducted by e-mail.

Tod Lippy: In your 1968 interview with Mike Nichols, he and you both seemed to agree that LA is, in fact, an easier place to live than New York. Nichols, though, concluded with, 'But who says that's good?' If New York isn't necessarily the easiest place to live, what makes it so valuable as a context for working (particularly, writing)?
Nora Ephron: Actually, I disagree with Mike about the premise. I have been in LA for several months now, and it is nowhere near as easy a place to live as New York. In fact, one of the most mystifying things to me is that people don't get how much easier New York is. I mean, the subway alone.

But to answer your question, I'm one of those people who grew up always knowing that when I got things sorted out, I'd live in New York. My parents had moved us to LA when I was four, and – I am not exaggerating – I knew at the very moment I saw it that a terrible mistake had been made. New York is the place where I feel most at home, where I feel I have to do next to nothing in order to belong, so that automatically makes it a wonderful place for me to work or write. And now that I'm in the movie business, it's even more thrilling to live there (as opposed to LA) because people there don't think the sun rises and sets on whether you have a deal. New York has always been a print-driven city, and it's still a place where the written word rules.

In an article about *You've Got Mail*, you said jokingly that the genteel, almost homey New York City the characters inhabit in the film was at its 'Giuliani-fantasy best'. Do you think one could characterize that New York as very 'Ephron' (much as one would characterize the NYC of *After Hours* or *Bringing Out the Dead* as very 'Scorsese')? Does it reflect in some way your actual experience of the city?
I've probably always had a very romanticized view of New York, and now, finally, the reality of New York has caught up with it.

You were raised in LA, the child of Hollywood screenwriters. You thought to yourself as a young woman that you 'would have committed suicide before (a) staying in LA and (b) going into the movie business'. You're one for two. Would you ever move back to LA?
I don't think I could ever live in Los Angeles all the time. There's nothing wrong

with it for a few months, although you have to use a lot of moisturizer.

In your first collection of essays, you likened your journalist's role as observer to being a 'wallflower at the orgy'. You're writing fiction these days, but I was curious to know how many of the details in your screenplays – at least the stuff that adds background texture to your films – come from witnessing people and things around you, particularly given the rich source material New York provides.

Most writers can only write what they know, and we were certainly raised to believe that. My mother must have said it once a week. And of course, the other thing she always said was Everything Is Copy. When we were doing *You've Got Mail*, Delia and I pretty much fed our view of New York right into every detail of the script. Our neighbourhood, our failed neighbourhood bookstores, our views on coffee, our passion for e-mail, etc. One night while we were writing *You've Got Mail*, Delia got stuck in the elevator, and the next day the character Tom Hanks plays in the movie got stuck in an elevator in the script. *When Harry Met Sally*, which is not at all autobiographical, is a script that I always thought of as a direct result of all those years I spent writing essays – in this case a movie version of an essay on love, or dating, etc. And it's full of my observations – and Rob Reiner's – from years of falling in and out of love and dating. There's always a certain amount of reporting involved in what I write. I try to make the scripts I write as specific as possible; one of the most frustrating things to me about some of the scripts I read is how generic they feel.

Numbers, as far as I can tell, is your first directing gig working with someone else's screenplay. How does it feel to be approaching a job solely from the directorial angle? Is it 'cleaner'? Did you work with Adam Resnick before or during shooting?

I met Adam Resnick after I read his script, and we worked for several months on the screenplay. He is a wildly funny writer. Since we began shooting, we've pretty much been shooting the script, and very few revisions have been needed.

When your novel _Heartburn_ was adapted into a film, more than one New York reviewer grumbled that it had been 'de-ethnicized' with the casting of Meryl Streep and Jack Nicholson (definitely not Jewish) as the two leads. Was that something that surprised you at the time?

I never thought of *Heartburn*, or of any of my writing, as 'Jewish'. Which is not to say that I'm not in a Jewish tradition, etc., etc. The whole idea of *Heartburn* – the whole tradition of turning a terrible story into a funny one – is probably profoundly Jewish. But it never crossed my mind that for it to work as a movie it had to be performed by – who? – Barbra Streisand? And if it didn't work as a movie, I don't think it was because it was 'de-ethnicized'.

Your most successful films to date (*You've Got Mail, Sleepless in Seattle*) feature leads who not only generate enormous box office (and who, of course, are enor-

mously appealing), but who also happen to be definitely not Jewish. Do you think middle America prefers it that way? Or am I being too cynical, or for that matter, paranoid? If the answer to the 'middle America' question is 'yes', does it reflect a conscious choice on your part (both in the writing and casting stages)?
Tom Hanks is Jewish.

Critic John Leonard once called you a 'blithe moralist'. If you think that's an accurate moniker, could you talk about how and why that attitude has informed your approach to the subject matter which interests you (whether it be *Deep Throat* or chain bookstores)?
I love that John Leonard once called me that, but I can't say that that's really how I respond to anything. But I do have a tendency to enjoy seeing both sides of things, and that certainly seems to me to be the thing that characterized my work as an essayist and as a film-maker. There are lots of ways to tell a story, and I like staying open to more than one of them. One of the things I like about *You've Got Mail* is the moment when Meg Ryan's character walks into the huge bookstore and suddenly realizes it's not all bad.

Do you read reviews? And if you do, are you ever inclined to respond to critics?
I don't read bad reviews if I can help it. I certainly have read some, though, and they kept me up at night thinking of ways to respond to the people who wrote them, and that's one of the main reasons I stopped reading them.

You once said that 'The romantic comedy was killed by sex.' Can you elaborate, and talk about how that's affected your take on the genre?
What I mean is that in the thirties and forties and fifties, when people didn't generally have sex before they got married, it was possible to write a romantic comedy that went on quite a while before sex reared its head, if at all. Then along came modern life, and people leapt into bed the minute they met, so it was hard to think of obstacles to becoming lovers. That's one reason why *When Harry Met Sally* works, I think – it found a very nice obstacle, the friends thing. And, of course, *Sleepless* works because it found the nicest obstacle of all – they don't know each other. But you pretty much have to go that far these days to come up with an obstacle that sustains you in a modern romantic comedy.

While we're on the subject of genres, do you have any interest in returning to more dramatic stuff, like the script you co-wrote with Alice Arlen for *Silkwood*? Or is there something inherently more satisfying to you about comedy, romantic or otherwise?
Alice and I wrote a wonderful movie about a correspondent in the Korean War, and I have been trying for several years now to get the money to make it – and to cast it so that I could get the money to make it. The studio I originally wrote it for was willing to make it last year, but the actress I wanted for it wouldn't cut her price so it would work. It's been very very frustrating and sad, to be honest,

because I certainly never wanted to make only romantic comedies or even comedies. Although I do truly enjoy making comedies.

For whom do you think your movies are best suited? Do you have an ideal audience in mind when you're writing?
No.

When *Scribble Scribble* came out, you were quoted in an interview as saying, 'The act of doing a column forces you into figuring out what you think about a subject.' Do you find yourself undergoing a similar process before you begin a new screenplay?
Not always. Sometimes. Sometimes you think things through beforehand, and sometimes you don't really get to thinking about themes until you're through with a first pass. Screenplays are very different from columns. I think the closest I ever came to the process of writing a column when writing a screenplay was *When Harry Met Sally*, which is a sort of series of essays about dating. But I didn't really figure out what the movie of *When Harry Met Sally* was about until we did the junket.

I know Lubitsch's *Shop Around the Corner* served as an inspiration for *You've Got Mail*. Are there any other classics you've thought might be particularly suitable for updating/contemporizing?
Probably, but I can't think what they are. I mean, there are all sorts of movies that work well whenever they're done – *Clueless* as a re-invention of Jane Austen's *Emma* is a perfect example – but then there are movies one probably shouldn't go near with a ten-foot pole. The problem with updating romantic comedies, of course, is that sometimes the obstacle to love that worked perfectly well in the thirties doesn't work at all now. *It Happened One Night*, which is probably the greatest romantic comedy ever, is all about class differences, but no one today would ever buy the idea that a journalist couldn't marry an heiress.

Do you feel like you're part of a film-making community in New York?
No. The good part of living in New York and working in the movie business is that you're not part of the film-making community. The film-making community is in Los Angeles, and many of the people there are obsessed with the details of that community – who just got cast in what, which script just got auctioned for a trillion dollars, who's about to be fired, etc. These things are not important, and it's nice to live in a place where that's understood, and where the culture is not dominated by film but by print and theatre and art, among others.

Do you find the production experience (attitude of crew, dealings with residents, etc.) to be different in LA from how it is in New York?
There's no question that dealings with residents are the same in New York and Los Angeles: people who live in either place are very used to film crews, and are basically bored witless by them. They are impatient with large lights and noise all through the night and traffic jams and the general inconvenience caused by

people making movies. This is one of the reasons why we went to Sacramento on the last film I did (the one I just finished shooting): we needed to shoot for ten nights, and to turn a small neighbourhood into a snowscape, and we knew we would never find a neighbourhood in Los Angeles that would agree to it. But the people in Sacramento were thrilled to have us there, and couldn't have been nicer about all of it. They stayed up all night for a glimpse of John Travolta, etc. I haven't noticed any difference in crews in Los Angeles and New York.

Some time ago, you remarked on 'the difficulty intelligent people have in distinguishing what is controversial from what is merely offensive'. Can you give any recent examples from the film world?
That remark rings a bell. From about twenty years ago, I think. I don't see that many examples of this in the film world, but I see it all the time on television, where it seems to me the urge to push the envelope has become pathological.

When you were writing your column on women and the woman's movement in *Esquire*, and later *New York*, you talked about how much easier it was to 'reach people by making them laugh than by shaking a fist and saying don't you see how oppressed you are'. Do you still think of your work as political, or 'politicized', at least with regard to feminist politics?
I don't think of myself as political. I think that I have politics, but I don't think they're what drives me in any way as a film-maker. I have certainly turned down a script because I was offended by its politics, but it was probably a script that wasn't particularly well written either. *Silkwood* was the most 'political' movie I've ever done, although my approach to it was as journalistic as it was political. I did a huge amount of reading about Karen Silkwood, and it seemed to me that the stuff that was written about her by people who were either 'for' or 'against' her told you absolutely nothing about her and why she did what she did. This is what we tried to do in the movie, just tell a story about how sometimes the most unlikely person does something heroic. But if you asked me, and Alice Arlen, and Mike Nichols what political point we wanted the movie to make, I think we'd all have different answers. Mine would be about the exploitation of labour by large American corporations, not about feminism.

Is there a particular characteristic you'd ascribe to the majority of films you've seen by New York film-makers?
Well sure. I think they're smarter than films made by Los Angeles film-makers. Don't you?

Sam Cohn

Sam Cohn has been a New York-based agent for nearly forty years; he served as the Director and Vice Chairman of International Creative Management from 1974 to 1999. His clients have included Woody Allen, Robert Altman, E. L. Doctorow, Nora Ephron, Bob Fosse, Arthur Miller, Mike Nichols, Arthur Penn, Susan Sarandon, Meryl Streep, Lily Tomlin, and Sigourney Weaver. Cohn was awarded the Independent Feature Project-East's Gotham Lifetime Achievement Award in 1994.

Tod Lippy: How did you get involved in the agency business? My understanding is you didn't start out in the mailroom . . .

Sam Cohn: I went to law school, like everybody goes to law school – there comes a time when you're graduating from college and somebody says, 'So what are you going to do next?' You don't have the slightest idea, so you opt for three more years of avoidance. After that, I got a job here in CBS's legal department. After a while, I became a so-called business-affairs person. When the head of programming at that time, Hubbell Robinson, left CBS to become a producer, he invited me and another fellow there, Tom Ryan, to go with him. MCA became our agents, and they sold a series of, I think, thirty-nine specials to the Ford Motor Company, in the person of a guy named Sonny Werblin, who later created the Jets. He promised Ford that those thirty-nine programmes were going to have thirty-nine of the MCA stars in them. You know, Marilyn Monroe, etc. etc. – a whole list of them. And we managed to produce six or seven programmes quite brilliantly, and the other thirty-two . . . well, they just weren't there. Without the machinery of CBS behind him, Hubbell couldn't do it. So MCA took it over, and I'm sure rebated an enormous amount of money to the Ford Motor Company.

So Tom and I decided to leave the company, and Hubbell remained on with MCA as his agent and financiers, and he made extremely generous settlements with us. We started a little company making prestigious specials – which we had just proved we didn't know how to do. That lasted for about a year, and then there was a company – still is – called Goodson–Todman, which was the king of the game shows, and the senior partner of an entertainment law firm called Marshall, Bratter, Greene, Allison & Tucker, had just died – well, the details are irrelevant. Mark Goodson or Bill Todman offered me the chance to become general counsel of that company, which I declined – I didn't want to serve one master – so I think the law firm got wind of it, and contacted me and asked me if I wanted to go there. I *really* didn't want to practice law, so I made a ridiculous proposal – which they accepted, because they wanted to help the client, I guess. I went there, and ironically ended up doing some work for Goodson–Todman. And I started to work with a client of the firm's named Herbert Siegel, who had started acquiring talent agencies – one of the first was General Artists Corporation. I worked on this acquisition, and because I'd produced a couple of off-Broadway plays —

You were producing around the same time?

No, during the time I was at CBS. *Red Eye of Love*, which actually was good, and, oh, a whole bunch – maybe five. On an avocational basis, because I couldn't bear what I was doing at GDC, I'd be working on contracts for programmes that had been broadcast a year earlier. It was like being in a Russian play.

So I started working for Herb, and started getting entwined in the business, so he suggested that I should come and work for him for a year or so. I did that, and that's how I first got involved – just as an advisor to him. Then I got more deeply involved, and Herb decided to make a bid to acquire Paramount Pictures, and immediately Paramount sued us and said you couldn't be an agency and a motion-picture producer – you cannot be an employer and an agent at the same time. Which made sense – we knew that was going to happen – so I organized a group, including myself, to buy the agency from Herb. That's how I *really* got in deep water, because I was now going back to the firm having become a principal in the ownership of the company.

Prior to Herb's leaving we had acquired a number of other agencies – small ones, whose names I can't remember – because in the middle of all of this, in '62 or '63, came the breakup of MCA, when between the government and SAG they essentially forced MCA to make an election between producing television and motion pictures or being an agent. MCA elected to go into the production business, and the agency broke up. There were a lot of splinter groups, some of which we acquired. So that's how I became an agent.

My understanding is that in this period of the early sixties, General Artists (GAC) was best known for representing night-club acts.
We had a big so-called 'personal appearance' area. The Copacabana, for example, was a big source of income. I guess that's called 'variety entertainment'. I really didn't have that much to do with it. We also had a theatre department – nothing to compare with MCA's – which was oddly enough acquired by International Famous Agency, whom we ultimately merged with to form ICM a decade later. IFA's department was run by Audrey Wood and Phyllis Jackson, two distinguished practitioners of the theatre. I mean, elegant, tasteful people who represented the major playwrights of the United States. When we got together, it was the twilight of these women. They were wonderful, wonderful people.

Did you first begin representing clients at GAC?
Oh, yes. My first client was Jackie Gleason. PHC was his agent. The guy who was responsible for him left the company, and Herb said to me: 'You're Jackie Gleason's agent.' So I got on a plane – I'll never forget, it was the Lindbergh plane – and we flew to Fred Waring's country-club resort place in Pennsylvania. I introduced myself as his new agent, and he couldn't have been nicer. We had a relationship that went on until he died. It was a wonderful experience. He probably went to the seventh or eighth grade. You know, I thought he was a genius. He was very generous and honest and absolutely conservative politically. A Nixonite. But

honest as the day is long. I can remember so many things that I learned from him.

Such as?

Well, he once said to me – he was about to go out and do one of those hour-long 'Honeymooners' – 'I'll give you a thousand dollars if there's a prop on the set that I haven't used by the time I'm finished.' I didn't get my thousand dollars . . . And he used to do a monologue during the beginning part of the show, where he'd come out and sit down with the little teacup which was supposed to be full of booze. The writers would write the monologue and he would insist that they slip it under the door. He would read one after another – and I would be sitting by him sometimes when he did – and just continue to turn them down, send them back. One time I just felt so bad for the writers, I said, 'Jackie, c'mon, that's the five-hundredth one of those you've gotten.' He said, 'Listen, Sam, if you think it's so funny, why don't you go out and do it.'

I remembered CBS wanted to have a morals clause in his contract – if he committed a felony, did this or that, etc. – and he said, 'You know what? I'll sign this if Bill Paley will sign one.' That was the end of that. Anyway, those were wonderful years with him. He was a real genius. I mean, the formula of the half-hour 'Honeymooners' was so simplistic-seeming, but you know, it's a little bit like Eugene O'Neill. You go to see *Long Day's Journey*, and the first hour, you're sitting there thinking to yourself, 'This guy couldn't pass a high-school writing class,' and then, suddenly, it overwhelms you. It was that kind of thing. When you see that embrace that came at the end of every episode, it's really moving.

Did your work with Gleason serve as a model for future client relationships for you?

Well, he was pretty singular. But I've been lucky. When I began, I really never dreamed that I'd work with some of these people, like Arthur Miller, Edgar Doctorow, Bobby Fosse, Paddy Chayefsky. And lots of the actors, too: Sigourney, Meryl for a long time, Susan Sarandon. Bill Irwin. You know, it's been very gratifying.

Have you ever been tempted to become a producer?

There have been occasions where people, particularly Bobby Fosse, would ask if I'd like to produce their movies. I remember saying to him, 'Look, Bobby, if I became a producer, my job would be to come in in the morning, make sure the coffee was hot, stand around all day while you shot the movie, go to the rushes – and if I made a comment that displeased you, you'd throw me out.' I don't want to live life that way. I'd rather be an independent person, free to express my views, free to involve myself in the exciting moments – you know, with the script and the casting, the cutting, the release and the marketing and all those things, and not have to be essentially part of a one-man band. And also, to go through the agony of being on a movie set without a specific role – you know, the long periods of time.

How about becoming a studio executive?

No. I never wanted to live in California. I really couldn't do that – I just wouldn't. And not because I hate it. I always used to say – whether it's true or not – that probably I'm just afraid I'd go out there and in two months or something I'd be driving around in a Porsche with a glove compartment filled with God-knows-what and a sixteen-year-old girl at my side. So maybe that was it – I knew myself too well.

But I've never really liked the environment there. I wouldn't go to Hollywood for the same reason I sold my house in East Hampton.

Because most of Hollywood is now there all summer long?

Well, Hollywood and other Masters of the Universe. That environment just doesn't work for me.

Do you spend much time in LA?

I used to go out there more often, but I go out very infrequently now. I'm flying out next week, but it's to see a rough cut. That's what I go there for mostly these days. You know, in terms of making a deal, it's really not that important with all of this stuff. [*Points to computer, fax.*] As a matter of fact, it's counterproductive – you're dancing to someone else's tune, and you're in a hurry to get back.

I'm a little bit like Woody. I like it here. The biorhythms are good for me.

Do you think the business is run differently here than it is there?

Yeah. Well, that's not fair. In the first place, eighty per cent of it is there. And ninety per cent of the decision-makers are there. But certainly, locally, it's different. Also, I spend a lot of time in theatre, which is located here. And in many ways, the theatre is a much more marginalized business than the motion-picture or television business.

But I don't want to exaggerate, because there are a lot of difficult people in and around the theatre, and it's changed from the days of the Robert Whiteheads, Robby Lantzes, people like that. But the ethos is still different. Not everybody cares about the work, but more people do than in film or television. People have higher aspirations. Also, for me it's much more exciting because it's a plastic art form – you know, you can continue working and changing.

You say that ninety per cent of the decision-makers are in California. Would you say New York played a more central role in the sixties and seventies?

Well, not really. I guess Paramount was here, but not for long. United Artists was here until the end of Orion – the lamentable end of Orion. But it was never really central – in my time, anyway. I think in an earlier generation, even than mine, it was a different story. But the so-called creative stuff was always centred in Hollywood. And the so-called front office was here – the people who controlled the money, dealt with the shareholders, held the reins in their hands. And there was always that tension between the two.

Just to back up with a second – could you talk briefly about the series of mergers that led to the formation of ICM?

Well, first GAC merged with CMA – Creative Management Associates – the principals of which were David Begelman and Freddie Fields. The purpose there was to get more involved with so-called movie stars. And from my point of view, you know, to put a little pepper in the steak, if you know what I mean. To be challenged. And I liked Freddie a lot; David was difficult. And then we merged with International Famous – that was '74, and became ICM.

Were you shifting into film at that point?

No, I was already representing film clients.

Who were your first?

Fosse was one. I think he was already at IFA – maybe in the theatre division. I remember Stevie Phillips was somehow involved. And Robert Benton, and Woody. Oh, a whole bunch of people . . .

How did you get involved with Woody Allen?

We represented him, I think, as a variety performer. He was a big success in clubs and things, and hated it. So I became friendly with his managers, and they let me know he wanted to do film. Edgar Sherick, who ran ABC Films, financed the first movie, which was *Take the Money and Run*. And for the second movie, *Bananas,* and God knows how many more, David Picker was the guy, at UA. Then when Transamerica forced Krim and Benjamin out, and they made their first Orion deal with Warner's, I was still involved in that. Then they became independent. And fortunately, I really felt it was a shitty situation, so our deal – Woody's deal – with Orion provided that if there were a material change in Arthur Krim's position or power, he could leave, which, when there was a bankruptcy, really allowed him to get out. Lucky thing, because a lot of people got stuck trying to unglue themselves. I loved representing Woody.

He left you for William Morris in 1998 after a thirty-year relationship. Are you still representing him in any way?

No. We're still friends. He's a wonderful artist. You know, with these relationships, I understand, even if I feel I've done a superb job, that it's work. I guess that's my background as a lawyer. I really can't rage at people because they've decided their circumstances require something else. People think I'm nuts on that score. So what.

Yet you've been described as harbouring an 'eye-watering loyalty' to your clients.

Well, that's nice to know. I'm the wrong person to ask about that.

Are there particular personality traits an agent should have?

Personality traits . . . You know, some of the agents, and I'm not going to name any of them, whom I've met over the years, and who have huge and important client lists – I would never let them near me when and if I needed the services of an agent. But that was also the case when I was a lawyer: the rainmakers ruled the day, even though some of them were almost incompetent. They had a way of relating to clients, bringing them in, while the guys in the back room were doing the actual work. So, the 'personality traits', to use your phrase, that help people acquire enormous and important client lists sometimes have very little to do with their actual accomplishments.

I mean, the ideal agent is somebody who – well, I guess there are a few things involved. One is to understand the business and be able to make an effective and *protective* deal. It's not a mystery; it's not that difficult to learn. There are intricacies involved in the equity positions, and the profit stuff, and one does occasionally get involved in unusual and interesting things, but I'm talking about the basic business aspects of making up the deal. You need to understand distribution, with respect to almost everything. How a play is distributed, how a book is distributed, how a movie is distributed, how a television show is distributed. Because, for example, in television, as you well know, if you have a wonderful show and it gets programmed opposite a huge success, it's a toxic decision. But they have to put something in those places, so you're often fighting with the networks or the cable networks not to be in one of those spots.

You should have a real knowledge of marketing – for example, when it's appropriate for a certain kind of movie to be released. For example, even though we weren't very successful in our plan, the way *Map of the World* was distributed was to get it into theatres by early December for Oscar consideration, which almost happened, and deservedly so. A great performance, and the debut of an interesting director. Anyway, that's just an example. That's number two.

Number three is, I think it's important to be literate, in the true meaning of that word. To be able to read and advise. Also to have the courage of your convictions, and not to be a go-alonger. To say to somebody, 'I'm sorry, I know how passionate you are, and you may be right, but it's my duty to advise you that this is a big mistake.' That's the hardest thing. Also, the hardest thing is to bring the bad news. That was the hardest lesson for me, at least.

You mean when a deal has fallen through, or someone hasn't gotten the job?
Exactly. It's not a problem for me any more, but it was a terrible problem for me early on. It's an analytic issue. One feels guilty, even though it's such an inappropriate feeling. When Jackie's career went through some arid stretches, I got to the point where I couldn't bear to talk to him, because I didn't have any good news. And he called me and said, 'Listen, I know how badly you feel, but believe me, I'd rather hear from you and get the unvarnished truth.' That was a terrific lesson, but a hard lesson for me to learn.

Any other tough lessons?

Well, I don't want to name the people – but sometimes you represent two people on the same project. I was in a situation once where, essentially, it was understood that an actress client of mine was going to play the part. And there was a reading of the script, and afterwards, the director – also a client – said to me, 'I think I've made a mistake, and I'm not going to cast her. Please treat this confidentially.' I said, 'Well, I can't withhold that information for long, but if you promise me you'll deliver this yourself . . .' And a day went by and it didn't happen, and then another day went by and it didn't happen, and I didn't really do what I should have done, which was to say, 'Well, I'm sorry, but I need to tell my client.' It led to a very serious thing – the actress called me when she finally learned about it and asked me if I'd known about this. I told her I had, and she left me. And she was right, even though we had a long, enormously successful relationship.

A terrible lesson. You really have to have the emotional strength to counsel against something that somebody's passionate to do, and to give them all the information that you have as quickly as you get it. Always. And if somebody says, 'I'm telling you this on a confidential basis,' and it involves a client of yours, you have to say, 'I'm so sorry, but you should have known this.' I don't know how to deal with that situation; it's still a tough one. I think that the way I did it, at the beginning, was correct – it was my follow-through that was awful. I should have said, 'Okay, I'll give you the rest of the day to tell her.' Not enforcing it was a big mistake.

Would you say that the agent-and-client relationship has other analogues, like, for instance, that of parent and child?
That way lies death. I had a client whom I loved – still do – but who got me confused with his father. That had never happened to me before. I went to see – at his request – his therapist seven or eight times, got involved in advising him on how to create a really marvellous rent-controlled apartment, stuff like that. He eventually came to me and said, 'I'm sorry, I had real problems with my father, and I'm getting them confused with you.' It was a tough one.

It seems that it could be a very emotional relationship.
Well, not in every case.

But you're good friends with a number of your clients . . .
I am. And then there are some clients who, in fifteen years, I've maybe had dinner with twice. But not because I don't like them; it's just because we're in different orbits. And I feel it's my prerogative to choose my friends.

You never worry about a potential 'business/pleasure' problem?
No. I don't think it makes any difference. In fact, I'd say just the opposite. That's the great pleasure of the job. If my personal, social life wasn't intertwined with my business life, I don't think I would be doing it. I would have done something else a long time ago.

I know you're loathe to use the word, but many have credited you with starting the whole 'packaging' trend that reached its apogee at CAA in the eighties.
Not really – I never did that.

But a film like *Eyewitness* had, I think, five or six of your clients in it. Peter Yates directed, Steve Tesich wrote it, Sigourney Weaver, Christopher Plummer, Irene Worth – they all were your clients at the time, right?
True. Well, I don't think we represented Irene at the time. Peter and Steve – their relationship came from *Breaking Away*. I had actually given Steve's original script to Peter because I liked it a lot. Then Peter had the idea of merging that script, called *The Cutters*, with another one of Steve's, and then they became good friends after that. So there wasn't any packaging, because there's no economic advantage to it, really, except that it's a job.

I mean, what 'packaging' connotes to me is putting different elements of an artistic work together regardless of the appropriateness of the elements. I refuse to say I've ever done that – I really mean that. If somebody calls and I feel that a non-ICM client is the best choice, I'll tell them. And I'll tell them on two levels: one, on a certain level of pride; but secondly, if you make good and valid suggestions to people, when it comes the time to honestly recommend a client, you've got real access. If, on the other hand, you make a suggestion from a list of people that varies anywhere from Cher to Irene Worth, you know, it's absurd. I have pretty good access with most directors because they know, even though I may be wrong, that I'm not just 'flogging the list', as it were.

In other words, if I represent a director or a star, and there's a project he or she wants to do, it's one thing to shoehorn the people you represent into it to make as much commission money as you can. I'm sure there are many, many agents who don't do that – I don't mean to say I'm the exception – but you need to talk about the right people. I mean, we all put movies together. But with Ovitz, the motivation was different.

What do you make of the whole 'Art of War' metaphor as applied to the agenting business?
I find it abhorrent. It doesn't seem to exist here, in this little group of people. But it's almost *opera buffa*, that kind of stuff.

In a *New Yorker* profile from the early eighties, you were described as being 'the single most important force of the motion-picture business in New York'.
Not really. Never was.

But you've wielded, and continue to wield, enormous power; it's hard to argue with that.
The basic psychological crisis that exists for all people is that distance between what you think is the essence of yourself and what others perceive. And closing that distance, and making yourself an integrated human being, I suppose is the

big casino. I haven't succeeded. I just don't have that self-image, and I'm not being modest. It's nice to hear it. Maybe if I hired a chorus to sit around all day and keep saying it, I might actually believe it.

It's not that I can't be aggressive and all of that, you know, when somebody's 'doing' me, but I don't feel like a centre of power. I don't. Nor do I feel denuded of it. I feel like I'm intelligent and articulate, and I try very hard – it's my wish – to be well-informed, about the business as well as the art of it. You know, the first section of the paper I read in the morning is the business section, so that indicates something.

How do you come across material? Do you read a lot of manuscripts, a lot of screenplays?
I have to read a lot of stuff. And I'm slow. I've been reading a new novel by Philip Roth – whom I don't represent, but one of my clients is interested in the movie possibilities. It's called *The Human Stain* – isn't that a wonderful title? – and it's taken me four weekend afternoons to read it. You know, when I start to read something, I finish it. And I've never used coverage. What's the point? If you read it and say to yourself, 'Gee, this sounds terrific,' how do you really know? And the same with the opposite – how do you know the person who's written the coverage is intelligent? Maybe he's wrong.

But there's only so much time. And I'm busy every night. I go to the ballet a lot, to theatre a lot. Music a great deal. There's much more of that here.

Do you see a lot of movies? I remember reading a quote of yours from a while ago about seeing at least one hundred a year.
Oh, yeah.

Do you attend screenings?
I go to screenings only when somebody tells me it's important to the company that I go. I prefer not to go. They always start a half an hour late; they're always tense. I like to go to the movie-movies. And I never watch video, unless there's no other way to see it. I've got two godchildren with whom I'm very close, so I'm an expert on children's movies. Not because I wish to be. They hate going to the Walter Reade, which has the best children's movie series on the weekends. They're afraid it's going to be in some foreign language. So I get to go see things like *Snow Day*, or *Toy Story 2*, which I actually thought was a wonderful movie.

Do you see a lot of independent films?
Sure. I go to mainstream American movies last.

I always think of you as representing major talent – do you have any clients from the independent world?
Well, Scott Elliott, certainly. And Lavinia Currier. I was astonished that *Passion in the Desert* didn't do well. It was amazing. I represent a lot of theatre directors, and a lot of musical theatre people, which is funny, because I never thought of myself

as an expert on musicals. I guess that started with Fosse and Tommy Tune.

How many clients do you represent?
I have no idea. I don't really count them.

Have you ever turned someone down because of a concern about being overextended?
Somebody who could be economically important, whom I like – somebody whose future I believe in – I'll do it. I mean, I don't feel overextended. Sometimes, you know, on the weekends when I'm trying to read this stuff, I get an anxiety attack that I'm not going to get it all done, or am not going to be able to do what I said I was going to do and all that.

How often do you talk to your clients?
That depends on *their* anxiety level. I probably speak to Nora Ephron six times a year; I speak to Scott three times a week. And also, when *Cradle Will Rock* was being put together by myself and several other agents, I talked to Tim two times a day for many, many weeks. Same was true with *Dead Man Walking.* You know, when you get into the middle of something with somebody, it increases. Like I'm talking to Claudia Shear right now every day, because we're moving to Broadway with *Dirty Blonde.*

What is the ratio of your theatre clients to film clients?
It changes. A lot of these people, like Sigourney, Kathleen Turner, Dianne Wiest, work in theatre as well as film. I encourage that. I think it's essential. It's invaluable to movie actors.

Are most of them based in New York?
No. A good portion of them are.

What's your opinion about the enormous salaries actors are now drawing?
I think in terms of commercial movies, they should get what the market will pay them. But I also think it's important for an actor to be elastic – as Tom and Nicole are, for example – and willing to do something like *Eyes Wide Shut* for nothing. Bruce Willis is another example. Actors should be willing to consider adapting themselves to working at different levels on better, or whatever the word is – more interesting – movies.

So you see it as sort of a payback?
It's not a question of paying back. It's the cinematic version of the theatre. And it's in your self-interest to work with those kinds of directors, and those kinds of scripts. And particularly since we are the dominant culture in the world, it's an important thing to do. I hope I would feel that way if I were an actor.

And you encourage your actors to do that.
Absolutely. But many don't require any encouragement.

Can you give me a sense of some of your most rewarding relationships with clients?
No, I can't do that. I think that's improper.

How often is your advice not taken by clients?
I'm trying to think of an honest answer, which means I have to push my ego to the back of my head. I'm going to say rarely.

How often are you right in the situations when it's not?
Not always. Of course not. For example, I begged Lily Tomlin – who's no longer a client of mine – not to finance her Broadway show, *Signs of Intelligent Life in the Universe*. I think what happened was we financed half from the Schubert Organization, and there was half left. She said, 'I want to do it myself.' I told her I thought it was too high-risk. It's a good thing she didn't follow that advice; I was dead wrong. That's an example that certainly sticks in my head.

What is your opinion of the state of the American film industry right now?
Well, I mean, with the success of some of these pictures like *American Beauty* – I'm not going to tell you whether I liked it or not – or David O. Russell's *Three Kings*, which I thought was terrific, and Soderbergh's arrival in the commercial world – I think that's all good. There are some very good movies being made. And of course there's the presence of the Weinsteins and the Octobers, the Good Machines, and Shooting Galleries, the GreeneStreet boys, Christine Vachon.

You know, I'm not sure what the motivation was for *American Beauty*. I suppose the idea was to make it for fifteen or sixteen million dollars, and I guess establish a relationship with Mendes, probably because Spielberg saw *Cabaret* or whatever. But I promise you that its success was a big surprise.

There was a lot of talk in the last several years about a somewhat pronounced antagonism between the New York and Los Angeles branches of ICM. Could you talk about that?
That's dissipated. There's no secret to the fact that Jeff Berg and I had real differences of opinion over about a year and a half, but that's been resolved, happily, as far as I'm concerned, and I think as far as he's concerned. And we're working together quite well. I'm very sorry that Jimmy Wiatt left – I'd be silly not to be. That was, I thought, a sad loss.

You know, as agencies go, I suppose I could go and work at any of them. But I certainly have no impulse to do so. It's no Plato's Republic here, but I have a sick identification with ICM.

Well, you're one of its founders.
It's a terrible thing to be a founder and/or a legend. Because the immediate response to that is to call Frank Campbell and reserve a spot.

In a recent issue of *Variety*, an agent in LA was quoted as saying 'New York has

lost its viability as a base to represent film clients'. How do you feel about that?
I don't think it's accurate. That's my answer. There are some people, some artists, who may feel that they want an agent on the 'battleground', if they think LA is the battleground. But there are others who actually remained with this agency because, even if they're based in LA, they want connections with the theatre and with the literary world. We have a great collection of literary agents downstairs. So we provide a lot of access to that which our artists – at least the thinking ones – want. Steve Martin, who is a very important motion-picture star, is here in part because the two plays that he did were terribly important to him, and the novel that he's just about to publish, and all the pieces that he's written for the *New Yorker*, have given him a new view of himself for which he's very grateful. And being able to do that kind of thing is what makes this kind of an enterprise work.

In the worst day of our arguments, Berg never contemplated changing this place. Me, maybe, but not this place. [*Laughs.*]

You sold your equity in the company recently, though, right?
I did. That was, I think, appropriate.

You're famous for the Sam Cohn 'telephone terror', or the infrequency with which you return phone calls —
Well, I don't think it's as much a problem now as it used to be, because I don't have as much management stuff as I used to have. For many years I was deeply involved in corporate policy, negotiating employment contracts with the CFO and General Counsel, who used to be here in New York. I'm not, now, and that's given me a lot more breathing room to return phone calls. It used to be that my telephone would be lighting up all day. It's not that way any more. It's surprising how much time that takes up.

Do you have any opinion about the recent move in the industry towards personal management?
I wouldn't want to be a manager in the sense that I could force myself on my client's movies as the executive producer, and all that other stuff that goes on. I find that tawdry. The connotation is that the manager is the guy who does the sound check, or meets the plane. That's probably not accurate, but it doesn't attract me.

You grew up in Pennsylvania; did you always want to come to New York?
No. I was frightened of New York. I was very provincial. I thought I was going to go back to Pennsylvania and be a judge, because I just didn't think I could deal with this place – I didn't think I could find a place in the field that interested me. But my then wife insisted, and this CBS thing came along as a result of an interview, which seemed like a miracle. I was sure I was going to end up in some sweaty law firm. I knew I wasn't going to make it to one of the great white-shoe ones, because in those days there was a slightly different attitude about Jews. Completely not the case any more.

Do you feel like an 'insider'?
In what world?

Well, in the entertainment world. I guess the irony of being in New York is that, however connected you are, you're still – by virtue of geography – on the outside.
I think that's correct. It certainly doesn't trouble me. LA is not the right environment for me. But I feel, and I've always felt, that being in New York creates a backdoor kind of insider-ness. I've deluded myself into thinking that there's a certain mystery connected with the fact that you're not there, and they don't see you every night. When they come to New York, they want to have lunch with you, go to the theatre with you. In some ways, it's a more advantageous relationship.

You develop a certain kind of stature, maybe a certain amount of envy – because there are many men and women in that city who wish they weren't living there. And also, I think – this may be a bad thing about me – there's a sense of cultural chauvinism, which may put some people off. And may draw others to me. Who knows? I hope it's not an affectation.

Juliet Taylor

Juliet Taylor has served as casting director for over seventy films, including every Woody Allen project since *Love and Death*. Taylor, who works frequently with the directors Mike Nichols, Alan Parker, Stephen Frears and Nora Ephron, has also cast *The Exorcist*, *Network*, *Taxi Driver*, *Close Encounters of the Third Kind*, *Pretty Baby*, *Terms of Endearment* and *The Sheltering Sky*.

Tod Lippy: When and why did you first come to New York?
Juliet Taylor: I moved to New York immediately upon my graduation from college in 1967, wanting to go into the theatre, but not really knowing what that meant. I realized that I was never going to have the nerve to act, so I thought I'd get a job in production – not having known anyone who'd ever done it. It wasn't exactly in my family's idea of job possibilities.

One reason I went to Smith was that it had a Theatre major. Lots of schools back then did not – it was always extracurricular. The college had a board of counsellors to every department that wasn't entirely an academic department, and the one for the theatre department was made up of this wonderful group of women that had gone on to work in the business. They set up field trips every year. They brought us to New York, and it was really wonderful – we had unbelievable access to things. My senior year, the original *Cabaret* had opened, and they organized a symposium with Harold Prince, Boris Aronson, Fred Ebb – all these people. That was the first time I'd ever met a casting director – Shirley Rich, who'd set up the whole thing – and it really stuck in my mind, because it seemed to be a way to get emotionally involved with a performance and actors without actually doing it yourself. But I didn't come to New York thinking that's what I would do.

Anyway, I arrived here and sort of tromped around, and I'd been told that people in the theatre were going to be very tough, and doors were going to slam in my face and all of that, but it didn't turn out to be like that. People were very nice. I went to a place that was extremely hot at the time, the Establishment Theater on East 54th Street. They were doing *Scuba Duba* and they didn't have anything, but they were so nice. So then I just started looking through the newspaper to see who was doing things, and during the days I'd go by and drop off my résumé at various places. I'd usher at the Jan Hus Playhouse at night.

Then, at the field trip for the seniors in the fall after I graduated, I ran into another Smith graduate who said she was leaving her job at the David Merrick office, and would I be interested? It was the receptionist, low-man-on-the-totem-pole job, but for me it was, you know, a dream come true. On the eighth floor of the St James Theater building, with a doorman, named Saul, who was out of an old movie – he smoked a stogie and had a little hat that sat on the top of his head. It was really Runyonesque. Merrick had a small staff, and we worked really long hours – I had to stay until the curtain went up, which was 8.30 then, and then I'd work on Saturdays until the matinee was half over. I was in heaven.

I recall your saying that Merrick had something like seven productions running concurrently when you were there.
Yeah, they did. My first day was the day after Pearl Bailey opened in *Hello, Dolly*.

How did that lead to the position with casting director Marion Dougherty?
I'd been at Merrick's office for about six months, and a woman who had worked with him as a casting director was taking a job as an associate to Marion. Movies then were becoming very busy in New York – production under John Lindsay had really increased. Marion was also looking for a secretary, but someone they could train, basically, and I thought it would be good to really learn something specific. Also, there was a kind of funny morale at the Merrick office. As I said, I felt like I was in heaven, but people were eager to get out of there. Everybody said, 'Take the job. If you stay here you'll just end up being somebody more important's secretary.' I'm not sure I would have had the courage to leave otherwise, because I really wasn't too interested in movies.

You must have felt like you were abandoning your true love.
A little bit, but casting interested me. Anyway, it was great. Marion was so fabulous.

She's been credited with revolutionizing the whole casting process. Can you talk about that a little bit?
She had a brownstone on 30th Street, which really gave the whole thing a kind of different, interesting spin. First of all, it was out of the main district where everybody usually is, and second of all, it was this little Victorian house that she had done up, and it was really cute. It lent a graciousness – a homeyness – to the whole situation. And it was a hilarious place to work in a certain way because we had wild, weird tenants, like this older man who lived in the basement who would sometimes come up in his bathrobe with his hair all askew in the middle of readings with some very fancy director. It was a goofy group of people, a funny place. And disgruntled actors – well, more like people who had fantasies of being actors, but were quite disturbed – would kind of push their way in because we had no security whatsoever.

Marion was a very interesting person to work for. I look back on it and realize that she was always kind of pushing the limits of a situation in ways that none of us has to do now. You know, she was sort of disciplining directors, in a way, to see casting as a more creative process. For instance, in the old style, a casting director would have a ton of people in for the same part, and they would all resemble each other. You know, thirty short blondes with an overbite or whatever. But Marion was a very creative thinker, and she would come up with very interesting, different ways to play a part, and then would have in just a handful of people. They would all look different, and each would bring something very different to it. And if a director said, 'But I want to see a ton of people,' she'd say, 'Well, tough. That's not the way I work.'

To be fair, if the director didn't like anyone, then you have to keep going. But directors liked it; they liked her intelligence and her certainty.

So in a sense she was providing a much denser filter than what casting agents had provided before?
That's right. And it's interesting how it's developed over the years, too. This is sort of a different subject, but when I worked with Marion, there were a lot of creative producers around, producers who sat in on your sessions or whatever. You don't see that so much any more. Directors tend to be their own producers; they have their own companies. And as a result, casting directors – not to mention other members of the creative team – have become more important in a director's support system, I think.

There were really people who wouldn't make a move without Marion. People like George Roy Hill. It became a very intimate process in a way. She contributed more than just an ordinary casting director.

At some point, she left to do studio work, right?
Well, she left to produce with David Picker, who was the head of UA, and who went off to produce movies independently. Shortly after that he was offered the presidency of Paramount, which he took, and he persuaded Marion to go out to LA with him and head the talent division there.

And you took over?
I took over when she left to produce with David, which was just short of three years before she went to LA. In that period, we called it Juliet Taylor/MDA. She still retained ownership of the company. And then I got married, and got pregnant, and Marion said to me, 'Why don't you make your life a little easier? You won't have to worry about a staff, all of that. Come to Paramount.' I was sort of thrilled not to have to be responsible for that house, the real-estate thing, so that's what I did.

But you stayed in New York, right?
Yes. I did East Coast casting. I was there for a year, and then my husband and I moved to Los Angeles in 1979 for six months for something he was doing, thinking we might stay. But we didn't. When we returned, I had another nice situation here where Paramount gave me an office, and I consulted on movies, and moved around for while – I spent some time at Warner's, again because Marion had switched over there – and then for many, many years I've been under the Woody Allen umbrella.

How did you meet Woody Allen?
Marion cast *Bananas*, and I was her assistant. And being a creature of habit, Woody came back to me on *Love and Death,* even though I was, like, twenty-six. It was crazy. I mean, I was kind of a wreck about it. So I got lucky. I inherited a lot of great directors from her.

Who else?
Well, Paul Mazursky and Martin Scorsese – I had worked with Marion on *Alice Doesn't Live Here Anymore*, and then did *Taxi Driver*. And John Schlesinger. I

don't think she ever actually worked for Mike Nichols, but Marion sent Mike my way when he was doing *Carnal Knowledge.* He got stuck. He was looking for one character he hadn't cast, so she asked me to look for someone. It was kind of a funny, odd little part.

Who did you find?
Carol Kane. I found her picture in the *Player's Guide.* He wanted someone with that sort of strange, pre-Raphaelite look. I remember he was in Vancouver, so I never actually met him. It was all done by telephone.

What was the first film you actually cast? *Panic in Needle Park?*
Well, Marion was really the person on that. She was very responsible for casting Al Pacino and Kitty Wynn, and then she handed the rest over to me. That was really the biggest responsibility I had ever had. The first one I was responsible for entirely was something she had nothing to do with, which was *The Exorcist.*

How did you find Linda Blair?
She had actually gone up for a number of commercials as a little girl – she was what we call a 'commercial kid'. I mean, I went to every school, every place you could imagine, to find children, but she happened to be a professional who came in through an agent.

I read somewhere that you cast actual junkies in *Needle Park,* as well as other non-actors —
I did. Here's what happened. *Hair* opened on Broadway in 1969, and all of their actors were on what they called 'pink contracts' – they only needed to give two weeks' notice to be released from the show. So the producers needed an ongoing casting situation. Marion really didn't have any interest, first of all, in casting for the theatre, but she especially had no interest in casting *Hair,* so I jumped at it, and did all sorts of odd stuff to build up our pool of talent. For instance, I had an open call on St Mark's Place, at Theater 80 St Mark's. My friends helped me – we would stand on the corner of 8th Street and also St Mark's Place, passing out flyers for it every night after work. We didn't advertise in any mainstream papers, only in the East Village *Other,* maybe *The Village Voice.* We sent stuff around to schools, tried to get a hold of some radio stations. But we passed out all of these of flyers. It was a huge event. People came and camped out in tents on the sidewalk the night before; kids came from all over. It was just wild.

Was anyone else doing this sort of thing?
Well, I don't know. I think there were others doing it a little bit, there must have been. But this particular milieu I was really into. I really loved that show.

Did any of the actors you cast become well known?
Some of them, like Jessica Harper. She was at Wesleyan, and she was one of the

kids that came in. We had a lot of good people for the show. Some of the crew, actually, now that I think back on it, also went on to other stuff. This was after Tom O'Horgan wasn't really around much any more. Dan Sullivan – every week he and I would hold auditions together. Wesley Fata was the assistant choreographer, who now teaches dance at Yale. And Barry Manilow was the rehearsal pianist. Isn't that funny?

But a lot of that pool of people ended up in *Panic in Needle Park*. It was a very streety crowd, so it was a good resource for me.

Do you still take business cards on the street with you?
Oh, yeah, I still have my cards. But with just my telephone number, not my address. I don't hand them out as much as I did.

The other great source for new talent in New York, of course, is theatre. How often do you go?
Well, before I had a family, I used to go almost every night. And a couple of things on Saturday, because they used to have midnight shows. You'd do one act here, one act there, that kind of thing.

Now that our kids are grown, we go fairly often. But even throughout, we would go a couple of times a week. My husband was a Tony voter for many years, and we would go every night for several months running. We still try to keep up, but I don't have as much tolerance for stuff that's not good any more. There's just not that much I want to see.

How often do you 'score' at more off-off-Broadway venues?
Well, you'd be surprised. With actors, you always see somebody kind of interesting. But I'm not as good about going to that kind of stuff any more. And now, of course, you have to keep up with independent films, too. Which I'm even less good at.

How many assistants do you have working for you?
It depends on the movie. Usually, two. I shouldn't admit this in print, but I probably do in some degree what Marion did with me – I count on an assistant in her twenties to be seeing stuff that I'm not seeing. And to be interested in a community that I'm a little less interested in.

You say 'her' twenties. Do you only work with female assistants? You've talked in the past how casting, for whatever reason, tends to attract more women than men.
I'd be interested to know if it is still more female statistically; I'm not so sure it is any more. In California I imagine it's probably equal. But I've always had an all-female office. It's a funny joke with us. It may be somewhat unfair, but I pretty much prefer it that way.

How many head shots do you get a week?

Well, when we're doing a movie, the postman brings sacks. Sacks. It's kind of discouraging.

And how do you get through them?
It's always sort of been our policy to try to be good about going through pictures, looking at them for good faces and interesting résumés. For instance, we have a Woody Allen cabinet filled with unusual faces, or faces that suggest something in particular – a very particular look that's hard to find, an odd ability, whatever. And then if someone just has a really substantial résumé and is interesting-looking, we might put them aside to interview.

It's hard to keep up with. You have to be really diligent about that. And your assistants have to be really diligent about it, too. But, you know, you do get unsolicited stuff that's interesting sometimes.

And you must get unsolicited stuff when you're not casting, too.
Right. All those pictures out there [*points to stacks in adjoining office*] are unsolicited.

How many of those people will actually be interviewed?
It's really hard to say. If you're very busy, you might find more interesting stuff.

How do you update your information on actors? Do you have files?
I used to keep index cards. That was the way Marion did it, and it's kind of a good way because you can slip it into an age group, alphabetically, and just record all your thoughts. Now I'm sort of switching over to another system, which is that I keep a notebook on every project, and every day that I interview someone or read someone a sheet goes into that notebook. That's probably slightly less effective, but I got tired of my card file, and I was never great at keeping it up.

The other thing I did when I was younger – I had a great memory, I really could remember practically everybody I'd ever met – was compile these lists, divided into folders based on age groups. I have tons and tons of them. Every time I sat down to do something I would go through the lists, because you would see a lot of stuff that might not apply but which would spark kind of interesting stuff, rather than getting too tightly into a type or a category.

Now, maybe it's motivational, or maybe it's age, but I don't really remember anybody I'm not really interested in. I just sort of flush it from my brain. Which isn't so great. So I'm trying to keep better notes.

You don't cast that many movies —
Well, but I used to. I'm sort of at this funny point in my life, at this crossroads where I'm trying to decide how much to do. It's true that I used to do less than other people, because I only did one movie at a time, or I would overlap a little bit. At my busiest I would do, maybe, three and a half movies a year. Three films plus maybe something that was only partially going to be done in the East, or a couple of consultant jobs in addition. I used to have an office of four people, and

it was kind of a really qualified office – almost top-heavy, in the sense that every-body there could really carry some weight.

Some people who have bigger offices and do more movies – I don't know how you do something without actually spending a lot of time with the director. I don't know how they do it. There were a few years there where I would excuse myself from a meeting with one director saying that I was going to the ladies' room and call another director from the reception area, because I was juggling. But you can't really let them know; they don't really like to know that.

Can you talk a bit about the casting agent–director relationship?
Other than having sort of good intuition and taste about actors, and a depth of knowledge – who you should know, etc. – I think one of the most important things is being able to talk to a director. The casting process is the first thing that happens in a production, and it's often the process that helps the director under-stand the characters – and sometimes you're surprised. Most good directors go in with no preconceived notions – I mean, some vague ones, but they don't come in saying, 'I've got to have a redhead.' Some lesser directors will be very rigid, but really good directors aren't. So often, as the piece evolves, they learn about the character. It's important to be able to talk to a director, talk about character. And as you cast one character, whoever you cast in that part is going to influence the chemistry of the other parts.

So the relationship is kind of intimate. The directors I work with are really close friends in a way – not that I see them socially necessarily, but there's kind of a real bond there that doesn't seem very businesslike. I always feel like it's kind of sisterly in a certain way, because they're mostly men, and there are some people I've worked with for so long. I say 'sisterly' because there's a certain kind of familial edge to it. A certain kind of affection that you have which is half the fun of it. You're hopefully giving good advice, and sometimes admonishing, and some-times saying, 'No, no, *no* – don't do that; that's not a good idea!' And yet ulti-mately there's such trust – that's what I'm talking about. That's great.

'Sisterly' has a aura of protection to it.
Right. It depends on the project. With Woody, I definitely, definitely stand between him and the outside world in many cases – that's one of the things that I definitely do. Because he doesn't really – he's not that interactive with the outside world. So I sort of have to protect him from that. But that's not my main job, really.

With some directors who are doing studio pictures, you have to protect them from the studio. This is what happens: you get a call from some really nice person who's the head of casting for a studio – and they're all quite nice, by the way. They say, 'Well, how's it going?!' And you say, 'Great!' And they act like they're just calling to be friendly, but they want to know who you're thinking of, because they want to go back and tell the president of the studio who the director's consider-ing. And you can't tell them, because if you say, 'Well, we're thinking of Arnold

Schwarzenegger, but he's actually fifth on our list,' then that call will come in the next day where they say, 'We hear you're interested in Schwarzenegger, and that's who you should go for.' You can't give them any information.

And do they give you suggestions?
In the end, they can make a director's life tough. You just don't want to say anything before you get your ducks in a row. Then, ultimately, of course, the studio has to say 'OK'. And almost every director is going to be susceptible to that, except for Woody, because he's so independent. You just have to be crafty.

Do you always pre-screen actors before they meet with a director?
Yes, unless I've seen a lot of their work on stage and I think they're really good. In that case, I won't, unless it's a part that I think is more unlikely for them. If it's an actor who is very, very new or unknown, I'll have them in to read for me even if I've liked their work in something else. But if it's someone who's really got a certain 'body of work', as they say in the business, I'll just sort of trust that what they'll do will be sort of interesting, even if in the end it isn't what we go for.

Let's do a case study, if you don't mind. I know you cast *Interview with the Vampire*, and I believe it was your first experience working with Neil Jordan.
Right, it was.

Let's start from the beginning. How did you get the script for that?
I'm pretty sure I got a call from Neil, telling me he was doing this movie. And I was very excited because I really admired his work, and especially loved *The Crying Game*. I was out in Los Angeles working on a movie – which I hardly ever do, by the way – and he was out there getting his movie set up. I met him and we had breakfast and whatever. They shot a lot of that movie abroad, so the amount of work I did on that picture was somewhat contained. A lot of it for me was finding the child.

Kirsten Dunst?
Mm-hmm. The two leads were already set, and Neil had always had Antonio Banderas in his mind for Armand. There were a handful of supporting roles – the ones that were shot in Louisiana – and the child. I had two people who went on the road, screening girls. And then we had the problem of River Phoenix dying before production. He was to be the interviewer. I was in Los Angeles at the time, and I remember reading Leo DiCaprio in my hotel room, and saying, 'This kid is so fabulous', and everyone telling me he was too young, and me saying, 'He's a student. Why can't he be a college student? He's so *great*.' And they wouldn't go for it.

How often does that happen?
Not that often. Most people really recognize it. I had suggested Christian Slater, too. It's just that I thought that Leo was a great idea. I was so excited by his reading, and his whole persona. I mean, they had a point – he was on the young side.

I just wasn't so sure it made a difference to the story. Actually, that's probably not the best example . . .

How about *Working Girl*?
Well, there are some interesting stories there. Although Melanie Griffith had started acting as a teenager, she wasn't really a 'star' yet. This was obviously a big break for her. She'd just done *Something Wild*, and was wonderful in it, and we flew her in to read for the movie. That was an exciting and dramatic moment, because, you know, she was terribly nervous – it was the biggest thing she had been up for. We had a screen test, with Campbell Scott reading with her – he's a good friend of Mike's, and has done a lot of things with him.

Actually, an interesting thing happened with the men on that movie. We had really talked about using Alec Baldwin for the lead. I don't know if he had done anything but *Married to the Mob* at that time; I don't think he had. He was dying to work with Mike. Actually, that picture was kind of the beginning of what I was talking about earlier, that kind of studio – well, I would call it 'interference', but I'm sure they would call it 'control'. I remember spending more time on the phone talking to studio executives than casting the movie; it felt as if a huge amount of my time and effort went into deflection.

Anyway, we had this interest in Alec, and the studio wanted a name. So, when Harrison Ford said he would do it, Mike offered Alec the old boyfriend role. But before that happened, Alec was up for a movie Robert Towne was doing – I guess it was *Tequila Sunrise* – and they offered it to him, but at that point he was still waiting to hear whether or not he was going to get the lead in *Working Girl*. And they started doing really manipulative things, which are not that uncommon, actually, by saying, 'If you don't answer us in twenty-four hours we're going to withdraw the offer.' In other words, trying to scare him so that he would lose both jobs.

People do that, but it's really not the right thing to do. You don't try to control which way somebody's going to go; you just sort of say, 'Well, we have to know within a reasonable amount of time; just keep us in close touch and let us know.' Interestingly, Alec was heroic, especially for a young actor for whom a lead role would be a big break, and he said, 'I think this a terrible, unethical thing to do to me,' and he withdrew. And even after he was offered only the smaller part on *Working Girl*, he still stuck to his guns and did it. It was impressive; a very sturdy thing to do.

Was Harrison Ford your first 'star' choice for the role?
As I recall, yes. And of course, he was wonderful. It was thrilling to have them both in the movie.

And I'm assuming that's the kind of situation where you just offered the role to him, without any kind of reading.
Right.

And Sigourney Weaver?
Well, that was also an interesting thing in terms of studio input. The studio really wanted a name in that part, too, and I was stunned. I thought, 'Whoa! We've got Harrison Ford, and Melanie and Alex, both on the rise,' but they were really quite insistent. They wanted a high-profile cast, which of course happens more and more now. And even though I disapprove of it, and think it's 'anti-creative', in a way, I kind of enjoy the intrigue in the process. There's a perverse part of me that sort of enjoys all of the negotiating.

How about *Dangerous Liaisons*?
Dangerous Liaisons was interesting, too, because Malkovich was already attached; Stephen Frears had already approached him by the time I had gotten on the movie.

How did Frears contact you?
He just called me out of the blue. I guess that was the first thing I did with him – *The Grifters* came later. What was interesting about that movie, which I can't really claim any kind of responsibilty for, is that Stephen made this really brilliant choice not to make it too 'Masterpiece Theatre' – he really broke it apart by using the people he used. It made the movie really interesting and daring.

For example, both Stephen and Christopher Hampton were really interested in Michelle Pfeiffer. But they felt that she had never done anything to indicate that she could handle the language, so they wanted her to come in and read for the part. And she was a big star then, but she still came in and really went after it, and it was just great.

Will name actors often read for a role?
Sometimes. Actors are just terrifically smart to do that. If they really want something, they'll audition for it. That's happened to me many times. I also remember reading it about Dan Ackroyd in *Driving Miss Daisy*. He wanted to prove he could do something other than *Saturday Night Live*-ish stuff, and he did. He has a lot of credibility, I think; he'd be fun to use.

Can you talk about the audition process? Every actor I know dreads it.
That's one of the things that Marion was particularly good about. She made a big point of telling those of us who sat in the outer office how welcoming we had to be to actors; how it was up to us to make them feel comfortable. And to never, if you could possibly help it, have two actors in for the same role back to back. You know, don't book people too tight, don't get behind, don't keep people waiting. That's not always possible, but generally speaking. And if you give someone a scene to look at, tell them as much as you can to make it sensible to them. And at the same time, do the same thing with the director. Tell him or her as much as you can about the actor. Directors are often not from New York; they don't see the same stuff we do, and if they see somebody cold, with no context, it can be hard for them.

So I was sort of 'brought up' to be very sensitive to actors. And it's interesting, the youngest of the two assistants I have has been working for other casting directors this winter while I've been fooling around, and she told me she was stunned to see the difference in style. I thought that was so interesting, because I wouldn't know; I would assume everybody was polite. For me, as I said, it was a matter of upbringing. Marion said it was important, so everyone who ever worked for her, or worked for me, would have that same speech delivered to them when they arrived.

You know, most casting directors really love actors. But I can see how it could be a really power-trippy kind of job . . .

I was actually going to ask you about that. Most would say that you wield enormous power in the industry —
It's funny, because I don't see it that way, but I know actors see it that way.

Well, I think actors assume you can really make or break their careers. That doesn't cross your mind?
It doesn't really. I always think actors have an overinflated idea of what I can do for them. And yet, I know that the truth of it is that that's actually naïve of me, because if I really believe in someone, and continually keep having them back and back and back, it will make a difference to their lives. But they're still the ones who have to get the job.

When do you first see a script from Woody Allen? As soon as it's finished?
With Woody, before. It's great, because he really includes me in what he's thinking about. For instance, this time he asked me if I would come over to the cutting room sometime to talk about his next project, and he told me about three ideas that he was fooling around with, and what did I think. And it was great, it was such an honour – I mean, it's such an honour to work with him anyway – to be in on it at the beginning. Anyway, I think he needs to talk out loud about what would be the next good project for him to do, or whether the idea works at all, whatever.

So we talked about it, and I think he was glad to find that I agreed with what he was thinking. Then he tried to write it, but didn't feel it was going that well, so he switched over to the idea that was the second best of the three. I haven't read it yet – he's still working on it – but we've been talking about casting already. He's moving his schedule up, actually, because he wants to start shooting in the spring.

That kind of stuff makes it really fun. But obviously that's not entirely typical.

What about with Mike Nichols? Same thing?
I usually hear from Mike very early on, but he usually has something in hand. Right now I'm working on something he's doing, in its very early stages, and we're doing a reading. He'll do that kind of thing sometimes because he likes to hear it aloud.

Do you cast readings often?
I do.

I'm assuming your first priority in that situation is finding an actor who reads well, but perhaps may not necessarily end up in the finished film.
Well, it depends how far along a project is, and how far along the director is in his or her thinking. For Mike, usually, he doesn't set his reading until he has his stars. Like, for instance, on *Primary Colors*, we did our reading with Emma Thompson and John Travolta, and a couple of people who turned out to be supporting actors in the film. And a number of actors who Mike uses all the time, who did end up in small parts in the film, or came in just to help out, or have been in other films of his.

Would you say that part of your *modus operandi* is casting against type?
Most casting directors are invested in being creative and different and original in their thinking. I don't set out to cast against type. I'm more interested in casting very interesting, charismatic and sort of electric people, actors who will bring dimension to their roles. So if what's really kind of 'on the nose' doesn't exist in an exciting form, I would rather move a little to the right or a little to the left. Of course, then you run into the thing where someone will say, 'Well, that's not how it's written.' And I'll say, 'Well, that really doesn't matter, because there's nobody who can play it as it's written that will be exciting, so it's better to have this person who's going to alter it slightly but give it a little punch.' I think that's kind of how it happens.

What is that 'punch' you're talking about? Is it something you can intuit?
I think it is. It's true that when someone walks into your office and you first see them, if they're right you'll go, 'OK. *Wow.*' You know? And then you just hope – you just hold your breath – that they're as good as they appear. It's interesting how seldom that little sort of magic is there. Because it's more than just being a great-looking person. It's definitely a vibe; that person fills up the room.

I remember the first time Emily Watson came in. You know, walking down the street, you wouldn't necessarily look at her and say she was remarkable. But when she came in to read, I just couldn't believe it. I remember the first time I met Tom Cruise. Now of course he was divine-looking; he was nineteen at the time and he made me feel like Mrs Robinson or something. [*Laughs.*] You just could tell. Even with character actors. There's a kind of an energy, a kind of a presence.

I'm guessing that many of the character actors you cast are theatre-based; is there ever any situation where the kind of actor that might be able to command a theatre doesn't 'work' for film?
You know, that's a question people used to ask me all the time, but I haven't heard it in a while. I think that if you have magic on stage, you're going to have it onscreen. Usually, I think the problem is that many actors who are touted as great are really quite dull. This is something that Woody and I talk about a lot.

People overinflate how wonderful actors are – every generation, they'll say so-an-so is so wonderful and brilliant. And they're really only OK, you know? They're not that great. I look back at my lists of actors and actresses in their twenties from years ago, and I swear seventy-five per cent of them aren't even acting any more. Did you see the article about comic genius in the *New York Times*? They were talking about how rare it actually is. Most people concurred that 'genius' is an overused word. It just doesn't come along that often.

People always say how hard it is for actors to make it, to be known. But if somebody's really good, believe me, they're going to make it. People are dying for actors to be good. I remember when Meryl Streep first moved to New York. I mean, forget it. It was five minutes. She'd hardly put her toe on the sidewalk and people were talking about her.

You've been credited with 'discovering' her.
Which of course I didn't. When she was at Yale, people were already raving about her. And then as soon as she got here, she did a couple of plays and that was it. There was a production of *Trelawny of the Wells* that was done at the Vivian Beaumont – it was the year that Papp ran Lincoln Center. The production included Meryl Streep, Mandy Patinkin and Mary Beth Hurt, and they were all just out of school. It was really something.

You're also well known for casting recognizable non-actors in cameos, like Calvin Trillin in *Sleepless in Seattle*, or Benno Schmidt in *Husbands and Wives*. It adds a sort of inside-joke angle to the whole thing.
Well, they aren't usually to wink at the camera. I'll tell you what it really is: the hardest thing to cast is middle-aged men – men from thirty-five to seventy, really – for parts that aren't that big. Men who have authority and weight, and seem like real people. Because when you get to that age, most men are either stars of television shows and movies or they look like soap-opera actors. It's very hard to find substance. So for those little parts, you're often attracted to using people who seem very real. That's why I go outside the acting pool. If I could do it inside, I probably would. Calvin Trillin is just a funny character, so that was sort of a fun idea. With Benno, he'd just done the *Delicate Balance* series on PBS, and he was so good. And he was a friend, too, so that wasn't so hard.

Sometimes I think people do it just to show their wares. It's a temptation of casting directors – you want to do something different from everyone else. You want to be the first or whatever. I think there are a couple of movies recently where people have used real people in a way that really called attention to itself, which isn't the point.

How did you find Greg Mottola for the opening scene in *Celebrity*?
I have to say I can't take credit for that, because Laura, who worked with me on *Celebrity*, knew him.

I can't imagine your ever having any resistance from an actor who you've offered a part in a Woody Allen movie to. Has anyone ever said, 'No thanks'?
Yes, we've been turned down, but we have a really good success rate. We really do. Every time somebody gets a lot of attention for a turn in a Woody Allen movie, I breathe a sigh of relief. That means next time will probably be easy. Actors love to be in Woody's movies, because frankly there's not that much good stuff around, and of course he's one of the few really original great directors. But, also, they always look good in his movies. They always do, and somebody almost always gets nominated. Great statistics, and that helps a lot.

What we did in the very beginning, which was really smart, was to say that everybody works for scale and gets the same amount of money. So it's never debatable; you're either in or you're out. So the agents don't bother you; they just accept it.

How often are you involved with a project where you ask an actor to take a pay cut to play a particular role? First of all, is that part of your job?
It is. I negotiate all the contracts. But you know, it's sort of your job to cast within a budget, so you have to think realistically. You can always make a stab, particularly in this new world of independent films, because more and more mainstream actors want to do independents – they can make a good back end, and they think it will show them off well.

You learn who cares about money and who doesn't. I mean, Jack Nicholson doesn't care how good the art is. He wants his money. He doesn't care if it's Woody Allen or Joe Blow. He never gets snowed by 'Oh my god, I have to do this because it's so beautiful and meaningful.' But some people do; they want to do something better than they've done before. You learn to gauge the enthusiasm level of actors. But the money thing is a constant hassle. And if an actor thinks somebody else is getting more, it sinks the whole deal.

Marshall Brickman once said that you were great at 'characterizing actors in a word or two'.
Right, but he then he always finishes the joke by saying, 'And that word or two was always devastating.' [*Laughs.*] And I thought, 'Am I really that mean?'

Can I run a few names by you?
Well, I don't want to say anything negative . . .

OK, we'll try out a few. Liev Schreiber.
Really talented. And he never hits a false note. In *Hurricane*, for instance, which was a little melodramatic for my taste, he never lost his way. I've seen him on stage being extremely touching in what some would call anti-heroic parts; he can be very moving.

Samantha Morton.
Mesmerizing. So fun to look at, and I loved her humour and whimsy in *Sweet and Lowdown*. So far this is easy. [*Laughs.*]

Robert Carlyle.
Well, I think he's also really talented. Very real.

Ralph Fiennes.
A dreamboat. I think he's divine. He's so handsome that I can't stand it, but I also think he's very moving. Particularly in *Quiz Show*. I cast *Schindler's List* and he was terrific in that, but I thought he was amazing in *Quiz Show*. He tends to pick quiet pieces and I think some people tend to associate that with a certain dullness, which is unfair.

Billy Crudup.
Oh, this is good – you're picking very good people. He's terrific. And he's not just a cute guy. I've had him in to read for things before he was well known, and I thought, 'Whoa.' Original, and has a great take on things.

One more: Julia Roberts.
Well, you know, she's a real movie star. And I'll tell you, I met her when she first came to New York, before she'd done anything, because I knew her brother, and her brother's manager asked me if I would see her. She was someone who when you were in a room with her just melted you. Not only really pretty, but a doll – lovable.

For some time you were on the board of the Sundance Institute. My impression, though, is that you don't do many low-budget films —
I don't.

That's a conscious choice?
I think it's mostly circumstantial. I've worked less since they've become more popular. Laura, who I mentioned earlier, does a lot of work for indie films, and she's got about eighty-five folders on her desk of things that may go some day. There's a huge amount of spinning of wheels, and since I'm sort of only working sometimes, I'm not really in the mood. Although I'll do it for friends.

Do you ever feel like you take on the role of shrink in your relationships with actors?
Sometimes, but not usually. I don't socialize that much with actors. I suppose if you did, you would. Occasionally there will be someone who is quite vulnerable, or who is having a tough time, who will take you into their confidence that something is upsetting or worrying them at a particular time in their life. You know, once I used an actress in one of Woody's movies whose marriage was on the rocks, and she was having a tough time deciding on whether she was going to come here and do the movie or stay there. But that doesn't happen that often.

Do you think the professional distance you talk about is easier to maintain in New York than it would be in LA?
Mmm . . . I don't think so. I have certain colleagues here who really like to be in the thick of it. It's a personal style choice, I think.

You alluded to the fact that you haven't spent much time in Hollywood —
So little that it's hilarious. I'll tell you something: I had never been to Los Angeles until I went to meet Billy Friedkin on *The Exorcist*. And then, until my son was a senior in high school, I think that I went there maybe two or three times – other than the six months I lived there. [*Laughs.*] The year he graduated, I went out for two different full weeks. I just didn't want to leave home, so what I did for years was, any movie that required travel, or time in LA, I shared with people; I split it.

So your decision has less to do with not wanting to be in LA than with not wanting to leave New York.
Yes. Actually, the few times I've gone out I've had a lot of fun. But I just wanted to have a sort of normal family life. You know, though, what's so funny now is that even though our kids are grown, I still resist leaving. Although I was more than happy to go to Ireland to do *Angela's Ashes*. They could have said, 'You're going to have to be here for six months' and I would have said, 'Fine.'

How critical are you about certain choices a writer or director has made in a script that you find either unrealistic or objectionable? I'm thinking, for instance, of pairing up fifty-five-year-old leading men with twenty-something female love interests.
Hmm. You mean onscreen or in real life? [*Laughs.*] I don't know, do you see that a lot in movies?

Well, yeah. For instance, the Michael Douglas/Gwyneth Paltrow pairing in *A Perfect Murder* —
I knew you were going to say that. That was the most obvious one, and I remember everybody talking about it. And then I know people certainly criticize Woody for that.

Well, that's true. One could argue that generally in his films the male characters are self-conscious about the situation —
They comment on the age difference.

Right. Does your input extend into that area?
Oh yeah, it does. A big part of my job is to bring the reality check into it, bring some sense to it. Unless it's a part of the plot, you'd say, 'Well, gee, I think Winona Ryder is too young for Sean Connery.' Absolutely, that's definitely the kind of thing I'd say.

Is it heeded?
Well, it is in the sense that I think a 'no' is more powerful than a 'yes'. If I bring up something negative about someone, everybody's ready to listen. If I say, 'I really think this is who you should have', it's harder to convince them to like somebody they don't like.

You've said before that to be a casting director, 'It's great to be obsessive; it's great to be a worrier.'

I was debating that with a colleague of mine the other day, because I think that's sort of what burned me out. There are only so many years you wake up in the middle of the night with a pit in your stomach worrying about who's going to play the part before you start to go nuts. It's a very detailed job, and there's a lot to keep under control. Like this reading I'm setting up – we've changed the time, and you need to make sure every person knows when and where they need to be . . . .

And making deals is a very detailed thing. Things can fall apart so easily, and agents don't always tell you the truth. You need to constantly read between the lines. And everyone thinks they know how to cast actors. Everyone has an opinion. It's not like you're in this kind of mysterious profession that nobody quite understands and that everyone thinks what you do is sort of miraculous. I've had people come in to me and say, 'You know, my daughter doesn't really like Brad Pitt.' Every one has strong opinions about what you do, and you're always afraid that when you say, 'Well, I think Joe Blow would be great', everybody's going to look at you and say, 'Joe Blow?! That idea sucks.' There's never a movie that I start – with a new director in particular – where I don't get butterflies. 'Oh, gosh, am I going to come up with good ideas this time? Am I going to come up with something new?'

Do you have a favourite casting experience?

Well, one of the most fun things I ever did was *Broadway Danny Rose*. It was a lot of work, but it was so much fun. I was dipping into so many different worlds – lounge singers and novelty acts and comics.

I remember reading something about how you discovered Nick Apollo Forte – who played Tony Canova – on an album cover.

Well, actually, we were looking everywhere. We'd seen well-known people as well as unknowns, and I asked my assistant, who was new to me, to go over to the Colony Records store and look in the bins of vocalists. She came back with several albums, and Nick Apollo Forte was one of them. You really need to be in New York to cast that kind of movie.

You've said a while back that being a casting director is like 'being the hostess at a great party'. Is that still true?

Yes, but there's also the potentially embarrassing feature of it, which is having to introduce people to each other, making sure they're comfortable. Making sure the director is nice to them, gives them the time they want. Making sure they aren't embarrassed by running into another person, that kind of thing. You feel very responsible for everybody being happy.

Jim Jarmusch

Jim Jarmusch has written and directed *Permanent Vacation*, *Stranger Than Paradise* (winner of the Camera d'Or at the 1984 Cannes Film Festival), *Down By Law*, *Mystery Train*, *Night on Earth*, *Dead Man* and *Ghost Dog: The Way of the Samurai*. He has also shot a documentary about Neil Young and Crazy Horse, *The Year of the Horse*, and several short films, including the acclaimed *Coffee and Cigarettes* series.

Tod Lippy: When did you first move to New York?
Jim Jarmusch: I came to New York in 1974, I think, after spending a year at Northwestern University in the Medill School of Journalism. I was pretty much asked to leave the school because I wasn't completing my requirements in journalism – I was taking classes in Literature and Art History and History and Philosophy. I transferred to Columbia, where I studied English and Comparative Literature, so that's how I got here.

Was the city everything you expected?
It was pretty intense, because I arrived here in late August to start classes in early September, and I had a dorm room right on whatever avenue is on the eastern border of Columbia – Columbus Avenue. It was really, really hot, and really, really loud, and I'd hear salsa music all night. It took me a little while to adjust, but I was amazed by the incredible energy of New York. And it was great to find a place that, no matter how strange you might be, you couldn't go a block without seeing someone much stranger. It was a great feeling to be here – it felt like anything was possible in a way.

What happened when you finished up at Columbia?
Well, they had a programme in Paris my last year, so I said, 'Where do you sign up?' And I went there and ended up coming back with a lot of incompletes because instead of studying much, I discovered the Cinématheque. Back then it was still run by Henri Langlois. And that was an amazing birth of something in me – a realization of how wide the diversity of films could be and what a beautiful form it was. I saw films from India by Sen and Ray, and films from Africa, and classic films from France and Japan and China and everywhere. Also, I learned a lot about Hollywood films from seeing them in that context. Nothing was presented in a hierarchical way; you just realized that the world of cinema was so huge.

When I came back here, I was still writing prose and poetry, but I started imitating film scripts in a way – not in a literal way, but making allusions to the form in my writing. And they became a little more visual. I realized from that that I was really thinking of movies all the time. So I applied to NYU Graduate Film School really on a whim, because I'd never made a film. But I submitted some writing and some photographs and I was accepted with financial aid really unexpectedly, so I decided to try that.

Weren't you also playing in a band around the same time, and a part of the whole Lower East Side music scene?

Yeah. We played the Mudd Club, CBGB's, Hurrah's, Tier 3, Irving Plaza, Danceteria – pretty much everywhere in New York. Actually, the aesthetics of that scene really gave me the courage to make films; it was not about virtuosity, it was about expression. It was that way with all those bands at the time – The Ramones and Talking Heads, Television, Blondie and Patti Smith, Mink DeVille, The Heartbreakers, The Voidoids, Suicide . . .

Anyway, in my third year of graduate school I went to tell László Benedek, who was the head of the school, that I wasn't coming back because I didn't have any money – I had a lot of student loans and I just really didn't see the point of returning to school for a third year. He said to me, 'That's really too bad, because I hired Nick Ray to teach here this year. He needs a teaching assistant and I thought you would be the perfect guy. He's in the next room, and he'd like to meet you.' And I was like, 'Oh, man . . .' So I went in there, and the first thing Nick asked me was to define the word 'dialectic' – which I did – and then we started talking. And he said, 'You're my assistant – I need your help, and I'm going to teach you.' In the end, László helped me get a fellowship – ironically, it was called the Louis B. Mayer Fellowship, after the guy who destroyed von Stroheim's *Greed*. So I went back for a third year.

Is that when you made *Permanent Vacation*?

Yeah, which the school hated. I didn't get a degree because I didn't fulfil the requirements at the time for a thesis film – you weren't allowed to make a film that long. But they didn't like the film anyway – not László, particularly, but the school. They also made a mistake, because I think the fellowship money was sent to me directly rather than for tuition at the school, and of course I spent it on the film. We shot it in ten days on the street in New York for twelve thousand dollars total – the whole budget, including post. Then, somehow, someone submitted *Permanent Vacation* to a festival in Germany, in Mannheim. They sent me a letter saying they wanted to screen the film there, that they were inviting me and would fly me there. I was surprised and really happy. So I went, and then the film was given a prize, which included two thousand dollars! I had no money – I owed, like, six months rent – and I was ecstatic. And then a guy came up to me from German TV, saying, 'We'd like to buy your film. We don't pay a lot, but we can give you twelve thousand dollars for five years.' And I was, like, 'Whoa!'

I'd left home assuming I'd never make another film again – 'So the school hates it; I'll be a writer, or a musician or something' – and I came back thinking, 'I've got to make another film!' Not only that, they invited the film to the Berlin Festival, and at the time it was very rare to have a film in two German festivals, but they made an exception. And I was so moved that they would respond at all to this odd, handmade, first-time film, which is not very good – I mean, it's a first film, and I haven't looked at it in a long time, but it's probably not a good film.

So I came home and wrote *Stranger Than Paradise*. Wim Wenders had seen my first film and he liked it, and I was Nick Ray's gofer when Wim worked with him on *Lightning Over Water*. So he offered me this black-and-white 35mm film stock that he had left over from *The State of Things*, just raw stock. It was this odd film material, like 4X – high speed, very grainy. But he had about 50 minutes of it that he gave to me, and I thought, 'If I'm very careful, I can make a half-hour film.' So John Lurie and I had this vague idea for a story and I wrote a half-hour script and we filmed it. That was the first third of *Stranger Than Paradise*.

You actually filmed the whole thing with that fifty minutes' worth of stock?
Yeah. Most scenes were shot in one, maybe two takes.

When you shot the rest of the film, did you use the extant footage for the first third?
Yeah, it was changed only slightly. I removed one little thing, maybe.

John Lurie and Richard Edson and Eszter Balint were all people you knew from this downtown scene?
Yeah, I hung out a lot – as everybody did – at the Squat Theater on 23rd Street, because it was a bunch of Hungarian weirdoes who were really amazing, inventive, creative people with no particular interest in traditional theatre. They weren't interested in anything commercial, anything like that. They lived communally. It was an incredible group of people. I still try to keep in touch with them although they've dispersed – some are back in Budapest. And they had a lot of music – Sun Ra played there, for instance – and a lot of people hung out there, like James Chance and Arto Lindsay and me and John and lots of different people. It was a really great atmosphere of ideas being exchanged. So I knew Eszter through that. I think she was fourteen when I first met her and she was seventeen or so when we were filming.

   Stranger Than Paradise was a very good lesson because I wrote it knowing the amount of material I had, so the style of the film reflected that – every scene being a single setup was by necessity. Learning to do that was something I have continued to benefit from. And then, when I was cutting the short in my Lower East Side walk-up apartment on an upright Moviola, I was also writing the rest of the script, because I got ideas for making it longer. So when I had the short film finished I also had a script to show. Then there's a whole thing I really don't want to go into – it was very hard for me to get the rights to the short film back from Wim's partner at that time. It was a big mess.

And that led to you insisting on the ownership of your negatives ever since?
Yeah. It was a lesson that almost entirely formed my way of working. So it was very valuable, but at the time it was heartbreaking having to try to steal your camera negative back out of DuArt and stuff like that.

Do you know of any other film-makers who own all their negatives?

I don't. I think John Sayles maybe owns some of his films. Cassavetes owned some of his films, some he didn't. I don't know of anyone else, other than, you know, film-makers like Michael Snow or Robert Frank. I own my own negatives and still produce all the films through my own company and am very, very attentive to all the details. Maybe obsessively so, but I learned from that first incident that people's intentions – or what they represent their intentions to be – are not always backed up by their actions. And keeping your word doesn't necessarily mean much in America.

Right after _Stranger Than Paradise_'s success, you were quoted as saying, 'Right now I could go out to LA and set up enough deals to buy a house and a swimming pool.' What held you back from doing something like that?
It's pretty much a personal reaction. I did get offers, but they were offers that I think were made by people who add up how many times your name or the name of your film appears in _Variety_. It really has nothing to do with your work or what it means, or what its content is. Also, I have always been drawn to things that were in the margins and not in the mainstream – this was true of me even as a teenager in Akron. I remember when I was fourteen or so, this friend of mine had an older brother who used to hitchhike to New York and other places, and while he was gone, we'd go into his room and find records by Ornette Coleman or The Mothers of Invention, and books by William Burroughs and Terry Southern. It was a revelation that there was more to the world than Akron, and that there were a lot of really interesting ideas that you could pursue and investigate that were very obviously not in the mainstream.

And also, let's face it: Hollywood, for the most part, is about status and money and power – that's like the Holy Trinity. And that is not and never will be my religion. At the time, I was living in New York very happily, finding a sort of 'bohemian' subculture here that was really invigorating and pretty adventurous. I met a lot of interesting artists, painters, writers, and musicians as well as plumbers and garbagemen and all kinds of people. So I don't know, to just transplant myself and go to LA and be a hack director of coming-of-age teen comedies or whatever was not my thing.

Could you define the niche that your films tend to fit into? Would you consider them to be 'arthouse' fare, for example?
I hope that they are really difficult to categorize. I'm very intuitive and I never calculated or made a path to be 'marginal'. I just do what I do and where it is is where it is; it's not something I have any desire to control. Those categories are somewhat annoying to me. Trying to categorize artistic movements or whatever is ridiculous – it's like looking at the ocean from a helicopter and trying to number all the waves to see where they align themselves. It's impossible. Those categories are mostly used for marketing or defining something, for reducing things.

So I don't know where I fit. I don't feel tied to my time period. I'm an American by circumstance. I'm not really interested in nationalities or borders, though I am very interested in cultures and what makes them different from other cultures. And I'm also very fascinated by those areas where the lines of cultures blur, because in those blurred edges is where synthesis occurs, and gardens grow. There are so many beautiful things that come from that blurring together of seemingly disparate elements.

Pardon my being literal, but your use of the word 'blurring' reminds me of those languorous tracking shots – usually from either a car or train window – that one can find in all of your films. Why are you drawn to them?
Well, I love moving and being in motion, and I love being off-balance by not knowing everything about the place you're in; it opens your imagination up. You have to fill in the blanks, and you fill them in with your imagination, not with facts. I like the simple landscape travelling shot because it's the most pure visual reduction of moving and things changing around you.

My sense is that your first four films – well, the four after *Permanent Vacation*, which I've never seen —
That's good. [*Laughs.*]

Those four films are really informed by the notion of travel – for instance, you picked a different location for each one, whether it was Louisiana for *Down By Law*, or Memphis for *Mystery Train*, or the several different cities visited in *Night on Earth*. And within those films, the characters themselves are all on their own various journeys through these places, which is, again, taken to a pretty literal extreme with *Night on Earth*. But your last two movies really have become more about interior – even metaphorical – journeys. Does that reflect a conscious decision on your part? You could almost call it a paradigm shift ...
You know, I prefer not to analyze it, because I'm not very analytical. I can see what you mean by that shift and I don't know how to respond to it that well. The only thing I can say – which is not a direct answer to the question – is that when I was twenty years old, I suspected everything; everything was a lie. I was inspired by the work of people like William Burroughs, or Sam Fuller (whose films really deal with the idea that the whole American Dream is a big lie, a deception). I suspected everything and always looked around to see who was controlling this and that, and what was being manipulated.

Now I'm in my forties, and I have seen so many weird things in my life that I'm willing to believe just about anything. So it's almost like being in the same place, but with a different consciousness. I still very strongly believe that nothing is what it seems, but I'm much more willing to believe the possibilities of almost anything. So that's kind of a big shift in perspective, and that may be why my films have shifted to being a little more interior in their themes. But I don't really know.

Greil Marcus wrote about *Dead Man*: 'There's no hint in Jarmusch's previous

work that he was into anything but irony. This movie has no irony.' Do you agree with that?

First of all, there are different forms of irony: there's an ironic attitude towards the world, which I don't think the films have, and then there's irony by situation. I don't think my characters are flippantly ironic in their attitudes, but their stories – their circumstances – are very ironic. At the end of *Stranger Than Paradise*, Willie is on the plane going to Hungary, the girl, Eva, is back in the hotel, and Eddie is at the airport, about to drive back to New York. That's ironic by situation. But I don't find them ironic in tone, or in attitude. So I don't know how I feel about that. One thing I've learned is that with anything that you create, your interpretation of it is no more valid than the person who sees it. In a way, your interpretation is less valid because you can't see it clearly. The beauty of cinema is that you can walk into a film, whatever it is, and if you've never seen it before, you are entering a new world, and you go with that world. Same with a new piece of music – it really takes you somewhere and you give yourself to it. I've seen each of my films a thousand times before it's finished – I wrote it, I directed it, I was there for the editing – so it can never be fresh; I can never not know where it's going to take me. Often other people explain things to me about my films that I wasn't conscious of or that aware of, which is very interesting and valuable.

That's also taught me to not be offended by any kind of criticism of my work. I'm not a person that has trouble with negative criticism at all – in fact, I generally prefer to read the negative criticism because maybe it'll be an angle or perspective that's different enough from my own and I might learn something from it. Greil Marcus, as a case in point, has explained a few things to me in his writing about *Dead Man* that I'm not sure I saw. To have someone with a mind like that looking at what I did and expressing his feelings or perception about it is really interesting.

In *Year of the Horse*, I was struck by how seldom during the concert footage we actually see shots of the audience and Crazy Horse in the same frame. You show lines of fans waiting to get into the concert in London, and you cut a few times between audience and performer during that same concert, but even then, the audience is shot in black-and-white and the band is in colour. I really felt a formal divide between artist and audience, and it called to mind that 'Warholian' distance a lot of critics have characterized your films as having. Would you say that's something you're aware of when you're working?

My job is definitely not to presuppose what the audience wants or expects. I'll leave that to a lot of other people. Commercial cinema is based on marketing analysis – you know, they show your film to a bunch of high-school girls in a shopping mall and then tell you to recut it because it was too slow. There are enough people who do that – that's not my job. My job is to make films that those people with whom I chose to collaborate would like to see. We're making a film for us. The rest of the world has to be ignored completely.

But I have to temper that by saying very sincerely that the film doesn't exist until somebody sees it and brings their energy, their life experience, to that moment. Even if it's purely for entertainment on a Friday night, they came to see this film and reacted to it, and they've completed an electric circuit. Without them there, it's like the light's not plugged in – the lamp is standing there but it's not going to light up. So it's sort of a yin-yang thing. With *Stranger Than Paradise*, we didn't think anyone would ever see it, so why should we try to gear it toward a certain prescribed audience reaction? Let's make what we want to make. I still do that, but I've learned that the film is really born when it gets disseminated and people see it, when it completes that full circuit.

I was wondering if you would talk a little about *Dead Man*'s relationship to the Western genre.
The Western is such an important genre in America, because it's like a fantasy world that people have used to stamp all kinds of ideology on. And it was really interesting to me to work with that, because I tried for the first time with *Dead Man* to make a film that had a lot of layers to it, if you wanted to think about them. And if you didn't, it was hopefully an alluring surface that you could follow as a story. But the themes in *Dead Man* include aboriginal cultures, William Blake, violence, the history of America, white European responses to nature versus aboriginal responses. Death, religion, philosophy. It's about language. It's about guns, it's about law, it's about the status of an outlaw – there are all these levels to *Dead Man*, and maybe that was the first time I was conscious of working in that way while writing. Something opened up for me, and I think the Western led me to that, because the Western is such an open form; it's such a strange frame, within which you can have things as diverse as *The Searchers* or a film by Monte Hellman. After I made *Night on Earth* or *Mystery Train*, if someone had said to me, 'You know, in a few years you'll make a Western', I wouldn't have believed it. But I don't know, I got drawn to it.

When did you decide to bring in the whole William Blake angle?
Blake walked right in at a certain point while I was writing. I was reading a lot of stuff written by Native Americans, about their language and their philosophy, and I was sort of getting overwhelmed by it. So I picked up a book of Blake just to clear my head. I was reading *Proverbs from Hell*, and parts of it sounded so much like Native thought – like 'The eagle never lost so much time as when he submitted to learn from the crow', or 'Expect poison from standing water'. This was William Blake! At that point he walked right into the story. And I always loved Blake for so many reasons – I mean, he's a really fascinating, amazing character.

A true 'visionary', in every sense of the word.
Exactly. And a guy who was able to publish only his first book legitimately – for the rest of his life he was considered to be an eccentric nutcase and had to publish everything himself. He really wasn't respected in his time. But he lived at a very odd time – he's the last great Christian religious poet, yet he's right on the cusp of

industrialization, and somehow he transcends both religion and science in his ability to be a visionary. He's also very contradictory, which I like a lot. A Christian who hates the church. It's like Pasolini – a Marxist homosexual Catholic. I love those kinds of contradictions.

Did the *Hagakure* serve as a similar kind of catalyst for *Ghost Dog*?
Very similar, because I was already in the process of writing the script when I discovered it. I had already read a lot about *bushido* and Samurai culture – not in preparation for the film, but in the past, out of a sort of dilettantish interest. And the *Hagakure* was the perfect thing to read – it gave me a map for the character and also a structural map for the film, in a way. The book is composed of little aphorisms, each separated by a *monsho*, a little round symbol, which is like a breathing space, and then it moves on to another text. I ended up using the reverse – a section of film, of story, and then a text, like the *monsho*, as a breathing space. And somehow it formally opened things up.

Would you consider either film to be an 'adaptation' of sorts, since both relate back to specific texts?
It was more that I was open to their influence – they both walked into the writing and affected me deeply, but without me having calculated or even expected that. So the texts got woven into the fabric of the film, rather than the stories of the film being adapted from them.

Ghost Dog was a big breakthrough for me. Though I refer to Chaucer or to Walt Whitman or things in passing in the earlier films, in this case I opened myself up to actually quoting other things, and that came, I really think, from my love of music. I love all kinds of music, but hard bebop, dub, and hip-hop, in particular, are forms that are very open about taking things from other places, and I think they gave me – well, 'courage' isn't the right word, but my love of those forms of music somehow spoke to me internally and said, 'Don't push things away just because they come from other sources', which is what I often used to do. 'Go ahead and open the windows and let them in, and don't hide that you let them in.' I'm not going to play a game like all these ideas are original and they're mine; I want to talk about where they came from, because if someone sees *Ghost Dog* and it leads them to see films by Melville or *Point Blank* by John Boorman or the films of Seijun Suzuki or to read *Don Quixote* or something that I mention in the credits, then that's a good thing. I didn't hide that in any way in *Ghost Dog*. Maybe *Dead Man* was a precedent, because that wacky poet William Blake walked right into my damn script.

You mentioned Melville – there are some very conscious nods to *Le Samouraï* in *Ghost Dog*, starting with their similar hit-men protagonists . . .
With their own moral code that the world doesn't really respect or respond to.

Can you talk more specifically about how you were influenced by Melville, and that film in particular?

I was interested in taking things from Melville that I found really moving. And some of them are minor things, like the fact that in various Melville films, before his killers kill someone, they put on white-cloth editor's gloves – I don't know if that was an inside joke with Melville and his editor – that he was saying his editor was a butcher or whatever, but I used that, too.

Also, Melville has been a teacher for me in something I love, which is cross-referencing cultures. His films are very, very French in their rhythm and certainly in the street language of Paris, yet the gangsters drive big American cars, and wear American-style sharkskin suits. And of course, Melville took his name from Herman Melville. Really, how more blatant can you be? So he was very interested in finding those things that he loved and mixing them up together and making something new out of it. So it's more of that kind of inspiration. There are specific details I took from *Le Samouraï*, but I wasn't conscious of where should I distance myself from Melville at all, or how should I make it different. It was just, 'These are things I love and they seem to intersect here, so I'm going to put them in.' They're like 'Variations on a Theme' in musical composition.

In the night scenes, in particular, there are all of these gleaming reflective surfaces – the cars Ghost Dog steals, the CDs he gracefully manoeuvres, even the guns he uses . . .
Locations have quite a different effect than in the previous film. In *Dead Man*, the landscapes were almost characters in the film. Since there were themes concerning America as a place, and nature and how different cultures relate to it, the landscapes became incredibly important – they're a really essential part of the fabric of the film. They are living things that people move through and they envelope the characters, like when they ride through the redwood forest – it's like a cathedral, or some gigantic thing that dwarfs them. In *Ghost Dog*, the locations are more background, in a way – it's almost the opposite way of using locations. The characters are always in the foreground and the backgrounds are all atmospheric surfaces, which surround them somehow. That's not really answering your question, but that's the extent of my consciousness of the locations in *Ghost Dog*.

Where was the film shot, by the way?
It was intended to be set in an undefined urban location, so we shot mostly in Jersey City because it's incredibly difficult to identify. The only thing we had to avoid was the Manhattan skyline, which isn't easy because there are views of Manhattan everywhere there. There was one scene where two of the Mob guys go up on a roof and they kill a guy who's keeping pigeons, but he's the wrong guy. In the wide shot facing them, you could see the World Trade towers, but I really needed that shot, so we put a clothesline up and carefully placed the material on it to block them out so we could use that angle. I really didn't want it to be a specific place. Even now, people ask me where we shot it – 'Is that Red Hook?' 'That

doesn't look like Brooklyn; is it the Bronx?' I really wanted to take a signature off the landscape, not let it identify itself.

In a way, the physical solitude of the 'samurai' in *Ghost Dog* is much more pronounced than in *Le Samouraï*, where we see scenes of Alain Delon with his girlfriend, or him showing up at clubs. In your film, Ghost Dog's connections to other people are minimal, to say the least – there's very little 'noise' in the background. Was that something that you thought about a lot?
Yeah, I always consider that. Some people say my films have always been abstractly depopulated, which may be true, but less is more for me. It reminds me of a beautiful essay by Carl Dreyer, where he talks about how the less you use in the location, the more identification with the character those objects you leave will have. Like if you have a roomful of furniture, your eye doesn't associate any of it with the character because there is too much information. Whereas if you strip it down and there's one chair and one table and one lamp, the very form of those objects has some effect on the viewer, because that is the atmosphere within which the character exists. I'm very conscious of those things. I don't want to have too much activity buzzing around. It's like using black-and-white for certain stories rather than colour – black-and-white gives you less information. That's the only real difference, psychologically speaking – you're not giving the audience the information about what colour a shirt is, so it has a very strong effect. Those little things become big.

There's a whole *Rashomon* subtext going on in the film, not only in the passing around of the paperback book, but also in the fact that you show two different versions of the scene where Louie saves Ghost Dog. The former remembers the assailant's gun pointing at him; Ghost Dog's version has it pointing directly at him.
Which is pretty subtle. Some people don't even get that.

It reverberates in so many interesting ways, because both men have built their relationship on the particulars of that remembered event.
Their whole lives are changed by that moment, and they remember it in a different way, a way that suits how each one's life has changed because of that moment. So your memory is not really to be trusted, because as your life goes on, you fashion your memories to fit the consequent results. You know, people always say, 'There are only twelve possible plots', or 'Only this many stories can exist', and that's true to a large degree. But what they seem to ignore is that even if there were only, you know, *three* plots possible, there are as many different perspectives on those plots as there are humans who have ever lived – and that's why *Rashomon* is such a resonant story.

Why did you decide to give Ghost Dog the carrier pigeons?
Because there was an old Italian guy who had pigeons on his rooftop right behind

my house. I used to watch him flying them. I loved the way the light would hit the birds – if they were backlit, they would look black and then they would flip and look white, and there was something magical about it. The guy would stand out there, smoking a cigar, and he'd have his flag to bring them back. That's the visual reason, but I also had them because I wanted Ghost Dog to be someone who uses ancient things and modern things at the same time – he doesn't differentiate between their value. (Oh, and it's a reference, of course, to *On the Waterfront*, but that was not primary, that was very secondary.)

It also showed Ghost Dog's respect for animals and other life forms, the absence of which I think is maybe at the heart of a lot of stupidity on the part of humans. This will get way off on to a long subject which my friends are, like, 'Oh, no, he's going to start talking about the food chain again . . .', but I really believe that once humans took themselves off the food chain they lost the understanding of the interconnectedness of all things. You know, the law of nature is Eat and Be Eaten, and life and death are part of the same thing, and animals that are predators are not more powerful than animals that are prey, because without prey there can be no predators. You can't evaluate things in a human-centric way when you think about nature and animals and plants – all things are part of one thing. And that's a part of *Ghost Dog* that certainly relates to Zen philosophy and to aboriginal philosophies, too. I've been interested in all of that since I was a child, but I really started to understand it more deeply while preparing and making *Dead Man*.

I love Ghost Dog's motion of deference paid to the dead in the graveyard every time he passes it.
Respect to the spirits. That's something Forest brought to the film, all those wonderful little moments. The first time we did just a run-through of that shot tracking alongside him, he gave that motion to the spirits. And we were like, 'Yeah, yeah, that's part of Ghost Dog.'

You generally write scripts with your actors already in place, don't you?
Yeah. The central actors. I do it backwards. [*Laughs.*] I cast before I start writing the main characters, because I have to visualize them. I can't write a vague character and then go out and see who fits it. I have to have them playing around in my imagination so I can visualize them moving down the street or whatever they're doing.

I loved the way the cartoons you selected for *Ghost Dog* played against – or even prefigured – certain scenes in the film. And their illogic – like the one with the bullets being shot up the drain and coming out of the showerhead – really deepened the poetry of the film when it referenced them. How did you choose which ones to use?
It was an odd thing, because first of all, the cartoons I originally wanted – like the Tex Avery stuff, Warner Brothers, Hanna–Barbera – I couldn't use, because they

refused to license any clip to a film that had any violence in it. The irony of that was kind of surprising, but predictable. Stacey Smith did a lot of research on who would license clips, and collected hours of odd cartoons. So then we just sort of amused ourselves hunting for things that I could license that did play off of stuff that was happening in the film. A more Hollywood, or commercial, way to do it would have been to have the cartoons always come right after the action, so you would see them echoing it. But instead, they usually come before, and you don't immediately get the connection. I just love animation, and I thought it was an interesting way to have another layer in the film that came from popular culture, and one more element in there that could make things that were happening in the story resonate even more. In the way that the *Hagakure* echoes things that are happening, the cartoons echo them from a totally different place. Cartoons are incredible because your imagination as an animator is not restrained by anything in the physical world at all. I love it when Heckle & Jeckle, for instance, always say in those cartoons, 'How did that happen? Because this is a cartoon, we can do anything!' [*Laughs.*] I love that freedom of imagination.

I love popular culture, and I hope all my work indicates that. When I was in college at Columbia, my friend Luc Sante and I used to argue with academics about the hierarchy of culture. We'd say, 'Okay, we love to listen to listen to Bach, but we love the Ramones just as much. We love Dante, but we love Charles Willeford, too.' And how can you say that Charles Willeford is just pulp crap, but Dante is classic stuff? Dante wrote in the vernacular of his time, which was unheard of. He was the first person to use spoken Italian – that's like hip-hop today! So how can that be different from listening to the Wu-Tang? I don't see the difference. Of course, now that I'm older, I find myself arguing the reverse side of the same thing, saying, 'You know, I love popular culture, but are you guys familiar with Dante?'

Speaking of the Wu-Tang Clan, I wanted to talk about RZA's score for *Ghost Dog*. In a piece in the *New York Times*, it was reported that you had a sort of clandestine meeting with him in a blacked-out van in the middle of the night, where he handed you a tape —

That was an abbreviation – it reduced the whole story of our collaboration to one little anecdote taken out of context. What happened was, I always listen to music before I write a script – I sort of hone in on things that are firing my imagination for the film's atmosphere. In this case, I was listening to a lot of dub stuff, outside jazz, and hip-hop – particularly instrumental mixes of different DJs, like DJ Premier and 4th Disciple. But RZA is my favourite, and I was madly taping off any instrumental mix by RZA I could find, because my dream was for him to do all the music for the film. I hadn't even started writing at this point. And then, after I finished the script, I tried to find RZA through his manager, his lawyer, his agent – and it was, like, forget it. As I said to RZA, it was like trying to find a criminal by going to the cops. That's not the way it works.

So I talked to my friend Nemo Labrizzi, who is so much like family I call him my 'nephew'. He's very street-connected, so he put me in touch with a friend of his, Dreddy Kruger, who's an associate of the Wu-Tang thing, and Dreddy hooked me up with RZA. I met with him a few times and I told him a little bit about the project. We come from different places, but it was very easy for us to talk with each other about a lot of different things, so after our second meeting, RZA said, 'Yeah, I'm down, I want to do this.' The film hadn't even been shot yet. When I had a rough cut – he has a brief cameo in the film – I showed it to him, and then he called me a few weeks later and told me to meet him in a blacked-out van on 50th and Broadway at two in the morning, which I did, and he handed me a little DAT tape with nothing written on it. A lot of the music on it was not exactly what I had thought it would be – I wanted that spooky, minimal, beautiful, slightly damaged, awkward sound of RZA's Wu-Tang stuff. Some of it was like that, but most of it was more like a traditional score – well, not necessarily 'traditional', but a score that would be perfect in, like, a John Woo film from Hong Kong. And it was great music – he should use it for another film – but I told him that those pieces were not what I was really looking for. And he said, 'Okay, I know what you want.' Three weeks passed, and he calls me and I get another tape from him, and this time the music is incredible, it's exactly what I want, all kinds of stuff. Then he came back a few weeks later with even more. By the end we had more music than we could use in the film, but it was incredible stuff.

The score is such a perfect marriage of music and image. That 'awkwardness' you talked about, for instance, plays so beautifully against the repeated images of the pigeons flapping their wings . . .
The weird thing is, RZA did it all by memory. He did it all via his feeling for the film. When he gave us music, rarely did he say anything about where it should go. He had a few ideas for the opening sequence, but otherwise, nothing was written for a particular place. So Jay Rabinowitz, the amazing 'samurai editor', and I played with the music and placed it. RZA said, 'Cut it up, edit it, mix it together – I don't care.' It was just incredible to me that his sensitivity to the soul of the film was so strong that he would create very different pieces of music that were all perfect for it, but it was up to us to choose how we used them.

There's a wonderful poignancy – not to mention hilarity – to the exchanges in the movie between Isaach De Bankolé and Forest Whitaker, where, even though they don't speak each other's language, it's clear that they've formed a deep bond. When the film came out in New York, weren't the subtitles for De Bankolé's French dialogue left out?
Yeah, that was a big mistake. It was only in New York, where Artisan released the film first. Fifteen screens with no subtitles. It was particularly painful because they had put the film in several 'urban' theatres – in other words, in predomi-

nantly Black neighbourhoods. Whatever – these kinds of categories are so foreign to me. But if you show the film in Newark to that particular audience and one-third of the humour and part of the plot is missing, then the guy with a similar theatre in Oakland is going to look at how it did in Newark and probably not book the film. So it was fucked up.

But Artisan came through, admitted the problem, and did free screenings, which is pretty much unheard of. I told them I wanted them to do that, and I think most film distributors would have said, 'Fuck you, you're crazy! We can't say that there was a fuck-up – are you nuts?' But they stepped up, and I respect that about them.

How involved are you in the marketing of your films?
I have some input and I make comments on details, but I don't evaluate the over-all thing – it's another world to me. As soon as the *Ghost Dog* marketing strategy started referring to separating 'arthouse' audiences from 'urban' audiences, you've lost me already, because that's against everything I stand for. But that's the way their thinking and their operations are, and I can't change that. So I look at it, I make comments; sometimes I change things in the trailers or TV ads. But I've begun to sort of step back more and more – I'm more open to them doing what they want, as long as I feel they're not really misleading the audience.

You know, when you think about it, getting people in to see a film is the old-est con in the world, because you are hooking them into paying for a product before they see it, and if they don't like it, tough shit, you've already got them in there. It's pure carnival hustle, with the poster, the trailer, all that stuff. I just don't want them to misrepresent the film and put some chick with no shirt on the poster if that has nothing to do with it – which they do all the time. A case in point was *Eyes Wide Shut*. They marketed it as a 'sexy' film, and yet the people who did that are the same fucking morons who blocked out the sex scenes in the actual movie! You can't get more transparent than that. That sums it right up: We'll use the sex to sell it, but we'll take the sex out.

Obviously the New York indie scene has changed enormously in the past fifteen years, particularly with the rise of Miramax, and, more recently, companies like Artisan, and with them the notion of the 'indie blockbuster'. Do you have a sense of where things are heading, or whether these developments are good or bad?
Well, I don't know how to predict anything any more. Everything is controlled by corporations now, and that's depressing. One thing you have to remember about New York is that there are no natural resources here. The city has always been based on trade, and that means con men, and money changing hands, and who can cheat who out of what. That's why we have Wall Street. You know, the tip of Manhattan was originally a trading post for Native people. So that means that things are always in flux here – if you don't like change, it's not a good place to

be. Many of those changes are really heartbreaking, like when they tore down Penn Station, or the way Times Square is now Disney World. But it's inevitable. Now we're at a particularly bad time because we live in Giulianiville, and it's all about selling out to the highest bidder and corporate greed. As far as independent film goes, that, too, is just a label they slap on to sell things, and now Hollywood imitates independent films. Todd Solondz made *Happiness*, which allowed Hollywood to make *American Beauty* – basically a watered-down version with no teeth to it. And it cleaned up at the Oscars.

But this is a culture that always usurps and repackages its own waste products and sells you the shit. They always do that. It's like what happened with the counter-culture in the sixties – *Time* magazine called them hippies, the government made them seem like whacked-out drug freaks and then a couple of years later they start selling tie-dyed shirts at the mall.

And suburban housewives are wearing peace symbols around their necks.
Exactly. That's just the way it works. So I don't know how to even assess or predict what will happen. New technology is always interesting as a tool, but it does always get usurped very quickly. My favourite example is television. What a beautiful, incredible idea. But it's become like a big river that everybody throws their garbage into. And people say, 'Oh, TV sucks, the river is ugly.' But the river isn't ugly, it's all the garbage that's in it. Similarly, it's not the concept of the Internet that makes it into a shopping mall, it's the way people use it.

Digital video is very liberating for a lot of people because they can avoid the middleman – now they don't have to get on their hands and knees and genuflect to the studios to get money out of them. But you know, it all gets turned around. Like with Sundance. I read some account a few years ago of someone who showed his first film there, and it was a nice film, and he was a promising director, but there was a feeding frenzy, and a distributor bought it for, like, eight million dollars. And of course on that level the film was a failure, and then the director's career was 'over'.

Do you feel that there's still a viable creative scene here in the city?
Less and less. It was much more evident back in the late seventies and early eighties, when there was a creative burst here, particularly in music. As people slowly got signed to major labels and pulled away, the scene was dismantled. Now I really feel like there's no scene in New York, which is partly an economic thing because so many young people – the new blood – can't afford an apartment in the city. It's no longer, well, you walk out at night and go to CBGB's and you're going to find something happening there. It seems like there is no centred new wave of energy coming from anywhere, because corporations decide what we're going to hear – what music they're going to push down our throats.

I'm sure there are little enclaves here and there where you'll find exciting things happening – probably in the places you'd least expect. Iran is a good example – their films are so good; there's a garden of beautiful things growing there in a place you'd least expect to find them. So I don't know. Also, I don't like getting too nostalgic, because things always change – it's like the ocean: they keep rolling and a lot of interesting things have happened during this change. But they're harder and harder to find. As RZA said, 'Wu-Tang shit is underground. And if a large audience reaches out for it, we want it to be there for them, but we aren't going to change what we do in order to facilitate them finding it. Our shit is still underground.'

That sounds pretty close to what you might say about your own work.
Yeah, it's very close. Same with someone like Neil Young. I love Neil because he doesn't give a fuck about what's fashionable. He's also completely contrary. If I was his advisor, I would have told him not to go back out on the road with Crosby, Stills and Nash, but that would just make him more inclined to do it. He'd say, 'Oh, you think that's a bad move, do you? Then I'll definitely do it.' Or Tom Waits. He lives in his own world. His last record was probably his best-selling one. It's a great record, but it doesn't really make sense that *Mule Variations* sold more than *Swordfish Trombones* – and it was certainly nothing he planned.

He doesn't give a shit. And we need people that don't give a shit, because there are already more than enough people who do – there's enough prefabricated garbage out there. I am very, very critical of people's expression. I have very particular tastes. Whether it's hip-hop or rock 'n' roll or gospel music, there's probably no more than ten per cent of it in any given genre that I'm going to respond to. But now, as I'm older, there may be parts of, say, *Gummo* that I think are embarrassing and horrible, but there other parts that I think are beautiful and sublime. So rather than saying, 'There's a lot of that film that's shit and I don't like it', I'm going to say, 'Bring on Harmony Korine and let him make more movies', because he's following his own vision. When I was twenty, I would have dismissed it; now I value it more, because I think that these days, the strange stuff – the more original stuff – is less valued in the marketplace, and everything is evaluated by the fucking marketplace. So even though I'm still very critical, I really try to look for the value in something if it's clear that the intention is not for profit or fame, or all that superficial stuff that means nothing to me.

Harmony Korine

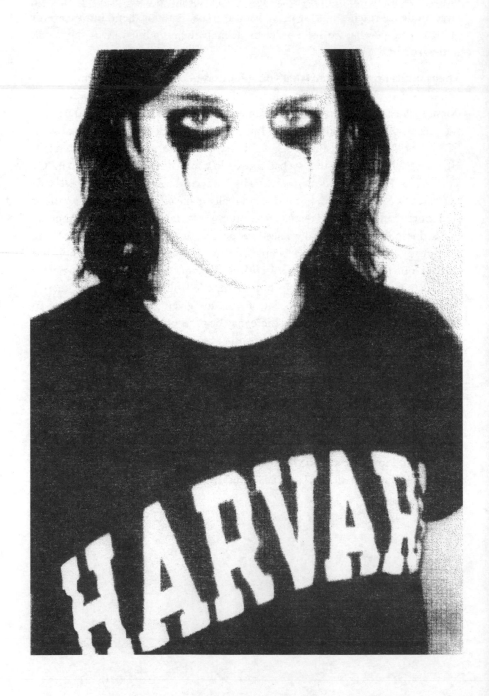

Harmony Korine's first involvement in film occurred when, at nineteen, he wrote the screenplay for *Kids*, directed by Larry Clark in 1995. He has since written and directed the features *Gummo* (Honorable Mention at the 1997 Venice Film Festival) and *julien donkey-boy*. Korine's recent movie projects include *Fight Harm* and the omnibus film, *Jokes*. His novel, *Crackup at the Race Riots*, was published in 1998.

The following interview with Korine was conducted by e-mail.

Tod Lippy: You recently remarked that, 'For a long time I was willing to die for film.'
Harmony Korine: I never meant that in a literal way. I have reconsidered it all, though, and I have skipped out on Ash Wednesday. At one point – the point most probably then remarked – I felt that something had to give in order to be received.

Literal or not, the comment intrigued me because I think it relates to a compulsion in your work to cross boundaries (narrative/non-narrative, art/life, objective/subjective) – to push through something finite in order to find out what's on the other side. It's like the kitchen scene in *Gummo*, where you can't imagine how much this guy's mastery over a wood-and-metal chair will mean until you watch him destroy it with his bare hands.
This idea of a man fighting a chair means very much to me. The outcome is central, because what would happen if the chair won? What would the man feel if the seat-cushion of the chair got the better of him, or if he got tangled up in its legs and felt that his opponent, although not necessarily alive, had been too worthy an adversary. I imagine the man's self worth would diminish as the chair stood there, bent and laughing.

The other people in the kitchen are so invested in it, too. They're continually upping the ante – 'C'mon! Kick his fucking ass!' It's an amazing film moment. Were you there for that? I remember reading somewhere that you wanted only Jean-Yves Escoffier in the room for a lot of that evening.
I was not in the room while the shooting was taking place. I felt that my presence would only hinder the actors, so I discussed with Escoffier the correct route. The room was lit only with strong practicals, and all the doors in the kitchen were closed so none of the crew and producers knew what was happening. It was very late at night on the last day of shooting. One of the men had just been released from prison that afternoon – I believe that's why he beat the chair with such zest. It was a celebratory notion. I turned off my monitor and only listened to what was happening through the closed door. We would shoot every take continuous for four minutes until the mag was spent. Between takes I would run in and whisper in their ears and refill their booze. After the scene was completed I vomited in a bucket to show my appreciation.

From anxiety, inebriation or just gratitude? Does the actual directing process ever make you anxious?

No, not anxiety. When the film is completed and I must go home, then I usually feel an overwhelming sense of disgust and heartbreak.

But during production, does the responsibility you bear as director ever feel overwhelming to you?

Only if there is a calm.

You described your script for *julien donkey-boy* as 'an assortment of scenes describing what could happen, what should happen, what might happen'. That kind of reliance on chance reminds me of a certain strain of Modern and Contemporary art (Duchamp, Fluxus, etc.). Is that a purely personal aesthetic, or do you feel you're coming out of a particular artistic tradition?

With *julien donkey-boy*, I was concerned with the documentation of science projects: if one actor in the film was sulphur-based, and the other actor was hydrochloric acid, then my sole duty was to shake them up and document the fizzle, the gurgle, the separation. Sometimes all things could just as easily evaporate or blow up in my face. This has more in common maybe with people like Otto Müller and Herman Nitsch, the Aktionists from Vienna. But even these are very different; the work appears to have almost no resemblance.

But I think there's a strain of seriousness and self-importance in Nitsch's work that I don't really get from your films. What about someone like Paul McCarthy, who seems to cover similar terrain but with a much better sense of humour?

I don't really see much of either, besides a sheer performance element, and documenting a 'set-up' that is manipulated to varying degrees. What is most important is the subject matter being photographed; the actual aesthetics are secondary or become more pertinent after the fact.

Speaking of 'after the fact', could you talk about how you go about editing your work? I seem to recall reading that there were something like a hundred hours of footage for *julien*; how did you distil that down into a feature-length film?

With *julien*, because I was working with so many cameras at once – up to fifteen – there was a lot of extra footage. I always work with a talented editor who can sort things and solidify my ideas into tangible scenarios, but I never allow the editor to watch the footage before the completion of production. This allows the editing process to follow the kinetic constructs that were laid down during the actual filming process. I guess you would call it a semi-improvised design through and through. But still the actual mystery of the process alludes me.

I thought I'd mention a couple of specific bits from your films, and, if you're inclined, ask you to riff off of them. I wanted to start with the image of the boy in the roach-ridden house repeatedly trying to rehang the picture on the nail in *Gummo*.

I don't necessarily have reasoning for the things I do, I just act upon intuition and prophetic gesture.

Speaking of prophetic gestures, how did you come up with the concept for *Fight Harm*, which, if I understand it correctly, consists of you picking fights with people much larger than you, and then being summarily beaten up while a hidden camera crew documents the whole thing?

I wanted to make the great American comedy. I felt that self-sacrifice in the name of a lost heathen tradition was and is the last fertile frontier. To embrace violence. To sip the blood. I felt as if I was Jolson on a unicorn. I wanted the feature film to consist only of brutality. But perhaps the film is short-lived if I want to raise my cup in the name of longer life outside the black circle.

How much of it was actually filmed? Will you ever resume work on it, or has – as you suggested a while ago – therapy permanently replaced your embrace of violence with one of self-preservation? And is that necessarily problematic for the kind of work you're trying to do?

Approximately six fights were recorded altogether. There is no winner or loser attached to the altercation. It is not about victory, it's more a spectacle of perseverance: how much heart does the bleeding man have. I can safely say that, for the time being, I have abandoned any and all notions of completing this film in the manner and length it was conceived. I will perhaps show it in its present form, or I might never.

When I first heard about the film, I couldn't help but view it as a sort of stripped-down, extreme representation of the physicality of life in New York – the fact that on any given day one literally collides with dozens of people. Would you agree, and could you talk more generally about if and how living in NYC has affected your work?

It only influenced me to move away. New York is a miserable place. I hope it burns.

But you lived here for close to ten years. Did you always have such antagonistic feelings about it?

I am not a good person to ask when it comes to geographical pleasure. I have never enjoyed living anywhere, nor have I ever thought of any place as being home.

A while ago, you said, 'The most subversive thing you can do with the most radical kind of work is to place it in the most commercial venue.' You've had great success in finding an established producer – Cary Woods – to help you finance, make and distribute films that have done just that, at least to a limited degree. Can you talk about your relationship with him, and his commitment to your work?

I ask him for a certain amount of money and he gives me half of it. I also remind him to take his blood pressure medicine. I was his biggest supporter when he had kidney stones as well.

Do you have a particular audience in mind when you're writing/shooting/editing your films?
No.

Does it make you uncomfortable to attend screenings of your films? Do you ever sneak into a theatre to check out an audience's response to them?
I will usually attend at least one screening in the beginning, for various reasons. Then I will never watch my movie again.

Why not?
The film becomes an annoying child that I wished my wife would have aborted, but it's too late – it already breathes and it has a name and it will survive past my own physical death and I will be judged on the merits of its afterlife. So my only option is to continue to plant my seed again and again, continuing to procreate, all the while never being the parent a proper director is supposed to be, neglecting all post-birth glory, hating those others who languish in pride at how well their child has held up, how sturdy, how smart, and how cute it looks. While in all actuality the child for the most part has become just another piece of shit, a whore whose patrons are those bored suckers who select your box at the video store brothel, stagger home with your child under their arm, then return her. Maybe a late fee is in order. I am an abusive father who has no need for his children once the umbilical cord is severed. It's just the fuck I'm concerned with. Copping the nut. I don't even know why I bother in this age when one can just adopt and then return it if you don't like it.

In your novel, *Crackup at the Race Riots*, you relate the anecdote of a woman on a train who notices two chow-chow dogs resting under a seat. After mentioning to her husband about how beautiful they are, she gets kneels down to pet them, and both dogs immediately get up and move away from her. Rejected, she says, 'Snob dogs', and then her husband, smiling, points to the dirt that's collected on the knees of her trousers. That sense of a prideful generosity backfiring into a kind of absolute vulnerability appears again and again in your work (i.e. the 'lump in your titty' scene in *Gummo*). Can you talk about why you're drawn to such moments?
It just seems to me that those people who think with a certain level of depth are destined to lose. The more vulnerable your work, the more people want to trample it. If you think freely, then everyone wants your head on a platter. In essence you become the sole white sheep standing on green Astroturf roped off in an exclusive part of the yacht, far out at sea, and it is here that the aristocracy, those men who own the boat, take turns one by one on their knees fucking you in the ass because they are aware that you are the only animal god gave the automatic anal-jerk reaction to fuck back without thinking, because this is your own specific animal talent. And all the wives of the humping aristocracy blush and smile, and some giggle, standing on the other side of the roped-off area,

watching the goings-on. And the bow rocks and this is how it is done.

It's funny, but I would never think of your work as particularly 'vulnerable' to attack, because it doesn't seem at all desperate to please. Sure, a critical Janet Maslin review may affect ticket sales, but my sense is that its financial success is of little or no consequence to you. I also sense that you have an enormous amount of confidence in what you're doing. Doesn't that combination make you feel impervious to the 'trampling'?
It depends if you are trampled on by a horse or a swine. The sigil of the cloven hoof marks thy path.

You've been exhibiting work recently in galleries. How does the different context ('white cube', rarefied demographic, etc.) affect your creative decisions? And do you think that context alters the meaning of your work?
Charles Eames was most notably an architectural engineer, a furniture designer, and a man of scientific theory, but most impressive to me were his films – films about toys, spinning tops, toy towns, toy soldiers, toy trains (most famous of the films were his two short masterpieces, *Power of 10* and *National Aquarium Presentation*). He will be remembered first and foremost as a creator of chairs. He did not give philosophical credence to his own separate and varied modes of creation: in essence, his chairs and his films were one and the same. The content was king, thus creating a 'unified aesthetic' that brought the house down, and allowed him to work free of any self-imposed constraints that most artists suffer. Personally, I have published books of fiction, books of photos, displayed my art in many galleries and in many forms, made recordings of banjo music, written and directed films, composed a symphony using only the same three black keys on the right-hand side of the piano, and, most importantly, I am now trying to revive the tap dance scene by developing an entirely new repertoire of semi-improvised, extremely technical, avant-garde dance structures. (Please do not think I am joking: it would be the deepest misunderstanding to interpret my intent, my dream, as somehow being an ironic display. I am admittedly not as advanced at the moment as I need to be before I showcase this next phase in my career. If my dream comes to fruition, and I am capable of a total tap revolution, then I declare without any hesitation or pause a complete and total abandonment of my current involvement in the cinema and all other areas of artistic contention. I need to go where I am most useful!) The point being: everything from me had been previously deposited inside of me, due to the force of a sacred entity whose identity I will take to my grave. This curse/blessing was bestowed upon my being without any previous knowledge and total disregard of personal choice in the matter, no consent. And when I am dead, perhaps I, too, will be best remembered for a chair I once built.

There's clearly an element of religiosity – a sense of a 'calling' – in the way you speak about your creativity, and in your willingness to make declarations

about art and your relationship to it. In that regard, it seems like you and the Dogme movement were a perfect match. Could you talk about what appealed to you about making a Dogme film? And if you'll do it again?

Faith is a requirement. Without belief you are lost. I need rules, I crave structure, I need to often be punished for my bad behaviour: this reminds of the world's reckoning. I work in order to redeem that which I have careened against. My work is all lies. I imagine that I am not a very good person, though not the worst of the bunch. I am sure that I have been bestowed many more faults and pains than goodness. Virtue sought through redemption. I am not a fan of life. I have never enjoyed the company of others. I continue because I know no other way. The Dogme 95 were militant in belief – a band of brothers who sought to flank the industry. *Vive la revolution!* Long live all the brothers everywhere in arms who resist the vortex with anger and contempt. I doubt I will return to the vow of chastity, though. Remember this, my friends: it is not enough to worship him, you must almost be him!!!

How were the Oscars? I saw you on TV.

I have forgotten.

I know that you once said 'I make movies because no one has made a film that I'd like to see at the cinema', but I was wondering if there were any films (recent or not) that had been particularly influential to you. And if so, could you talk about why and how they affected you?

This question is a bit too difficult for me to respond to in full. Actually, that was not what I said. What I said was that no one at present was presenting the types of images in the way I wished to see them presented, thus: 'I create what is not there for me to see at the moment.' I actually stole this point of view from a friend of mine. It is not profound, but it is the truth. It seemed to suit my views, though, so I adopted it as my own. As far as speaking of movies that have moved me, there are far too many to speak of. The history of cinema is vast and my attention is not so. Please forgive me. In order to answer this question we would have to play a lengthy guessing game.

Fair enough. Can you talk a little bit about the *Jokes* omnibus film? I understand Gus Van Sant is filming (or has completed filming) one segment, you're doing one, and possibly Claire Denis the third?

Jokes is a film that I wrote about two years ago. I have always been a fan of vaudeville, and I have for a long time had the desire to direct and revive the classic blackface minstrels of yesteryear, in particular those early Al Jolson and Eddie Cantor classics that helped inspire me to become the person I am today. In fact, my two life-long dream projects are both epic in scope: the first is to star as a tap-dancing minstrel in a film called 'The Grace of Blackface'. The other film would be a historical period drama, tracing in great detail the history of molestation in the Boy Scouts. I would go decade by decade, showcasing the most infamous Boy Scout molesters of the day. I would focus particularly on the evolution of the scout-master molester: how with each passing era his methods and sophistication would increase accordingly, in essence becoming more and more uniformly perverse, reflecting the times and attitudes of the day, ending up with the common flat-out paedophilic mantra that is the Boy Scouts of America. In fact I have already been working on a script that combines both themes, a period minstrel drama about the history of Boy Scout molesting. But *Jokes* is a separate undertaking. Written in conjunction with the former, it is a movie in three parts. Each chapter, so to speak, is based on a Milton Berle joke, usually a one-liner in the vein of Henny Youngman. Basically, I picked three separate jokes and embellished each one in order to stretch it out into a simple narrative of sorts. At the time, I was watching all the Alan Clarke films I could see, and I was very much excited by his technique: his use of long, flowing steadicam, no-frills organic film-making. So I was inspired to approach each joke/chapter in a similar way, a return to a place I had never before felt any interest. The idea of three different directors, including myself, came later, after the script was written. My main interest for making it an omnibus film was so that if the movie turned out terrible, I would only have to share a third of the negative critical brunt. Claire Denis is not going to direct the last instalment, although I admire her extremely. Logistically it could not happen in time. The third director will not be revealed until the film's completion.

Can you talk more about your interest in jokes? So many pages of your novel, for instance, are filled with little bits that have that 'set-up, pay-off' structure found in the Berle/Youngman stand-up tradition, but often the content (murder, rape, etc.) has an interestingly dissonant relationship to the form.

I am a showman. I will paint myself black and spark a jingle. I am the last living minstrel, and trickery is part of my trade. But I also have a soft spot in my heart for those pale-faced darkies who had, before I was yet born, painted themselves negro with burnt cork and shoe polish, and the pride these men had as they hocked their asses on the bright light stages for their nickel-tossing patrons. And as such, I will dance on their graves. This, I'm sure, would make them proud.

In your novel, you place celebrity's names ('Jessica Tandy') in odd contexts, often giving off a weird *frisson* ('Jessica Tandy had an elongated vagina'). I thought that your casting of Werner Herzog as the father in *Julien* had a similar effect. His fame – his history – kept bouncing off his character in interesting ways. Can you talk about 1) your take on 'celebrity' in this culture, and 2) your interest in playing with it in your work?

In this case, I am not sure why I do these things.

Can you name a specific film (or even a film moment) that has had an effect on you, and why?

Every Which Way But Loose, 1978, dir. James Fargo. I love when Clint Eastwood splits his beer with the chimp. This is the only movie moment that seems to be coming to my mind at the moment.

Buck Henry

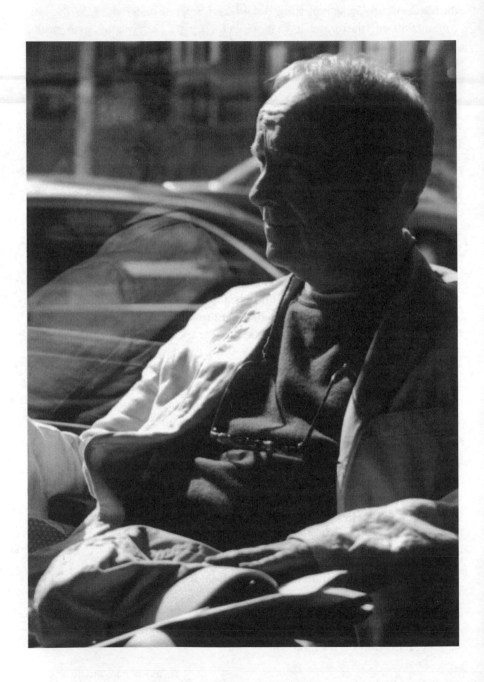

Buck Henry wrote the screenplays for *The Graduate* (with Calder Willingham), *Candy*, *Catch-22*, *The Owl and the Pussycat*, *What's Up, Doc?*, and *To Die For*, among many others. He co-directed *Heaven Can Wait* with Warren Beatty, wrote and directed the political satire *First Family*, and has acted in over forty films, including *The Player*, *Short Cuts*, *The Man Who Fell to Earth*, *Gloria*, *Taking Off* and *Defending Your Life*. Henry, who has also had a longstanding involvement with both theatre and television, created the *Get Smart* series with Mel Brooks in 1965.

Tod Lippy: You were born here, weren't you?
Buck Henry: So I've been told. There's a family myth that my father, who had a lot of friends in politics, and who was a member of what was then called 'Café Society', was running the riding board of a police car to take my mother at two in the morning down one-way streets the wrong way, sirens blaring, to Doctor's Hospital. But then, many years ago, I found out that Doctor's Hospital didn't exist in the year of my birth – it was built afterwards. So I'm angry, because my mother and father are long-deceased, and I don't have anyone to ask. But yes, I'm pretty certain I was born here.

Your mother was an actress, right? I read that she had been a Mack Sennett girl.
She was, among other things, a Mack Sennett girl – a Mack Sennett 'Bathing Beauty', as they called them. So her affairs were followed rather closely in the late twenties and early thirties, up until she quit totally, cold when she got married. So cold, in fact, that I always had to remind myself that she'd done it. She'd ask me what was going on, and I'd tell her some dopey show-biz story, and think, 'Wait a minute, she probably knows more about this than I do . . .'

Didn't she date Howard Hughes?
She did. She was a California girl – actually, a Portland, Oregon girl – who went to seek fame and fortune in Hollywood, and found a certain amount of both. Then she went on a publicity tour for a movie and came to New York, where she met my father. They were married three weeks later, and that was it.

You were in New York exclusively up until you were eleven or twelve, weren't you?
Not exclusively. We went to California a lot, because my mother's family was there. And my parents would vacation there. I started going to LA when I was about two. Some of my earliest memories are of the Chief, one of the last great American trains. One took the Twentieth Century Limited from Grand Central to Chicago, and then it was out to the Coast on the Chief. It was an extraordinary two-and-a-half, three-day train ride into the West, where everything, especially in those days, really opened up. You could stand on the rear platform of the train, which I usually did alone, and watch the country spread out behind you. It was a great, great adventure, always. So LA is built into me almost as much as New York is.

They're both 'in your blood'.
Yeah. I've always understood both places, so none of that stuff that comes as a great surprise to people who go there was ever a surprise to me. It's like a language. There are certain people who want to be in the film business, and you know they're going to have a struggle because they don't get the language out there, which is radically different from the language in New York. Los Angeles behaviour blends more easily with other cultures and subcultures. But New York has much a more specific, jagged and idiosyncratic sound to it, which reflects the personality of the place.

Did you pick up on these fundamental distinctions between New York and LA as a kid?
It never occurred to me; I never thought about it until later in life. Because I knew them both, and I had family in both places, they were both home. LA maybe not so much as New York, but I was an only child and I was very mischievous – or as they like to say in films today, 'mischeeveous'. In the opening scene of a film I saw recently – made by a really interesting film-maker whose name will go unmentioned – a guy playing a teacher pronounces it 'mischeeveous'. Whether that was a choice on the part of the actor or not I don't know, but it just rattled me – for fifteen minutes I couldn't concentrate on the film. 'Heineeous' is another one that seems to be making the rounds. In *To Die For*, I had everybody making carefully structured – on my part – grammatical errors. Like the 'I'/'me' thing. It's tricky, though, because every time I do it in a script I think it's going to make somebody talk that way – somebody else will think it's all right, and the next time it crops up it will be an English professor in a film saying, 'Me and my sister went to the movies last night', and I'll want to just slash the screen. I have only a small handful of friends now who are able to make the distinction between the nominative and the objective. In California it's meaningless.

To a lot of people, of course, this seems like petty dreck. But if you are interested in the language being part of what we laughingly refer to as our 'art form', then you damn well better attend to it. It's hard for me to think that film writers can get to be as famous and well-paid as they are without ever having thought about, or read about, the language.

Why do you think that is?
Because the business attracts a lot of facile but skilled intelligences that have a certain amount of contempt for the nuts and bolts of what they deal with.

Would you say New York is a more literate film culture?
Oh, there's no question about it. It's a more literate film culture because it's a more literate culture. There are people here who do care about what things mean. There's not a lot of care about meaning in LA. In the last few years, the Valley has spawned some enormous talent – Paul Thomas Anderson, for example – but for the most part, New Yorkers train themselves in a kind of dialogue

with the city that isn't available to people who live in California.

I think it's because of all of that time spent in cars in LA – at least two hours in the source of a typical day – time you would be spending talking to somebody, or listening to someone talk, or *something*, in New York. This is a cliché that Californians deplore, but it's a cliché because it's true. One trip on the subway is worth a hundred limousine rides.

Do you find that a ride like that will get your juices flowing as far as writing is concerned?
Oh, no. That's personal – I'm totally lazy and operate out of desperation and anxiety, wherever I am. Actually, I probably work better in LA because I'm not tempted to go to the theatre, or this museum, or that concert, or any of the one hundred thousand things you can do here every day. I was just cutting things out of the Sunday *New York Times* section for stuff that's coming up this summer. Unbelievable. The music section alone – I mean, Los Angeles prides itself on its music, but in the course of one day here you can find more than six months' worth of stuff in LA.

There are millions of people here, all the time, moving towards things that have ideas in them. In Los Angeles, most of the time, there are hundreds of thousands of people moving towards things that have success or failure written in neon above them. Trying to find the right door. It isn't to say you can't talk about ideas in Hollywood – you can. But it's on a vastly different level. It's all keyed to marketability. Again, it's a different language.

You split your time pretty much fifty-fifty between the two places, right?
Yep.

It's surprising to me, judging from what you've said, that you're not spending ninety per cent of your time here.
Well, I really like LA – I'm happy there in a different way. I have a great house, great friends and I love to drive, so it doesn't bother me the way it bothers other New Yorkers. And I do know book readers and theatre-goers there – you know, it's not a desert. It's just different.

My theory is that it all had to do with the stock exchange. Los Angeles was founded first by rich farmers and then by industrialists and media people, who made their money the same way all Americans of wealth did – off the stock market. The stock market opened at nine in the morning, which meant that people in California had to get up at six – which meant that they really got up at five so they could play a little golf before they attended to the business aspect of their lives. Which meant, of course, that they had to go to sleep at ten. So they couldn't go to operas and theatre and stuff. Only by the grace of a few extremely wealthy people out there were some theatres built, but it's minimal for a city of that size. You can find more theatre in Minneapolis, for instance.

You went off to military school in LA for several years when you were a teenager, didn't you?

Correct. From around eleven or twelve to fifteen, I think. During the Second World War.

In a piece you wrote several years ago, you talked about your experiences as a kid, mixing with the personalities of the time at places like the Garden of Allah bungalows in LA, or at the Palm Springs Racquet Club. You know, watching Chico Marx cavort at the pool, or Jack Warner playing tennis while Bogart offered encouragement from the sidelines . . .

Well, I was aware of all this stuff because I'd grown up around actors and writers. They spoke a language that seemed relatively normal to me. What was perceived of even then as glamour, and now as kind of iconic, was not that unusual for me – I saw both the upstairs and the downstairs. But I was still aware of the 'larger-than-life' way in which they lived – and they did live in a more interesting style than they do today.

Also, back then, the public didn't know things. Now, the public knows everything, including all the false things – the bad stuff about you that never happened. Back then, the public knew all the good things that didn't really happen. It was like under Stalin – the information was really carefully controlled, and only a few people controlled it. The dark side of things was very rarely made public.

My impression is that the Louella Parsons and Hedda Hoppers of the world ran the show – not like now, when celebrities, through their publicists and other 'handlers', seem to hold so much leverage.

Yeah, sure. But the weird thing is that now it sometimes seems that everyone just rises on this tide of scum. It's very interesting. There were reputations for incredibly bad behaviour in the celebrity world out there when I was a kid, but it was kept in the family, except for the more dramatic examples, like when somebody really ran afoul of the law. Gossip is always interesting – we can't live without it, and history is built on it – but the gossip is radically different today when no holds are barred.

In that same piece you talk about seeing Louella Parsons at the Palm Springs Racquet Club late in her life. You described a steady stream of celebrities approaching her, kissing her hand, and then you noticed when she finally got up to leave that she'd left a puddle of urine in her chair. Such an arresting image . . .

It's an ugly image. She was – as all doyennes are – closely watched and petted by her intimates all her life. And she did monstrous, awful things – all of them did. I'm not being entirely fair. I didn't know her well, I only knew her through my mother. I'd listen in on their conversations, and I have to say I never heard her say anything interesting. But in those last few years, the couple of times I saw her, it wasn't a pretty sight.

Hedda Hopper also did her damage, but she was a much more interesting, articulate woman, who had been a good actress. She had to dig in the same dirt in order to compete. There was another guy who's totally forgotten now, named Jimmie Fiddler, who had a daily or weekly fifteen-minute show about the business.

And then Walter Winchell in New York.
And of course Winchell, to whom everyone was beholden. I met him when I was about fifteen at Toots Schor's. It was right out of *Sweet Smell of Success*: he was holding court at a table, and there were a couple other famous people around – you know, somebody like DiMaggio, and somebody like Gleason. I really can't remember, because I was so fascinated by Winchell. I wasn't aware, until much later, of his politics, or his peculiar, twisted journey through the American experience of the forties and fifties.

So when you returned to New York as a teenager, you were already getting into show business?
I joined Equity when I was fifteen, I think. I toured with *Life with Father* one summer during high school.

What did your mother think about that?
I think she thought it was swell. Nobody in my family ever tried to discourage me from any of this. Although I think my father hoped I would turn to something more serious than show business, even though he was very good friends with a lot of actors, as well as an inveterate film-goer and theatre-lover. I don't think he had a lot of admiration for it as a life choice. Also, I think he was concerned about how difficult and 'iffy' the whole thing was.

And your acting at the time was all in the theatre?
All theatre. It never occurred to me that I would have anything to do with film. I'd been going to the theatre since my fourth birthday, so by the time I was fifteen I'd seen every famous actor in the work of every famous playwright of our time, and that obviously fed more of my sensibilities than other art forms. I love film, but I have a feeling about the theatre that's different, which is not shared with most of my compatriots – including a lot of directors I know who have been very successful in the theatre but cannot sit through a play.

When did you first begin writing?
I was writing when I was a kid. Writing stories, playlets, things like that. And when I got out of the Army, in '54, I was trying to write for television here in New York. I was turning out scripts that I hoped would become material for *GE Theater*, *Studio 90*, that kind of thing. I'd acted in a few of them – I actually did some small parts on them even before I went into the service. So I was basically making just a scrape-though living as an actor for a number of years during the fifties – I'd go on tour with a show, do summer stock. Do just enough to live without having to take a real job. And I lived cheap in Greenwich Village. Got free

tickets to plays from Equity. Or snuck in, which one used to be able to do. New Yorkers who live on the edge know how to do an awful lot for free. And then, free was a lot cheaper than free is now. [*Laughs.*]

Anyway, I was trying to write, but I never sold anything. I was very young, and I wasn't that good at what I was doing. But there were a few story editors on those shows who were very kind to me, and encouraging, even though I could never sell anything. Finally, I got a job in an improvisational theatre which was famous for a few years.

This was The Premise?
Yeah. And that led, step by step, to everything else.

Around this time weren't you also involved in something called the Society for Indecency to Naked Animals?
Right. A lunatic friend of mine named Alan Abel, who is a drummer, a lecturer and a kind of comedy writer, was also a professional trickster – he became famous later on for several other stunts, including having his own obituary published in the *New York Times*. Anyway, he invented this 'organization', and then we kind of refined it together. I became the front man for it: G. Clifford Prout, Jr, President of SINA. It never made us any money, but we got trips and accommodations to various places.

And people swallowed this? The title is so absurd —
The title makes no sense at all. But I guess it was hard for people to find fault with this pair of earnest men. Alan was the vice-president – Bruce something. We spent a week in San Francisco under the auspices of the *San Francisco Chronicle*, whose reporter followed us around for a week as we tried to put underwear on the animals in the San Francisco Zoo, or picketed the city dog pound, condemning various animal exhibits as being prurient and part of the downfall of American youth, leading them ultimately to alcoholism, juvenile delinquency and suicide. A lot of people bought it, including some people on the television shows that covered us.

The story goes that even Walter Cronkite was duped.
The last piece I ever did for SINA was at the zoo in Los Angeles, and I talked to a very well-known reporter for CBS. Robert something – he had been a very good foreign correspondent for them, and then somehow got stuck doing things like this. Anyway, he interviewed me at the zoo there, and I talked to him about indecency, and sang the SINA marching song while accompanying myself on a ukulele. They put it at the end of one of the fifteen-minute CBS newscasts, and someone at the network recognized me. By that time, I'd been around for a while. And according to rumour, Cronkite was very annoyed about being conned.

I was wondering if the kind of improvisation you, George Segal and other members of The Premise were doing was similar to the Second City model.

It was less open-ended than Second City. If Second City was doing something they thought was going interestingly, they'd go on for twenty minutes. And sometimes the magic happened, and that twenty minutes was breathtaking. We'd do a lot of improvisation, but we'd be very careful to limit ourselves to five to seven minutes. The point was to get an idea that would come around and finish itself. Then, if things were really interesting, we'd work on it as a piece. So half the show would be pieces that we'd already refined, and half of it would be improvisation. It was great for anyone who needs to think on their feet. And it opens up areas that are hard to get open in other ways.

Every night, something strange happened. In truth, something strange happens every night on stage, in anything. Otherwise actors would have nothing to talk about. There's always a conversation after a performance where somebody says, 'Did you see what happened in Act Two?!' But in the case of improvisation theatre, it's filled with that.

What do you think attracted you to comedy, as an actor and as a writer?
In college, I always had this problem: if I had a part in a serious play, the audience would come and always be deeply disturbed, because they weren't getting a barrel of laughs. I remember in my third year – by then I'd been in a lot of plays – we did *The Lady's Not for Burning*, and I played the Richard Burton part. The curtain goes up on me cleaning the floor of the lead's study, and the audience began to laugh in expectation of these fabulous, hilarious things that would happen while I was cleaning the floor. And, of course, nothing fabulous happened.

I don't know why I gravitated to comedy. Maybe it's because it covers a lot of faults. You can be superficial in a much more interesting way if you can write comedy. If you're writing serious stuff, you're either good or you're boring.

Same with acting?
I'd like to think it's a gift, but most serious actors can also do comedy. And I don't think it's true that most comic actors can do serious stuff. I don't know, maybe it's fifty-fifty.

What happened after your time with The Premise?
After about six months with them, I was asked to come out to LA and write for Steve Allen's show. I lived in an apartment so appalling that when I drive by it these days I am immediately depressed. It was the loneliest place I've ever lived in. To a certain extent, I lived the kind of life New Yorkers who hate Los Angeles think they have to endure if they live out there. I don't really know why. I wasn't making a lot of money – well, I was making a lot of money for me, because I'd come out of off-Broadway, but I wasn't really happy in the job. Part of the fact was that I thought it was going to be an ideal situation – the one person I wanted to work for on television was Steve Allen. But I didn't think I was successful on the show, except for meeting my partner, Stan Burns, who was a great, great comedy writer.

So you didn't actually own a house out there until later on?

I had a house when I was doing *Get Smart*, but I didn't own it. And then I bought a house sometime between *Get Smart* and *The Graduate*. I wrote *The Graduate* in that house. And I didn't come back to New York to live – except for renting places occasionally, like when I did *Taking Off* – until the early eighties, when I did *The New Show*.

Why did you decide to come back here and buy a place?

Well, I was always going back and forth, and I'd rented various apartments in the building I'm in now for a long time. Actually, it never occurred to me that I wouldn't live in LA and New York. I knew I'd be going out there to work, and always will. And I like running away from the weather in either place. The rain in Los Angeles drives me nuts, by the way. I find nothing romantic about it – it's just a total pain in the ass. If it isn't seventy-five to eighty-three degrees, and the sun isn't out, I see no excuse for Los Angeles at all.

You made another taxi vs limo reference in an interview from some years back, where you said, 'You can't just take taxis or limousines or you forget what the streets are like. You've got to take a bus or subway now and then.' Was that meant to be a metaphor for the Los Angeles/New York thing, or were you being more specific?

What I always meant by that was that I do believe that a lot of directors, and writers, and sometimes producers just lose their edge because they haven't seen anybody or talked to anybody or been with anybody who isn't a kind of replica of themselves for a long period of time. If you're massively talented, you can intuit the way people think and behave who have absolutely nothing to do with your life. But you have to be pretty damned talented to do it. In the kiddie movies that are made today – I am being condescending – almost everyone talks like everyone else all the time. There are some distinctions to be made, but for the most part, everyone has the same language and the same approach to life situations. So the differences between people and between voices just gets wiped out, unless you're there to hear them. We're always bemoaning the fact that there are great directors around who haven't made a decent film in twenty years, or writers who have run out of stuff, but I don't think it's that so much as they simply lose their ear – or maybe their eye – because they haven't been looking and listening. You know, we're voyeurs and eavesdroppers, and if everyone is voyeuring and eavesdropping on what's being said at Spago, you're not going to get a lot of really good material.

Your mention of voyeurism reminds me of the scene in *The Owl and the Pussycat* where George Segal is spying on Streisand with his pair of binoculars —

Yes, indeed. [*Laughs.*] The voyeurism thing is a part of my life that I've managed to put into a couple of films.

The work you're doing at the moment is almost a distillation of your bi-coastal

existence. You've been involved for the last several years in the highly publicized rewrite process for *Town & Country* – whose budget, at last count, was estimated as having doubled (some say it's near one hundred million dollars) since production began. But you're also developing a project with Greene-Street Films – one of a number of smaller independent production companies here in New York. How did you get involved with both of those?

I came into the Hollywood situation because they started shooting, and two or three months in, they felt like they needed some new material. And it's one of these peculiar situations, which had never happened before in my experience, but I'm sure it's happened in a lot of other writers' experiences, where the direction of the film had changed as they were shooting – things didn't seem to go together – so I came in as yet another writer. They'd been through two or three people already, I think. And for one reason or another, this film staggered over – well, I like to think of the fact that it's been shot over two separate centuries. A Film That Spans the Millennia – I think that's a fine selling point. It's been a long, difficult road, with a lot of problems. But I was just a hired hand. I mean, almost everyone in Hollywood has had a job like that.

Have you had them yourself?
Never one quite like this. I've done rewrites very infrequently.

Mostly uncredited?
All uncredited, as a matter of fact, until this one. They can't uncredit me on this one because I've been there for the better part of two-and-a-half years. But I feel spooky having a credit on it, because it wasn't any of my sensibilities or ideas that generated the story, so I'm potshotting kind of from the outside.

And how did *Bathing Suits*, the script for GreeneStreet Films, come about?
Charles Webb, who wrote the novel of *The Graduate*, wrote a script and sent it to me. Charles and I have conducted an epistolary relationship for almost thirty-five years. Until last year, I had not seen him since before we started shooting *The Graduate*. But we did correspond all of that time, and I've always felt a debt to him. He, in turn, always says the same thing about me. But in truth, without Charles Webb there would be no *Graduate*, and my career would have gone in a different direction. So he sent me this script, which I thought was terrific, and had great possibilities. I spent a year or so trying to convince several producers in LA of that fact, who were unable to go another step with it for one reason or another. Then I acted in a short film that was directed by Curtis Clayton, longtime editor of Gus Van Sant, and produced by a woman named Cathy Main, who is an independent producer in California. They were looking for a feature, so I showed Charles's script to them. They fell in love with it, and then, a few steps later, they asked me to rewrite it for them, and I did. I didn't want to get in this far, but I thought it was worth doing, because I think it will make a wonderful film, and also because of my feelings for the Webbs. So I did the rewrite, and it

took them some months to set it up at GreeneStreet, and then I came on it as a co-producer in order to help push it along.

If I were a producer somewhere, I personally would not be particularly thrilled to hear 'Buck's going to be a co-producer'. 'Wow! Let's move!' Anyway, that's where it is. We're looking for a cast as we speak. Actors with names, basically, to help us get the money.

So it's sort of a tinier version of what you would be dealing with in Hollywood.
It's a smaller, more eccentric version. We're talking about a three-to-five-million-dollar film. But those are just as hard to make.

Is one world more pleasant to work in than the other?
It depends. As an actor, I like the independent film process better. It's quicker, it's leaner. I like being on location, too. I've never had to be in a really bad place for a long time. And the really bad places are often bearable and sometimes really interesting for a few weeks. I like the idea that people are moving fast. In an ideal world, you'd always take a crew of six out to make a film, which kids are doing these days. That's pretty great.

On the other hand, I understand and admire the system. I love crews – I think the professionalism of real Hollywood or New York crews is just terrific. If they're working well, it's a dream to watch. When we were making *Gloria*, John Cassavetes had a lot of women in the top spots on the crew – something I've missed recently. I think it fundamentally changed the atmosphere of the shoot. I was only there for a week or so, but there was a lowering of the temperature. Not physically, because we were shooting in a boiling summer in an abandoned apartment in the Bronx. But it lowered the temperature of the temperament of the set in a really interesting way.

Actually, in a truly ideal world, I'd like to go out on location with six very beautiful female crew members. Beautiful, powerful grips, beautiful camera operators, gorgeous cinematographers . . .

Looking over your filmography as an actor, I would say that a majority of films you've appeared in would be classified as independent, ranging from things like *Eating Raoul* in the early eighties all the way up to *1999* or *I'm Losing You* last year.
Oh, absolutely. Even from *Taking Off*, if you want to characterize that as an independent film.

Is it simply that the *Grumpy Old Men* parts aren't as interesting to play?
Oh, no. They don't ask me. All of the films I've been in are either because somebody connected to the company is a friend of mine or because someone involved knows me, and has a weird idea for casting a part. Usually, it's because another actor has said, 'What about Buck?' Or a director has happened to see something I've done, which was the case in *Grumpy Old Men*. Donald Petrie had this idea to

cast me; nobody else did. They're all kind of accidents. I think I've gotten maybe one acting job in my life through an agency.

Even with the films I've written, I never really wrote a part for myself. They all happened after the fact. Like in *To Die For*, somebody at some point said to me, 'So which part do you want to play?' They're all accidents. I've never made any money at all acting in film. And I like it, but not nearly as much as I like acting on stage.

You've written a number of unproduced scripts. Didn't you do an adaptation of Vonnegut's novel *Jailbird* some years back?
Oh, yeah. It's pretty heavy, because I tried to be as faithful to the book as I could, which means a lot of locations and a lot of actors. It's complicated, with lots of great characters, and it would need a heavyweight director. I wrote it for an old friend of mine, the Danish film-maker Henning Carlsen, who made the world-famous film *The Hunger* in the sixties, and who has made a lot of films since that haven't been seen in the United States. He came to me and said he loved the book, and asked me to adapt it.

If I'd thought about it for five minutes I would have realized it had about an eight per cent chance of being made. Because it needed big money, and it had a foreign director attached, all this stuff. So it's never been made. Every couple of years, some director asks me about it, and wants to know if I'd be willing to sit down and do some rewrites on it. And I'll give them a half-hearted 'yes', because I think it's less likely than more that it will ever get going. And it's political – all the things the audience doesn't want. Literary, political, poetic.

You also adapted Elmore Leonard's *La Brava* a while ago. Whatever happened with that?
I don't know what happened.

You'd think with the relative successes of several of the other recent Leonard adaptations . . .
There have been several unsuccessful adaptations of his as well, though, so it balances out. It needs two or three heavyweight actors to get it going. I wouldn't be surprised to hear that someone's rewriting it, which is okay.

What about your screenplay from the early seventies, *Cells*?
It's funny you mention it – I'm working on that as we speak. I wrote it originally in 1970. Somebody got interested in it again a couple of years ago, and I went back and read it. It needed to be rewritten, which I'm in the process of doing. It was written not only before there was an Internet, but before anyone had a computer, and it needs to be startlingly brought up to date. And the dialogue is weirdly old-fashioned.

You can't do it as a period thriller?
No.

It sounds like it would be something along the lines of *The Matrix*.
No, it's not quite that. It's more a kind of an – oh, God, I hate to use this term – existential thriller. It's a mystery that doesn't reveal itself very easily.

What's it like to go back to material you wrote almost thirty years ago?
It's awful. I just read it for the first time a couple of months ago. And as I read along, I'll say to myself, 'What was I *thinking* there? What was I trying to do?' It's like someone else wrote it. I know the intention of it, and I know why I wrote sequences, but there are moments where I'm really wondering, you know, what the characters are talking about. And it also has to be pumped up, because the rules of language have really changed. I used to have to really struggle to put what we'd refer to as 'bad language' into a script. I remember when I was writing *Catch-22*, and I was looking at the page – we looked at pages then, not screens – for a long time before I wrote 'prick'. You know, Yossarian yells, 'Milo, you prick.' It was unthinkable. Nobody had ever used that word in a film. Now, it's on every television show.

You co-directed *Heaven Can Wait* with Warren Beatty, but I believe your only other directing credit is for the 1980 political satire *First Family*.
That was a long road. I wrote the original script for that right after Nixon left office, and that's what it was meant to be about. Then the years went by. Among other things, I had written a third act which caused a threatened copyright lawsuit to take place. To my horror, I didn't understand the copyright laws in the area of satire and parody I went into, and was completely vulnerable. So I had to completely rewrite the last third of the film. The studio gave me an actual A, B, and C actor list – the only time that's ever happened. A one-, two-, and three-point list – put ten points together and you've got a 'go'. And then I just lost control of it.

There's a very funny sight-gag scene near the beginning – Richard Benjamin, the press secretary, and Rip Torn, the Chairman of the Joint Chiefs of Staff, are having a policy discussion in an office in the White House. Through the window behind them, Gilda Radner, who plays the president's nymphomaniac/ virgin daughter, scales down the side of the building and attacks the White House gardener, finally being apprehended by the Secret Service.
There are some good things in it. You know, we were talking earlier about audience expectations – they can sometimes really put a crimp in your plans. That happened on *Catch-22*, also. Because of *M*A*S*H*, erroneous expectations were made about *Catch-22*; that it was going to be this laugh riot. But they are simply not alike in any way. And this happened, I think, to a certain extent with *First Family*. What it was supposed to be about on a serious level I couldn't dig out of what it was; I just couldn't find a way to make it come to life.

Was that your last experience directing?

I've done some television. Frankly, I don't much like the procedure. I'm not good getting up early in the morning – I'm an insomniac. I don't really like answering questions all day. I don't like thinking about one thing all the time. I don't like looking at dailies. So it's tough for me. And I don't think I'm good enough to handle heavy stuff. If I ever do it again, I want to do it with a small crew on location. I just don't like being responsible for 110 people.

Do you find that you're often recognized on the street here in New York?
I'm much more recognizable in Los Angeles, because in Los Angeles, you go to places where people are used to recognizing other people. Here, I get recognized when I go to the theatre, or at certain restaurants. But for the most part, no. I can walk down Broadway and not a soul will take a second look.

And you prefer that?
I do. It's nice because it allows me to – well, this isn't so true any more, but it used to allow me to go into peep shows without people yelling at me. In the *Saturday Night Live* days, I used to get it here a lot – 'Hey, Uncle Roy!' as I was slipping into some place in Times Square.

There is something weirdly appropriate about that whole scenario.
Yeah, there is. In those days, when I did more television guest appearances, you know, on Carson, or Letterman, or *Saturday Night Live*, I'd get it more. But I like anonymity, except when I want to get a table at a restaurant or a ticket to a theatre.

You once said, 'Certain things that are funny in California are just not funny in New York.'
Well, you know, you could take out the city names and substitute thousands of others. For that matter, countries. I think it's more true the other way around, though. There are things that are funny in New York that are not funny in California. It has to do with recognition. Milos Forman used to say that when he was a kid, they sat in the cafés and read Kafka out loud and laughed and laughed, just fell on the floor. They read it in the way one here would read *Catch-22* or *Portnoy's Complaint*. So yeah, comedy doesn't always carry. What would a Russian in the fifties or sixties have conceivably made of *The Graduate*? This guy who lives in this house with a swimming pool, and has a problem communicating. They'd get laughs out of it? I don't think so.

Well, I think of Woody Allen's films as being quintessentially 'New York' in their sense of humour, but don't they play well in LA, too?
Not as well as they play in New York, because their core audiences aren't the same. Fairly well-educated, middle-class white Jewish boys and girls do not go to the theatre en masse in Los Angeles the way they do in New York. And the core audience makes things happen.

By the way, Woody Allen is just about the only person left who makes New York movies. Or for that matter, city movies. I hope that the sensibilities of all the new good writers and directors – and there are a whole bunch of them, like Alan Ball, or Alexander Payne, Todd Solondz, among others – can be tuned to an urban environment, and they can get something going that isn't just about the suburbs. Because America is still very urban – there are a lot of large cities here.

You mentioned the scarcity of peep shows these days, due in large part to the Giuliani administration's 'cleaning up' of the city. What's your opinion about all of that?

Oh, it's not only Giuliani. It's the real-estate powers, too. I go at it from two sides. I think it's great that the theatres are coming back to life, but I hate to see 42nd Street changed quite so radically. To try to stamp out that quality of life – the raffishness, which is a polite word for it – of New York is not only pompous, but injurious to a sense of what the city is, and of what it can do. It's New York – it's a place where people with radically different dispositions and temperaments live together, and always have, in a wonderful way. It's sort of like going to Paris and finding out that the food police were in every restaurant and issued a dictum that you can't cook with butter.

Walter Bernstein

Walter Bernstein's screenplays include *Fail-Safe* (both for the 1964 Sidney Lumet film and Stephen Frears's 2000 remake), *Heller in Pink Tights*, *The Molly Maguires*, *The Front*, *Semi-Tough*, *Yanks* (with Colin Welland), and *The House on Carroll Street*. He also wrote and directed the 1980 remake of *Little Miss Marker*. Bernstein's book, *Inside Out: A Memoir of the Blacklist*, was published by Knopf in 1996.

Tod Lippy: I know you grew up in Brooklyn, and other than college at Dartmouth and time in the Army during World War II, have made New York your home, but didn't your first feature film credit – *Kiss the Blood Off My Hands* – come from a stint in Hollywood?

Walter Bernstein: Yeah. I first went out to Hollywood in the summer of '47, on a ten-week deal with Columbia Pictures to work for Robert Rossen. The original idea was that I would come out and adapt a Chekhov story called 'The Grasshopper' that he wanted to make a movie of. As soon as I got there, he changed his mind. He was working on *All the King's Men* then, so he put me to work on that. And I was green – I didn't know anything. So basically, for the ten weeks I just listened to him. He used me as a sounding board on various things – plot, character, political things. It was a great education for me on how to write a script, essentially, because he was very experienced, and very good.

At the end of the ten weeks, my agent, Harold Hecht, had just started an independent production company with Burt Lancaster, and they had optioned this book called *Kiss The Blood Off My Hands*. They had a deal at Universal. I think I had been getting two hundred and fifty dollars a week from Rossen, and Harold offered me five hundred dollars. Rossen was very nice about it. He said, 'I can't match that, so go, good luck.' I went to work for them, and because of my lack of experience, Hecht put me together with a more experienced writer named Ben Maddow. And Ben and I worked for several months, doing essentially a treatment first. I forget now whether we did a script or whether we did a script equivalent, but we worked out this story, which we both liked very much.

I haven't seen it, but it sounds like it must be film noir.

Well, it was – it was a neo-Hitchcockian piece with a lot of odd stuff in it. Burt and Harold liked it very much, and on the basis of that draft they got Joan Fontaine. And I think Gregg Toland was going to shoot it. Then, of course, it became the old 'tomato soup' story – the one about the two producers who are lost in the desert and they're dying of thirst, and they come across this can of tomato soup. One takes out his knife and opens it and is about to drink it, and the other one says, 'Wait!' And the guy says, 'What is it? What's wrong?' And the other guy says, 'First we piss in it.' [*Laughs.*] In other words, they hired another writer to rewrite the script. And I didn't really much care for what came after. So that was my first experience.

How did you like LA? I remember reading a comment of yours in your book

about how you noticed the flowers there had no scent.
Right. But I've really had very happy experiences in Hollywood, although I never wanted to live there. I only went out there to work – my home was always in New York. LA is an awful place to be unemployed in, much more than most places, because it's a company town. You can't be anonymous there and unemployed – everybody knows what you're doing. On my trips out there, I was always working, getting paid – I was doing something I liked doing. And I had a lot of friends there, you know. Played tennis, that kind of thing.

Do you think it was easier to live through the blacklist here than there?
I never really knew what the situation was like out there, but I would think, simply because of that 'company town' aspect, it was probably easier here. A lot of the writers there who were blacklisted moved to New York – Polonsky, Ring Lardner, Ian Hunter, Waldo Salt. I imagine it was probably better here.

Your memoir about that period recounts the devastating effects of the blacklist on you and your colleagues, but I was also struck by how close-knit and supportive a group you and the other blacklisted writers managed to form – particularly you, Abe Polonsky, and Arnold Manoff.
Looking back on it, I really do feel that that community we formed really enabled us to get through it. And I miss it, I do miss it. I miss that help that everybody gave everyone else. It was very important.

Is that something that evaporated after the blacklist ended?
Yeah, because it was dictated, essentially, by economic necessity. That was the basis of it. We helped each other find jobs – we needed to do it. It was really kind of a socialist framework in a way, and very hard to impose on a capitalist system. And when the blacklist was over and we all went back to work – although we kept up individual friendships – it was back to the whole individual dog-eat-dog Hollywood.

You also edited a newsletter for a while during the period called *Facts About Blacklist*, which, as you described it, allowed you to feel like you were making some kind of effort against this monolithic thing. Can you talk about that a little bit?
I guess in any of those kinds of situations, you are made to feel helpless. And you are constantly having to fight against those feelings of victimization, and impotence, too. There was nothing you could do. You weren't allowed to work in your field. So in putting out *Facts About Blacklist*, however minimal it might be, we felt we were doing something. It was a sporadic four- or six-page sheet, put out primarily by a wonderful writer who had been the head of the Radio Writers Guild, Sam Moore, and myself. All the networks and advertising agencies – which ran a lot of the television in those days – were saying there was no blacklist, so we would collect facts, like that CBS was doing this or BBDO was doing that, in order to prove that they were lying. And we found that people working at the networks or the agencies would help us – they wouldn't want their names used, but

they would feed us information. We published it and gave it away, or dropped it off at various places. We did three or four different issues of it over a year or so, and then it kind of petered out.

You used the term 'guerrilla warfare' in the book to describe your experience writing for *You Are There* – the CBS series in which reporters 'interviewed' historical figures played by actors. Especially when you were writing about the trial of Joan of Arc, or the Salem witch trials.

That was Polonsky's phrase. He said, 'It's guerrilla warfare, it's guerrilla warfare!' *You Are There* was just a happy confluence of people. There was Sidney Lumet directing it, and the producer, Charles Russell, and then Manoff, Polonsky and me. We were all on the same page. And Lumet and Russell were risking much more than we were – they would have been blacklisted and lost their jobs if anyone had figured out we were writing it and using fronts. A year or so ago I ran into Walter Cronkite, who was the narrator of the programme, and I asked him if he knew that blacklisted writers were writing it – I was always curious about what he knew. And he said he didn't know anything the first year. He said he thought it was curious that no writers were ever around on the set or anything. And then, after about the first year, or a number of months anyway, Sidney and Charlie Russell took him out for a drink and told him it was blacklisted people.

It sounds like it was a wilful denial – or avoidance – on the part of nearly everyone in the industry.

The head of dramatic programming at CBS was a Hollywood producer by the name of William Dozier, who was married to Joan Fontaine. Everyone was scared that he would catch on, and worried what he would do if he found out. After the blacklist, when I was working again, I got a letter from him asking me if I was interested in writing something – a project that he had or something like that – and at the end of the letter he had a postscript: 'P.S. Please give my regards to . . .' And he named all the fronts for everybody. So obviously he knew what was going on but didn't say anything. It's a good example of the fact that nobody liked the blacklist, and nobody wanted it except the people who were profiting from it – or the zealots, like Ward Bond. And if people could help without hurting themselves, they were sympathetic.

Didn't Sidney Lumet get you the writing job on your first post-blacklist film, *That Kind of Woman*?

Yes. I was still blacklisted, though the blacklist was beginning to crack – it was right around the time Kirk Douglas had hired Trumbo for *Spartacus*. Carlo Ponti and his partner at the time, Marcello Girosi, had this movie they wanted to do with Sophia Loren. It was her second English-language movie – I think she'd done one before with Cary Grant. It was being shot in New York, and I think they had a script already that they didn't like – it was based on a short story – which I hadn't read. So Sidney, who was going to direct it, suggested me. They didn't know anything about the blacklist, so they hired me. I remember Girosi was kind of nervous about my lack of experience. I had given him, like, the first ten pages, and because I really didn't know much about technique – didn't know what I was doing, basically. I really thought I was going to lose the job. So I spoke to a good friend of mine, a director named Robert Parrish. I said, 'What am I going to do here?' And he said, 'Just put a lot of shots into it. Break it up'. You know, I had just written the scenes. So I went back to it and put in 'Close Shot' here, 'Medium Shot' there, and I gave Girosi back the pages. He was ecstatic: 'You've learned how to write a movie!' [*Laughs.*] Anyway, I wrote that and we shot it, and it was a very happy experience.

Were you on set most of the time?
Yeah, it was a very convivial kind of group. We would break for lunch and bring in the bottles of Soave, and people would drink. Sidney was very brilliant and prided himself, particularly in those days, on working very fast. He worked fast and wore funny hats. I haven't seen the film in a long time, but my friend Jay Cocks called me recently to tell me that he and Scorsese had screened it. They were so excited about it. They kept saying, 'It's *Shopworn Angel*, it's *Shopworn Angel*! It's wonderful!' I don't think it's wonderful, but it was a good experience.

And that led to a three-picture association with Ponti, right?
Ponti and Sophia had a deal with Paramount, so on the basis of *That Kind of Woman*, they were about to sign me to a contract there. I was still finishing up the script for it when I got a call from my agent, Irving Lazar, telling me that Paramount wouldn't sign the contract because there was a subpoena out for me to appear before HUAC. So I said, 'Thank you very much,' and basically went on the lam. I made my way up to Rhode Island and finished the script there, but Paramount wouldn't go through with the deal, so I was back where I started. Actually, United Artists had originally offered me the job of writing *The Magnificent Seven* – Yul Brenner was supposed to direct it and Marty Ritt was supposed to produce it – but I had said 'no' because of the impending Paramount deal. Well, they had hired another writer named Bob Aurthur – Robert Allen Aurthur – and I didn't really know him very well, but he came to Marty and Yul quite spontaneously and said, 'Look, I can work anywhere. I'm getting jobs. I'll step aside if I have to.'

So UA hired me, taking the position that they didn't know anything about any subpoena, and I wrote a first draft of *The Magnificent Seven*. Then I had a meeting with Ponti and my lawyer, a wonderful man named Leonard Boudin, basically to explain my position. Ponti didn't know English very well, so there was an interpreter there, too. My lawyer explained everything – which was that I would not give names; I would be an 'unfriendly witness'. The interpreter translated it for Carlo, and then there was a big long stream of Italian from him. When he was finished, the interpreter turned to us and said, 'Mr Ponti would like to know who has to be fixed and for how much?' He kept throwing up his hands and saying, 'It's politics, it's politics!' It was all bullshit to him. Making movies, that was important, but politics, you pay somebody off and you go on with your business. [*Laughs.*] Anyway, I got a call shortly after that from Paramount, when they found out that UA was willing to hire me, and after a meeting with the head of the studio, they hired me to write *Heller in Pink Tights*.

That's a terrific film.
It's fun. It has great style.

You were working for George Cukor on that one?
Cukor was going to direct it. Dudley Nichols had already been hired, and had written a treatment or outline of some kind, but he was dying, unfortunately – he couldn't do any more, and Ponti called me on it. And I ended up essentially writing the entire thing during production, a day ahead of shooting.

The role of Tom Healy, the flamboyant leader of the theatre troupe, was an unusual one for Anthony Quinn.
It's interesting, Cukor at first didn't want Quinn. He wanted someone much lighter. I remember he mentioned this young British actor he liked a lot who nobody had heard of – Roger Moore – but Ponti and Girosi kept saying no, they needed someone 'very masculine' to stand up to Sophia. So they hired Tony, who was a pain in the ass through the whole thing. And he felt a little bit like a fish out of water in that part – he wasn't quite secure in it, really. And Sophia's English was still quite shaky. But Cukor was wonderful, he was just wonderful. He wanted to do a Western because he was interested in the style. And he hired George Hoynigen Huene to work on the colour and the look of it, and Gene Allen as art director. I think George had found Gene on *A Star is Born* – he'd been an LA cop, and he looked like an LA cop – but he had this wonderful sensibility and talent. The three of them made a very odd but really quite wonderful combination. Nobody paid too much attention to the story – it wasn't that great – but the whole style of it I loved. That sequence when the Indians raid the troupe's caravan and try on all of their theatre costumes is just great. Unfortunately, what happened was that Paramount didn't know what to do with the picture when they saw it.

Because it didn't comfortably fit into the Western genre?
Exactly. So they made me write and George direct a couple of action sequences that he wasn't happy with and didn't care about particularly. When it was finally released, it got quite good notices, but again, the studio didn't know how to market it. But anyway, I loved it, and I liked Cukor very, very much.

What did you do after that?
I went and spent seven miserable weeks in Vienna working on this movie based on the Molnar play, *Olympia*. I took my name off the picture, which was called *A Breath of Scandal*. I think Ring Lardner had worked on the script previous to me. I remember that every ten minutes Girosi would come in and say to me, 'You have to put in a Swedish actress here' or 'You have to put in an Italian actress

there' and I would say, 'This is Vienna in 1890 – what are you talking about?!' He'd say, 'Never mind, we can get six hundred thousand lire from Italy if we use the Italian actress.' They were putting the picture together that way. Michael Curtiz came in to direct it, and he was senile, I think, by that time, so Vittorio De Sica, who was actually in it, was kind of directing behind his back.

Were you working with either Curtiz or De Sica on rewrites?
No, I had done pretty much what I had done. De Sica had to be paid in cash at the end of every day so he could go gamble – it was a mess, it was really a mess. [*Laughs.*] But while I was there, Cukor came over to direct a movie about Franz Lizst called *Song Without End*. Charlie Vidor, who was supposed to do it, had died, and Cukor, as a favour, had promised the family he would take over and direct it. He arrived in Vienna just as I was about to leave, and asked me to read the script. He had Dirk Bogarde playing Lizst, and after I read it I said to him, 'Don't touch the script, but fire Dirk Bogarde and get Sid Caesar.' He said, 'No, come on, will you work on it? Just for two weeks?' And I said, 'There's nothing to be done – it's just too bad,' and I flew back to Paris. Then he sent Charlie Feldman, who was the producer – mainly because his mistress, Capucine, was in it – to Paris after me, and for really the only time in my life, I was wooed. He found out where I was, took me out to dinner every night, offered me the two-week gig at twice my normal salary, promised other fabulous jobs afterwards. It's so fascinating, because ninety-nine per cent of you is laughing at it, but one per cent is saying, 'Who knows?. . .'

I finally agreed to go back and do the two weeks. I met with Cukor, and we decided to start working on the material he was going to shoot first. There was a scene between Lizst and Wagner, and I rewrote it and took it back to Cukor. He read it and said, 'It's not right.' And I said, 'I know it's not right, but is it better? It's better, isn't it?' 'Yeah, it's better, but it's not right.' And for two weeks I worked on that one scene – he would not let it go until he felt it was 'right'. I kept saying to him, 'We've got to move on . . .' So there's one decently written scene between Dirk Bogarde and Lyndon Brook in this terrible, terrible movie. The promised jobs, of course, never materialized.

You also worked with Cukor on Marilyn Monroe's last film, didn't you?
Later on, yes. But before that, I went back to Paris and got a job working for Anatole Litvak, who wanted to do a picture about corruption in Italy. He liked to play gin rummy, he liked to gamble, and he didn't like to work particularly. He took me on a tour. I remember we went to the Venice Film Festival, where we were supposed to be 'working'. He would sleep in the morning and I would get up and tool around. Then I would meet him for lunch, and then afterwards he would have to play gin rummy with Willie Wyler and Sam Spiegel and that crowd. In the evenings he had to go to the casino. We stopped in Rome for a couple of days, and Fellini was shooting *La Dolce Vita*. He invited Litvak and me to see some scenes from it that he had started to cut together. After seeing them, I said to Lit-

vak, 'Let's pick another subject to do, because we are never going to get anywhere near this.' I did write the script, but nothing really happened to it. We had a big fight over something, and I got very upset and angry and I told him to go fuck himself, and I don't think anybody – especially not a writer – had ever spoken to him like that. I remember he looked at me and sputtered, 'Go fuck yourself *yourself!*' [*Laughs.*]

It was after that that the Monroe movie – *Something's Got to Give* – happened. And I went out to LA to work on that. They were getting ready to shoot it when I arrived. But there again, I did very little, because not long after I started writing it the whole thing blew up. But Cukor was very good with Monroe.

I'm assuming at this point she was probably not in very good shape.
It was interesting, because the First Assistant had worked with her before – he was an old Hollywood hand. And I'll never forget the first day she came in – everyone was kissing and hugging, and she was in great form. When she left at the end of the day, he said to me, 'She won't be back tomorrow.' And I said, 'What are you talking about? She's up and she's fine.' And he said, 'I'm telling you, she won't be here tomorrow.' And she wasn't. He knew her well, and could see the signs. But as I said, Cukor was very good with her. And the other one who was very professional on it was Dean Martin – he was always there on time, and he was always patient with her, too. She was out of control, or in control, depending on how you want to look at it.

Did you ever work directly with Monroe on any rewrites?
At one point George asked if I would go and meet with her on some scene. And I went out to her house and she was very nice, very sweet. She showed me around, and was very proud of everything. But she was also very shrewd about the scene – about herself in the scene – and that was what interested me. She would refer to herself in the third person: 'No, Monroe wouldn't do that, really.' It was shortly before she died. Soon after that she stopped showing up at the set – things got out of hand. The money was piling up, and they just finally pulled the plug on the picture.

You have a writing credit on the 1961 Martin Ritt film *Paris Blues,* that starred Newman, Woodward and Poitier.
I had very little to do with that. I did about a month's work on it, but very little. Mostly dialogue stuff and some internal writing. I was surprised when I got a credit on it because I really didn't think I deserved one.

And that was due to your association with Martin Ritt?
Yeah, that was the whole thing. Marty called me and asked if would I do some work on it that he wanted done.

How did *Fail-Safe* come about?
It was a producer thing. Max Youngstein at UA, whom I knew socially and also through *The Magnificent Seven,* called me. He had gotten the rights to the book and

asked me to do it. Whether he had already approached Sidney Lumet yet, I really don't remember. Anyway, I was delighted. And I wrote the script in three weeks in the Henry Hudson Hotel on a diet of tuna fish sandwiches and black-and-white milkshakes. I remember that very well; I just hunkered down in the hotel. UA paid for a room – something like thirteen dollars a week – and I wrote it. It was really just about organizing the material. And it was a very good picture for Sidney. He had that kind of energy and drive, and he was also so good with actors.

Wasn't there an issue with Kubrick, whose similarly themed *Dr Strangelove* came out at around the same time?
There was a lawsuit. We were scheduled to come out first, and Kubrick didn't like that; he wanted *Strangelove* to come out first. So I don't know who the hell he sued, whether it was UA or Max or Columbia or something, but he claimed that the book *Fail-Safe* was plagiarized from the short story he had based *Strangelove* on. It was a nuisance suit, but it scared Columbia enough so that Columbia bought the rights to the book from Max, or whoever it was, and let *Strangelove* come out first. And it's too bad, because actually they hurt us a lot, and we wouldn't have hurt them. You can do a satire after you have the straight one, but you can't do it the other way.

In the film, I was struck by the conversation at the end between the American general and the Soviet general, when they start sharing their impressions of London, finding a commonality in the midst of this mounting crisis.
That's not in the novel.

It reminded me of a passage from your book, where you mention the phone call between you and the FBI agent who's been following you around for months, and the two of you have a fairly intimate discussion about how similar your lives are. Was that something you drew on for this?
No, not really, but I love that moment. You know, they're doing *Fail-Safe* again for TV. Stephen Frears is directing, and George Clooney is producing and starring. But unfortunately, CBS or Clooney or whoever it was who originated this whole thing couldn't get the rights to the script from Columbia, but they were able to get the rights to the book, which were available again. So in doing the script again, I could use what I had taken from the book, but I couldn't use what I had invented – like that moment between them. I had to find something else. And it works so well, that moment there. But I had to bring in a whole other kind of conversation for that.

The Train, I believe, was the only movie you worked on with Arthur Penn. Wasn't he taken off the picture by Burt Lancaster?
Burt fired him after the first day of shooting, which seemed to me totally unjustified, absolutely unjustified. There was no basis for it. He didn't like Arthur for some reason. I just got a new biography of Lancaster, and of course the first thing

you do is look up your own name in the index and see what they said about you. [*Laughs.*] But what the author says about *The Train* was that Lancaster had not had a commercial success with his last several pictures, and he wanted something very commercial. I think he felt that Arthur wanted something different, which is true, because what he and I were trying to do there was tell a story, really, about the ass-end of the war – when everybody was tired and crippled and beaten down.

I remember the first scene that Arthur shot with Burt. It was with him and Michel Simon, a French actor, and it was quite an emotional moment between them in the cab of the locomotive. Arthur was directing Burt, and Burt was resisting him. And finally Burt turned around and said, 'Here, I'll give it the grin.' He was making it plain that he wasn't going to do what Arthur wanted, wasn't going to give it any real or true emotion – just his trademark grin. The next day was a holiday, and I was home having dinner that night with Alexandre Trauner, a marvellous set designer, when I got the call from Lancaster saying that Arthur had been fired and John Frankenheimer was taking his place. And I'll never forget what Burt said about John: 'He's a bit of a whore, but he'll do what I want.' Then he told me he'd like me to stay on and finish the script, and I said, 'No thanks.' And that was it. So there's very little, if anything, of mine in the film.

But Burt was an interesting man. I liked him. During that period that I was doing *Kiss the Blood Off My Hands*, I didn't have a car. I was staying in an apartment someone had loaned me in Beverly Hills, and Burt would pick me up and drive me to the studio – he was shooting *All My Sons*, I think. We'd talk – he was very anxious to learn. He would ask me questions about books or art or what music to listen to.

It seems that you were travelling back and forth between LA and New York quite a bit in the sixties.
It all depended on the picture. With Sidney Lumet, I always worked in New York. But some of the other directors, like Michael Ritchie and Cukor, were in LA.

Did you ever feel like you weren't getting offers on things because you weren't living out there?
It's easy to say that. I do think my career was hurt by being here in those days. Unless you were a firmly established writer with a lot of hits and stuff like that, executives would want you in their office in ten minutes. So it's not really worth it to them to book the flight, pay your airfare and bring you out – it would have to be for a particular reason. Although, with Marty Ritt I worked out there a lot. He had clout. If a director of his stature wanted you out there, you went out. But yeah, I think I probably would have gotten more work if I'd lived there.

Speaking of Ritt, can you talk a bit about *The Molly Maguires*? How did you get involved with the project? You've got a producing credit on the film.
I first read about those militant Pennsylvania coal miners in college, and I remember thinking, 'Wow, this would make a great movie.' I forget how the subject came

up with Marty, but I brought it to him and he set it up at Paramount, with the usual proviso: 'Get some stars and we'll do it.' We flew to the south of Spain, where Sean Connery was doing a Western, and he liked the idea and agreed to do it – although I think he would have done anything to get away from the James Bond stuff. And then we searched around for an actor to play the Pinkerton detective who infiltrates the gang. We went to Albert Finney, who would have been very good, but he didn't want to do it, and we finally settled on Richard Harris. The only other thing Paramount insisted on was a love story, which I had not thought of having originally, so it became a question of writing in a love story that was thematic in some sense.

It was a very happy experience, because it was something we both felt very strongly about, and loved doing. But when the picture came out, it got mixed reviews. Ordinarily, the studio would have let it sit for a while to see if it could find its audience, but around the same time they had had four or five big-budget movies that had flopped – *On a Clear Day*, Harold Robbins' *The Adventurers*, *Paint Your Wagon*. A big budget in those days was around ten million. And in a corporate decision, they just dumped them all to save on prints and advertising and whatever else.

I'm surprised that the film didn't get any Oscar nominations. Harris and Connery were both fantastic.
They were wonderful, but it didn't. The Academy very rarely nominates something that doesn't make money. It's too bad; it never really got its shot.

The subject matter – capital exploiting labour, and labour's attempts to fight back – obviously struck a chord with both you and Ritt. There was also a lot of blacklist subtext in the film – particularly the whole idea of an informer who befriends and gains the trust of the people he will eventually betray.
Right – the betrayal, and the choices one has to make in that kind of situation. I screened that movie for a bunch of Black Panthers, figuring this was their kind of movie – I was sure they were going to love it. They hated it.

Why?
They said to me, 'We're getting shot at, we're getting killed, the cops are kicking the shit out of us. Why do we have to go to movies to see it done again?' It was very interesting. They said they didn't need to see a bunch of people fighting for what they believe in only to get hanged at the end.

That reminds me of a quote of yours from some years back: 'In certain pictures of mine, the protagonists go to jail at the end or get hanged or suffer some sort of unpleasant fate, because it's their struggle that counts. What interests me most is a person who will fight, even if reluctantly, someone who will ultimately take a stand.'
It is the kind of theme that interests me most: somebody who, at the end, makes a stand that goes against his better judgement or his self-interest – the kind of character Woody played in *The Front*. And that theme is very connected to the

blacklist experience. Because what they were saying to you all the time – and it's essentially what they say to you in Hollywood, too – was, 'What's your bottom line? How far can we push you?' And that seems to me a great subject to deal with.

You were good friends with Martin Ritt for many years; can you talk about your relationship with him a little bit?
I revered Marty as well as loved him. He was an extraordinarily moral man – he would not do anything that he didn't feel in some way had a moral component to it. We'd argue a lot, and there was an 'evenness' about his directing that I some-times didn't like, but he was a wonderful man – somebody once said about him that he had 'made integrity into a style'. And it really does fit him. We were always thinking of projects. We wanted to do one in particular about labour unions, but we couldn't really get anyone interested – at least not in the way we wanted to do it. We were always thinking about improbable kinds of stories to tell.

Was *The Front* hard to sell?
We had always wanted to do a movie about the blacklist and our experience of it, and the idea was basically to tell it straight. We couldn't get anyone interested at all in that. But then we came up with the idea of doing it sideways, as a comedy. We went to David Begelman, who was the head of Columbia at that point, and who had been our agent at one time. He was perverse enough to go for something like this, and he commissioned a script. I did a first draft, and they liked it, and as usual, the studio said, 'We need a star.' They mentioned Redford, Newman, Jack Nicholson. I said, 'That's not the type we were thinking of.' But we couldn't come up with anybody. Then one day, Marty and I were playing tennis and he said, 'What about that kid?' I said, 'What kid?' He couldn't think of the name: 'That funny kid.' We went back and forth and finally I realized he was talking about Woody Allen. I thought it was a great idea. Begelman said he would do it with him, and we sent it to Woody, and he agreed. And that got it made. We cast it with as many ex-blacklisted people as we could.

Having read your book, I was shocked to realize how much of what happens to Zero Mostel's character in the film actually happened to him during the black-list.
That incident in the hotel in the Catskills, where they cut his pay, was a true inci-dent. I drove him up there. He needed the rent money – it was down to that – and the hotel guy cut his fee in half. But he went onstage and he did his show. And he was in such a rage. He went before this big audience – it must have been 1,200 people – and he cursed them, screamed at them in Yiddish. And the more he did it, the more they liked it, the more they laughed. They couldn't get enough of him. He couldn't get the rage out. Finally, after the show, he went off and drank most of a bottle of whiskey. I put him to bed and we got up the next morning and came home.

Making *The Front* must have been cathartic for all of you.
Well, it was cathartic, and, in a way, there was also this kind of triumphant feeling: 'Fuck you, we're still here. We're still working.' It was a very nice shoot. But that moment with Zero, I'll never forget it. It was too terrifying for him to do again in the film – I don't know if he could have recreated the intensity and the rage that was in him. It was very tough.

After *The Front*, you wrote the screenplay for *Semi-Tough*, which was directed by Michael Ritchie. How did that come about?
Well, Michael had a script by Ring Lardner which he didn't like for whatever reason – I don't know, I never read it. He called and asked me if I would do another draft. And I called Ring, as a matter of fact, and asked him what was going on, and he said he was out of it. So we just threw the novel out – it had no story, really. We kept the names of the characters and the fact that they're headed for the Super Bowl, and we really just ended up doing a satire on the consciousness-raising movement that was going on – EST and pyramid power, all that kind of stuff. And we had a great time. I like that movie, I think it's fun. And Reynolds was very good. He was really a first-class comedian – a leading-man comedian, like Cary Grant.

And was Ritchie also open to you being involved during production?
Oh, yeah. I've been very lucky with most of the directors I've worked for. If they wanted changes, they would call me, or I would go down to the set if I could. In the case of *Semi-Tough*, I went down to Dallas when they were shooting there, and went down to Florida when they shot in the Orange Bowl. But I'm lucky, as I say, because I didn't have directors or, for that matter, stars who wanted to rewrite it themselves.

I'm assuming that in the sixties and seventies there were fewer situations with actors coming in with their own script doctors . . .
No, it was not out-of-hand the way it is now, where it's taken for granted that there will be four or five writers on a movie. It wasn't like that at all then. I felt, rightly or wrongly, that if I wrote a script, that would be the script that would be shot, along with whatever changes I made along the way.

Why do you think that's changed so drastically?
I don't know. I think it reflects the whole change in the culture – the whole kind of corporate attitude that you have now. Whatever else you might say about the Harry Cohns, the Zanucks, or those kind of guys, they really cared about movies in their own crazy, despotic way. You don't get the feeling now that anyone gives a shit, essentially.

I have a director friend who just recently got a job, and his agent called and said, 'What writer are you bringing on?' And he said, 'What do you mean? I like the script, and if there's any work to do I'll deal with the original writer.' And the agent said, 'No, the studio won't respect you unless you bring your own writer.'

Do you do a lot of script doctoring, or rewriting?

I did a lot in the past. I haven't been doing as much lately. I remember one experience along those lines I had with Marty Ritt – I rewrote a script called *The Electric Horseman* for Ray Stark. Marty was going to direct it, and it was going to be for Steve McQueen originally. But then McQueen got lung cancer, and Stark called and said, 'Redford is interested in doing it, would you meet with him?' He was here in New York at the time, and Marty flew in, and we all had a script meeting. Redford had certain criticisms – certain notes – but he was generally positive about it. Afterward, Marty and I left his office and went to see Sam Cohn, our agent. We were very pleased and told him what had happened, and Sam said, 'I'll tell you what's going to happen. You're out, the two of you.' And we said, 'What are you talking about? We just had this nice meeting . . .' He said, 'Redford will hire Sydney Pollack to direct it and David Rayfiel or Alvin Sargent to rewrite it. That's what's going to happen.' And that's exactly what happened – he wanted his people to do it.

Did the film with Redford resemble anything you had written?

I remember I had written a scene which McQueen would have done very well, where the protagonist, who was kind of a bum, is visited by his ex-wife. She wants him to sign over to her a piece of property that they jointly own. And he says he'll think about it – he doesn't do it right away. That night, he comes to visit her in her motel room. He holds up the piece of paper, smiling. She's so thrilled she grabs him and they fuck on the floor. When they finish fucking, she rolls over and looks at the paper, and says, 'You didn't sign it,' and he says, 'No, I didn't,' and walks out. [*Laughs.*] That's a scene that Redford would never play in a million years. And in the current thing, Valerie Perrine comes to see him in Vegas and he signs the paper – he's this nice guy.

Is that a vanity issue, do you think?

I think it's an image issue, really, about what he sees himself as. And from his point of view, what succeeds for him – what the audience wants to see him as. McQueen saw himself as much rougher, much harder-edged. Not so much 'macho', but mean – he would let himself be mean.

How did you get involved with *Yanks*? Had you worked with John Schlesinger on anything else?

No, that was the only thing we worked on together. He reminded me a lot of Cukor, really, in the sense that he was wonderful on individual scenes, in the texture he would give to them. I enjoyed working with him very much. That picture, which I like, is really all texture. That's what makes it. The story is a soap opera story. But I find the film very moving every time I see it. And it all comes from John.

The screenplay is credited to you and Colin Welland.

The original script was written by Colin Welland – it was based on his experiences when he was a little kid. He had worked for many years on it, and it was not easy to have an American writer come in and start rewriting it.

It's weirdly appropriate for the story, though, which is centred on this culture clash between the Americans soldiers in World War II and their interactions with English civilians.

Well, I wrote the American stuff, really. The basic structure is Colin's, and the English characters are his. And I don't know if I would have handled it as graciously as he did, but we became friends and hung out together during the shoot.

There's an element to that film which I've noticed recurs in many of your screenplays – women characters often tend to be the conscience of the male characters, like Samantha Eggar in *The Molly Maguires*. It's not just that the women are 'strong', which I think might be a more typical way to do it; it's that they represent a potential that the men haven't yet reached. In *Yanks*, Lisa Eichorn's character is constantly asking Richard Gere's character to 'do better'.

Well, as I said about *The Molly Maguires*, when I do a love story, I really try to relate the relationship – or the woman's role – to the theme of the film. And that usually means that the female characters turn out to be carrying the conscience of the film. And it isn't just a matter of strength – it's a moral strength that Samantha Eggar's character has, to a great extent. I hadn't thought about it consciously, but it's true – I tend to look at the women that way.

From my understanding, you've only ever directed one feature film – the 1980 remake of *Little Miss Marker*.

I never really had a fire in my belly about directing, but at one point I thought I should try it. Jennings Lang, a producer, had asked me to write the remake of that film, and I said, 'I'll write it if I can direct it.' He said, 'Sure. I've started a lot of directors.' He was an extremely nice man. I remember I called Marty Ritt, and he said, 'Don't do it. That's the kind of movie that should be done by either someone who's twenty-two years old and just starting, or someone who's done fifty movies.' I didn't listen to him, and I should have, really, because I wrote a nice script – mild, but nice – but it required a style to pull it off that I just didn't have.

I thought I would balance Walter Matthau off with Julie Andrews, and that didn't work at all – there was negative chemistry there between them. And then I hired Tony Curtis – who I like as an actor very much – for a part that should have been played by Jack Palance or somebody like that. Also, Tony at that time was heavily into coke, and that became a problem. I remember one time we were shooting a pretty long one-take scene and he just couldn't remember his lines. Finally, he excused himself and went to his camper for a few minutes. When he came back, he knew all the words, except not in their proper order. [*Laughs.*] And I had a little girl playing the Shirley Temple part who had the most beautiful face, and I cast her off the face, but then discovered there was nothing beyond.

Can you give me a idea of how often you've felt that the actor who ended up playing a role you'd written had been perfectly cast?
I was very pleased with the casting of *The Molly Maguires*. I really, really, really thought that was great casting. And I thought Woody did the best acting of his career in *The Front*. The casting of *Yanks* was very good, although I didn't like William Devane in it. He's a heavy.

He's got that vaguely malicious smile.
He's the smiler with the knife. But John had directed him in *Marathon Man* and liked him, and Devane really went after this part – he really wanted it very much. I thought it needed a young Fonda – that's the kind of actor that part was for. In the television movie I wrote, *Miss Evers' Boys*, I thought that Alfre Woodard was beyond great acting, she was extraordinary.

***Miss Evers' Boys* was about the Tuskegee Experiments in Alabama, where the government purported to offer treatment to a group of Black men with syphilis, when in fact they were giving them placebos so they could study the course of the disease. You're obviously still managing to write projects with a social conscience.**
That's the side of the street I work.

You've used the Scylla and Charybdis analogy to characterize the struggle you're often faced with – to do work that is informed by your political convictions, but to not go so 'far' as to scare off financers or alienate audiences.
I work in a commercial medium – that's what I chose to do and that's what I've always done – and it's a balancing act. You're always testing to see how far can you go, trying to push it as much as you can. But I have to say, I don't think so much of the audience; it's more of a question of how I'm going to get it made. And when you think that *The Molly Maguires* cost ten million in 1970 – it would cost at least seventy today. I just wrote an original script for an English company, a movie that takes place in Germany in 1942. It's based on fact – Goebbels, who, of course, was in charge of propaganda, decided that he would spice things up by having a jazz band play on his radio programme. But jazz was forbidden in Germany, so he would beam it directly to American and English troops. That's the basic subject. Anyway, it's a question now of where do Michael Ritchie – who's going to direct it – and I go with it, how do we raise the money, who do we find to play in it. If you get so-and-so, you'll get this amount of money, and if you get so-and-so, you'll get this much more. There's an American character in it, for example, and we were talking about how we've got to boost up this part because we want to get an American actor with a half-assed name for it. So you're up against that. But I don't generally think about what's going to please the audience.

You once said your goal as a writer was to make 'audiences go away dissatisfied in a satisfied way'. Can you elaborate on that?

This sounds rather grand, but I am interested in affecting people – in changing people. I want what I write to have an effect on them, and I want to present the world to them in a truthful, dramatic way – to show them the conflicts. I want them to go away feeling gratified that they've had an experience that has filled them with pleasure, but there should be a little bit of a burr under the saddle. That happens, I think, in all my movies. You know, *The Front* ends with Woody Allen going off to jail, and it's funny in a way, but I hope an audience goes away thinking 'What's going to happen to him there?' The same thing for the ending of *The Molly Maguires*. These guys get hanged at the end, and the man who caused that is going to become very successful because of it. What's going on there? You know, you come away from *Death of a Salesman* very shaken, very moved, but wow, is that enormously satisfying.

Is there any particular subject you haven't yet treated that you'd like to?
I don't know, there's a subject I've toyed with that revolves around the Palmer Raids after the First World War, in New York. And I just took an option on a novel that I think would make a very good small movie that I'd like to write and direct if I can.

Can I ask how old you are?
Eighty.

What do you attribute the longevity of your career to?
I don't know; I really don't know. Right now, I've lucked into a relationship with HBO, which has been a very happy and fruitful one for me. I don't have too much of a career in feature films at the moment. Maybe it's because it's a business run mostly by and for fifteen-year-olds. [*Laughs.*] Although maybe that's why I get work – they think I'm in my second childhood.

Do you think your experience during the blacklist somehow contributed to your resilience?
I survived.

But you did more than survive. You never named names, you managed to somehow find work —
Well, I survived on my own terms, I suppose.

Just to wrap up, how do you think New York has affected your work and your life?
It's my town. It's the one place I can come in the world and know I'm home. I feed off of it – I love the anonymity of it when I step out of the house or I get on a bus or I get in the subway. And the heterogeneity of it, and the energy. It's gotten more crowded, it's gotten dirtier – it's gotten a lot of other stuff – but I can't see myself disconnected from it. I love travelling, and I can imagine at this stage of my life, if I could afford it, living maybe three, four months in Europe and then back here – just like I lived in Los Angeles happily for months. But I have to keep my feet on the ground here. That's why the name of my company is Antaeus.

Karyn Kusama

Karyn Kusama's first feature, *Girlfight*, won both the Grand Jury Prize and the Director's Prize at the 2000 Sundance Film Festival. It was also selected for the Directors' Fortnight at Cannes, where it won the *Prix de la Jeunesse*.

Tod Lippy: When did you come to New York?
Karyn Kusama: I came here when I was eighteen to go to NYU Film School.

What was NYU like?
It was a mixed blessing, because it's such a huge school. I didn't realize how big it was going to be and how unfocused, frankly; how so many students would be at the undergraduate level. I thought everyone who arrived at the school was going to feel very certain about wanting to be a film-maker. I have no problem with people changing their minds midstream and going on to become dentists, [*laughs*] but they take up a little too much class space, in my opinion. But at the same time, I did have a couple of really key teacher/mentors who understood me and encouraged me. I think at any big private university, you really have to look for that support, because there is a huge financial incentive to just keep churning out the students. So I found that I had to aggressively seek out the breaks, the teachers, the students that I could connect with, and be very cut-throat, in a way, about getting what I wanted out of this very expensive education. That said, I think I did.

The other thing that struck me about the students there was how, even at the time – over twelve years ago – there was such an interest in achieving a certain level of status or celebrity or wealth. That just blew my mind. I was surprised at how many people wanted to make movies like other movies, had favourite movies that they wanted to make again for themselves. There was a real resistance – and I think this is reflected in the larger world – to your own ideas and your own expressive power. People were very afraid to be personal. And it strikes me that the film-making that we all grow up on as powerful film-making comes out of some deeply personal place.

Was the work you were doing more personal?
It was, and I felt that I kept having to legitimize my odd little movies that were very influenced by experimental film and documentaries – I think you get a kind of weird fighter spirit after doing that over and over.

What kind of films were you looking to for inspiration?
Well, I had taken a really formative class early on in school called 'Underground Film', which I believe was sort of a one-off that year. It was taught by J. Hoberman, and I believe it was the first class he ever taught, so he was really in this zone of, 'I'm just going to show you work you're not going to see in the rest of the school.' So we saw stuff by Jonas Mekas, we saw Joseph Cornell movies, of course Stan Brakhage and Kenneth Anger and Jack Smith and some Warhol movies. It was a really great thing because it made this progression all the way through to

George Romero and John Waters and David Lynch. What was largely absent was work by women, but there were some films by Beth B. and Vivienne Dick, who I thought was really incredible. Of course, some of the kids in my class practically spat at the screen – they had no patience for most of it.

And then there was a documentary class taught by George Stoney. I saw some great Michael Roemer films, and other films by a couple of women. I hadn't seen documentaries like that. I'd always thought of them as this sort of PBS, rarefied, factoid world, and the class opened my mind to what documentaries essentially do when they're good, which is that they find the story at the same time the audience does. So that's what I've been trying to make my film-making do on some level. It's never been a mandate, but it's been an interest of mine. So I was very lucky to see those movies.

Were the films you made for school documentaries?
One was a documentary that I shot on film that was in that 'personal documentary' realm, just about all of these fresh, raw friendships that I had developed over two years, and how some of them felt very stable, and some of them felt extremely unstable and a bit unhealthy. I look back on it now and I can't believe I made it because I just filmed my friends and then put in this voiceover that dissected the relationships. I was really working in the unconscious. I didn't understand the power of the medium, which was a good thing, I think, but sometimes you just unearth stuff you shouldn't really unearth. One girl wept in class after I showed it and I thought, 'Wow, I guess it meant something', but then somebody else said, 'How could you do that to people in your life?' And I was just like, 'I don't know, it didn't occur to me . . .'

That was my first thesis film, and then my second one was a much more narrative film, but it was part of an experimental narrative workshop which I had taken with this teacher named Pat Cooper, who really encouraged us to find the narrative logic of our expressive realms. So that even if you're kind of going into a dream logic, make it somehow resonate on a plain emotional level. If I hadn't learned some of those formative lessons, I wouldn't even be able to write or explore anything. So here I am bashing NYU, and as I keep talking I realize that I got a lot out of it.

Were you seeing many films on your own at the time?
Oh, yeah. When I first moved here, the Thalia Soho was still a functioning rep theatre. Actually, I had always gone to a lot of movies as a child, often by myself. There was a great theatre a lot like the Thalia in St Louis, where I grew up. I remember one weekend my parents dropped me off at eleven in the morning and picked me up at around six, because there was a triple feature of *Splendor in the Grass*, *McCabe and Mrs Miller* and *The Parallax View*. It was like a Warren Beatty weekend, and I went for the whole stretch of it. In retrospect, the best thing about it to me was not understanding a lot of it – being too young to really comprehend themes.

Intuiting that there was something there you weren't getting now, but would get at some point?
Exactly. It's like the Surrealists making a point to walk into a movie halfway through – once the plot made any sense they would get up and leave. That's probably how I felt the whole time that I was sitting and watching these movies, because they were simply too mature for me then, but they made impacts in more abstract ways – like single images. I think of seeing Warren Beatty alone in the snow in *McCabe and Mrs Miller*, not understanding the scope of the story at all. Or I just think of how physically dark *The Parallax View* was, how hard to see it was.

And when I got here, New York was great because there was still that excitement around older movies, almost a sense of preserving movies in some way. It's been really interesting to see how those theatres disappeared – were just kind of decimated – and now are rising to the surface again. But I think it's still going to be a struggle. It's weird to me to think that a little town like St Louis had theatres like that and now doesn't have any – not one. Which is sad, because it's our last link to being educated in a way.

And VHSs or DVDs are never the same.
I know. I just recently learned the difference between alpha and beta waves, and I was so shocked that alpha waves, which come out of film, sort of trigger the active part of your brain – I don't really know the science of it. Beta waves are what come off a TV screen or off a video projection. And beta has the opposite effect, it triggers into your passive brain. That's scary, because think of how many people decide on the Academy Awards watching those goddamn Academy screeners. [*Laughs.*] Or just think of how few people who make decisions about who gets money to make movies even watch them on the big screen.

Why did you decide to stay in New York after you graduated?
I think street life is a really key element to living. The first moment I set foot on New York City pavement, I was like, 'OK, I'm home, I know what's going on with the world because I'm being faced with difference.' It's easy to be lulled by enclosure and isolation in the suburbs or in areas or cities where there's so much segregation. That's the thing about St Louis – it's so segregated. I mean, there were kids bussed into my school from the city, and it was like, 'OK, I know Black people exist, but why don't I ever see them in my neighbourhood?' That shit drove me crazy.

It's such a miracle to me that New York runs as well as it does. I'm always amazed that people don't open fire on each other or kill each other with butter knives. I think it's because there's a lot of generosity in people here, and in a funny way, despite the complaints – many true – that it's a hard city to live in, I think people here ultimately are trying to work together. They're really interacting. I was just thinking about all of this, because I recently had a trip out to LA for the first time in maybe six years, having to do with the sale of the movie, meeting some new people and all of that. And I was so stunned by how much time I spent in a car; how much time I spent alone, with no ability to reach beyond the confines of the vehicle. It started to depress me. And I know there's a secret to it – you should only be driving when there's no traffic, and of course I was driving at the worst times of day and all that stuff, but I couldn't believe how bad it was, that there's just constant traffic. New York is full of traffic, too, but it's a constant traffic of energy, and that energy moves.

How did you become an assistant for John Sayles? Is that a job you took right after film school?
It was a while after, because I had gone into film right after school, editing and working mostly in documentary films, and actually meeting interesting people, but never really finding a sort of 'mentor' – you know, a person who could give me a real clear sense of what the various avenues of the industry were. And I was also writing a screenplay with a partner who died midway through. That was kind of a devastating experience, and I just started to feel like, you know, 'This whole industry is bullshit.' I was feeling very, very cynical, so I left it altogether to take care of kids and do work painting houses – getting back into the life that isn't film.

I was looking after some kids whose parents worked with John, and I met his assistant, Martha Griffin – who is now my producer. She was leaving the position and thought I might be a good match for John. We hooked up and I met with him and got the job. I spent almost three years working for him, and it was a very formative, very enriching time. I'm still marvelling at how different his way of working is from so many film-makers, at least in the US. There's no rush on his part to work with the 'status symbols' of this industry, and even though we have entirely different aesthetics, and sometimes very different concerns, I'm so impressed by his intentions and his execution and the way he works.

What do you mean by his 'intentions'?
He's not looking to manipulate a place for himself in the industry. He just exists and wants to continue to exist as a film-maker. Maybe it's because I'm younger, but I'm a bit more self-conscious, perhaps, about where I stand or where I might stand someday. I hope soon that I just don't care. But it's hard not to care, especially when you admire other film-makers who have these bodies of work that stand up to time. That's a really huge achievement, and I feel like there has to be some kind of cunning involved. I don't think you can be this sort of *naïf* wandering through your own career – I actually think you have to fight very hard. So maybe it's just that John is so humble about his fight.

What kind of work did you do for him?
I was in the office a lot, initially, taking care of the minutiae – the bills and the roof caving in and all those little things that sometimes he wasn't even physically in town to deal with. After a while, I think, he started to share a little bit more of the decision-making with me. He's always working on scripts that he was helping

to rewrite or that he was writing for other companies – Hollywood stuff. And then he was always researching for his own next project. So there was always a dual mission. There were the relationships with the James Camerons and the Rob Reiners and the Ron Howards – this whole Byzantine world of phone calls and hierarchies and all that sort of stuff in the Hollywood system – and then there was the relationship with the New York Public Library and seeking out information and delving into a topic. Being involved in both was a really great thing for me, because I saw there is quite certainly more than one way to make movies. And one way just requires a lot of compromise, every step of the way. If I had to work with a big star, the little curmudgeon in me would say, 'It's not a good thing that I have to cast this person. Who cares if they like the film, I don't like them!' I have that kind of bristling thing towards it. So it was very interesting to see that process and then to see John working so organically in another direction towards his own work. He's so story-oriented in terms of making choices. One of the things he encouraged in me while making *Girlfight* was to make choices that were really relevant in that regard – which really opened up the story and drove it. That's not really my strong point, so that was great.

When did you first come up with the idea for *Girlfight*?
It's a funny story. I had been boxing myself, and I sparred for the first time with this beautiful kid in the gym who, I admit, I sort of had my eye on. I was, like, 'I can't believe a person could be this beautiful.' And his name was Adrian.

The name of your protagonist's boyfriend in the film. That's funny.
Yeah. And a lot of the time he would literally wear green satin shorts – nothing else – and then a rosary. And I was just like, 'Oh man, I am a goner!' [*Laughs.*] He was just too beautiful. So I sparred with him, because he wasn't the kind of guy who was going to fuck with me and be 'gentle', but he also wouldn't just whack me to show me a lesson. And I was being very tentative with him and he was being very tentative with me in the ring, and he got me into a clinch and whispered in my ear, 'Hit me.' Like, 'Don't be afraid,' essentially. And I was so flipped out in a way because I think guys would do that to each other, also – they would say, 'C'mon, don't be afraid, let's just go.' But the intimacy of it is really like a courtship, and I think that kind of skin-on-skin contact and the weird privacy of that space between word and ear is just so odd. Weird emotional exchanges really do happen in the ring.

Also, I was just struck by how many young guys really walk into the gym pissed off and unfocused and just begging for punishment or guidance or father figures, and often they find something from that process if they keep going, and they do change. And then, sometimes, they disappear – something pulls them back into the world that they are attempting to escape – and you never know what happened to them. That old story of those forties and fifties melodramas – 'I want to be somebody, I want to get out of this neighbourhood' – is real. And I just kept thinking to myself, when is a girl who is the sister of one of these guys, who's just as pissed-off, as fucked-up, as unable to deal with problems in a manner that allows them to survive, going to walk in the door?

When did you actually begin putting all of these ideas together?
It must have been '92 when I was starting to think about it. I almost don't want to admit how long it's been. But I didn't start writing it until maybe two years later, and made a promise to myself that I would write it in three weeks just to get it out of my system. And I did. Such a different draft, such a painfully awkward piece of work. But it did contain a couple of simple things that were very basic to the story – the conflict with the father, the development of the relationship with the trainer, and then this sort of love that emerges within the confines of the ring.

It sounds like it must have been a pretty protracted process of rewriting that followed . . .
Well, it was hard for me to write while I was working for John, because I really had to make the time. And I spent a lot of time at the gym. There were days that I would go there and not work out, I would just spend the day there and watch all my guys play their dominoes and see the relationships that walked in and out. Every day was exciting – every day, something insane would happen. It's sort of a circus in a way – I think that's what people complain about in boxing, and I completely understand that the purity of the sport really has been corrupted over the years in many different ways. But the fact remains that boxing is still a world where you can be yourself in some crazy way. Don King can exist as a businessman in boxing, you know? What a crazy, almost great thing. My mission, initially, was to just be accepted in this environment, because soon I was asking everyone questions and it became this ongoing research, but research based on friendships, which is a great way to work, a great way to get ideas. And because of that I think it came out so organically in the end – I was so close to my subject that I really felt like I knew what I was talking about on some level.

As you were writing, were you showing drafts to Sayles?
I think I showed John the second draft – he was always saying to me, 'What's going on with that boxing story?' When he first read it, he was so generous. He said, 'This is a great story – I love that all of her issues that are happening in the outside world are getting crystallized and worked out in the tiny world of the ring.' But he also said, 'I know she's your main character, but maybe you need to focus on Adrian a little bit and figure out who he is. Why does he fall for her, and not just go for the trophy girlfriend?' Which is a very heavy question. So he really encouraged me to think in the direction of making each character a total character, even if they're only there for five seconds, which is really great advice.

The successive drafts were also about giving more complexity to the relationship. One of the themes I wanted to work on was that kind of hormonal nightmare of adolescence. That's such a fertile ground for building characters because they can do almost anything crazy, or make bad choices, and you believe it. And the fact of it, too, is I think we are so afraid to see characters just make mistakes or blow it a little bit. So I started thinking, 'OK, once they fall for each other, just on the pure romance level, it can be a real boy-girl teenage relationship, where it never feels solid or stable at all.'

When did you line up a producer?
Well, Martha was always producing it from the beginning. She and I had actually spent several years trying to find money for another project of mine – kind of a dark, perverse, unpleasant script that John had read previous to *Girlfight*. He said, 'This is very well-written, but these are not the kinds of people I would want to hang out with for two hours.' But he did feel that it was strong enough for him to put his name on as an executive producer. So when he read the *Girlfight* thing, he said, 'This is really what I think you need to do.' And so we went with what we thought was the more 'commercial' fare. And my fear was and still is that it's too commercial. But what can you do? It plagues me.

Anyway, money came together and fell through so many times that we just needed more support. And Maggie Renzi and Sarah Green came on as producers – they have a deal with Sony and are in a partnership called Green-Renzi – which gave us some more legitimacy to work with. And then John said he would invest into half of the budget as long as we stayed under one million dollars. And we thought, 'OK, *now* we can find the money.' And still it would fall through. I think it's really because people just hadn't seen this story before. I think the thing about a female in this kind of trajectory is really unsettling to people who invest money on tried-and-true formulas.

Is that sexism, do you think? Or is it more lack of imagination?
Perhaps studies will prove that there's a relationship between lack of imagination and sexism. [*Laughs.*] But there was just this general sense of 'Who is going to watch this movie?' The fact is, I still don't know. But I think there is something undeniably appealing to a lot of people about it, because I think we crave women in more active, engaged roles in the world. I think men want it and need it as much as women do. We're not all just living in this fantasy world of men somehow having a leg up.

Anyway, finally we got to a point where we were negotiating with somebody, and we'd gone into pre-production because we were *that sure*, and then the financing just collapsed, literally a day before official pre-production was to begin. My DP and I had finished our last storyboard: 'Well, you know, we made it through the entire movie – we storyboarded all 683 shots – too bad we're not shooting it.' [*Laughs.*] That night I got home at like eleven and there was a message on the machine saying that John had gotten wind of this bad news and he was going to put up all the money until we found money from someone else. That's just the kind of thing that – you can't even *measure* the magnitude of that choice on his part.

Martha and I think about it a lot. What if Maggie and John didn't agree to do this, what would we be doing? I'd be scooping ice-cream cones. [*Laughs.*]

What an incredible vote of confidence.
Yeah, but it's a lot of pressure, too, because you're suddenly dealing with his money. We said to him, 'We'll guard every penny,' because there was such a fear of fucking up – it was Martha's first producing gig and my first directing and writing job. But yeah, it was great to have that vote of confidence. Also, once John was the person bankrolling the movie, his work philosophy was how choices got made. So I was an important voice in decisions that other directors wouldn't even go near or get the opportunity to go near. I was able to really say, 'Why can't we spend money on this if we're going to spend money on that?' – I could still be a part of that dialogue. I think it can really make you a better film-maker if you can deal with it, if you can really not let it corrupt your creative process.

How did you find Michelle Rodriguez?
It was a long process. When we met with our casting directors – and this was maybe two years before we really found the money – I said, 'You know, I want this character to be a kind of watershed cultural icon.' Which is a really heavy thing to say to a casting director. But I was thinking that, you know, people really felt like something unique was happening when they were watching Travis Bickle or Tony Manero or Stanley Kowalski. There is a tradition of a kind of presence that just sort of electrifies the screen and holds you captive. So I told them I wanted Brando as a teenage Latina. And they said, 'OK, we'll find her.'

When we were finally really bankrolled enough to do the casting, we had this steady stream of girls coming in to read for the part wearing push-up bras, and tiny little tank tops – when it was two degrees outside. I was shocked. There was an obsession with being small, an obsession with frailty, and it was just really interesting, because I never knew until I saw all of these talented, often very articulate young women coming in who had to literally sell their bodies. We read some great actors, but a lot of times there was a sort of polish, almost a finish, to how they interpreted scenes. Midway through casting, I just said, 'This isn't working.' We weren't finding the girl who, like the character I'd written, can sort of take us or leave us, the girl with that kind of raw energy. So we did an open casting call, and Michelle emerged as one of the last people out of the three hundred and fifty or so we saw that day. She was close to two hours late, and she kept cracking up during the reading – she'd laugh when she made a mistake and make these crazy faces like, 'Oh, I'm such a fuck-up.' The minute she walked out of the room, I wrote her off. Then we went back and looked at the tape, and it was like 'Ahhh!' She converted beta into alpha. So we brought her back, and she was late again.

I remember your mentioning her lateness problem after a screening of the film here at the Directors' Guild.
She has a little bit of a different time sense, which really concerned me a lot ini-

tially because it was one of those kind of things that made me think, 'Is she going to show up on the set?!' I was terrified about that. And the thing is, she had no experience, had never acted before. So I decided to just put her in the ring and see how she was physically. Within the first hour, people were coming up to me and saying, 'We haven't seen anyone like this in the gym in two years.' She learned so fast, and just had this animal pride – this unwillingness to be humiliated. Of course, for boxers, that's something you want to train out of yourself, because it's really important to know when you're in trouble and to try to seek help somehow with whatever tricks you have. But that aggression was something a lot of the trainers noticed. People were so excited, and you could feel the bloodlust in the air. And I just knew I had to cast her. So then it became this thing of working on the script every now and then – because she trained five or six days a week for four-and-a-half months – and we were really able to take a long period of time and talk about character, talk about narrative scenarios.

The other great thing was, she read with all the other actors when we were try-ing to find the right match for her, and it seemed like every time she was learning something more just through the audition process. It also became clear that the actor who played Adrian had to be someone that she didn't demolish on screen. I mean, she would just be standing there and it still would seem she was walking all over these guys. It was really interesting – we realized we'd hit the jackpot.

And I've got to say, she pulled it together and she had a focus, a natural abil-ity. I'd say, 'Michelle, stop climbing the walls and singing the *South Park* theme – calm down for one second, we're shooting in two minutes.' She would just be spazzing out on the way to her mark, and then she would get there and it was like everything would fall away and she was an actor. Actually, even more than an actor – she's almost a 'channeller' of some kind. She's very raw in some ways and I'm sure has a lot to learn before her next movie, but I hope she gets a lot of atten-tion from good directors because I think she's a huge talent.

You've used the term 'melodrama' when talking about the film, but I have to say that, despite *Girlfight*'s storyline, I found the style of the film to be much more in the vein of the cinematic realism of film-makers like the Dardennes brothers, or even someone like Erich Zonca.

That's interesting. I knew that would be a part of how people would experience it, but I think what I meant with 'melodrama' was that this film, like the most expres-sive and interesting melodramas, has a clear emotional logic. You can watch a Douglas Sirk movie like *Written on the Wind* and you can think it's insane and 'out there', but within the context of what it is, it makes perfect sense. And the big tra-jectory of the story is that people finally express what they're feeling, and that everyone finally is in this kind of a fantasy zone where stuff gets released. I was interested in that in terms of *Girlfight* because I did see her narrative trajectory as being one from emotional paralysis to emotional openness and vulnerability. And all of that came from the opposing and parallel story of her finding focus for her violence and her rage and her aggression. So even if it wasn't going to be big and 'out there' in terms of my personal expression of those themes, I really feel that that desire to be noticed is a part of the melodramatic tradition.

I love the fact that, throughout the movie, we keep returning to those vaguely disquieting scenes at the dinner table with her and her brother and father. The apartment is literally the 'home base' – physically and emotionally – for the whole movie, in a way.

I really encouraged the other two characters to be comfortable on some level in that space – less so with Tiny, her brother, but definitely with Sandro, the father. I wanted them feeling like they were where they *belonged*, no matter how untrue that was. Whereas with Michelle, I wanted her character to be someone who had presence to burn, but nowhere to put it. So in those scenes she was constantly hunched in this weird, almost cowering position – but she's not someone who cowers . . .

Except in that context.

Yeah, definitely. That the home is not a place where she can be a developed human being, which I find might be something I'm going to explore a lot. I feel like that was the thing that survived out of the family scenes in the script, because a lot of that stuff was overwritten – or not as well-written or clear as the rest – so a lot of it got peeled away. And the only thing that really seemed to stay was the discomfort, which is what I really wanted to try and preserve. I think we did an OK job, although the movie's got problems. [*Laughs.*]

What kind of problems?

Well, I would have liked to see even more of that coyotes-circling-each-other dynamic between the boy and the girl. Even more of a sort of overt fear of connection, with that overwhelming need for connection working at the same time. I think young actors see so many examples of that falling-into-the-screen-kiss stuff that they forget how awkward it is when it really happens, so I kept trying to get that awkwardness back in. But I felt at times that things were, even with the complications, still too easy. And that's also a function of my writing. I think I should have explored instability a little bit more. That's one thing, but there are so, so many things. The final fight I wanted to be a true battle of wills in every possible way – including, obviously, the physical – and we just didn't have the time to really express that. We had two days in this enormous location filled with extras. It was really hard to shoot there.

That's a lot of really tricky choreography, too.

Oh yeah. It was really tough. And mistakes happen. People get hit accidentally in a big way and feelings get hurt. And it's heavy, because I think the two actors really had a lot of respect for each other and a lot of love for each other, which I think shows on the screen – but, you know, I was asking them to bring a lot of animus into the ring, and I think that was difficult for both of them.

But, in a Machiavellian way, that must be great, right? The characters they're playing are experiencing those same emotions.

Oh yeah, absolutely. But it's not pleasant while it's happening. Both of them got hit 'accidentally', and it was one of those ugly moments where you say, 'Wow, this is what this would really be like.' Anyway, that sequence is something I would change.

In those fight scenes, you did this really nice thing with the POV shot of either boxer, where there's a white 'flash' every time they get punched . . .

That's John Sayles. When we were editing, I was saying, 'I'm really frustrated, because I think the footage is strong, but it literally needs some 'pop' to feel impact and I don't know what to do.' I didn't want it to be a sound effect. And he said, 'Well, there's something really cheap you can do – just cut in a frame of white leader.'

Just one frame?

It's interesting – every cut was different. Some were two frames, some were three, some were one. It just depended on the flow of it. But we did it, and it really made a difference – really gave you that sense of being stunned. That was such an easy thing to do, and it cost, like, one cent. It also gave the film a sort of homemade feeling, like there was something unfancy about it. From the beginning, I really wanted to make the movie very bluntly – I didn't want to get too poetic.

Girlfight won the Grand Jury Prize – as well as a directing award – at Sundance this year. Could you talk about the whole process of showing the film there?

Well, we submitted a rough cut – something on tape with no sound work, no music – and I was really horrified to do that. But it got accepted. I had high hopes for the film, but I didn't necessarily think it would win any awards. Sundance was great because it got everything rolling, and it was a great forum for that first time to have five really enthusiastic audiences see the movie. But it was an exhausting experience for me – I really look forward to going to a festival when I either don't have a film there or I'm not in competition. Because I felt like a monk or something – I couldn't stay out late and I couldn't drink because I had to always get up and deal with 'the grind'.

In a sense, you're playing out the ultimate fantasy of a first-time director: Your film won major awards at Sundance, you've gotten a distributor, Screen Gems, who's clearly behind the film, and now you've been selected for the Directors' Fortnight at Cannes. Is this anything you can honestly say you had prepared yourself for?

I think I did kind of hope for it at some point – whether this was the movie, I don't know. It's a lot of pressure on some level. I have these conversations a lot with prospective agents, and I'm sure they all think I sound either pessimistic or insane, but I've told them all that a lot of my favourite film-makers are the ones who have brutally failed, who have really gone off the deep end with a couple of movies and lost their way. Those are the most interesting film-makers to me – the ones who explore what they're doing deeply enough that they just fall flat on their face. The funny thing about this kind of moment for me personally is that it creates a certain sense of expectation about me – that I'm very craft-oriented or technique-oriented and very story-driven, and I'm not sure if I will always be those things. Sometimes the pure aesthetics is actually the story to me.

So in a way, the real pressure for me is to continue to explore what I want to do in a very complete way and create an environment for myself to do that – I think that's going to be hard. But I want people to understand that I'm not going to be one of those directors who gets a list of people I can cast – List A, List B, List C. I'm not going to do that. I'm not going to be someone who will do a test to see if I should re-shoot the ending, and I'm not going to have a board of twenty accountants tell me how to rewrite my script so that it's more suitable for this or that demographic. Once you get those factors out of the way, I think you can get a lot of really expressive work made. But sometimes even the most expressive work, crazy as it is, beautiful as it is, fails. And I need to be reminded of those kinds of moments when I say this, because I really believe it. Of course, I've set this precedent now of experiencing some degree of success so early that it's a little scary. I don't know, though – I'm pretty resilient.

Who are some of your influences?
I'm really into Shohei Imamura. I feel that he goes into this zany territory that is purely about his own obsession – and I just love to see people's obsession get worked out on screen. For that reason I could say the same of Stanley Kubrick. I think a lot of his film-making was about control – or the loss of control – and that obsession is just explored right in front of you, which is so gratifying to see. Right now I'm going bananas for Claire Denis. I saw *Beau Travail* at Sundance the day before *Girlfight* premièred, and I just thought, 'OK, this is all I could ever hope for in a long career' – moments of purity and beauty, and buried tenderness. It really humbled me. Some Kurosawa films give me a whole new belief in narrative film-making. And Douglas Sirk – there are so many people who think it's too campy and wacky, but god, I feel so much passion from his work. And I saw *Velvet Goldmine*, like, seven times in the theatre. Todd Haynes is a real hero.

So there are those film-makers out there that I go to for inspiration, and the best thing about all of them is that you never feel anything but the stamp of their personal cinema on the work. I'm not looking to brand my work particularly, but I do hope that a sensibility emerges where my natural concerns in life continue to get worked out in an organic way. I think the reason we don't see distinctive work a lot of the time in Hollywood is people always want to be working, so they just grab on to the next project that's available that has a star attached – 'We've got the money, let's go!' That's just no way to explore personal cinema. But you know, I'm a really work-oriented person, so of course I've been thinking to myself, 'If I don't get the next thing off the ground in the next year, I'm really going to start to lose my mind.' I want to be working on something right now. I want to be shooting in the fall. And the fact is, I'm not ready, and I know it.

I meant to ask you earlier; did you hit Adrian, the kid in the gym, after he asked you to?
Yes, I think I did. [*Laughs.*] I did hit him, I granted him his wish. And it was probably pretty satisfying, for both of us.

David O. Russell

David O. Russell's films include the critically acclaimed *Three Kings*, *Flirting with Disaster* and *Spanking the Monkey*, which was the winner of the Audience Award at the 1994 Sundance Film Festival, as well as recipient of Best First Feature and Screenplay Independent Spirit Awards.

Tod Lippy: I know you're planning to move back to New York, but you've been in LA for close to two years now. How does the city strike you?
David O. Russell: I'll just start out by saying that, you know, there are ghosts in America. Cultural ghosts – just certain, very American ghosts. And in Los Angeles, they're really strong – stronger than they are anyplace else.

Why is that?
Because this is their home territory. I'm talking about a particular American hopefulness and energetic-ness that translates into certain narrative conventions – like always requiring a narrative resolution. A certain narrative drive. Those ghosts are just really strong, and if you come out here, they will get into your cerebellum and you don't even realize it. It's like ether – you're breathing it and suddenly it's influencing you. Even if you're making an irreverent or different or independent film, these narrative ghosts will still inhabit it.

And this is only in LA?
Well, it's very potent here. I was watching a French movie last night, *When the Cat's Away*. Have you seen that?

Yeah, it's wonderful. That's about to be remade, isn't it?
Well, Miramax wants to do it; that's why I was looking at it. I would do it, but what's the point of a remake? I think there's something fundamentally corrupt about them. Anyway, as I was watching that movie – which I thought was brilliant – I was thinking, 'This movie doesn't have any American ghosts in it.' Every single thing about it is so real, and upsetting, you know? The fact that the guy you think she's going to get together with turns out not to be the right one. And the Arab who's taking her around is not the right one. And her gay roommate's not the right one. And his friend who comes to visit is not the right one. Everybody's really lonely and disconnected in a very consistent way – there's such a consistency of missed connection that's so real. I think Americans find that unbearable. I was aware of my *own* anxiety while I was watching it. There is a terrible loneliness in America that we work really hard to deny through all kinds of luxurious, glossy entertainment, and theme parks, and Nike shoes.

Why did you come out to LA initially?
I came here to make *Three Kings*, which I just sort of stumbled into. After the film was over, we ended up staying to finish out the school year for our son, because we didn't want to bounce him around so much.

What did you think of the city when you first arrived?

When we moved here, LA was this magical place to me. I think – probably like a lot of people who end up making films – I wanted to escape my home, and the emotional environment of my home as a kid, and LA became this very alluring place. You know, you watch movies and TV shows, and they look cool – you want to go be there with those people. Even when I visited here as an adult, it still had that quality to me. I would come here for short periods of time, and I would get to meet certain people at a studio, or certain movie stars, and it still had a magical quality to me. And then when we came here – I brought my wife and my son with me to make the movie, having cavalierly jumped into this endeavour without even thinking what it would be like to uproot us from New York – I was just willing to try it for a while. I don't know, what can I tell you about LA? Number one, the car became all-important. At first, that was a really nice thing. You have all your CDs in it, and you can talk to your friends on the phone – it's this little travelling cocoon. And it's a big purse which you can keep important personal stuff in, which you don't really have in New York. But then it became extremely oppressive to me, and I realized if I did two or three things in a day I was spending four to five hours in a car. I felt like my legs were atrophying into these vestigial appendages. I wasn't walking anywhere.

That's actually one of the major things I miss about New York, and when we went back for Christmas this year, I was struck by it so objectively for the first time. When you live there, you walk or ride your bike everywhere, at least I do, even in the winter. I don't know how you quantify that, but all I can say is it's something that I love. The secondary part about it is that you're surrounded by humanity, and by life, by the city. All kinds of people, and all kinds of buildings – just swarming life. You can be lonely in the middle of that, but it can also be comforting in some strange way. You can engage somebody on the street, or walk into a store and talk to somebody, and it's all different kinds of people. I miss that more than anything. It's very alive. LA, in comparison, is very isolated and sterile, in the sense that you're either in your car, or in your house, or in somebody's office. You're never really in a public space. I'm not saying anything new, I just experienced it really intensely. Also, West LA is a very homogeneous colony – not a lot of diversity.

You know what else I realized? When you're in LA, there's a different perception about how a film's going to do. In New York, you have a colder, clearer sense of things, because you're not swept up in the whole culture of it. Recently, there was some film that was coming out here, and I remember thinking, 'Everybody in LA thinks this is going to be really huge, but it's not.' If you were in New York, you would know, because it would barely register on your radar.

There are certain cool things about LA, though. For instance, because everybody here is in the business, they all understand what you go through when you're writing something or making something – there's a lot of kinship here. And a certain 'hometown' rooting for you, which, as I said, can distort the potential of a movie.

Do you feel like you're more accessible to the industry?

That's something I like about it. And for some reason, I've found it really easy here to hook up with other directors and actors, so you can have a lot of fun evenings with people. I've become friends with other directors here. Then there's the occasional celebrity evening – you find yourself at dinner with, or the private screening room of, some legend – it's almost like Hollywood as theme park. Not something you'd want to do every night, but it's an amazing experience to talk about – touching on history, in a way.

You didn't find that in New York after *Spanking the Monkey* came out?

No, I didn't really have that so much in New York. I got to meet Woody Allen there, for instance, but I've also seen him here, because his agent is out here. It didn't happen that much for me there, and for some reason, it did here. You know, in a funny way, LA is more democratic than New York. New York is more hierarchical, more clique-ish, whether it's business, or art, or theatre, film, publishing. Here, just about anybody can go to any party. Everyone's self-made here; you've all invented yourselves.

Would you say that in LA it's more about money?

It's about money, but it's also about, you know, if you're the guy who made an interesting independent film that got attention last week, even if you don't have any money and you never will, you are somebody they're interested in talking to at a party. Maybe only for a week, but it's a good week. [*Laughs.*] But what I miss about New York, and why I want to move back there as soon as we can get a school for our son, is being very far away from the business, and being able to just create your own world.

There are different ghosts in New York for me: the Italian and Russian relatives on both sides of my family. And then the long train of writers and filmmakers who have always had at least one foot out of Hollywood.

Are you working on another project now?

Yeah.

Is it as easy to write out here as it is in New York?

Yeah, which means it's equally excruciating and hateful. [*Laughs.*]

Are the ghosts infiltrating the writing process?

They're there at the very inception of things. That's why, if you're conscious of them, you have to hire some ghostbusters. Sort of like one of those virus-searching programs you have on your computer. You have to run that every once in a while to make sure they haven't crept in. Friends can help.

Did you find working for Miramax on *Flirting with Disaster* a good primer for making a studio film?

Miramax can in some ways be more intrusive than the average studio – that's part of the power of Harvey's personality. My experience with Warner Bros. on *Three Kings* was that they were not very intrusive at all.

You were quoted as saying that they were attempting to 'sand down the edges' of *Three Kings* at certain points. I'm thinking, in particular, of the reference to Michael Jackson and 'little boys' from the torturer's monologue.
They always go after the craziest things – the things that they think are going to alienate a mass audience. That one was just a red flag to them, and when anything pops up like that they're afraid. But anyway, I'll work with Miramax again – the next couple of films I do could be for Miramax, or possibly financed out of Europe or something like that.

So you're going back to a smaller budget again?
Absolutely.

Fifty million dollars is a lot of money –
It sure is.

Especially for a film that's so subversive – that's got to almost be a record. How much was *Fight Club*'s budget?
I think *Fight Club* was sixty-seven million dollars, and that film was ballsier in a way. But it had sex in it, and that always makes it more accessible. On the other hand, it was more relentlessly alienating. I liked most of it a great deal, and I think it's impressive that it was made at that budget.

Why do you want to go back to a smaller-budgeted film?
I didn't enjoy working with a big crew – it was over a hundred people at times. This is nothing new, either, but I'm trying to find a way to work with the tiniest crew possible – a skeletal crew – because it gives you so much more freedom. Basically, it should be about you, the script, and the actors. And the more people who get involved, the more you have to fight your way through all of that to keep it to you, the script, and the actors.

And also, the crew on these big shoots is just doing a job. You know, your picture is the one between *Grumpier Old Men* and *Major League 3*. And they just think you're another loser on the train of crap that's being generated. That can affect the creative environment.

Did the crew for *Flirting with Disaster* have a similar attitude?
No, not nearly as much. In New York, there's a world of independent crews which you can't find here, at least not that I'm aware of. In New York, there's this whole subculture. Also, there's the East Coast Council deal – a special union deal where under a certain budget you can make a union picture, but you can cut the rates. The only problem with shooting in New York is that it's such a dense city, unlike Paris or LA, where you can just grab a street. In Manhattan, you can't do that – it's harder to get locations. The script says 53rd Street, but you always find

yourself up on 160th Street or something, saying to yourself, 'How the hell did I end up here?'

In interviews around the time of *Three Kings'* release, you talked about how your intention was to 'disorient' and 'destabilize' the audience with the film's presentation of the subject matter. On a purely technical note, did you ever cross the eyeline? It looked like you did.
I don't know. I know I didn't give a shit, whereas on the first two movies the script supervisor, the DP and myself were constantly going off on some horrific, endless conversation about eyelines. I know that this time I approached it in a much more reckless way. It was definitely supposed to feel like you'd driven into a chaotic landscape.

That feeling was compounded by those low-angle shots with only sky in the background, which made it even harder for the viewer to get his bearings.
Well, that's what's so beautiful about the desert.

I remember Kenneth Turan's review of *Three Kings* talking about how the film resorted to a very 'conventional' ending, which I actually disagree with. The film's ending, however 'happy', is drenched in irony and cynicism. The only reason the prisoners are finally escorted to the border is because the gold these guys have recovered is literally 'buying' the consciences of the commanding officers.
I agree with you about that. That was my original intention, to have the ending have the cynicism to it. But I think that the ghosts got me a little bit. Especially when it came time to score; I let the score get away from me. These were things that were imperceptible to me at that time – I think because of the air I was breathing, you know? Also, the producer on the picture – who is an excellent producer – had certain ideas about the film and encouraged me in that direction. Don't get me wrong – I made all the choices, but I think that without my even recognizing it, something insidiously crept in, even at the writing stage. I was experimenting with genre – take a typical heist structure, and layer it with political and provocative ideas. I'm still not happy with the conventional aspects of it, so I wouldn't want to try it again.

But the fact that the film is still a 'difficult' film is shown by the fact that it only did sixty million dollars – which is respectable, but it didn't explode. I think what held it back was how difficult it was for mass consumption. This was a very idea-driven movie, and it was driven in part by the fact that I thought the end of the Gulf War – our supposed 'victory' – had never been examined in a big public way. And if you let things like that slide, a country can talk itself into doing some pretty bad things dressed up as honourable.

You spent a good deal of time before making films writing for Socialist papers like *In These Times*. Do you still consider yourself a Socialist? The film is from a pretty leftist point-of-view.

That's a tough question. I think a managed economy is a good thing; does that mean I'm a Socialist? I mean, if some really smart people could figure out a way to direct capital without inhibiting it, I think that would be cool. Directing it towards certain things that are socially good. And it would avoid a lot of waste.

There's a scene in the film where the reporter, played by Nora Dunn, visits a site where some dying birds are covered in oil. After pronouncing, 'This story has been so done', she bursts into tears. Do you think that somehow reflects the authorial voice of the movie – that sense of absolute cynicism combined with a sort of heartfelt humanism?
Yeah, yeah, that's very good. That's, in a nutshell, the movie's approach to a lot of things that people feel numb to. And you can't approach it without approaching the numbness in addition to the penetration of the experience and how real or how upsetting it may be. Unfortunately, the film sometimes gets too sentimental.

That humanism is even more evident when one compares several of _Three Kings_' scenes to similar ones from other films. I was thinking, for instance, of the slowing down of bullets in the scene by the bunker in the film, and how that technique has an emotional weight – a quality of dread – that becomes all the more evident when it's compared to something like _The Matrix_, which uses that same motif to a much poppier effect.
The depiction of violence interested me greatly, as something to do in a way that was re-sensitized. The other thing is, _The Matrix_ is a world of fun and ideas, so when the bullets are going off, it's more like a video game. It's deeply stimulating, and really good film-making, but a different thing altogether.

And of course, you can compare Mark Wahlberg's torture scene with the one in _Reservoir Dogs_...
Well, you know, in _Reservoir Dogs_, as good as that film is, that scene felt almost to me like an exercise in torturing the film-goer.

I have to say, that scene with Mark Wahlberg – especially when the oil is poured down his throat – was heavy-handed. We had that in, we had it out. I find some of the moralization in the movie a bit tedious – I think that's something to move away from.

I love the way you play with the term 'shoot', a word used by both the troops and the news crews with equal abandon.
That wasn't that intentional, but it just kind of naturally occurs because in that war the journalists were everywhere, and the fire-fighting was everywhere, and the Americans controlled both. Also, because the shooting seemed so strangely optional at the war's end, 'Which shooting are they talking about?' is a question more likely to be posed during the Gulf War than in any other war.

You used a lot of pop music – the Beach Boys, and Chicago's 'If You Leave Me

Now' when Saddam's Republican Guard is fleeing their bunker – to great effect in the film. Was that in any way a nod to *Apocalypse Now*?

I think *Apocalypse Now* was a good ghost, which was kind of floating over my head – good terrain travelled by good film-makers helps you along your way. But again, I didn't think of it consciously, like I was paying homage. I looked at all these journals from the war, and you'd read about all the music these guys were listening to on their CD Walkmans in their tanks as they went along, and so I just had to litter it with a lot of that.

Many people have commented on the fact that *Three Kings* is a kind of 'infected' genre movie – it's a war movie, but it's also a political film, with certain strains of absurdist comedy. What draws you to a particular genre in the first place, and then, why you are you interested in subverting it? The same could be said of *Flirting With Disaster*.

Part of it is what Nora's character says in the movie: 'This story's been so done.' It's been done to death. Part of it is wanting to inhabit a genre, while at the same time growing it beyond the expectations. Also, part of it is some form of ADD on my part as a film-maker. I think I would do better to try to unify my tone a little more – that's something I feel I can be very frank with you about, although I can already imagine my own words being used against me by some critic.

You've talked in the past about how the post-production on your films is always rather protracted – I recall that you spent something like a year in post with *Flirting with Disaster*. Was there a similarly long period with *Three Kings*?

With *Three Kings*, we had to make a release date. What happens with these films is that you're jockeying for a date against other big films, so we had to have three editors going at the same time. I'd go from room to room. I liked it, actually, because it's a nicer space at Warner Hollywood than you'd get, you know, in the Brill building, for instance. And Spike [Jonze] was editing *Being John Malkovich* on the same lot, so we could visit each other while we were both editing. So yeah, it was a long process, but the process was shorter than with *Flirting with Disaster*, because there was no deadline on that – we were able to just keep going for, like, nine months. *Three Kings* took, I think, five months, which is not that long for a movie of that size.

Did you get involved in the marketing of the film at all?

Yeah.

What was that like?

I think that, in retrospect, the film may have been mis-marketed. Marketing departments in general can be frustrating, because even when they're trying to be accommodating – and they do try to be accommodating and inclusive – they're doing a whole slate of movies. They're a machine. I think it's hard for them to step out of that and look at the market and the film in a fresh way. Especially when you're in the fifty-million-dollar range. They just want to hit the broadest target possible, and I can't blame them – they want to make their money back. But from the very first time I saw the materials they produced for *ShoWest*, the marketing seemed too 'rock 'n' roll' to me. There's a more poetic stance that could have been struck, that had the absurdity in it and the poignancy in it rather than the rock 'n' roll and the big, big emotion. They kind of went for the broadest stuff. And I participated in those decisions.

But again, you get sucked up in that. There's this insidious process – you don't like what they've done, but you can only talk to them in their own language, so you end up compromising more than you realize.

Do you think because of that marketing strategy the film completely missed a certain demographic, or do you just think the audience drawn into it didn't respond well to it or recommend it to others?
I have to admit, I don't think it's the easiest film in the world to market. Harvey Weinstein said to me that the film should have been presented from the get-go as a Very Special Undertaking. The studio wouldn't want to do that, of course, because they're afraid of freaking people out and alienating a mass audience, but I think what he had in mind was to present it as an amazingly special film of great quality. I think the studio was terrified to do that. It's very hard to say if the film could have done better.

It was definitely being sold as an action movie, I assume to attract the teenage male population . . .
Yeah, that's who they were selling to really hard, but they never got that audience. The studio people thought that was because at some point we went off that message too much and into the weird and emotional stuff, but I wonder if they would have been better off to never have gone after that demographic. Women were the ones who it tested the highest with, ironically. Maybe because of George, and the more human approach to action.

I remember an interview with you right after *Spanking the Monkey* came out – you talked about how Gus van Sant's *Mala Noche* had such an impact on you, because it spurred you on to look into the dark recesses of your own life for dramatic material. Has that continued with your other films?
There has been some degree of that in every film. But *Three Kings* wasn't a personal experience.

Can you recognize when you're hitting that point in your writing?
It feels a little queasy in general. It feels uncomfortable. But I have to say I'm still completely learning what it is to be a good writer. I'm not totally sure how to answer that otherwise.

Who are you learning from?
From working. Talking to friends, watching other film-makers I respect a lot.

Right now I'm mostly struck by how there are these two different kinds of movies – of course there are many kinds, but there are two that I'm very struck by. There are movies that say, 'We're going to hang out with these people for a while', and the story's not particularly compelling. It's more like *Raging Bull* or *Rushmore*, where you're just going to hang out in a world. And then there's *Being John Malkovich* or *Election*, which is like a Swiss watch. There's nothing there that isn't propelling the story one step forward.

You wouldn't put *Flirting with Disaster* in that latter category?
It's in that direction. I've been told by people that it's actually used in structure classes in film schools, but I don't think it's nearly as tight as *Election*.

Were you aware of the fact that male characters are often referred to as 'bitches' or 'bitch-boys' in your movies? Nora Dunn calls Jamie Kennedy's character 'bitch' in *Three Kings*, and David Patrick Kelly's character refers to Ben Stiller as a 'bitch-boy' in *Flirting With Disaster* . . .
I don't think it's in *Spanking*, though.

Not in the film, but there's actually an interview with you where you refer to the character as a 'bitch-boy'.
[*Laughs.*] Let me think what I could say about that. The only thing I could say is that it's directly out of the house where I grew up – the psychological jousting that used to go on in my house between the mother/father/son/sister kind of a thing.

Right around the time *Flirting with Disaster* came out, you said, 'Being a director is kind of like being a pimp.' You were talking about your attempts to convince Mary Tyler Moore to —
Get down to her skivvies. Fortunately, for me, most of the actors I've worked with are eager to be in the films I make and are willing to try anything. But even then, actors are putting themselves out there, and there's usually a negotiation that has to go on. How much are they going to show? Are they really going to be able to do that? I had this whole thing with Mark Wahlberg – and God bless him, he was willing to try it – where his character sings all of these Beach Boys songs whenever he's anxious. It was in the script – there's really horrible things going on and he's singing these Beach Boys songs. Ultimately, it just seemed too psychotic, but it was the kind of thing that I wanted to try. And Mark was willing to do it, which meant learning all these songs – and it wasn't like he loved the Beach Boys in the first place. We actually went to see them at a concert of theirs in Phoenix when we were shooting, and we went backstage and hung out with them. It was funny. Maybe I should make a little compilation reel for Mark.

Speaking of actors, I know for the first three films you had some difficulty casting leads, based, I assume, on the off-centre nature of the screenplays. Do you think that will always be an issue with the kind of films you're writing?
A lot of casting is a matter of luck and timing. Who's available when you're

shooting. I do feel that my choices are expanding, rather than shrinking, with actors. Also, I think now people will get my scripts more. It's not like they're extremely esoteric or anything, but a lot of times agents read them and they just don't get it. Now they can see several of my films, and get the sensibility, and imagine what the next one will look like more.

So when are you coming back to New York?
We're planning to come back this summer.

Are you going to shoot the next movie there?
Yeah, that's what I want to do. The next one or two. One of the things I learned after making this desert movie is that I do want to make more films about the area of my life where I'm from, which is New York and the outskirts of New York. And I suppose I needed to depart from that before I realized it. Because there was something about it that felt well-trod by other film-makers, and conventional in its own way. I think having separated from New York for a while, I can see it in a more particular and personal way. I think I can do it in a way that I just couldn't see a few years ago.

Acknowledgements

The editors wish to thank Carole Eastman, Paul Feldsher, Martin Fox, Robert Haller, David Hariton, Lee Ann Hileman, Kent Jones, Michael LaHaie, Annie Nocenti, John Pierson, Steven Starr, Willard Taylor, Becky Tesich, Barbara Turner and Irwin Young for their invaluable assistance, support and counsel during the course of this volume's production.

Thanks should also be extended to the individuals who helped to secure and arrange the participation of the interviewees: Laird Adamson, Susan Anderson, Will Battersby, Nadia Benamara, Lili Jacobs, Merritt Johnson, Stefanie Koseff, Jason Lampkin, Emilie Larew, Jawal Nga, Paula Orndoff, Jen Porst, J.J. Sacha, Stacey Smith, Will Sweeney, and Melinka Thompson-Godoy.

Heartfelt appreciation for the support and attention to detail of the Faber production team: Sarah Hulbert, Rafaela Romaya, Jude Young, Kristin Cooper and Shona Andrew.

All interviewee photographs © Tod Lippy except for the following: Thérèse DePrez photo by Tim Spellman; Spike Lee photo by David Lee; Tim Robbins photo by Michael Williams; Sidney Lumet and Nora Ephron photos by Brian Hamill; Harmony Korine photo by Roman Barrett; David O. Russell photo by Mark Crosby.